worlds
in the making

probes for students
of the future

MARYJANE DUNSTAN

communications department
college of marin

PATRICIA W. GARLAN

studies in nonverbal behavior
langley-porter neuropsychiatric institute

worlds
in the making

probes for students of the future

prentice-hall, inc., englewood cliffs, new jersey

worlds in the making:
probes for students of the future
by maryjane dunstan/patricia w. garlan

C–13–969055–7
P–13–969048–4

library of congress catalog card number 77–103318

current printing (last number)
10 9 8 7 6 5 4 3

printed in the united states of america

prentice-hall international inc., london
prentice-hall of australia, pty. ltd., sydney
prentice-hall of canada, ltd., toronto
prentice-hall of india private limited, new delhi
prentice-hall of japan, inc., tokyo

acknowledgments

We wish to thank the production team at Prentice-Hall, who had faith that we knew what we were doing, and in particular the book's designer, Jim Beggs, who devoted his time and talent to make WORLDS come alive on the page.

The authors wish to thank the following for the use of photographs and artwork:

Mr. Gottschalk of Gottschalk-Kalender for the cover and the photograph facing page 2. These photographs are taken from the Macro Color calendar (Universe Books, 381 Park Avenue South, New York, N.Y. 10016).

Miss Betty Wilson for the artwork facing pages 22, 158, 356, and on pages 114, 160, 213, and 236, and Sydney Goldstein for her assistance with the art facing page 158.

The National Aeronautics and Space Administration for the photograph facing page 112.

Philco-Ford Corporation, Space & Re-entry Systems Division, for the photograph facing page 192.

Metro-Goldwyn-Mayer, Inc. for the photograph from *2001: A Space Odyssey* facing page 288.

dedication

CRAZY BLUE BALLOON

Walking in a blue land,
Trudging round a bend,
   Feeling like an old man
   Feeling like a baby
Feeling that the world should end.

It's all yours, baby. Don't you see,
You don't have to take it—
Only try to make it
The way that you want it to be.

Then I saw an old man
Sitting in the sun.
   Smiling like an old man
   Smiling like a baby
Smiling like a guy who'd won.

Looked like the Buddha
Looked like Socrates
Looked like J.S. Bach
Looked like Einstein
Looked like Kennedy
Looked like Benjamin Spock.

It's all yours, baby. Had to be—
From the day when your brother
Took hold of that other
Fork in the family tree.

Then he bent his grey head
Something in his hands
   Glittered like an emerald
   Glittered like a meteor
Glittered like the desert sands.

Looked like an hourglass
Looked like a yardstick
Looked like a man in a moon.
Looked like a spaceship
Looked like a planet
Looked like a crazy blue balloon.

It's all yours, baby. Glory be.
I was just holding it,
Couldn't help molding it
A little in the shape of me.

Then he threw his hands wide
Tossed it in the air.
   Never said a word, but
   Never said a word, but
Told me what I had to hear:

It's all yours, baby. Here's the key.
Yours to have and enfold
Till your children can be told:
"It's all yours, baby. Set me free!"

Patricia W. Garlan

contents

PART IV **the machine—enemy or ally?**

thirteen
the threat   **159**

fourteen
the promise   **176**

catching up with technology

P A R T V **evolution or revolution?**

fifteen
world enough, and time

trying on a new life

sixteen
work-play

designing life styles: 1

seventeen
communication-transportation

designing life styles: 2

eighteen
education-evolution   **237**

designing life styles: 3

PART VI   **discovering human nature**

nineteen
defining the quest   **289**

conquest or civilization?

the search for the self

other as brother

the self and the world

developing a creed

**twenty
the taste of space, the scent of time**   **334**

**twisting the kaleidoscope
the creative process**

the "aha!" experience

big—little, etc.

the universe within

PART VII inventing the future

worlds
in the making

probes for students
of the future

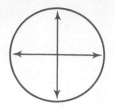

Change is avalanching down upon our heads, and
most people are utterly unprepared to cope with it.

Alvin Toffler,
"The Future as a Way of Life"

PART I

grokking
the problem

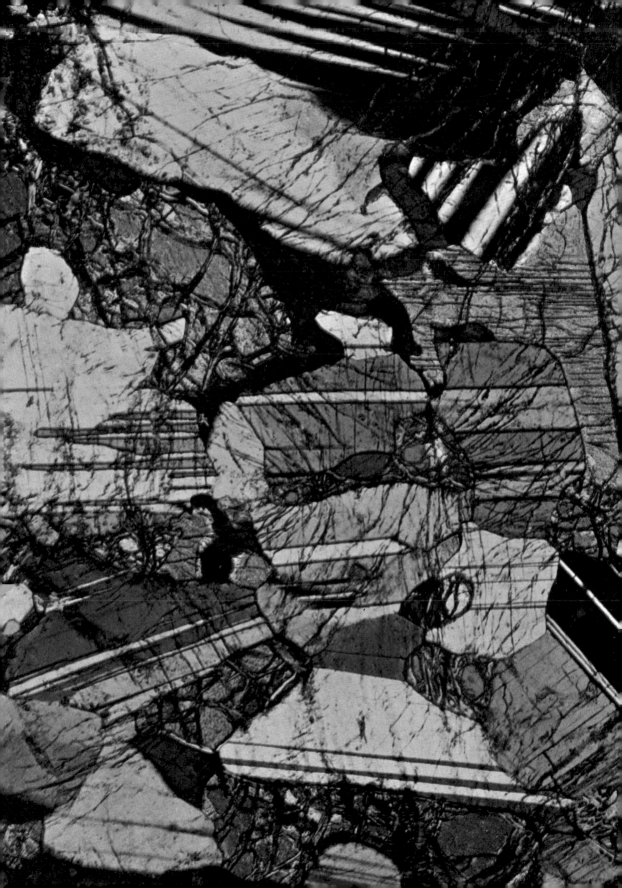

one

stranger in
a strange land

This young man Smith was busy staying alive. His body, unbearably compressed and weakened by the strange shape of space in this unbelievable place, was at last relieved by the softness of the nest in which these others placed him. He dropped the effort of sustaining it, and turned his third level to his respiration and heart beat.

He saw that he was about to consume himself. His lungs were beating as hard as they did at home, his heart was racing to distribute the influx, all in an attempt to cope with the squeezing of space—and this while smothered by a poisonously rich and dangerously hot atmosphere. He took steps.

Robert A. Heinlein,
Stranger in a Strange Land

In the science fiction novel *Stranger in a Strange Land,* Smith has been brought to earth from Mars on a spaceship. The captain of the spaceship describes him:

"Smith is an intelligent creature with the ancestry of a man, but he is more Martian than man. Until we came along he had never laid eyes on a man. He thinks like a Martian, feels like a Martian. He's been brought up by a race which has *nothing* in common with us— they don't even have *sex*. He's a man by ancestry, a Martian by environment. If you want to drive him crazy and waste that 'treasure trove', call in your fat-headed professors. Don't give him a chance to get used to this madhouse planet." . . .

Smith may think and feel like a Martian, but the sensation he feels —of mortal danger from an alien and hostile environment—could become painfully familiar to those of us for whom the earth is home. For, the ever-changing world is pulling a fast one this time; and we, like Smith, may find ourselves unfit to live in it.

Smith, however, has mysterious techniques for coping with change:

When his heart rate was twenty per minute and respiration almost imperceptible, he watched long enough to be sure that he would not discorporate while his attention was elsewhere. When he was satisfied he set a portion of his second level on guard and withdrew the rest of himself. It was necessary to review the configurations of these many new events in order to fit them to himself, then cherish and praise them—lest they swallow him.

Where should he start? When he left home, enfolding these others who were now his nestlings? Or at his arrival in this crushed space? He was suddenly assaulted by lights and sounds of that arrival, feeling it with mind-shaking pain. No, he was not ready to embrace that configuration—back back! back beyond his first sight of these others who were now his own. Back even before the healing which had followed first grokking that he was not as his nestling brothers ... back to the nest itself.

None of his thinkings were in Earth symbols. Simple English he had freshly learned to speak, less easily than a Hindu used it to trade with a Turk. Smith used English as one might use a code book, with tedious and imperfect translation. Now his thoughts, abstractions from half a million years of wildly alien culture, traveled so far from human experience as to be untranslatable.

The word "grokking" describes a psychological state unknown to us; it is a total assimilation of something, through understanding, identifying with, empathizing and feeling. "To discorporate" is to die by vanishing or dissolving, and dying can be controlled by the person. Science fiction, yes. But other new words hint at experiences equally strange to us but no longer viewed as impossible. "Teleportation"—the *instantaneous* transference of matter (yourself, for instance) from one place to another—and "holograph"—a three-dimensional image thrown in space by a laser—are examples.

The shock of change—physical and cultural—almost destroyed Heinlein's stranger in a strange land, even though he had highly sophisticated personal machinery for grokking a new kind of reality. But what of ourselves? Are we becoming strangers in our own land?

Let us imagine a particular space and time circa 1986: a home in the suburbs of Phoenix. A man is sitting in the middle of a circular room, and on the curved walls around him he can see the ocean—surf breaking over the rocks and foaming up the beach; a fish hawk trembling in the luminescent sky. Across from him sits another man, and the two of them are talking to each other. Once in awhile, the boom of the bursting surf and the cry of the hawk intrude upon their conversation.

Let us now say that the room is underground and has no "real" view at all; that what is experienced on the curved walls is an image on a "flat wall" television screen, prerecorded in Hawaii, and now being replayed electronically.

Let us further say that the first man is "real," but that the second man is being broadcast by laser beam from a satellite and recreated, in color and full dimension (you could walk around his image and see the back of his head), by "holography," so that though he is "there" in Phoenix at the moment, he is "in reality" at the same moment sitting in his study at the University of Edinburgh.

Where, in this situation, does "reality" begin and end? This will be a question that—by 1986—we will, individually, be asked to answer. There is nothing in the situation just described that does not appear to be perfectly feasible within perhaps the next ten years; certainly within the next twenty. We have already entered a new world of experience.

Don Fabun,
The Dynamics of Change

Reprinted from *The Dynamics of Change*, Kaiser Aluminum & Chemical Corporation, © 1967.

from THE FUTURE AS A WAY OF LIFE

Alvin Toffler

As more Americans travel abroad, the term "culture shock" is beginning to creep into the popular vocabulary. Culture shock is the effect that immersion in a strange culture has on the unprepared visitor. Peace Corps volunteers suffer from it in Borneo or Brazil. Marco Polo probably suffered from it in Cathay. Culture shock is what happens when a traveler suddenly finds himself in a place where "yes" may mean no, where a "fixed price" is negotiable, where to be kept waiting in an outer office is no cause for insult, where laughter may signify anger. It is what happens when all the familiar psychological cues that help an individual to function in society are suddenly withdrawn and replaced by new ones that are strange or incomprehensible.

The culture-shock phenomenon accounts for much of the bewilderment, frustration, and disorientation that plague Americans in their dealings with other societies. It causes a breakdown in communication, a misreading of reality, an inability to cope. Yet culture shock is relatively mild in comparison with a much more serious malady that might be called "future shock." Future shock is the dizzying disorientation brought on by the premature arrival of the future. It may well be the most important disease of tomorrow.

Future shock will not be found in *Index Medicus* or in any listing of psychological abnormalities. Yet, unless intelligent steps are taken to combat it, I believe that most human beings alive today will find themselves increasingly disoriented and, therefore, progressively incompetent to deal rationally with their environment. I believe that the malaise, mass neurosis, irrationality, and free-floating violence already apparent in contemporary life are merely a foretaste of what may lie ahead unless we come to understand and treat this psychological disease.

Future shock is a time phenomenon, a product of the greatly accelerated rate of change in society. It arises from the superimposition of a new culture on an old one. It is culture shock in one's own society. But its impact is far worse. For most Peace Corps men, in fact most travelers, have the comforting knowledge that the culture they left behind will be there to return to. The victim of future shock does not.

Take an individual out of his own culture and set him down suddenly in an environment sharply different from his own, with a different set of cues to react to, different conceptions of time, space, work, love, religion, sex, and everything else; then cut him off from any hope of retreat to a more familiar social landscape, and the dislocation he suffers is doubly severe. Moreover, if this new culture is itself in a constant turmoil of revolutionary transition, and if—worse yet—its values are incessantly changing, the sense of disorientation will be still further intensified. Given few clues as to what kind of behavior is rational under the radically new circumstances, the victim may well become a hazard to himself and others.

Now imagine not merely an individual but an entire society, an entire generation—including its weakest, least intelligent, and most irrational members—suddenly transported into this new world. The result is mass disorientation, future shock on a grand scale.

This is the prospect that man now faces as a consequence of accelerated change—the prospect of dislocation far more subtle, complex, and continuous than any we have known. Change is avalanching down upon our heads, and most people are utterly unprepared to cope with it.

"Culture shock is what happens when a traveler suddenly finds himself in a place where "yes" may mean no, where a "fixed price" is negotiable, where to be kept waiting in an outer office is no cause for insult, where laughter may signify anger."

Has this happened to you?

Try to recapture what it was like when "all the familiar psychological cues . . . were withdrawn."

"The culture shock phenomenon accounts for much of the bewilderment, frustration, and disorientation that plague Americans in their dealings with other societies. It causes a breakdown in communication, a misreading of reality, an inability to cope."

Does this phenomenon exist **within** our own society?

Can you think of examples?

Can you think of ways in which future shock is already occurring?

Change has occurred in all ages.

What is different about change today?

ARE YOU READY?

Your child may live to be 100. And, in his lifetime, he may take drugs to raise his intelligence, may have a "talking" computer as a colleague, and may select the characteristics of *his* children before they are born.

These developments were forecast by Theodore Gordon of the Douglas Space Systems Center. Speaking at Stanford University, Gordon said that an international panel of experts felt a 100-year life expectancy might be achieved by the turn of the century.

Co-author of *Social Technology*, a RAND Corporation report on long-range forecasting, Gordon predicted that the median age of the U.S. population, now below 25, may move up to 30 or more. "As life expectancy is extended," he says, "the older people

"100-Year Life Expectancy Predicted for 2000 A.D." Reprinted by permission of *Today's Health* and Stanford University from *Today's Health*, January 1968, published by the American Medical Association.

of the community may form a political group of considerable power and significance."

Availability of artificial organs will lead to biological production lines, says Gordon, "both for the devices themselves and their installation in human beings. Millions of these units will be installed before the end of the century, probably by teams of specialized doctors working in 'new-installation hospitals.'

"The units themselves will have very long lifetimes," he predicts. "If they are owned by their wearers, they may be passed on from generation to generation... Since the devices will be expensive, they may be provided by insurance companies or social security...."

More than 20 private organizations in the United States are now attempting to solve future-oriented social problems. Describing "mainstream developments," and the median estimates for their likely attainment, Gordon said: "The biological age starts with 'the pill', includes creation of artificial life (1988 A.D.), pharmaceutical treatment of many forms of psychoses (1992 A.D.), stimulation of the growth of new organs and limbs (2005 A.D.), and even using drugs to raise human intelligence (2005 A.D.).

"There is even a chance that potentially inheritable defects could be detected (and corrected) before reproduction (2000 A.D.). (This could lead to genetic engineering in which the characteristics of progeny are selected before birth.)

"The new biology will provide man freedom from disease, and probably age, revolutionize his inheritance, and profoundly affect his concepts of love, family, and God. Psychological, chemical, and physical techniques will give man the ability to control the behavior of other men without force." But, he added: "Our freedom may be lost in the process.

"Typically, we may find drugs that destroy the will to resist (1977 A.D.), invite forgetfulness, provoke artificial courage, and distort perception in determinable ways," Gordon noted. "Perhaps tomorrow we will have the pharmaceutical equivalent of the liquor store in which chemicals can be obtained to buy any mood, from euphoria to mystic contemplation. Wives, perhaps, will slip antigrouch pills into their husband's coffee."

Experiments both in mice and men have revealed the existence of "pleasure centers" in the brain, which can be triggered by electrodes. Gordon predicts that, with this kind of stimulation on the horizon, people in some future society may wish to be wired to be happy. "The operation which places the little connector in the scalp can be quite simple, and the plug can be hidden cosmetically. Perhaps it will even be a mark of beauty.

"The use of these control means is odious and foreboding because, to a large degree, they may rob the freedom of individual action and decision... Yet it is a feature of these techniques that the individual may derive enjoyment and satisfaction from their use, and therefore feel it is his freedom to be controlled.

"The dilemma will be great."

Advances in computer technology may lead to a common network for stores and banks in this country (1973 A.D.), and then throughout the world, in a system of personal-credit transfers which might ultimately replace money. Computer networks may be used in tax collection, with access to all business records (1988 A.D.), or for automated voting, providing for legislation through an automated plebiscite (2000 A.D.). Medical symptoms and effective treatments may be kept on file for use by doctors throughout the world (1985 A.D.).

"Computers will be developed into intelligent machines which can serve as colleagues in research," Gordon forecasts. "These devices might typically score 150 on standard IQ tests and be able to respond to questions in spoken English (1990 A.D.) ...

"In the distant future, man might

be able to extend his intelligence directly by electro-mechanical connection to a computer (2010 A.D.). "The chosen few, with electrodes in their brains, can be stimulated by machines possessing a large portion of the accumulated knowledge of man, at their thought command."

Director of advanced space stations and planetary systems for Douglas, Gordon said, "In the years to come, space will provide an important antidote to leisure. It will provide a massive economic stimulant with heroic goals... Space enterprises will provide an important vicarious thrill which accompanies exploration. In an overpopulated, perhaps largely idle society, this may be necessary for man to maintain psychological equilibrium —to maintain a feeling for the value of life in an otherwise degrading and value-diminishing society."

Current differences in population trends around the world may be accentuated, with the U.S. and other industrialized nations becoming relatively older and smaller. The Caucasoid race, which now accounts for 25 per cent of the world's population, may comprise only 15 per cent by the year 2000 A.D., if present trends continue.

"It will not be an easy problem to carve out of this seeming morass a world which preserves freedom and individuality, creativity, and personal dignity," Gordon concluded. "Only if we understand the possible consequences for our actions and innovations, only if we choose our goals and pursue them, only if we believe that social responsibility cannot be delegated or avoided, can we remove our future from the domain of chance and actively seek the best for all."

two

star light, star bright

Behind every man now alive stand thirty ghosts, for that is the ratio by which the dead outnumber the living. Since the dawn of time, roughly a hundred billion human beings have walked the planet Earth.

Now this is an interesting number, for by a curious coincidence there are approximately a hundred billion stars in our local universe, the Milky Way. So for every man who has ever lived, in this universe there shines a star.

But every one of those stars is a sun, often far more brilliant and glorious than the small, nearby star we call *the* Sun. And many—perhaps most—of those alien suns have planets circling them. So almost certainly there is enough land in the sky to give every member of the human species, back to the first apeman, his own private, world-sized heaven—or hell.

How many of those potential heavens and hells are now inhabited, and by what manner of creatures, we have no way of guessing; the very nearest is a million times farther away than Mars or Venus, those still remote goals of the next generation. But the barriers of distance are crumbling; one day we shall meet our equals, or our masters, among the stars.

Arthur C. Clarke,
2001: A Space Odyssey

Wishing on a star is a ritual. The child, no less than the scientist, artist or philosopher, feels the human need to tune in to the largest reality imaginable. And what could be more practical? For the future of man

Reprinted by permission of the World Publishing Company from *2001: A Space Odyssey* by Arthur C. Clarke. An NAL book.

*"What do you think, Professor? Is it a laser, a maser,
a quasar, or just a little ray of hope for all mankind?"*

rests, quite literally, with the capacity of each one of us to be at home in the universe.

To be at home in the universe, we need to know who we are. We also need to know where in the universe we are, and the latter is every bit as difficult to determine as the former.

We have only to consider that the fish is not aware that his medium is water to recognize the difficulty of being aware of our environment. To become more aware of what our environment is, we must somehow achieve a perspective of it from outside of it.

Why is it important that we become aware of our environment? In a world where change is slow, it is perhaps not very important; our past ways of coping may suit us well enough in the present. But our contemporary environment is as much like the future as it is like the past; and with increasing rapidity it is becoming less like the past. The danger, to use Marshall McLuhan's analogy, is that we are driving rapidly into new and unexplored terrain with our eyes firmly fixed on the rear-view mirror. Instead of looking at where we are and where we are going, we focus on where we have been. Our perceptions, conceptions, values, systems of mental, emotional, personal, and social organization, our very consciousness—all have been developed in interaction with past environments, and these do not prepare us to see a different road ahead.

Today, in every domain, all forms of imagination are rampant—except in those spheres where our historical life goes on, stifled, unhappy and precarious, like everything that is out of date. An immense gulf separates the man of adventure from humanity and our societies from our civilization. We are living with ideas of morality, sociology, philosophy, and psychology that belong to the nineteenth century. We are our own great-great-grandfathers. As we watch rockets rising to the sky and feel the ground vibrating with a thousand new radiations, we are still smoking the pipe of Thomas Graindorge. Our literature, our philosophical discussions, our ideological conflicts, our attitude toward reality—all this is still slumbering behind the doors that have been burst open.

Louis Pauwels and Jacques Bergier,
The Morning of the Magicians

How, then, can we learn not to deal with today in yesterday's terms? One way is to launch ourselves into imagined futures; from the vantage point of possible tomorrows, today may take on new meanings. For example (as Marshall McLuhan points out), when we see our planet from outer space, we can perceive it as a space probe.

Consider the electronic computer. If we think of it in terms of the past, we may say that it is the culmination of the Machine Age. But if we see it from the perspective of the future, we may say that it is the beginning of the Electronic Age. When we think of the computer in terms of the future, we can see that its *differences* from other machines, rather than its similarities to them, are the important things; these differences will for all time change the life experience of man.

We are about to embark upon a journey—a journey in and out of space and, more importantly, forward (and backward) in time. It will be a journey from which there is no returning—and that will be the point of going.

Do not think of a space ship as one more ingenious scientific experiment, whatever the electronic engineers and astrophysicists may say. See, rather, the image of this pale blue spinning ball on which we live, this dancing dust-mote of a world, miracle of self-contained, self-sustaining life, hurtling vertiginously through the vast silence of interstellar space; and daring at last to shoot out its infinitesimal seeds, its atoms of living matter, towards other remotely spinning worlds, pinpoint targets millions of miles away—in the forlorn, crazy, inextinguishable faith of finding new possibilities of survival and growth. The manned spaceship is no scientific toy. It is a unique and numinous symbol—a union of opposites, of the very old and the very new—whose ultimate meaning may one day reverberate through the galaxies and fatefully alter the majestic pattern of the cosmos. To have a part in so great a venture is an inconceivable honor for that handful of dust which is the mortal part of man.

Alan McGlashan,
The Savage and Beautiful Country

coping with change

You will need to leave behind much of the equipment you have been accumulating for years. This will not be easy, because that equipment has become part of yourself—so much so that it will be hard to know what is *it* and what is *you*. But it must be done. To go where we are going, we travel light.

What an abyss of uncertainty, whenever the mind feels that some part of it has strayed beyond its own borders; when it, the seeker, is at the same time the dark region through which it must go seeking, where all its equipment will avail it nothing. Seek? More than that: create. It is face to face with something which does not so far exist, to which it alone can give reality and substance, which it alone can bring into the light of day.

Marcel Proust,
Remembrance of Times Past

exploring spaceship earth

The lands we will be traveling through do not exist–yet. Part of the terrain will be familiar; you will have seen it before, from a different perspective.

the machine —enemy or ally?

Strange creatures will appear. (Are they human? Are they hostile?)

evolution or revolution?

We will find segments of an interior landscape–the texture of men's lives, the tenor of their minds, the hue of hope and of fear. The pieces are there–but the landscape has no pattern. The pattern will be in *you*.

discovering human nature

But who are you? You might answer by giving your name, but when you tell someone your last name, you are in effect saying, "I am the child of my parents." Is that all? "No, I also have a first name; and I am the sum of my experiences." If, however, you move into a world where you are identified by a number instead of a name, then who are you? Society's child? A mathematical probability? And is that *all*?

You might say instead, "I am studying to be a doctor (or teacher or butcher or baker)." If, however, you move into a world where these functions are performed by machines, then who are you?

"I can think."
"So can a machine. Is that all?"
"I can feel."
"So can a dog. Is that all?"
"I create values. I believe in peace and
 brotherhood and the worth of my fellow man."
"Then why do you make war?"
"*I* don't make war! My fellow man makes war."
" . . . ? . . "
"I can make choices. I can plan, I can
 develop new patterns. I, alone among
 animals and machines, can invent the future."
"Ah, then show me."

inventing the future

To imagine what does not exist may turn out to be the one distinguishing ability of man, and inventing the future his best and only work. For the journey we are about to take, the only indispensable piece of equipment will be your imagination. The farther we travel the more clearly you will see that you must invent the future or it will invent *you*.

By the end of the journey, you will be seasoned. Hopefully, you will be more comfortable with change than with fixity. You will be able to anticipate—and to some extent control—the world into which we are moving. You will have a clearer notion of who you are, what it means to be human, and what kind of world can best enhance the growth and well-being of man.

The paramount distinction between human and animal intelligence, so far as we know, lies not in complexity, or profundity, or creativity, or memory, but in man's capacity for conceptual thought, and his power to see ahead. . . . Both foresight and the capacity to form a mental concept reflect the same intellectual capacity: imagination.

Robert Ardrey,
African Genesis

Reprinted from Robert Ardrey, *African Genesis* (New York: Atheneum Publishers, 1961), by permission of the publisher.

three

this madhouse planet
—spaceship earth

Motion is the condition of existence. We are indeed travelers in more than a metaphorical sense. When we invent expressions like "our journey through life," our metaphors are the literal truth.

You are being asked to take a journey of the imagination into your future and into some of the many alternative futures of our planet. So that you will not be lost, you might want to hold in your mind four words: *change, environment, man,* and *future.*

These, if you will, are the four points on our compass; these will guide our venture. And so that you will know where you have been and can measure changes in yourself, you will be asked to map or chart your journey.

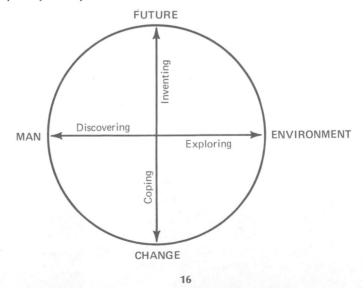

"Spaceship Earth," Buckminster Fuller calls it, to dispel any illusion we might have that we are a fixed point in a static universe. All is in motion. We lack awareness that we are at each instant moving through space and through time because we can experience nothing else with which to compare it. It might be interesting to try to imagine and describe what it would be like to be absolutely still.

Worlds in the Making is a book of problems. Some of them are explicit. Some will be found in the connections that your own imagination draws from the materials. Some are hidden. Some are tangential—byways to explore if they intrigue you.

Be wary. Take nothing for granted. Of the dozens of questions, puzzles, probes, and projections you encounter here, you may find that some don't lead you very far. Spend the most time on those that happen to take you farthest. Your own treatment of these problems will be the map of your journey. Whether you work with them

The complete human faculty of thought requires speech, communication, the formation of symbols, and the necessary warehouse space ...for the storage of symbols for future use.... Until experience can be summarized by symbols—whether words or manual gestures—and the symbols grouped, filed, isolated, and selected to perform the thinking process, then experience is no more than an endless silent film.

Robert Ardrey,
African Genesis

verbally or visually, in discussion, on paper, on tape, or on film, you will be creating, observing, expressing, and communicating your own experience. The future you invent will be your own.

Inventing the future is a game any number can play. The rules are flexible. Buckminster Fuller's 200-word, one-sentence statement of his life objectives, written for *Who's Who*, describes one approach. We present it here, first to shock you mildly ("*This* is communication?"); second to reassure you ("After this, anything will be easy"); third to propose one of the few problems in the book to which there is a single solution; and fourth to give you a hint of the book's bias.

THE PROBLEM: Find the twelve words that are the gist or essence of Fuller's life objectives.

WHAT I AM TRYING TO DO

Acutely aware of our beings' limitations and acknowledging the infinite mystery of the a priori universe into which we are born but nevertheless searching for a conscious means of hopefully competent participation by humanity in its own evolutionary trending while employing only the unique advantages inhering exclusively to the individual who takes and maintains the economic initiative in the face of the formidable physical capital and credit advantages of the massive corporations and political states and deliberately avoiding political ties and tactics while endeavoring by experiments and explorations to excite individuals' awareness and realization of humanity's higher potentials I seek through comprehensive anticipatory design science and its reductions to physical practices to reform the environment instead of trying to reform men being intent thereby to accomplish prototyped capabilities of doing more with less whereby in turn the wealth augmenting prospects of such design science regenerations will induce their spontaneous and economically successful industrial proliferation by world around services' managements all of which chain reaction provoking events will both permit and induce all humanity to realize full lasting economic and physical success plus enjoyment of all the Earth without one individual interfering with or being advantaged at the expense of another.

Buckminster Fuller,
Aboard our 1,000-miles-per-minute speeding spaceship Earth within the outer reaches of the cosmically spiraling and expanding Milky Way, the Galactic Nebula

Reprinted by permission of R. Buckminster Fuller.

THE SOLUTION ". . . I seek . . . to reform the environment instead of trying to reform men."

planning strategies

This is the first of the 16 explorations we have called *projections*. A projection is an act of make-believe, in which you imagine for the moment that you are someone else or that you are in some other time or place. The projections suggested in this book demand as great an investment of imagination as you are willing to make. They may open up for you inner and outer worlds only guessed at before. They are ways to awareness.

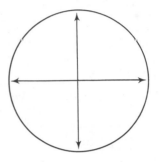

Planning Strategies is a projection into your own immediate future. It is simply a way to awareness of the scope of the task of shaping the future, a way to begin to grasp the future and make it yours.

Find out how far you will be going.

> Familiarize yourself with the book: read the Table of Contents; browse a little. Notice what is covered; be aware of what is there so you can use it when you want it. *Make the book your own.*

Take stock of your resources.

> **Time**. How much time do you have? For reading? For writing? For projects? For discussing? How do you want to use your discussion time? Can you decide on devices or procedures to keep discussion relevant but not restrictive? (One device is described on page 250.)

> **People**. Your richest resource might be people. Find out the relevant talents and interests of the persons in your group.

> Can someone make films, build models, draw, etc? Is anyone particularly concerned with conservation, population control, new communications or transportation media, computers, electronics, the new sciences, experiments in education, etc.?

> What resources in your community can you draw on?

> **Materials**. What would you like to have available? Would you like to have a class copy of any of the books quoted in *Worlds in the Making*? If you de-

cide on a few books only, general books about the future might be most useful. The following are exciting, wide-ranging books:

The Dynamics of Change, by Don Fabun, Prentice-Hall, Inc., 1968.
Profiles of the Future, by Arthur C. Clarke, Harper & Row, Publishers, 1963.
Education and Ecstasy, by George Leonard, Dell Publishing Co., Inc., 1968.
Dialogue on Technology, Dialogue on Education, Dialogue on Science, Dialogue on Youth, edited by Robert Theobald, part of the Campus Dialogue Series, the Bobbs-Merrill Co., Inc., 1967.

What about films, records, newspapers, magazines? For example, there is a magazine called *The Futurist;* a record, *Buckminster Fuller Thinks Aloud*; a film series, *Twenty-first Century.*

What resources can you draw on for collecting and presenting ideas? A notebook for clippings? Materials for art work? Audio-visual equipment? Construction board? Blackboard? Bulletin board?

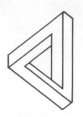

In the coming world the capacity to face the new appropriately is more important than the ability to know and repeat the old.

Carl Rogers,
*quoted in Kaiser Aluminum
NEWS* © **1967**

PART II **coping with change**

four

meeting change
with change

If all environments were stable the well-adapted would simply take over the earth and the evolutionary process would stop. In a period of environmental change, however, it is the adaptable not the well-adapted who survive.

Kenneth Boulding,
The Meaning of the
Twentieth Century

How adaptable are you? Do you really know who you are? How can one best prepare to cope with change?

Change in our natural, technological, and cultural environment is occurring at such a rapid pace that the future is interpenetrating the present, somewhat like a gas mixing with air. Thus, future shock is experienced in the present, in each present, by more and more persons, as more and more of our environment undergoes change. Later on in our journey, we will be projecting into environments that we ourselves can create in imagination. By anticipating, we will be ready to meet—perhaps even to choose—changes to come.

First, however, we will prepare by experimenting with two kinds of disorientation. The first is one in which you feel *yourself* to be different from the person you thought you were. This is a form of identity crisis, of being caught in the question: "Who am I?" The second is one in which you feel your *environment* to be different from what you thought it was. This is a form of alienation, a confronting of the question: "Where am I?"

The persons in the readings to follow are experiencing culture shock. Each undergoes a change so profound that to cope with it he must break through to a new level of awareness of who or where he is. In imagination, we will try to experience culture shock with each of them.

five

imprisoned
in the flesh of
an utter stranger

In principle, the sense impressions from any living creature—animal or human—might be wired directly into the
appropriate sections of the brain. And so one could look
through another man's eyes.

Arthur C. Clarke,
Profiles of the Future

In 1960 *Sepia Magazine* published an account of a white man's experience as a black man traveling through the South. That man was
John Howard Griffin who, through pigmentation treatments, changed
the color of his skin from white to black. His account grew into a
book, *Black Like Me*. The following selection is an episode from that
book. Mr. Griffin, about to embark on his own journey, makes a
startling discovery.

from BLACK LIKE ME

John Howard Griffin

I had my last visit with the doctor in the morning. The treatment had
not worked as rapidly or completely as we had hoped, but I had a dark
undercoating of pigment which I could touch up perfectly with stain.

Reprinted from John Howard Griffin, *Black Like Me* (Boston: Houghton Mifflin
Company, 1961), pp. 14–17, by permission of the publisher.

We decided I must shave my head, since I had no curl. The dosage was established, and the darkness would increase as time passed. From there, I was on my own.

The doctor showed much doubt and perhaps regret that he had ever cooperated with me in this transformation. Again he gave me many firm warnings and told me to get in touch with him any time of the day or night if I got into trouble. As I left his office, he shook my hand and said gravely, "Now you go into oblivion."

A cold spell had hit New Orleans, so that lying under the lamp that day was a comfortable experience. I decided to shave my head that evening and begin my journey.

In the afternoon, my host looked at me with friendly alarm. "I don't know what you're up to," he said, "but I'm worried."

I told him not to be and suggested I would probably leave sometime that night. He said he had a meeting, but would cancel it. I asked him not to. "I don't want you here when I go," I said.

"What are you going to do—be a Puerto Rican or something?" he asked.

"Something like that," I said. "There may be ramifications. I'd rather you didn't know anything about it. I don't want you involved."

He left around five. I fixed myself a bite of supper and drank many cups of coffee, putting off the moment when I would shave my head, grind in the stain and walk out into the New Orleans night as a Negro.

I telephoned home, but no one answered. My nerves simmered with dread. Finally I began to cut my hair and shave my head. It took hours and many razor blades before my pate felt smooth to my hand. The house settled into silence around me. Occasionally, I heard the trolley car rattle past as the night grew late. I applied coat after coat of stain, wiping each coat off. Then I showered to wash off all the excess. I did not look into the mirror until I finished dressing and had packed my duffel bags.

Turning off all the lights, I went into the bathroom and closed the door. I stood in the darkness before the mirror, my hand on the light switch. I forced myself to flick it on.

In the flood of light against white tile, the face and shoulders of a stranger—a fierce, bald, very dark Negro—glared at me from the glass. He in no way resembled me.

The transformation was total and shocking. I had expected to see myself disguised, but this was something else. I was imprisoned in the flesh of an utter stranger, an unsympathetic one with whom I felt no kinship. All traces of the John Griffin I had been were wiped from existence. Even the senses underwent a change so profound it filled me with distress. I looked into the mirror and saw reflected nothing of the white John Griffin's past. No, the reflections led back to Africa, back to the shanty and the ghetto, back to the fruitless struggles against the mark of blackness. Suddenly, almost with no mental preparation, no advance hint, it became clear and permeated my whole being. My inclination was to fight against it. I had gone too far. I knew now that there is no such thing as a disguised white man, when the black won't rub off. The black man is wholly a Negro, regardless of what he once may have been. I was a newly created Negro who must go out that door and live in a world unfamiliar to me.

The completeness of this transformation appalled me. It was unlike anything I had imagined. I became two men, the observing one and the one who panicked, who felt Negroid even into the depths of his entrails.

I felt the beginnings of great loneliness, not because I was a Negro but because the man I had been, the self I knew, was hidden in the flesh of another. If I returned home to my wife and children they would not know me. They would open the door and stare blankly at me. My children would want to know who is this large, bald Negro. If I walked up to friends, I knew I would see no flicker of recognition in their eyes.

I had tampered with the mystery of existence and I had lost the sense of my own being. This is what devastated me. The Griffin that was had become invisible.

The worst of it was that I could feel no companionship with this new person. I did not like the way he looked. Perhaps, I thought, this was only the shock of a first reaction. But the thing was done and there was no possibility of turning back. For a few weeks I must be this aging, bald Negro; I must walk through a land hostile to my color, hostile to my skin.

How did one start? The night lay out there waiting. A thousand questions presented themselves. The strangeness of my situation struck me anew—I was a man born old at midnight into a new life. How does such a man act? Where does he go to find food, water, a bed?

The phone rang and I felt my nerves convulse. I answered and told the caller my host was out for the evening. Again the strangeness, the secret awareness that the person on the other end did not know he talked with a Negro. Downstairs, I heard the soft chiming of the old clock. I knew it was midnight though I did not count. It was time to go.

point of departure

What avenues can we explore which will help prepare us to live in a world in which "all the familiar psychological cues are gone"? Here are a few.

What discovery did Griffin make about himself and about his attitudes toward Negroes?

Why did changing the color of his skin make such a profound change in Griffin? Can you imagine a situation in which changing one's skin color would not make this difference?

What other changes might be comparable? Changing one's sex? One's hair style? Why?

If 80 per cent of the United States' population were black, would you rather be black or white? (Ask yourself: "What does my racial identification mean to me?")

The overwhelming majority of the world's population is nonwhite. And the world, in Marshall McLuhan's words, "is becoming a global village." What implications for change do these facts suggest? What will this mean for you?

What will be changed?

What that you have assumed as "fixed" in yourself would have to change if you changed your appearance as completely as Griffin did?

trying on a different self

We all play roles much of the time, and it is difficult to know sometimes what is **us** and what is **a role.** First, you will be asked to play roles very different from your accustomed ones. Among the insights you might get from this will be the discovery of how **you** differ from your roles or perhaps just the awareness that there is a "you" which goes deeper than your roles. (Later you will be asked to "try on" that real you.) Seeing the distinction between you and your roles can free you for change. Roles suitable to a receding past may be useless or pointless in the advancing future; one needs to be free to discard them without fear that one is discarding his very self.

> Imagine that you are a Negro, or a Caucasian, a South African Bushman, a Vietnamese, a Japanese, a Chinese, a boy, a girl, etc. Place yourself in an appropriate setting. What does the setting look like? What do you look like? What are your feelings? Your thoughts? Jot down phrases.

> Study how Griffin has developed his episode—how he has structured the scene; how he uses detail; how he conveys information and evokes emotional response from the reader. Make notes on this.

> Using Griffin's episode as a model for your own imagined episode, develop your own "different self."

six

i wish
i was a fish

[Aldous Huxley] compared the brain to a "reducing valve." In ordinary perception, the senses send an overwhelming flood of information to the brain, which the brain then filters down to a trickle it can manage for the purpose of survival in a highly competitive world. Man has become so rational, so utilitarian, that the trickle becomes most pale and thin. It is efficient, for mere survival, but it screens out the most wondrous part of man's potential experience without his even knowing it. *We're shut off from our own world.* Primitive man once experienced the rich and sparkling flood of the senses fully. Children experience it for a few months—until "normal" training, conditioning, close the doors on this other world, usually for good.

Tom Wolfe,
*The Electric Kool-
Aid Acid Test*

Trying on a different self gave Griffin insights into his real self. The following episode from T. H. White's novel *The Sword in the Stone* shows us that by exploring the experience of being a nonhuman form of life, we can learn to experience nature differently.

When the Wart, who is the young King Arthur, rebels against the boredom and irrelevance of his studies, his teacher, the magician Merlin, supplies an alternative.

Reprinted from Tom Wolfe, *The Electric Kool-Aid Acid Test* (New York: Farrar, Straus & Giroux, Inc., 1968) by permission of the publisher.

from THE SWORD
IN THE STONE

T. H. White

They went out into the courtyard, into a sun so burning that the heat of hay-making seemed to have been nothing. It was baking. The thunder-clouds which usually go with hot weather were there, high columns of cumulus with glaring edges, but there was not going to be any thunder. It was too hot even for that. "If only," thought the Wart, "I did not have to go into a stuffy classroom, but could take off my clothes and swim in the moat."

They crossed the courtyard, having almost to take deep breaths before they darted across it, as if they were going quickly through an oven. The shade of the gatehouse was cool, but the barbican, with its close walls, was hottest of all. In one last dash across the desert they had achieved the drawbridge—could Merlyn have guessed what he was think-ing about?—and were staring down into the moat.

It was the season of water-lilies. If Sir Ector had not kept one section free of them for the boys' bathing, all the water would have been covered. As it was, about twenty yards on each side of the bridge were cut each year, and you could dive in from the bridge itself. The moat was quite deep. It was used as a stew, so that the inhabitants of the castle could have fish on Fridays, and for this reason the architects had been careful not to let the drains and sewers run into it. It was stocked with fish every year.

"I wish I was a fish," said the Wart.

"What sort of fish?"

It was almost too hot to think about this, but the Wart stared down into the cool amber depths where a school of small perch were aimlessly hanging about.

"I think I should like to be a perch," he said. "They are braver than the silly roach, and not quite so slaughterous as the pike."

Merlyn took off his hat, raised his staff of lignum vitae politely in the air, and said slowly, "Snylrem stnemilpmoc ot enutpen dna lliw eh yldnik tpecca siht yob sa a hsif?"

Immediately there was a loud blowing of sea-shells, conches and so forth, and a stout, jolly-looking gentleman appeared seated on a well-blown-up cloud above the battlements. He had an anchor tattooed on his tummy and a handsome mermaid with Mabel written under her on his chest. He ejected a quid of tobacco, nodded affably to Merlyn and pointed his trident at the Wart. The Wart found he had no clothes on. He found that he had tumbled off the drawbridge, landing with a smack on his side in the water. He found that the moat and the bridge had grown hundreds of times bigger. He knew that he was turning into a fish.

"Oh, Merlyn," cried the Wart. "Please come too."

"Just for this once," said a large and solemn tench beside his ear, "I will come. But in future you will have to go by yourself. Education is experience, and the essence of experience is self-reliance."

The Wart found it difficult to be a fish. It was no good trying to swim like a human being, for it made him go corkscrew and much too slowly. He did not know how to swim like a fish.

"Not like that," said the tench in ponderous tones. "Put your chin on your left shoulder and do jack-knives. Never mind about the fins to begin with."

The Wart's legs had fused together into his backbone and his feet and toes had become a tail fin. His arms had become two more fins—also of a delicate pinkish color—and he had sprouted some more somewhere about his tummy. His head faced over his shoulder, so that when he bent in the middle his toes were moving towards his ear instead of towards his forehead. He was a beautiful olive-green color with rather scratchy plate-armor all over him, and dark bands down his sides. He was not sure which were his sides and which were his back and front, but what now appeared to be his tummy had an attractive whitish color, while his back was armed with a splendid great fin that could be erected for war and had spikes in it. He did jack-knives as the tench directed and found that he was swimming vertically downwards into the mud.

"Use your feet to turn to left or right with," said the tench, "and spread those fins on your tummy to keep level. You are living in two planes now, not one."

The Wart found that he could keep more or less level by altering the inclination of his arm fins and the ones on his stomach. He swam feebly off, enjoying himself very much.

"Come back," said the tench solemnly. "You must learn to swim before you can dart."

The Wart returned to his tutor in a series of zig-zags and remarked, "I don't seem to keep quite straight."

"The trouble with you is that you don't swim from the shoulder. You swim as if you were a boy just bending at the hips. Try doing your jack-knives right from the neck downwards, and move your body exactly the same amount to the right as you are going to move it to the left. Put your back into it."

Wart gave two terrific kicks and vanished altogether in a clump of mare's tail several yards away.

"That's better," said the tench, now quite out of sight in the murky olive water, and the Wart backed himself out of his tangle with infinite trouble, by wriggling his arm fins. He undulated back towards the voice in one terrific shove, to show off.

"Good," said the tench, as they collided end to end, "but direction is the better part of valor."

"Try if you can do this one," said the tench.

Without apparent exertion of any kind he swam off backwards under a water-lily. Without apparent exertion; but the Wart, who was an enterprising learner, had been watching the slightest movement of his fins. He moved his own fins anti-clockwise, gave the very tip of his own tail a cunning flick, and was lying alongside the tench.

"Splendid," said Merlyn. "Let's go for a little swim."

The Wart was on an even keel now, and reasonably able to move about. He had leisure to observe the extraordinary universe into which the tattooed gentleman's trident had plunged him. It was very different from the universe to which he had hitherto been accustomed. For one thing, the heaven or sky above him was now a perfect circle poised a few inches above his head. The horizon had closed in to this. In order to imagine yourself into the Wart's position, you will have to picture a round horizon, a few inches above your head, instead of the flat horizon which you have usually seen. Under this horizon of air you will have to imagine another horizon of under water, spherical and practically upside down—for the surface of the water acted partly as a mirror to what was below it. It is difficult to imagine. What makes it a great deal more difficult to imagine is that everything which human beings would consider to be above the water level was fringed with all the colors of the spectrum. For instance, if you had happened to be fishing for the Wart, he would have seen you, at the rim of the tea saucer which was the upper air to him, not as one person waving a fishing-rod, but as seven people, whose outlines were red, orange, yellow, green, blue, indigo, and violet, all waving the same rod whose colors were as varied. In fact, you would have been a rainbow man to him, a beacon of flashing and radiating colors, which ran into one another and had rays all about. You would have burned upon the water like Cleopatra in the poem by Heredia. The reference may possibly be to Shakespeare.

The next most lovely thing was that the Wart had no weight. He was not earthbound any more and did not have to plod along on a flat surface, pressed down by gravity and the weight of the atmosphere. He could do what men have always wanted to do, that is, fly. There is practically no difference between flying in the water and flying in the air. The best of it was that he did not have to fly in a machine, by pulling levers and sitting still, but could do it with his own body. It was like the dreams people have.

point of departure

This selection takes us out of our human form and helps us to see the possibilities of a different kind of relationship to our environment.

How does being a fish differ from being a person?

What does being a fish do to one's experience of space? Of time? Of self?

As a fish, what aspects of the self become most important? Least important?

As a person, which of your senses give you most experience? Which least? Would the world seem different to you if these were reversed? In what ways?

What role does your mind play in your experience of nature?

"A child is a genius till he is five because all his senses are in active inter-relation," says Marshall McLuhan. What does he mean?

How could you communicate sensory experience without words?

What changes in our technological environment could make practical thinking less important than sensory experience in the future?

[E]ducation is an understanding of life, and ... life flows out from man through nature (or the other way, if you please) so that birds and beasts see aspects of it which are necessary for sympathy.

Henry Seidel Canby,
quoted from the book jacket of
The Sword in the Stone

Where in this episode do you find clues to White's attitude toward education?

What underlying view of man's relationship to his world justifies such views about education?

Unlike Griffin's experience, the Wart's is enjoyable. What circumstances can make a change of identity an agreeable experience?

trying on a nonhuman form

Imagine that you are an animal—a bird, a mammal, a fish, etc.

What are the sights, sounds, scents, tactile qualities of the scene? What do you look like? Feel like? What are your thoughts? Jot down phrases.

Study how White has developed his episode: how he has structured the scene; how he uses detail and imagery; how he uses language and sentence patterns; how he conveys information, establishes tone, and evokes emotional reaction in the reader. Make notes on this.

Using White's episode as a model, write your own imagined episode.

seven

when i discover who i am, i'll be free

Ralph Ellison's novel *Invisible Man* first appeared more than twenty years ago, but the problems it deals with and many of the attitudes it expresses are with us still. It is a novel written in the first person. We never learn the hero's name. Chapter One begins:

> It goes a long way back, some twenty years. All my life I had been looking for something, and everywhere I turned someone tried to tell me what it was. I accepted their answers, too, though they were often in contradiction and even self-contradictory. I was naïve. I was looking for myself and asking everyone except myself questions which I, and only I, could answer. It took me a long time and much painful boomeranging of my expectations to achieve a realization everyone else appears to have been born with: That I am nobody but myself. But first I had to discover that I am an invisible man!

As a young black man growing up in the South, "the invisible man" tried to conform to the confusing, often conflicting, expectations of a number of persons. One such person was his grandfather. As the invisible man says, it was his grandfather who caused the trouble.

From *Invisible Man*, by Ralph Ellison. Copyright 1952 by Ralph Ellison. Reprinted by permission of Random House, Inc.

On his deathbed he called my father to him and said, "Son, after I'm gone I want you to keep up the good fight. I never told you, but our life is a war and I have been a traitor all my born days, a spy in the enemy's country ever since I gave up my gun back in the Reconstruction. Live with your head in the lion's mouth. I want you to overcome 'em with yeses, undermine em with grins, agree 'em to death and destruction, let 'em swaller you till they vomit or bust wide open." They thought the old man had gone out of his mind. He had been the meekest of men.

The family is disturbed by the grandfather's dying words, and the children are told to ignore them. But telling isn't always doing.

It had a tremendous effect upon me, however. I could never be sure of what he meant. Grandfather had been a quiet old man who never made any trouble, yet on his deathbed he had called himself a traitor and a spy, and he had spoken of his meekness as a dangerous activity. It became a constant puzzle which lay unanswered in the back of my mind. And whenever things went well for me I remembered my grandfather and felt guilty and uncomfortable. It was as though I was carrying out his advice in spite of myself. And to make it worse, everyone loved me for it. I was praised by the most lily-white men of the town. I was considered an example of desirable conduct—just as my grandfather had been. And what puzzled me was that the old man had defined it as *treachery*. . . . The old man's words were like a curse. On my graduation day I delivered an oration in which I showed that humility was the secret, indeed, the very essence of progress. (Not that I believed this—how could I, remembering my grandfather?—I only believed that it worked.) It was a great success. Everyone praised me and I was invited to give the speech at a gathering of the town's leading white citizens. It was a triumph for our whole community.

The invisible man's fortunes rise and fall in a series of humiliating encounters with the community leaders he tries to impress. He is given a scholarship to a Negro college, and he believes that his future is assured. He is deeply honored when the college's black president asks him to drive a visiting white trustee around town. He is further encouraged by the deep interest the trustee, Mr. Norton, shows in him. The sight-seeing tour turns into a disaster, however, when the trustee, shocked to discover how black people are forced to live, suffers a stroke.

The infuriated president, Dr. Bledsoe, expels him from college and sends him to New York with letters of "recommendation" he discovers to be phony when he tries to get a job.

The humiliating treatment he has endured from persons in authority, both black and white, has not weakened his trust in such persons. He goes to New York still fervently believing that his surest road to advancement is deference, diligence, and trust. After many lonely and frustrating weeks living in the (to him) astonishing Harlem and seeking in vain for a job, he meets Emerson, the liberal son of a company president who helps him get a job at the Liberty Paint factory. He is assigned to the part of the plant which prepares the high-quality white paint for which the company is famous. At last, he believes, he will have a chance to prove himself.

However, on the very first day the boiler explodes, something heavy falls on him, and he slips into unconsciousness, "transfixed and numb with the sense that I had lost irrevocably an important victory." It is here that we pick up his story.

from INVISIBLE MAN

Ralph Ellison

I was sitting in a cold, white rigid chair and a man was looking at me out of a bright third eye that glowed from the center of his forehead. He reached out, touching my skull gingerly, and said something encouraging, as though I were a child. His fingers went away.

"Take this," he said. "It's good for you." I swallowed. Suddenly my skin itched, all over. I had on new overalls, strange white ones. The taste ran bitter through my mouth. My fingers trembled.

A thin voice with a mirror on the end of it said, "How is he?"

"I don't think it's anything serious. Merely stunned."

"Should he be sent home now?"

"No, just to be certain we'll keep him here a few days. Want to keep him under observation. Then he may leave."

Now I was lying on a cot, the bright eye still burning into mine, although the man was gone. It was quiet and I was numb. I closed my eyes only to be awakened.

"What is your name?" a voice said.

"My head . . ." I said.

"Yes, but your name. Address?"

"My head—that burning eye . . ." I said.

"Eye?"

"Inside," I said.

"Shoot him up for an X-ray," another voice said.

"My head . . ."

"Careful!"

Somewhere a machine began to hum and I distrusted the man and woman above me.

They were holding me firm and it was fiery and above it all I kept hearing the opening motif of Beethoven's *Fifth*—three short and one long buzz, repeated again and again in varying volume, and I was struggling and breaking through, rising up, to find myself lying on my back with two pink-faced men laughing down.

"Be quiet now," one of them said firmly. "You'll be all right." I raised my eyes, seeing two indefinite young women in white, looking down at me. A third, a desert of heat waves away, sat at a panel arrayed with coils and dials. Where was I? From far below me a barber-chair thumping began and I felt myself rise on the tip of the sound from the floor. A face was now level with mine, looking closely and saying something without meaning. A whirring began that snapped and cracked with static, and suddenly I seemed to be crushed between the floor and ceiling. Two forces tore savagely at my stomach and back. A flash of cold-edged heat enclosed me. I was pounded between crushing electrical pressures; pumped between live electrodes like an accordion between a player's hands. My lungs were compressed like a bellows and each time my breath returned I yelled, punctuating the rhythmical action of the nodes.

"Hush, goddamit," one of the faces ordered. "We're trying to get you started again. Now shut up!"

The voice throbbed with icy authority and I quieted and tried to contain the pain. I discovered now that my head was encircled by a piece of cold metal like the iron cap worn by the occupant of an electric chair. I tried unsuccessfully to struggle, to cry out. But the people were so remote, the pain so immediate. A face moved in and out of the circle of lights, peering for a moment, then disappeared. A freckled, red-haired woman with gold nose-glasses appeared; then a man with a circular mirror attached to his forehead—a doctor. Yes, he was a doctor and the women were nurses; it was coming clear. I was in a hospital. They would care for me. It was all geared toward the easing of pain. I felt thankful.

I tried to remember how I'd gotten here, but nothing came. My mind was blank, as though I had just begun to live. When the next face appeared I saw the eyes behind the thick glasses blinking as though noticing me for the first time.

"You're all right, boy. You're okay. You just be patient," said the voice, hollow with profound detachment.

I seemed to go away; the lights receded like a tail-light racing down a dark country road. I couldn't follow. A sharp pain stabbed my shoulder. I twisted about on my back, fighting something I couldn't see. Then after a while my vision cleared.

Now a man sitting with his back to me, manipulating dials on a panel. I wanted to call him, but the *Fifth Symphony* rhythm racked me, and he seemed too serene and too far away. Bright metal bars were between us and when I strained my neck around I discovered that I was not lying *on* an operating table but *in* a kind of glass and nickel box, the lid of which was propped open. Why was I here?

"Doctor! Doctor!" I called.

No answer. Perhaps he hadn't heard, I thought, calling again and feeling the stabbing pulses of the machine again and feeling myself going under and fighting against it and coming up to hear voices carrying on a conversation behind my head. The static sounds became a quiet drone.

Strains of music, a Sunday air, drifted from a distance. With closed eyes, barely breathing I warded off the pain. The voices droned harmoniously. Was it a radio I heard—a phonograph? The *vox humana* ot a hidden organ? If so, what organ and where? I felt warm. Green hedges, dazzling with red wild roses, appeared behind my eyes, stretching with a gentle curving to an infinity empty of objects, a limpid blue space. Scenes of a shaded lawn in summer drifted past; I saw a uniformed military band arrayed decorously in concert, each musician with well-oiled hair, heard a sweet-voiced trumpet rendering "The Holy City" as from an echoing distance, buoyed by a choir of muted horns; and above, the mocking obbligato of a mocking bird. I felt giddy. The air seemed to grow thick with fine white gnats, filling my eyes, boiling so thickly that the dark trumpeter breathed them in and expelled them through the bell of his golden horn, a live white cloud mixing with the tones upon the torpid air.

I came back. The voices still droned above me and I disliked them. Why didn't they go away? Smug oncs. Oh, doctor, I thought drowsily, did you ever wade in a brook before breakfast? Ever chew on sugar cane? You know, doc, the same fall day I first saw the hounds chasing black men in stripes and chains my grandmother sat with me and sang with twinkling eyes:

Godamighty made a monkey
Godamighty made a whale
And Godamighty made a 'gator
With hickeys all over his tail . . .

Or you, nurse, did you know that when you strolled in pink organdy and picture hat between the rows of cape jasmine, cooing to your beau in a drawl as thick as sorghum, we little black boys hidden snug in the bushes called out so loud that you daren't hear:

Did you ever see Miss Margaret boil water?
Man, she hisses a wonderful stream
Seventeen miles and a quarter,
Man, and you can't see her pot for the steam . . .

But now the music became a distinct wail of female pain. I opened my eyes. Glass and metal floated above me.

"How are you feeling, boy?" a voice said.

A pair of eyes peered down through lenses as thick as the bottom of a Coca-Cola bottle, eyes protruding, luminous and veined, like an old biology specimen preserved in alcohol.

"I don't have enough room," I said angrily.

"Oh, that's a necessary part of the treatment."

"But I need more room," I insisted. "I'm cramped."

"Don't worry about it, boy. You'll get used to it after a while. How is your stomach and head?"

"Stomach?"

"Yes, and your head?"

"I don't know," I said, realizing that I could feel nothing beyond the pressure around my head and on the tender surface of my body. Yet my senses seemed to focus sharply.

"I don't feel it," I cried, alarmed.

"Aha! You see! My little gadget will solve everything!" he exploded.

"I don't know," another voice said. "I think I still prefer surgery. And in this case especially, with this, uh... background, I'm not so sure that I don't believe in the effectiveness of simple prayer."

"Nonsense, from now on do your praying to my little machine. I'll deliver the cure."

"I don't know, but I believe it a mistake to assume that solutions—cures, that is—that apply in, uh ... primitive instances, are uh ... equally effective when more advanced conditions are in question. Suppose it were a New Englander with a Harvard background?"

"Now you're arguing politics," the first voice said banteringly.

"Oh, no, but it *is* a problem."

I listened with growing uneasiness to the conversation fuzzing away to a whisper. Their simplest words seemed to refer to something else, as did many of the notions that unfurled through my head. I wasn't sure whether they were talking about me or someone else. Some of it sounded like a discussion of history...

"The machine will produce the results of a prefrontal lobotomy without the negative effects of the knife," the voice said. "You see, instead of severing the prefrontal lobe, a single lobe, that is, we apply pressure in the proper degrees to the major centers of nerve control—our concept is Gestalt—and the result is as complete a change of personality as you'll find in your famous fairy-tale cases of criminals transformed into amiable fellows after all that bloody business of a brain operation. And what's more," the voice went on triumphantly, "the patient is both physically and neurally whole."

"But what of his psychology?"

"Absolutely of no importance!" the voice said. "The patient will live as he has to live, and with absolute integrity. Who could ask more? He'll experience no major conflict of motives, and what is even better, society will suffer no traumata on his account."

There was a pause. A pen scratched upon paper. Then, "Why not castration, doctor?" a voice asked waggishly, causing me to start, a pain tearing through me.

"There goes your love of blood again," the first voice laughed. "What's that definition of a surgeon, 'A butcher with a bad conscience'?"

They laughed.

"It's not so funny. It would be more scientific to try to define the case. It has been developing some three hundreds years—"

"Define? Hell, man, we know all that."

"Then why don't you try more current?"

"You suggest it?"

"I do, why not?"

"But isn't there a danger ... ?" the voice trailed off.

I heard them move away; a chair scraped. The machine droned, and I knew definitely that they were discussing me and steeled myself for the shocks, but was blasted nevertheless. The pulse came swift and staccato, increasing gradually until I fairly danced between the nodes. My teeth chattered. I closed my eyes and bit my lips to smother my screams. Warm blood filled my mouth. Between my lids I saw a circle of hands and faces, dazzling with light. Some were scribbling upon charts.

"Look, he's dancing," someone called.

"No, really?"

An oily face looked in. "They really do have rhythm, don't they? Get hot, boy! Get hot!" it said with a laugh.

And suddenly my bewilderment suspended and I wanted to be angry, murderously angry. But somehow the pulse of current smashing through my body prevented me. Something had been disconnected. For though I had seldom used my capacities for anger and indignation, I had no doubt that I possessed them; and, like a man who knows that he must fight, whether angry or not, when called a son of a bitch, I tried to *imagine* myself angry—only to discover a deeper sense of remoteness. I was beyond anger. I was only bewildered. And those above seemed to sense it. There was no avoiding the shock and I rolled with the agitated tide, out into the blackness.

When I emerged, the lights were still there. I lay beneath the slab of glass, feeling deflated. All my limbs seemed amputated. It was very warm. A dim white ceiling stretched far above me. My eyes were swimming with tears. Why, I didn't know. It worried me. I wanted to knock on the glass to attract attention, but I couldn't move. The slightest effort, hardly more than desire, tired me. I lay experiencing the vague processes of my body. I seemed to have lost all sense of proportion. Where did my body end and the crystal and white world begin? Thoughts evaded me, hiding in the vast stretch of clinical whiteness to which I seemed connected only by a scale of receding grays. No sounds beyond the sluggish inner roar of the blood. I couldn't open my eyes. I seemed to exist in some other dimension, utterly alone; until after a while a nurse bent down and forced a warm fluid between my lips. I gagged, swallowed, feeling the fluid course slowly to my vague middle. A huge iridescent bubble seemed to enfold me. Gentle hands moved over me, bringing vague impressions of memory. I was laved with warm liquids, felt gentle hands move through the indefinite limits of my flesh. The sterile and weightless texture of a sheet enfolded me. I felt myself bounce, sail off like a ball thrown over the roof into mist, striking a hidden wall beyond a pile of broken machinery and sailing back. How long it took, I didn't know. But now above the movement of the hands I heard a friendly voice, uttering familiar words to which I could assign no meaning. I listened intensely, aware of the form and movement of sentences and grasping the now subtle rhythmical differences between progressions of sound that questioned and those that made a statement. But still their meanings were lost in the vast whiteness in which I myself was lost.

Other voices emerged. Faces hovered above me like inscrutable fish peering myopically through a glass aquarium wall. I saw them suspended motionless above me, then two floating off, first their heads, then the tips of their finlike fingers, moving dreamily from the top of the case. A thoroughly mysterious coming and going, like the surging of torpid tides. I watched the two make furious movements with their mouths. I didn't understand. They tried again, the meaning still escaping me. I felt uneasy. I saw a scribbled card, held over me. All a jumble of alphabets. They consulted heatedly. Somehow I felt responsible. A terrible sense of loneliness came over me; they seemed to enact a mysterious pantomime. And seeing them from this angle was disturbing. They appeared utterly stupid and I didn't like it. It wasn't right. I could see smut in one doctor's nose; a nurse had two flabby chins. Other faces came up, their mouths working with soundless fury. But we are all human, I thought, wondering what I meant.

A man dressed in black appeared, a long-haired fellow, whose piercing eyes looked down upon me out of an intense and friendly face. The others hovered about him, their eyes anxious as he alternately peered at me and consulted my chart. Then he scribbled something on a large card and thrust it before my eyes:

WHAT IS YOUR NAME?

A tremor shook me; it was as though he had suddenly given a name to, had organized the vagueness that drifted through my head, and I was overcome with swift shame. I realized that I no longer knew my own name. I shut my eyes and shook my head with sorrow. Here was the first warm attempt to communicate with me and I was failing. I tried again, plunging into the blackness of my mind. It was no use; I found nothing but pain. I saw the card again and he pointed slowly to each word:

WHAT . . . IS . . . YOUR . . . NAME?

I tried desperately, diving below the blackness until I was limp with fatigue. It was as though a vein had been opened and my energy syphoned away; I could only stare back mutely. But with an irritating burst of activity he gestured for another card and wrote:

WHO . . . ARE . . . YOU?

Something inside me turned with a sluggish excitement. This phrasing of the question seemed to set off a series of weak and distant lights where the other had thrown a spark that failed. Who am I? I asked myself. But it was like trying to identify one particular cell that coursed through the torpid veins of my body. Maybe I was just this blackness and bewilderment and pain, but that seemed less like a suitable answer than something I'd read somewhere.

The card was back again:

WHAT IS YOUR MOTHER'S NAME?

Mother, who *was* my mother? Mother, the one who screams when you suffer—but who? This was stupid, you always knew your mother's name. Who was it that screamed? Mother? But the scream came from the machine. A machine my mother? . . . Clearly, I was out of my head.

He shot questions at me: *Where were you born? Try to think of your name.*

I tried, thinking vainly of many names, but none seemed to fit, and yet it was as though I was somehow a part of all of them, had become submerged within them and lost.

You must remember, the placard read. But it was useless. Each time I found myself back in the clinging white mist and my name just beyond my fingertips. I shook my head and watched him disappear for a moment and return with a companion, a short, scholarly looking man who stared at me with a blank expression. I watched him produce a child's slate and a piece of chalk, writing upon it:

WHO WAS YOUR MOTHER?

I looked at him, feeling a quick dislike and thinking, half in amusement, I don't play the dozens. And how's *your* old lady today?

THINK

I stared, seeing him frown and write a long time. The slate was filled with meaningless names.

I smiled, seeing his eyes blaze with annoyance. Old Friendly Face said something. The new man wrote a question at which I stared in wide-eyed amazement:

WHO WAS BUCKEYE THE RABBIT?

I was filled with turmoil. Why should he think of *that?* He pointed to the question, word by word. I laughed, deep, deep inside me, giddy with the delight of self-discovery and the desire to hide it. Somehow *I* was Buckeye the Rabbit . . . or had been, when as children we danced and sang barefoot in the dusty streets:

Buckeye the Rabbit
Shake it, shake it
Buckeye the Rabbit
Break it, break it . . .

Yet, I could not bring myself to admit it, it was too ridiculous—and somehow too dangerous. It was annoying that he had hit upon an old identity and I shook my head, seeing him purse his lips and eye me sharply.

BOY, WHO WAS BRER RABBIT?

He was your mother's back-door man, I thought. Anyone knew they were one and the same: "Buckeye" when you were very young and hid yourself behind wide innocent eyes; "Brer," when you were older. But why was he playing around with these childish names? Did they think I was a child? Why didn't they leave me alone? I would remember soon enough when they let me out of the machine . . . A palm smacked sharply upon the glass, but I was tired of them. Yet as my eyes focused upon Old Friendly Face he seemed pleased. I couldn't understand it, but there he was, smiling and leaving with the new assistant.

Left alone, I lay fretting over my identity. I suspected that I was really playing a game with myself and that they were taking part. A kind of combat. Actually they knew as well as I, and I for some reason preferred not to face it. It was irritating, and it made me feel sly and alert. I would solve the mystery the next instant. I imagined myself whirling about in my mind like an old man attempting to catch a small boy in some mischief, thinking, Who am I? It was no good. I felt like a clown. Nor was I up to being both criminal and detective—though why criminal I didn't know.

I fell to plotting ways of short-circuiting the machine. Perhaps if I shifted my body about so that the two nodes would come together—No, not only was there no room but it might electrocute me. I shuddered. Whoever else I was, I was no Samson. I had no desire to destroy myself even if it destroyed the machine; I wanted freedom, not destruction. It was exhausting, for no matter what the scheme I conceived, there was one constant flaw—myself. There was no getting around it. I could no more escape than I could think of my identity. Perhaps, I thought, the two things are involved with each other. When I discover who I am, I'll be free.

It was as though my thoughts of escape had alerted them. I looked up to see two agitated physicians and a nurse, and thought, It's too late now, and lay in a veil of sweat watching them manipulate the controls. I was braced for the usual shock, but nothing happened. Instead I saw their hands at the lid, loosening the bolts, and before I could react they had opened the lid and pulled me erect.

"What's happened?" I began, seeing the nurse pause to look at me.

"Well?" she said.

My mouth worked soundlessly.

"Come on, get it out," she said.

"What hospital is this?" I said.

"It's the factory hospital," she said. "Now be quiet."

They were around me now, inspecting my body, and I watched with growing bewilderment, thinking, what is a *factory* hospital?

I felt a tug at my belly and looked down to see one of the physicians pull the cord which was attached to the stomach node, jerking me forward.

"What is this?" I said.

"Get the shears," he said.

"Sure," the other said. "Let's not waste time."

I recoiled inwardly as though the cord were part of me. Then they had it free and the nurse clipped through the belly band and removed the heavy node. I opened my mouth to speak but one of the physicians shook his head. They worked swiftly. The nodes off, the nurse went over me with rubbing alcohol. Then I was told to climb out of the case. I looked from face to face, overcome with indecision. For now that it appeared that I was being freed, I dared not believe it. What if they were transferring me to some even more painful machine? I sat there, refusing to move. Should I struggle against them?

"Take his arm," one of them said.

"I can do it," I said, climbing fearfully out.

I was told to stand while they went over my body with the stethoscope.

"How's the articulation?" the one with the chart said as the other examined my shoulder.

"Perfect," he said.

I could feel a tightness there but no pain.

"I'd say he's surprisingly strong, considering," the other said.

"Shall we call in Drexel? It seems rather unusual for him to be so strong."

"No, just note it on the chart."

"All right, nurse, give him his clothes."

"What are you going to do with me?" I said. She handed me clean underclothing and a pair of white overalls.

"No questions," she said. "Just dress as quickly as possible."

The air outside the machine seemed extremely rare. When I bent over to tie my shoes I thought I would faint, but fought it off. I stood shakily and they looked me up and down.

"Well, boy, it looks as though you're cured," one of them said. "You're a new man. You came through fine. Come with us," he said.

We went slowly out of the room and down a long white corridor into an elevator, then swiftly down three floors to a reception room with rows of chairs. At the front were a number of private offices with frosted glass doors and walls.

"Sit down there," they said. "The director will see you shortly."

I sat, seeing them disappear inside one of the offices for a second and emerge, passing me without a word. I trembled like a leaf. Were they really freeing me? My head spun. I looked at my white overalls. The nurse said that this was the factory hospital . . . Why couldn't I remember what kind of factory it was? And why a *factory* hospital? Yes . . . I did remember some vague factory; perhaps I was being sent back there. Yes, and he'd spoken of the director instead of the head doctor; could they be one and the same? Perhaps I was in the factory already. I listened but could hear no machinery.

Across the room a newspaper lay on a chair, but I was too concerned to get it. Somewhere a fan droned. Then one of the doors with frosted glass was opened and I saw a tall austere-looking man in a white coat, beckoning to me with a chart.

"Come," he said.

I got up and went past him into a large simply furnished office, thinking, *Now, I'll know. Now.*

"Sit down," he said.

I eased myself into the chair beside his desk. He watched me with a calm, scientific gaze.

"What is your name? Oh here, I have it," he said, studying the chart. And it was as though someone inside of me tried to tell him to be silent, but already he had called my name and I heard myself say, "Oh!" as a pain stabbed through my head and I shot to my feet and looked wildly around me and sat down and got up and down again very fast, remembering. I don't know why I did it, but suddenly I saw him looking at me intently, and I stayed down this time.

He began asking questions and I could hear myself replying fluently, though inside I was reeling with swiftly changing emotional images that shrilled and chattered, like a sound-track reversed at high speed.

"Well, my boy," he said, "you're cured. We are going to release you. How does that strike you?"

Suddenly I didn't know. I noticed a company calendar beside a stethoscope and a miniature silver paint brush. Did he mean from the hospital or from the job? . . .

"Sir?" I said.

"I said, how does that strike you?"

"All right, sir," I said in an unreal voice. "I'll be glad to get back to work."

He looked at the chart, frowning. "You'll be released, but I'm afraid that you'll be disappointed about the work," he said.

"What do you mean, sir?"

"You've been through a severe experience," he said. "You aren't ready for the rigors of industry. Now I want you to rest, undertake a period of convalescence. You need to become readjusted and get your strength back."

"But, sir—"

"You mustn't try to go too fast. You're glad to be released, are you not?"

"Oh, yes. But how shall I live?"

"Live?" his eyebrows raised and lowered. "Take another job," he said. "Something easier, quieter. Something for which you're better prepared."

"Prepared?" I looked at him, thinking, Is he in on it too? "I'll take anything, sir," I said.

"That isn't the problem, my boy. You just aren't prepared for work under our industrial conditions. Later, perhaps, but not now. And remember, you'll be adequately compensated for your experience."

"Compensated, sir?"

"Oh, yes," he said. "We follow a policy of enlightened humanitarianism; all our employees are automatically insured. You have only to sign a few papers."

"What kind of papers, sir?"

"We require an affidavit releasing the company of responsibility," he said. "Yours was a difficult case, and a number of specialists had to be called in. But, after all, any new occupation has its hazards. They are part of growing up, of becoming adjusted, as it were. One takes a chance and while some are prepared, others are not."

I looked at his lined face. Was he doctor, factory official, or both? I couldn't get it; and now he seemed to move back and forth across my field of vision, although he sat perfectly calm in his chair.

It came out of itself: "Do you know Mr. Norton, sir?" I said.

"Norton?" His brows knitted. "What Norton is this?"

Then it was as though I hadn't asked him; the name sounded strange. I ran my hand over my eyes.

"I'm sorry," I said. "It occurred to me that you might. He was just a man I used to know."

"I see. Well"—he picked up some papers—"so that's the way it is, my boy. A little later perhaps we'll be able to do something. You may take the papers along if you wish. Just mail them to us. Your check will be sent upon their return. Meanwhile, take as much time as you like. You'll find that we are perfectly fair."

I took the folded papers and looked at him for what seemed to be too long a time. He seemed to waver. Then I heard myself say, "Do you know him?" my voice rising.

"Who?"

"Mr. Norton," I said. "Mr. Norton!"

"Oh, why, no."

"No," I said, "no one knows anybody and it was too long a time ago."

He frowned and I laughed. "They picked poor Robin clean," I said. "Do you happen to know Bled?"

He looked at me, his head to one side. "Are these people friends of yours?"

"Friends? Oh, yes," I said, "we're all good friends. Buddies from way back. But I don't suppose we get around in the same circles."

His eyes widened. "No," he said, "I don't suppose we do. However, good friends are valuable to have."

I felt light-headed and started to laugh and he seemed to waver again and I thought of asking him about Emerson, but now he was clearing his throat and indicating that he was finished.

I put the folded papers in my overalls and started out. The door beyond the rows of chairs seemed far away.

"Take care of yourself," he said.

"And you," I said, thinking, it's time, it's past time.

Turning abruptly, I went weakly back to the desk, seeing him looking up at me with his steady scientific gaze. I was overcome with ceremonial feelings but unable to remember the proper formula. So as I deliberately extended my hand I fought down laughter with a cough.

"It's been quite pleasant, our little palaver, sir," I said. I listened to myself and to his answer.

"Yes, indeed," he said.

He shook my hand gravely, without surprise or distaste. I looked down, he was there somewhere behind the lined face and outstretched hand.

"And now our palaver is finished," I said. "Good-bye."

He raised his hand. "Good-bye," he said, his voice noncommittal.

Leaving him and going out into the paint-fuming air I had the feeling that I had been talking beyond myself, had used words and expressed attitudes not my own, that I was in the grip of some alien personality lodged deep within me. Like the servant about whom I'd read in psychology class who, during a trance, had recited pages of Greek philosophy which she had overheard one day while she worked. It was as though I were acting out a scene from some crazy movie. Or perhaps I was catching up with myself and had put into words feelings which I had hitherto suppressed. Or was it, I thought, starting up the walk, that I was no longer afraid? I stopped, looking at the building down the bright street slanting with sun and shade. I *was* no longer afraid. Not of important men, not of trustees and such; for knowing now that there was nothing which I could expect from them, there was no reason to be afraid. Was that it? I felt light-headed, my ears were ringing. I went on.

Along the walk the buildings rose, uniform and close together. It was day's end now and on top of every building the flags were fluttering and diving down, collapsing. And I felt that I would fall, had fallen, moved now as against a current sweeping swiftly against me. Out of the grounds and up the street I found the bridge by which I'd come, but the stairs leading back to the car that crossed the top were too dizzily steep to climb, swim or fly, and I found a subway instead.

Things whirled too fast around me. My mind went alternately bright and blank in slow rolling waves. We, he, him—my mind and I—were no longer getting around in the same circles. Nor my body either. Across the aisle a young platinum blonde nibbled at a red Delicious apple as station lights rippled past behind her. The train plunged. I dropped through the roar, giddy and vacuum-minded, sucked under and out into late afternoon Harlem.

point of departure

While both John Howard Griffin and the Wart changed their identities willingly and with something of a spirit of experiment and adventure, the character in Ellison's novel was changed against his will. They acted; he was acted upon. They had to cope with the consequences of an active choice; he was assigned a passive role. More importantly, while Griffin and the Wart retained some sense of their former selves against which to measure the new experiences, Ellison's character lost sight of his former self altogether. As we shall see, the heart of his experience was the struggle between different, conflicting parts of himself.

How did Ellison's character cope with the experiences forced upon him by the environment in which he found himself? He found himself! That is the simple answer. But our probe does not end here. Paradoxically, the same process by which he lost himself plunged him deeply into an experience of himself. Let us see if we can resolve the paradox.

We can begin by becoming more aware of the *development* of the episode. We may notice first that the invisible man goes through not one but several experiences that deepen with each succeeding shock. He meets each of these with a response that is his way of coping. There is a progression from an inner-outer conflict to an internal one.

The invisible man had to cope first with physical pain. Next, he had to cope with his own feelings, his reactions. Finally, he had to cope with his own muddled thoughts, his confusion about his identity. If you look back at the episode, you will see that Ellison gives us some clues about how he copes with these. But the clues themselves are confusing. What about the *"Fifth Symphony"*? Does he really hear this? Is this his coping?

What were the people trying to do to him? Did they succeed? Before the events of this chapter occurred, Ellison's hero could be described as a young man who believed that only through attitudes of submission and respect could he avoid the wrath and enlist the help of the white man, that such was the correct pose for the Negro.

In what ways does he change? How can we describe him after these events? Toward the end of the selection, after his discussion with the director, he makes some observations about himself. What answers can you find there?

---

taking another look

In reading and thinking about this episode so far, you have probably noticed some puzzling sentences. Perhaps you have discovered that some of these lead to a second and even a third level of meaning.

"Their simplest words seemed to refer to something else, as did many of the notions that unfurled through my head. I wasn't sure whether they were talking about me or someone else...." (p. 38)

"It would be more scientific to try to define the case. It has been developing some three hundred years...." (p. 38)

"...still their meanings were lost in the vast whiteness in which I myself was lost." (p. 39)

"I could no more escape than I could think of my identity. Perhaps, I thought, the two things are involved with each other. When I discover who I am, I'll be free." (p. 42)

Have you found others?

Let us look at the episode again, but first let's draw a distinction between *the real self* and *the self-structure*. With these two concepts as tools, we may then be able to fathom the second and third levels of meaning.

The expression "real self" refers to a person's *inner reality*, to his spontaneous feelings, wishes, thoughts, memories, and fantasies. The real self is a *process*, not a thing. To be in touch with one's real self, to be able to express it, to behave in accordance with it is to be a *healthy* person, as distinguished from an *adjusted* one. (For a fuller presentation and development of these ideas see Sidney Jourard, *Personal Adjustment*.)

A person's *self-structure* is the view he holds of himself. He develops his self-structure on the basis of his experience with people and situations. He believes he has certain qualities, values, and goals because, perhaps, he has been brought up to hold those beliefs. For example, the invisible man grew up with the belief that he was a submissive, cooperative person. If a person has a self-structure which is very different from his real self, we say that he is *alienated* from his real self. In other words, he does not know who he really is.

One plays many roles in society, according to the dictates of the self-structure. If the self-structure is not closely similar to the real self, one may never *be* one's real self at all.

On one level, as we have seen, the invisible man was *responding* to an immediate, alien environment—the machine, the people, and what they were trying to do to him. But his response was not merely passive; he was actively engaged in a struggle—not just with his surroundings, but also with himself. In fact, he found it difficult to distinguish between the environment and himself. "Where did my body end and the crystal and white world begin?" (p. 39)

Worse still, he lost sight of the *here* and *now*. He was experiencing —or re-experiencing—other times and other places. (p. 37)

He no longer knew who he was. He was searching for himself. But where did that search take him, and what did he find?

Looking again through the first part of the episode, we can see that he was given at least four separate "shocks." He reacts to these with questions and changing attitudes. (What are they?) With each shock, another layer of his self-structure is stripped away.

His search for his identity takes him back through his childhood. And yet he does not seem to find himself there. As he tries to remember who he *is* he can only discover who he *was*. And that, he felt, was dangerous. (p. 41)

Why does the question "what is your name" throw a spark and fail, while the question "who are you" excites him? (p. 40)

Is it possible that the shock treatments take him all the way back to *before his birth*? Is there a sense in which he is *reborn*? What can we make of the way in which he thinks about the machine—"A machine my mother?" (p. 41)

"I felt a tug at my belly and looked down to see one of the physicians pull the cord which was attached to the stomach node. . . . I recoiled inwardly as though the cord were part of me. Then they had it free and the nurse clipped through the belly band. . . ." (pp. 42–43)	What *is* the machine? Of course he does not mean that it is literally his mother. But clearly, it is not merely a machine, either.

Could the machine be society—white man's society, which has formed and shaped him, which has given him his self-structure? If so, then who is *he*? Is it possible that this whole episode is a metaphorical treatment of the relationship of the black man to (or his identity in) the white man's world?

"I had no desire to destroy myself even if it destroyed the machine; I wanted freedom, not destruction." (p. 42)

What other lines point to this possibility? Does the invisible man achieve freedom? From what?

"The machine will produce the results of a prefrontal lobotomy without the negative effects of the knife." . . . "[T]he result is [a] complete . . . change of personality." (p. 38)	Is this what Ellison sees society doing to the black man? Is this what society is doing to all of us?
"I wasn't sure whether they were talking about me or someone else. Some of it sounded like a discussion of history." (p. 38)	

May we go one step further and consider whether the episode has not only a second level, depicting the life experience of "the Negro," but also a third level, depicting the history of the Negro through generations? If so, what historical period is represented by the doctors and nurses? (Take a look at p. 37.)   What period is represented by the director of the hospital-factory? (Is it a hospital or a factory; if it is a factory, what does it produce?) Is the shock treatment the Civil War?

When we look at the episode at this level, we see that the self-structure imposed upon the young man is one that has been built up through generations; he has not been a *person* at all, but a *Negro*. That is why he was an invisible man.

Were there any imprints from the invisible man's early social contacts which were out of harmony with his self-structure?

Three statements are usually made about the effects of early experience. The first is that early habits are very persistent and may prevent the formation of new ones. This, of course, refers not only to the study of experimental animals but also the rearing of children. The second statement is that early perceptions deeply affect all future learning. This concept leads to the difficult question whether basic perceptions—the way we have of seeing the world around us—are inherited or acquired. The third statement is simply that early social contacts determine adult social behavior. This, of course, is imprinting.

Eckhard Hess,
"Imprinting in Animals"

ways and meanings

Perhaps, after all this, you are curious about Ellison's technique as a writer. To understand this, one must look not through his language to his meaning, but at his use of language itself. One would examine his use of sensory description, for example, and the ways in which he juxtaposes his character's experience of the internal and the external world.

The words "white" and "black" occur many times. They are, in fact, a primary "pivot" among the levels of meaning. Examining all of Ellison's uses of these two words yields some surprising insights into his meanings and how he conveys them. Of particular interest is the passage which concludes the last shock treatment and describes the beginning of the "awakening":

I rolled with the agitated tide, out into the blackness.... When I emerged, the lights were still there.... [S]till their meanings were lost in the vast whiteness in which I myself was lost. (p. 39)

trying on your real self

Probably few of us have experienced so profound and rapid a change in ourselves as Ellison's hero. Yet most of us have experienced in less extreme ways what it is like to penetrate a self-structure that has been hiding our real or genuine self. One might say that this is what growth is.

> How closely does your own self-structure fit your real self? Can you think of attitudes, values, or feelings you might have acquired that are in conflict with your inner reality?
>
> Can you recapture an occasion when you had a sudden insight into your real self?

Attitudes, values, and feelings which have been implanted by early social contacts have been called imprints. The biologist Konrad Lorenz has described in **King Solomon's Ring** how newly hatched ducklings will identify the first creature they see as their mother; by much the same process, some biologists believe, human beings form impressions at a very young age about themselves and the world. The process is called **imprinting.**

If we bear in mind that the world we are moving into may have little resemblance to the past, the need for each of us to re-examine his early imprints appears acute. Whether those imprints helped us accept the world as we have traditionally known it, they might be totally inappropriate to a changed and changing world. The real self, because it is a process of interaction with one's environment, is more flexible than a self-structure imposed by early imprinting. We can outgrow a self-structure as we outgrow clothes.

> Granting the enormous difficulty of breaking one's early imprints, do you think it can be done?
>
> In your own experience, what early imprints are you aware of which you have (or have not) been able to break?
>
> What kinds of experience do you think can break a person's imprints? Or do you believe that this is even desirable?
>
> How is imprinting related to culture shock, to future shock, and to the need to cope with change in a rapidly changing world?

Child of Darkness

Calvin Scott

What should the child
of darkness born
be made to know,
what should this child be told
that he may bear the weight of
manhood
in the valley of death
where from the mother land
he was sold?

How can the child of darkness born
walk the valley of the snake
of three lies,
know the lies
and still be whole?
What should this child be told?

The child of darkness
walks a prince,
and this the vipers know
and so they sting him
and so they scorn him,
this child of night,
and so they give him woe.

What should this child be told?
This must the child of
darkness know,
this should the child be told:
This color of yours is as the night
holy as the night;
it is pure
and it is strong.
So look you to your mother land,
oh, child of darkness
look you home.

What should the child of darkness born be made to know?
How would Ellison answer this question?
In this poem, written over twenty years later, how does Scott?

From *Pretty Black Is the Color Soul*, reprinted by permission of the author. (Calvin Scott is a young California poet.)

eight

i'm no wolf and you're no rabbit

In the presence of some people, like certain friends, teachers, relatives, or employers—even a barber, bartender, or stranger on a train—an individual may feel more whole, more worth while, surer of himself, and perhaps unusually inspired with hope and self-confidence. . . . These therapeutic people may simply be good, sympathetic listeners. Or, they may be busy people, strongly committed to the pursuit of some goal, as for example artists, scientists, or politicians. Whatever their vocation, they tend to inspire hope and imagination in the persons around them, such that the latter feel more fully alive and strongly motivated to cope with problems outside themselves. They feel the better for having known these people.

Sidney M. Jourard,
Personal Adjustment

In our explorations so far, we have been looking at the *effects* on the personality of a profound and new experience. In each case, the character had an experience that forced him to change his idea of who he was. As a result of his insights into himself and his environment, and of his method of coping with his insights, he was a changed person—or, more accurately, he functioned at a more "real" level.

Our purpose in making these explorations has been to extend our own capacity for coping with change by changing ourselves. But we must now face a key question: *Change to what?* Though we may understand and accept the need to be flexible and adaptable in a changing world, still we would not want to accept just any change forced upon us by our environment. There may be circumstances in which we would choose not to change. Unless the change were con-

Reprinted with permission of The Macmillan Company from *Personal Adjustment* by Sidney Jourard. © by The Macmillan Company 1958.

ducive to our health and well-being, we might seek to change our environment instead—or to withdraw from it.

With *One Flew Over the Cuckoo's Nest*, a novel by Ken Kesey, we will begin to look more closely into two aspects of our problem: *evaluating change* and *recognizing agents of change*. This is not to say that these aspects were not present in the earlier excerpts, or that the elements we examined there are not also present here. For example, the agent of change in *Invisible Man* was shock treatment, which produced an experience so profound as to shatter the imprints inhibiting the young man's growth as an individual. In *One Flew Over the Cuckoo's Nest* the agent of change is a person.

The setting for this novel, like the setting for the excerpt from *Invisible Man*, is a hospital—in this case a mental hospital somewhere in Oregon. From this rich and provocative novel we have drawn four scenes—two near the beginning and two near the end. While these scenes cannot show fully the depth and scope of the novel, they do give us a vivid glimpse of some rather unusual people, deeply engrossed in a battle for survival.

Most of the action takes place in a ward for acute and chronic patients. Two key figures have been introduced before we take up the story. One is the story-teller himself, called variously "The Chief," "Chief Broom," and Chief Bromden. The Chief is a huge half-breed Indian. The staff and the other patients think that he is deaf and dumb and capable only of pushing a broom around the ward. He has been an inmate in the hospital since his participation in the Second World War. He views the hospital as a great "Combine"—a powerful machine, a network of wires and buttons and devices built into the walls—that holds all the inmates in a crippling grip. When the pressures are strong, Chief Broom hides in a mind-clouding fog that he believes is ejected into the ward by the machine.

The other key figure is Big Nurse, a cold, hard, powerful woman, who hides her malevolence behind a coating of icy politeness. She has absolute authority on the ward. She is the enemy.

As we pick up the story, a new patient is being brought into the locked ward.

from ONE FLEW OVER
THE CUCKOO'S NEST

Ken Kesey

Admission. Everybody stops playing cards and Monopoly, turns toward the day-room door. Most days I'd be out sweeping the hall and see who they're signing in, but this morning, like I explain to you, the Big Nurse put a thousand pounds down me and I can't budge out of the chair. Most days I'm the first one to see the Admission, watch him creep in the door and slide along the wall and stand scared till the black boys come sign for him and take him into the shower room, where they strip him and leave him shivering with the door open while they all three run grinning up and down the halls looking for the Vaseline. . . .

But this morning I have to sit in the chair and only listen to them bring him in. Still, even though I can't see him, I know he's no ordinary Admission. I don't hear him slide scared along the wall, and when they tell him about the shower he don't just submit with a weak little yes, he tells them right back in a loud, brassy voice that he's already plenty damn clean, thank you.

"They showered me this morning at the courthouse and last night at the jail. And I *swear* I believe they'd of washed my ears for me on the taxi ride over if they coulda found the vacilities. Hoo boy, seems like everytime they ship me someplace I gotta get scrubbed down before, after, and during the operation. I'm gettin' so the sound of water makes me start gathering up my belongings. And *get* back away from me with that thermometer, Sam, and give me a minute to look my new home over; I never been in a Institute of Psychology before."

The patients look at one another's puzzled faces, then back to the door, where his voice is still coming in. Talking louder'n you'd think he needed to if the black boys were anywhere near him. He sounds like he's way above them, talking down, like he's sailing fifty yards overhead, hollering at those below on the ground. He sounds big. I hear him coming down the hall, and he sounds big in the way he walks, and he sure don't slide; he's got iron on his heels and he rings it on the floor like horseshoes. He shows up in the door and stops and hitches his thumbs in his pockets, boots wide apart, and stands there with the guys looking at him.

"Good *morn*in', buddies."

There's a paper Halloween bat hanging on a string above his head; he reaches up and flicks it so it spins around.

"Mighty nice fall day."

He talks a little the way Papa used to, voice loud and full of hell, but he doesn't look like Papa; Papa was a full-blood Columbia Indian— a chief—and hard and shiny as a gunstock. This guy is redheaded with long red sideburns and a tangle of curls out from under his cap, been needing cut a long time, and he's broad as Papa was tall, broad across the jaw and shoulders and chest, a broad white devilish grin, and he's hard in a different kind of way from Papa, kind of the way a baseball is hard under the scuffed leather. A seam runs across his nose and one cheekbone where somebody laid him a good one in a fight, and the stitches are still in the seam. He stands there waiting, and when nobody makes a move to say anything to him he commences to laugh. Nobody can tell exactly why he laughs; there's nothing funny going on. But it's not the way that Public Relation laughs, it's free and loud and it comes out of his wide grinning mouth and spreads in rings bigger and bigger till it's lapping against the walls all over the ward. Not like that fat Public Relation laugh. This sounds real. I realize all of a sudden it's the first laugh I've heard in years.

He stands looking at us, rocking back in his boots, and he laughs and laughs. He laces his fingers over his belly without taking his thumbs out of his pockets. I see how big and beat up his hands are. Everybody on the ward, patients, staff, and all, is stunned dumb by him and his laughing. There's no move to stop him, no move to say anything. He laughs till he's finished for a time, and he walks on into the day room. Even when he isn't laughing, that laughing sound hovers around him, the way the sound hovers around a big bell just quit ringing—it's in his eyes, in the way he smiles and swaggers, in the way he talks.

"My name is McMurphy, buddies, R. P. McMurphy, and I'm a gambling fool." He winks and sings a little piece of a song: " '... and whenever I meet with a deck of cards I lays ... my money ... down,' " and laughs again.

He walks to one of the card games, tips an Acute's cards up with a thick, heavy finger, and squints at the hand and shakes his head.

"Yessir, that's what I came to this establishment for, to bring you birds fun an' entertainment around the gamin' table. Nobody left in that Pendleton Work Farm to make my days interesting any more, so I requested a *transfer*, ya see. Needed some new blood. Hooee, look at the way this bird holds his cards, showin' to everybody in a block; man! I'll trim you babies like little lambs."

Cheswick gathers his cards together. The redheaded man sticks his hand out for Cheswick to shake.

"Hello, buddy; what's that you're playin'? Pinochle? Jesus, no wonder you don't care nothin' about showing your hand. Don't you have a straight deck around here? Well say, here we go, I brought along my own deck, just in case, has something in it other than face cards—and check the pictures, huh? Every one different. Fifty-two positions."

Cheswick is pop-eyed already, and what he sees on those cards don't help his condition.

"Easy now, don't smudge 'em; we got lots of time, lots of games ahead of us. I like to use my deck here because it takes at least a week for the other players to get to where they can even see the *suit*...."

He's got on work-farm pants and shirt, sunned out till they're the color of watered milk. His face and neck and arms are the color of oxblood leather from working long in the fields. He's got a primer-black motorcycle cap stuck in his hair and a leather jacket over one arm, and he's got on boots gray and dusty and heavy enough to kick a man half in two. He walks away from Cheswick and takes off the cap and goes to beating a dust storm out of his thigh. One of the black boys circles him with the thermometer, but he's too quick for them; he slips in among the Acutes and starts moving around shaking hands before the black boy can take good aim. The way he talks, his wink, his loud talk, his swagger all remind me of a car salesman or a stock auctioneer—or one of those pitchmen you see on a sideshow stage, out in front of his flapping banners, standing there in a striped shirt with yellow buttons, drawing the faces off the sawdust like a magnet.

"What happened, you see, was I got in a couple of hassles at the work farm, to tell the pure truth, and the court ruled that I'm a psychopath. And do you think I'm gonna argue with the court? Shoo, you can bet your bottom dollar I don't. If it gets me outta those damned pea fields I'll be whatever their little heart desires, be it psychopath or mad dog or werewolf, because I don't care if I never see another weedin' hoe to my dying day. Now they tell me a psychopath's a guy fights too much and fucks too much, but they ain't wholly right, do you think? I mean, who-ever heard tell of a man gettin' too much poozle? Hello, buddy, what do they call you? My name's McMurphy and I'll bet you two dollars here and now that you can't tell me how many spots are in that pinochle hand you're holding *don't* look. Two dollars; what d'ya say? God *damn,* Sam! can't you wait half a minute to prod me with that damn ther-mometer of yours?"

The new man stands looking a minute, to get the set-up of the day room.

One side of the room younger patients, known as Acutes because the doctors figure them still sick enough to be fixed, practice arm wrestling and card tricks where you add and subtract and count down so many and it's a certain card. Billy Bibbit tries to learn to roll a tailormade cigarette, and Martini walks around, discovering things under the tables and chairs. The Acutes move around a lot. They tell jokes to each other and snicker in their fists (nobody ever dares let loose and laugh, the whole staff'd be in with notebooks and a lot of questions) and they write letters with yellow, runty, chewed pencils.

They spy on each other. Sometimes one man says something about himself that he didn't aim to let slip, and one of his buddies at the table where he said it yawns and gets up and sidles over to the big log book by the Nurses' Station and writes down the piece of information he heard—of therapeutic interest to the whole ward, is what the Big Nurse says the book is for, but I know she's just waiting to get enough evidence to have some guy reconditioned at the Main Building, overhauled in the head to straighten out the trouble.

The guy that wrote the piece of information in the log book, he gets a star by his name on the roll and gets to sleep late the next day.

Across the room from the Acutes are the culls of the Combine's product, the Chronics. Not in the hospital, these, to get fixed, but just to keep them from walking around the streets giving the product a bad name. Chronics are in for good, the staff concedes. Chronics are divided into Walkers like me, can still get around if you keep them fed, and Wheelers and Vegetables. What the Chronics are—or most of us—are machines with flaws inside that can't be repaired, flaws born in, or flaws beat in over so many years of the guy running head-on into solid things that by the time the hospital found him he was bleeding rust in some vacant lot.

But there are some of us Chronics that the staff made a couple of mistakes on years back, some of us who were Acutes when we came in, and got changed over. . . .

I'm the one been here on the ward the longest, since the Second World War. I been here on the ward longer'n anybody. Longer'n any of the other patients. The Big Nurse has been here longer'n me.

The Chronics and the Acutes don't generally mingle. Each stays on his own side of the day room the way the black boys want it. The black boys say it's more orderly that way and let everybody know that's the way they'd like it to stay. They move us in after breakfast and look at the grouping and nod. "That's right, gennulmen, that's the way. Now you keep it that way."

Actually there isn't much need for them to say anything, because, other than me, the Chronics don't move around much, and the Acutes say they'd just as leave stay over on their own side, give reasons like the Chronic side smells worse than a dirty diaper. But I know it isn't the stink that keeps them away from the Chronic side so much as they don't like to be reminded that here's what could happen to *them* someday. The Big Nurse recognizes this fear and knows how to put it to use; she'll point out to an Acute, whenever he goes into a sulk, that you boys be good boys and cooperate with the staff policy which is engineered for your *cure*, or you'll end up over on *that* side. . . .

This new redheaded Admission, McMurphy, knows right away he's not a Chronic. After he checks the day room over a minute, he sees he's meant for the Acute side and goes right for it, grinning and shaking hands with everybody he comes to. At first I see that he's making everybody over there feel uneasy, with all his kidding and joking and with the brassy way he hollers at the black boy who's still after him with a thermometer, and especially with that big wide-open laugh of his. Dials twitch in the control panel at the sound of it. The Acutes look spooked and uneasy when he laughs, the way kids look in a schoolroom when one ornery kid is raising too much hell with the teacher out of the room and they're all scared the teacher might pop back in and take it into her head to make them all stay after. They're fidgeting and twitching, responding to the dials in the control panel; I see McMurphy notices he's making them uneasy, but he don't let it slow him down.

"Damn, what a sorry-looking outfit. You boys don't look so crazy to me." He's trying to get them to loosen up, the way you see an auctioneer spinning jokes to loosen up the crowd before the bidding starts. "Which one of you claims to be the craziest? Which one is the biggest loony? Who runs these card games? It's my first day, and what I like to do is make a good impression straight off on the right man if he can prove to me he *is* the right man. Who's the bull goose loony here?"

He's saying this directly to Billy Bibbit. He leans down and glares so hard at Billy that Billy feels compelled to stutter out that he isn't the buh-buh-buh-bull goose loony yet, though he's next in luh-luh-line for the job.

McMurphy sticks a big hand down in front of Billy, and Billy can't do a thing but shake it. "Well, buddy," he says to Billy, "I'm truly glad you're next in luh-line for the job, but since I'm thinking about taking over this whole show myself, lock, stock, and barrel, maybe I better talk with the top man." He looks round to where some of the Acutes have stopped their card-playing, covers one of his hands with the other, and cracks all his knuckles at the sight. "I figure, you see, buddy, to be sort of the gambling baron on this ward, deal a wicked game of blackjack. So you better take me to your leader and we'll get it straightened out who's gonna be boss around here."

Nobody's sure if this barrel-chested man with the scar and the wild grin is play-acting or if he's crazy enough to be just like he talks, or both, but they are all beginning to get a big kick out of going along with him. They watch as he puts that big red hand on Billy's thin arm, waiting to see what Billy will say. Billy sees how it's up to him to break the silence, so he looks around and picks out one of the pinochle-players: "Harding," Billy says, "I guess it would b-b-be you. You're p-president of Pay-Pay-Patient's Council. This m-man wants to talk to you."

The Acutes are grinning now, not so uneasy any more, and glad that something out of the ordinary's going on. They all razz Harding, ask him if he's bull goose loony. He lays down his cards.

Harding is a flat, nervous man with a face that sometimes makes you think you seen him in the movies, like it's a face too pretty to just be a guy on the street. He's got wide, thin shoulders and he curves them in around his chest when he's trying to hide inside himself. He's got hands so long and white and dainty I think they carved each other out of soap, and sometimes they get loose and glide around in front of him free as two white birds until he notices them and traps them between his knees; it bothers him that he's got pretty hands.

He's president of the Patient's Council on account of he has a paper that says he graduated from college. The paper's framed and sits on his nightstand next to a picture of a woman in a bathing suit who also looks like you've seen her in the moving pictures—she's got very big breasts and she's holding the top of the bathing suit up over them with her fingers and looking sideways at the camera. You can see Harding sitting on a towel behind her, looking skinny in his bathing suit, like he's waiting for some big guy to kick sand on him. Harding brags a lot about having such a woman for a wife, says she's the sexiest woman in the world and she can't get enough of him nights.

When Billy points him out Harding leans back in his chair and assumes an important look, speaks up at the ceiling without looking at Billy or McMurphy. "Does this...gentleman have an appointment, Mr. Bibbit?"

"Do you have an appointment, Mr. McM-m-murphy? Mr. Harding is a busy man, nobody sees him without an ap-ap-pointment."

"This busy man Mr. Harding, is he the bull goose loony?" He looks at Billy with one eye, and Billy nods his head up and down real fast; Billy's tickled with all the attention he's getting.

"Then you tell Bull Goose Loony Harding that R. P. McMurphy is waiting to see him and that this hospital ain't big enough for the two of us. I'm accustomed to being top man. I been a bull goose catskinner for every gyppo logging operation in the Northwest and bull goose gambler all the way from Korea, was even bull goose pea weeder on that pea farm at Pendleton—so I figure if I'm bound to be a loony, then I'm bound to be a stompdown dadgum good one. Tell this Harding that he either meets me man to man or he's a yaller skunk and better be outta town by sunset."

Harding leans farther back, hooks his thumbs in his lapels. "Bibbit, you tell this young upstart McMurphy that I'll meet him in the main hall at high noon and we'll settle this affair once and for all, libidos a-blazin'." Harding tries to drawl like McMurphy; it sounds funny with his high, breathy voice. "You might also warn him, just to be fair, that I have been bull goose loony on this ward for nigh onto two years, and that I'm crazier than any man alive."

"Mr. Bibbit, you might warn this Mr. Harding that I'm so crazy I admit to voting for Eisenhower."

"Bibbit! You tell Mr. McMurphy I'm so crazy I voted for Eisenhower *twice!*"

"And you tell Mr. Harding right back"—he puts both hands on the table and leans down, his voice getting low—"that I'm so crazy I plan to vote for Eisenhower again this *November.*"

"I take off my hat," Harding says, bows his head, and shakes hands with McMurphy. There's no doubt in my mind that McMurphy's won, but I'm not sure just what.

All the other Acutes leave what they've been doing and ease up close to see what new sort this fellow is. Nobody like him's ever been on the ward before. They're asking him where he's from and what his business is in a way I've never seen them do before. He says he's a dedicated man. He says he was just a wanderer and logging bum before the Army took him and taught him what his natural bent was; just like they taught some men to goldbrick and some men to goof off, he says, they taught him to play poker. Since then he's settled down and devoted himself to gambling on all levels. Just play poker and stay single and live where and how he wants to, if people would let him, he says, "but you know how society persecutes a dedicated man. Ever since I found my callin' I done time in so many small-town jails I could write a brochure. They say I'm a habitual hassler. Like I fight some. Sheeut. They didn't mind so much when I was a dumb logger and got into a hassle; that's *excusable*, they say, that's a hard-workin feller blowing off steam, they say. But if you're a gambler, if they know you to get up a back-room game now and then, all you have to do is spit slantwise and you're a goddamned criminal. Hooee, it was breaking up the budget drivin' me to and from the pokey for a while there."

He shakes his head and puffs out his cheeks.

"But that was just for a period of time. I learned the ropes. To tell the truth, this 'sault and battery I was doing in Pendleton was the first hitch in close to a year. That's why I got busted. I was outa practice; this guy was able to get up off the floor and get to the cops before I left town. A very tough individual . . ."

He laughs again and shakes hands and sits down to arm wrestle every time that black boy gets too near him with the thermometer, till he's met everybody on the Acute side. And when he finishes shaking hands with the last Acute he comes right on over to the Chronics, like we aren't no different. You can't tell if he's really this friendly or if he's got some gambler's reason for trying to get acquainted with guys so far gone a lot of them don't even know their names.

He's there pulling Ellis's hand off the wall and shaking it just like he was a politician running for something and Ellis's vote was good as anybody's. "Buddy," he says to Ellis in a solemn voice, "my name is R. P. McMurphy and I don't like to see a full-grown man sloshin' around in his own water. Whyn't you go get dried up?"

Ellis looks down at the puddle around his feet in pure surprise. "Why, I thank you," he says and even moves off a few steps toward the latrine before the nails pull his hands back to the wall.

McMurphy comes down the line of Chronics, shakes hands with Colonel Matterson and with Ruckly and with Old Pete. He shakes the hands of Wheelers and Walkers and Vegetables, shakes hands that he has to pick up out of laps like picking up dead birds, mechanical birds, wonders of tiny bones and wires that have run down and fallen. Shakes hands with everybody he comes to except Big George the water freak, who grins and shies back from that unsanitary hand, so McMurphy just salutes him and says to his own right hand as he walks away, "Hand, how do you suppose that old fellow knew all the evil you been into?"

Nobody can make out what he's driving at, or why he's making such a fuss with meeting everybody, but it's better'n mixing jigsaw puzzles. He keeps saying it's a necessary thing to get around and meet the men he'll be dealing with, part of a gambler's job. But he must know he ain't going to be dealing with no eighty-year-old organic who couldn't do any more with a playing card than put it in his mouth and gum it awhile. Yet he looks like he's enjoying himself, like he's the sort of guy that gets a laugh out of people.

I'm the last one. Still strapped in the chair in the corner. McMurphy stops when he gets to me and hooks his thumbs in his pockets again and leans back to laugh, like he sees something funnier about me than about anybody else. All of a sudden I was scared he was laughing because he knew the way I was sitting there with my knees pulled up and my arms wrapped around them, staring straight ahead as though I couldn't hear a thing, was all an act.

"Hooeee," he said, "look what we got here."

I remember all this part real clear. I remember the way he closed one eye and tipped his head back and looked down across that healing wine-colored scar on his nose, laughing at me. I thought at first that he was laughing because of how funny it looked, an Indian's face and black, oily Indian's hair on somebody like me. I thought maybe he was laughing at how weak I looked. But then's when I remember thinking that he was laughing because he wasn't fooled for one minute by my deaf-and-dumb act; it didn't make any difference *how* cagey the act was, he was onto me and was laughing and winking to let me know it.

"What's your story, Big Chief? You look like Sittin' Bull on a sitdown strike." He looked over to the Acutes to see if they might laugh about his joke; when they just sniggered he looked back to me and winked again. "What's your name, Chief?"

Billy Bibbit called across the room. "His n-n-name is Bromden. Chief

Bromden. Everybody calls him Chief Buh-Broom, though, because the aides have him sweeping a l-large part of the time. There's not m-much else he can do, I guess. He's deaf." Billy put his chin in hands. "If I was d-d-deaf"—he sighed—"I would kill myself."

McMurphy kept looking at me. "He gets his growth, he'll be pretty good-sized, won't he? I wonder how tall he is."

"I think somebody m-m-measured him once at s-six feet seven; but even if he is big, he's scared of his own sh-sh-shadow. Just a bi-big deaf Indian."

"When I saw him sittin' here I *thought* he looked some Indian. But Bromden ain't an Indian name. What tribe is he?"

"I don't know," Billy said. "He was here wh-when I c-came."

"I have information from the doctor," Harding said, "that he is only half Indian, a Columbia Indian, I believe. That's a defunct Columbia Gorge tribe. The doctor said his father was the tribal leader, hence this fellow's title, 'Chief'. As to the 'Bromden' part of the name, I'm afraid my knowledge in Indian lore doesn't cover that."

McMurphy leaned his head down near mine where I had to look at him. "Is that right? You deaf, Chief?"

"He's de-de-deef and dumb."

McMurphy puckered his lips and looked at my face a long time. Then he straightened back up and stuck his hand out.

"Well, what the hell, he can shake hands can't he? Deef or whatever. By God, Chief, you may be big, but you shake my hand or I'll consider it an insult. And it's not a good idea to insult the new bull goose loony of the hospital."

When he said that he looked back over to Harding and Billy and made a face, but he left that hand in front of me, big as a dinner plate.

I remember real clear the way that hand looked: there was carbon under the fingernails where he'd worked once in a garage; there was an anchor tattooed back from the knuckles; there was a dirty Band-Aid on the middle knuckle, peeling up at the edge. All the rest of the knuckles were covered with scars and cuts, old and new. I remember the palm was smooth and hard as bone from hefting the wooden handles of axes and hoes, not the hand you'd think could deal cards. The palm was callused, and the calluses were cracked, and dirt was worked in the cracks. A road map of his travels up and down the West. That palm made a scuffing sound against my hand. I remember the fingers were thick and strong closing over mine, and my hand commenced to feel peculiar and went to swelling up out there on my stick of an arm, like he was transmitting his own blood into it. It rang with blood and power. It blowed up near as big as his, I remember. . . .

"Mr. McMurry."

It's the Big Nurse.

"Mr. McMurry, could you come here please?"

It's the Big Nurse, That black boy with the thermometer has gone and got her. She stands there tapping that thermometer against her wrist watch, eyes whirring while she tries to gauge this new man. Her lips are in that triangle shape, like a doll's lips ready for a fake nipple.

"Aide Williams tells me, Mr. McMurry, that you've been somewhat difficult about your admission shower. Is this true? Please understand, I appreciate the way you've taken it upon yourself to orient with the other patients on the ward, but everything in its own good time, Mr. McMurry. I'm sorry to interrupt you and Mr. Bromden, but you do understand: *everyone*...must follow the rules."

He tips his head back and gives that wink that she isn't fooling him any more than I did, that he's onto her. He looks up at her with one eye for a minute.

"Ya know, ma'am," he says, "ya know—that is the ex-*act* thing somebody *always* tells me about the rules..."

He grins. They both smile back and forth at each other, sizing each other up.

"...just when they figure I'm about to do the dead opposite."

Then he lets go my hand.

Do you like McMurphy? Why? What kind of person is he? Think of four or five words which catch your impression of McMurphy. (Don't describe him.) Then check back to see how Kesey gave you your impression. What words does he use?

How does the Chief feel about Big Nurse? What tactics does she use with the patients?

What initial effect does McMurphy have on the patients? What tactics does he use? How does he get the patients to play along with him?

Does Kesey give any clues to suggest that McMurphy is more than just a "dedicated gambler"?

The next episode follows a group therapy session, which is a regular part of the Acutes' routine. The patients are encouraged to talk about each other's weaknesses and to report any infractions or "undesirable" behavior. The effect of this particular session has been to humiliate and demoralize Harding. McMurphy realizes that Big Nurse is not interested in therapy but in power, in control over other people. In a conversation with Harding, McMurphy says:

"I've seen a thousand of 'em, old and young, men and women. Seen 'em all over the country and in the homes—people who try to make you weak so they can get you to toe the line, to follow their rules, to live like they want you to. And the best way to do this, to get you to knuckle under, is to weaken you by getting you where it hurts the worst...."

The men have been talking over the session, and Harding has expressed his hatred and fear of Big Nurse.

"She *doesn't* accuse. She merely needs to insinuate, insinuate anything, don't you see? Didn't you notice today? She'll call a man to the door of the Nurses' Station and stand there and ask him about a Kleenex found under his bed. No more, just ask. And he'll feel like he's lying to her, whatever answer he gives. If he says he was cleaning a pen with it, she'll say, 'I see, a pen', or if he says he has a cold in his nose, she'll say, 'I see, a cold', and she'll nod her neat little gray coiffure and smile her neat little smile and turn and go back into the Nurses' Station, leave him standing there wondering just what *did* he use that Kleenex for." . . .

The episode continues.

Harding hushes all of a sudden and leans forward to take McMurphy's hand in both of his. His face is tilted oddly, edged, jagged purple and gray, a busted wine bottle.

"This world . . . belongs to the strong, my friend! The ritual of our existence is based on the strong getting stronger by devouring the weak. We must face up to this. No more than right that it should be this way. We must learn to accept it as a law of the natural world. The rabbits accept their role in the ritual and recognize the wolf as the strong. In defense, the rabbit becomes sly and frightened and elusive and he digs holes and hides when the wolf is about. And he endures, he goes on. He knows his place. He most certainly doesn't challenge the wolf to combat. Now, would that be wise? Would it?"

He lets go McMurphy's hand and leans back and crosses his legs, takes another long pull off the cigarette. He pulls the cigarette from his thin crack of a smile, and the laugh starts up again—eee-eee-eee, like a nail coming out of a plank.

"Mr. McMurphy . . . my friend . . . I'm not a chicken, I'm a rabbit. The doctor is a rabbit. Cheswick there is a rabbit. Billy Bibbit is a rabbit. All of us in here are rabbits of varying ages and degrees, hippity-hopping through our Walt Disney world. Oh, don't misunderstand me, we're not in here *because* we are rabbits—we'd be rabbits wherever we were—we're all in here because we can't *adjust* to our rabbithood. We *need* a good strong wolf like the nurse to teach us our place."

"Man, you're talkin' like a fool. You mean to tell me that you're gonna sit back and let some old blue-haired woman talk you into being a rabbit?"

"Not talk me into it, no. I was born a rabbit. Just look at me. I simply need the nurse to make me *happy* with my role."

"You're no damned rabbit!"

"See the ears? the wiggly nose? the cute little button tail?"

"You're talking like a crazy ma—"

"Like a crazy man? How astute."

"Damn it, Harding, I didn't mean it like that. You ain't crazy that way. I mean—hell, I been surprised how sane you guys all are. As near as I can tell you're not any crazier than the average asshole on the street—"

"Ah yes, the asshole on the street."

"But not, you know, crazy like the movies paint crazy people. You're just hung up and—kind of—"

"Kind of rabbit-like, isn't that it?"

"Rabbits, *hell!* Not a thing like rabbits, goddammit."

"Mr. Bibbit, hop around for Mr. McMurphy here. Mr. Cheswick, show him how *furry* you are."

Billy Bibbit and Cheswick change into hunched-over white rabbits, right before my eyes, but they are too ashamed to do any of the things Harding told them to do.

"Ah, they're bashful, McMurphy. Isn't that sweet? Or, perhaps, the fellows are ill at ease because they didn't stick up for their friend. Perhaps they are feeling guilty for the way they once again let her victimize them into being her interrogators. Cheer up, friends, you've no reason to feel ashamed. It is all as it should be. It's not the rabbit's place to stick up for his fellow. That would have been foolish. No, you were wise, cowardly but wise."

"Look here, Harding," Cheswick says.

"No, no, Cheswick. Don't get irate at the truth."

"Now look here; there's been times when I've said the same things about old lady Ratched that McMurphy has been saying."

"Yes, but you said them very quietly and took them all back later. You are a rabbit too, don't try to avoid the truth. That's why I hold no grudge against you for the questions you asked me during the meeting today. You were only playing your role. If you had been on the carpet, or you Billy, or you Frederickson, I would have attacked you just as cruelly as you attacked me. We mustn't be ashamed of our behavior; it's the way we little animals were meant to behave."

McMurphy turns in his chair and looks the other Acutes up and down. "I ain't so sure but what they should be ashamed. Personally, I thought it was damned crummy the way they swung in on her side against you. For a minute there I thought I was back in a Red Chinese prison camp..."

"Now by God, McMurphy," Cheswick says, "you listen here."

McMurphy turns and listens, but Cheswick doesn't go on. Cheswick never goes on; he's one of these guys who'll make a big fuss like he's going to lead an attack, holler charge and stomp up and down a minute, take a couple of steps, and quit. McMurphy looks at him where he's been caught off base again after such a tough-sounding start, and says to him, "A hell of a lot like a Chinese prison camp."

Harding holds up his hands for peace. "Oh, no, no, that isn't right. You musn't condemn us, my friend. No. In fact..."

I see that sly fever come into Harding's eye again; I think he's going to start laughing, but instead he takes his cigarette out of his mouth and points it at McMurphy—in his hand it looks like one of his thin, white fingers, smoking at the end.

"...you too, Mr. McMurphy, for all your cowboy bluster and your sideshow swagger, you too, under that crusty surface are probably just as soft and fuzzy and rabbit-souled as we are."

"Yeah, you bet. I'm a little cottontail. Just what is it makes me a rabbit, Harding? My psychopathic tendencies? Is it my fightin' tendencies, or my fuckin' tendencies? Must be the fuckin', musn't it? All that whambam-thank-you-ma'am. Yeah, that whambam, that's probably what makes me a rabbit—"

"Wait; I'm afraid you've raised a point that requires some deliberation. Rabbits are noted for that certain trait, aren't they? Notorious, in fact, for their whambam. Yes. Um. But in any case, the point you bring up simply indicates that you are a healthy, functioning and adequate rabbit, whereas most of us in here even lack the sexual ability to make the grade as adequate rabbits. Failures, we are—feeble, stunted, weak little creatures in a weak little race. Rabbits, *sans* whambam; a pathetic notion."

"Wait a minute; you keep twistin' what I say—"

"No. You were right. You remember, it was you that drew our attention to the place where the nurse was concentrating her pecking? That was true. There's not a man here that isn't afraid he is losing or has already lost his whambam. We comical little creatures can't even achieve masculinity in the rabbit world, that's how weak and inadequate we are. Hee. We are—the *rabbits*, one might say, of the rabbit world!"

He leans forward again, and that strained, squeaking laugh of his that I been expecting begins to rise from his mouth, his hands flipping around, his face twitching.

"Harding! Shut your damned mouth!"

It's like a slap. Harding is hushed, chopped off cold with his mouth still open in a drawn grin, his hands dangling in a cloud of blue tobacco smoke. He freezes this way a second; then his eyes narrow into sly little holes and he lets them slip over to McMurphy, speaks so soft that I have to push my broom up right next to his chair to hear what he says.

"Friend . . . *you* . . . may be a wolf."

"Goddammit, I'm no wolf and you're no rabbit. *Hoo,* I never heard such—"

"You have a very wolfy roar."

With a loud hissing of breath McMurphy turns from Harding to the rest of the Acutes standing around. "Here; all you guys. What the hell is the matter with you? You ain't as crazy as all this, thinking you're some animal."

"No," Cheswick says and steps in beside McMurphy. "No, by God, not me. I'm not any rabbit."

"That's the boy, Cheswick. And the rest of you, let's just knock it off. Look at you, talking yourself into running scared from some fifty-year-old woman. What is there she can do to you, anyway?"

"Yeah, what?" Cheswick says and glares around at the others.

"She can't have you whipped. She can't burn you with hot irons. She can't tie you to the rack. They got laws about that sort of thing nowadays; this ain't the Middle Ages. There's not a thing in the world that she can—"

"You s-s-*saw* what she c-can do to us! In the m-m-meeting today." I see Billy Bibbit has changed back from a rabbit. He leans toward McMurphy, trying to go on, his mouth wet with spit and his face red. Then he turns and walks away. "Ah, it's n-no use. I should just k-k-kill myself."

McMurphy calls after him. "Today? What did I see in the meeting today? Hell's bells, all I saw today was her asking a couple of questions, and nice, easy questions at that. Questions ain't bonebreakers, they ain't sticks and stones."

Billy turns back. "But the wuh-wuh-*way* she asks them—"

"You don't have to answer, do you?"

"If you d-don't answer she just smiles and m-m-makes a note in her little book and then she—she—oh, *hell!*"

Scanlon comes up beside Billy. "If you don't answer her questions, Mack, you *admit* it just by keeping quiet. It's the way those bastards in the government get you. You can't beat it. The only thing to do is blow the whole business off the face of the whole bleeding earth—blow it all up."

"Well, when she asks one of those questions, why don't you tell her to up and go to hell?"

"Yeah," Cheswick says, shaking his fist, "tell her to up and go to hell."

"So then what, Mack? She'd just come right back with 'Why do you seem so *upset* by that par-tik-uler question, Patient McMurphy?'"

"So, you tell her to go to hell again. Tell them all to go to hell. They still haven't hurt you."

The Acutes are crowding closer around him. Frederickson answers this time. "Okay, you tell her that and you're listed as Potential Assaultive and shipped upstairs to the Disturbed ward. I had it happen. Three times. Those poor goofs up there don't even get off the ward to go to the Saturday afternoon movie. They don't even have a TV."

"And, my friend, if you *continue* to demonstrate such hostile tendencies, such as telling people to go to hell, you get lined up to go to the Shock Shop, perhaps even on to greater things, an operation, an—"

"Damn it, Harding, I told you I'm not up on this talk."

"The Shock Shop, Mr. McMurphy, is jargon for the EST machine, the Electro Shock Therapy. A device that might be said to do the work of the sleeping pill, the electric chair, *and* the torture rack. It's a clever little procedure, simple, quick, nearly painless it happens so fast, but no one ever wants another one. Ever."

"What's this thing do?"

"You are strapped to a table, shaped, ironically, like a cross, with a crown of electric sparks in place of thorns. You are touched on each side of the head with wires. Zap! Five cents' worth of electricity through the brain and you are jointly administered therapy and a punishment for your hostile go-to-hell behavior, on top of being put out of everyone's way for six hours to three days, depending on the individual. Even when you do regain consciousness you are in a state of disorientation for days. You are unable to think coherently. You can't recall things. Enough of these treatments and a man could turn out like Mr. Ellis you see over there against the wall. A drooling, pants-wetting idiot at thirty-five. Or turn into a mindless organism that eats and eliminates and yells 'fuck the wife', like Ruckly. Or look at Chief Broom clutching to his namesake there beside you."

Harding points his cigarette at me, too late for me to back off. I make like I don't notice. Go on with my sweeping.

"I've heard that the Chief, years ago, received more than two hundred shock treatments when they were really the vogue. Imagine what this could do to a mind that was already slipping. Look at him: a giant janitor. There's your Vanishing American, a six-foot-eight sweeping machine, scared of its own shadow. That, my friend, is what we can be threatened with."

McMurphy looks at me for a while, then turns back to Harding. "Man, I tell you, how come you stand for it? What about this democratic-ward manure that the doctor was giving me? Why don't you take a vote?"

Harding smiles at him and takes another slow drag on his cigarette. "Vote what, my friend? Vote that the nurse may not ask any more questions in Group Meeting? Vote that she shall not *look* at us in a certain way? You tell me, Mr. McMurphy, what do we vote on?"

"Hell, I don't care. Vote on anything. Don't you see you have to do something to show you still got some guts? Don't you see you can't let her take over completely? Look at you here: you say the Chief is scared of his own shadow, but I never saw a scareder-looking bunch in my life than you guys."

"Not me!" Cheswick says.

"Maybe not you, buddy, but the rest are even scared to open up and *laugh*. You know, that's the first thing that got me about this place, that there wasn't anybody laughing. I haven't heard a real laugh since I came through that door, do you know that? Man, when you lose your laugh you lose your *footing*. A man go around lettin' a woman whup him down till he can't laugh any more, and he loses one of the biggest edges he's got on his side. First thing you know he'll begin to think she's tougher than he is and—"

"Ah. I believe my friend is catching on, fellow rabbits. . . ."

The argument continues, with Harding apparently winning, until McMurphy makes a grandstand play. He bets each of the other patients five dollars that—without doing anything which will give Big Nurse an excuse to send him up for shock treatment—he can force her to lose her cool.

By this time you may be caught enough by the story to read the full novel and find out:

   —how McMurphy instills in the men a feeling of being men again.
   —how he tricks the Chief into revealing that he can hear and, in the deepening friendship which develops between them, leads him to talk again.
   —how he arranges, despite Big Nurse's opposition, a game room for the Acutes separate from the Chronics.
   —how he organizes a basketball team on the ward.
   —what happens when he takes ten of the patients "outside" for a day-long fishing trip.

In his series of encounters with Big Nurse, McMurphy wins some battles and loses some. The patients have a personal stake in the outcome of these battles, and their spirits rise and fall with McMurphy's successes and failures. Gradually he is breaking her hold. But he makes a fatal mistake. When he sees the ward boys tormenting some of the weaker patients, he leads an angry assault aaginst them and gives Big Nurse the break she has been waiting for.

As we take up the story again, McMurphy and the Chief are about to receive shock therapy at the order of Big Nurse.

We're sitting in the day room, those faces around us in a circle, when in the door comes the Big Nurse herself, the two big black boys on each side, a step behind her. I try to shrink down in my chair, away from her, but it's too late. Too many people looking at me; sticky eyes hold me where I sit.

"Good morning," she says, got her old smile back now. McMurphy says good morning, and I keep quiet even though she says good morning to me too, out loud. I'm watching the black boys; one has tape on his nose and his arm in a sling, gray hand dribbling out of the cloth like a drowned spider, and the other one is moving like he's got some kind of cast around his ribs. They are both grinning a little. Probably could of stayed home with their hurts, but wouldn't miss this for nothing. I grin back just to show them.

The Big Nurse talks to McMurphy, soft and patient, about the ir- responsible thing he did, the childish thing, throwing a tantrum like a little boy—aren't you *ashamed?* He says he guesses not and tells her to get on with it.

She talks to him about how they, the patients downstairs on our ward, at a special group meeting yesterday afternoon, agreed with the staff that it might be beneficial that he receive some shock therapy—unless he realizes his mistakes. All he has to do is *admit* he was wrong, to indicate, *demonstrate* rational contact, and the treatment would be canceled this time.

That circle of faces waits and watches. The nurse says it's up to him.

"Yeah?" he says. "You got a paper I can sign?"

"Well, no, but if you feel it nec—"

"And why don't you add some other things while you're at it and get them out of the way—things like, oh, me being part of a plot to overthrow the government and like how I think life on your ward is the sweetest goddamned life this side of Hawaii—you know, that sort of crap."

"I don't believe that would—"

"*Then*, after I sign, you bring me a blanket and a package of Red Cross cigarettes. Hooee, those Chinese Commies could have learned a few things from you, lady."

"Randle, we are trying to help you."

But he's on his feet, scratching at his belly, walking on past her and the black boys rearing back, toward the card tables.

"O-kay, well well well, where's this poker table, buddies . . .?"

The nurse stares after him a moment, then walks into the Nurses' Station to use the phone.

Two colored aides and a white aide with curly blond hair walk us over to the Main Building. McMurphy talks with the white aide on the way over, just like he isn't worried about a thing.

There's frost thick on the grass, and the two colored aides in front trail puffs of breath like locomotives. The sun wedges apart some of the clouds and lights up the frost till the grounds are scattered with sparks. Sparrows fluffed out against the cold, scratching among the sparks for seeds. We cut across the crackling grass, past the digger squirrel holes where I saw the dog. Cold sparks. Frost down the holes, clear out of sight.

I feel that frost in my belly.

We get up to that door, and there's a sound behind like bees stirred up. Two men in front of us, reeling under the red capsules, one bawling like a baby, saying, "It's my cross, thank you Lord, it's all I got, thank you Lord. . . ."

The other guy waiting is saying, "Guts ball, guts ball." He's the lifeguard from the pool. And he's crying a little too.

I won't cry or yell. Not with McMurphy here.

The technician asks us to take off our shoes, and McMurphy asks him if we get our pants slit and our heads shaved too. The technician says no such luck.

The metal door looks out with its rivet eyes.

The door opens, sucks the first man inside. The lifeguard won't budge. A beam like neon smoke comes out of the black panel in the room, fastens on his cleat-marked forehead and drags him in like a dog on a leash. The beam spins him around three times before the door closes, and his face is scrambled fear. "Hut *one*," he grunts. "Hut *two!* Hut *three!*"

I hear them in there pry up his forehead like a manhole cover, clash and snarl of jammed cogs.

Smoke blows the door open, and a Gurney comes out with the first man on it, and he rakes me with his eyes. That face. The Gurney goes back in and brings the lifeguard out. I can hear the yell-leaders spelling out his name.

The technician says, "Next group."

The floor's cold, frosted, crackling. Up above the light whines, tube long and white and icy. Can smell the graphite salve, like the smell in a garage. Can smell acid of fear. There's one window, up high, small, and outside I see those puffy sparrows strung up on a wire like brown beads. Their heads sunk in the feathers against the cold. Something goes to blowing wind over my hollow bones, higher and higher, air raid! air raid!

"Don't holler, Chief. . . ."

Air raid!

"Take 'er easy. I'll go first. My skull's too thick for them to hurt me. And if they can't hurt me they can't hurt you."

Climbs on the table without any help and spreads his arms out to fit the shadow. A switch snaps the clasps on his wrists, ankles, clamping him into the shadow. A hand takes off his wristwatch, won it from Scanlon, drops it near the panel, it springs open, cogs and wheels and the long dribbling spiral of spring jumping against the side of the panel and sticking fast.

He don't look a bit scared. He keeps grinning at me.

They put the graphite salve on his temples. "What is it?" he says. "Conductant," the technician says. "Anointest my head with conductant. Do I get a crown of thorns?"

They smear it on. He's singing to them, makes their hands shake.

" 'Get Wildroot Cream Oil, Cholly. . . .' "

Put on those things like headphones, crown of silver thorns over the graphite at his temples. They try to hush his singing with a piece of rubber hose for him to bite on.

" 'Mage with thoothing lan-o-lin.' "

Twist some dials, and the machine trembles, two robot arms pick up soldering irons and hunch down on him. He gives me the wink and speaks to me, muffled, tells me something, says something to me around that rubber hose just as those irons get close enough to the silver on his temples—light arcs across, stiffens him, bridges him up off the table till nothing is down but his wrists and ankles and out around that crimped black rubber hose a sound like *hooeee!* and he's frosted over completely with sparks.

And out the window the sparrows drop smoking off the wire.

They roll him out on a Gurney, still jerking, face frosted white. Corrosion. Battery acid. The technician turns to me.

Watch that other moose. I know him. Hold him!

It's not a will-power thing any more.

Hold him! Damn. No more of these boys without Seconal.

The clamps bite my wrists and ankles.

The graphite salve has iron filings in it, temples scratching.

He said something when he winked. Told me something.

Man bends over, brings two irons toward the ring on my head.

The machine hunches on me.

AIR RAID.

Hit at a lope, running already down the slope. Can't get back, can't go ahead, look down the barrel an' you dead dead dead.

We come up outa the bullreeds run beside the railroad track. I lay an ear to the track, and it burns my cheek.

"Nothin' either way," I say, "a *hundred* miles. . . ."

"Hump," Papa says.

"Didn't we used to listen for buffalo by stickin' a knife in the ground, catch the handle in our teeth, hear a herd way off?"

"Hump," he says again, but he's tickled. Out across the other side of the track a fencerow of wheat chats from last winter. Mice under that stuff, the dog says.

"Do we go up the track or down the track, boy?"

"We go across, is what the ol' dog says."

"That dog don't heel."

"He'll do. There's birds over there is what the ol' dog says."

"Better hunting up the track bank is what your ol' man says."

"Best right across in the chats of wheat, the dog tells me."

Across—next thing I know there's people all over the track, blasting away at pheasants like anything. Seems our dog got too far out ahead and run all the birds outa the chats to the track.

Dog got three mice.

...man, Man, MAN, MAN...broad and big with a wink like a star.

Ants again oh Jesus and I got 'em bad this time, prickle-footed bastards. Remember the time we found those ants tasted like dill pickles? Hee? You said it wasn't dill pickles and I said it was, and your mama kicked the living tar outa me when she heard: Teachin' a kid to eat *bugs!*

Ugh. Good Injun boy should know how to survive on anything he can eat that won't eat him first.

We ain't Indians. We're civilized and you remember it.

You told me Papa When I die pin me up against the sky.

Mama's name was Bromden. Still is Bromden. Papa said he was born with only one name, born smack into it the way a calf drops out in a spread blanket when the cow insists on standing up. Tee Ah Millatoona, the Pine-That-Stands-Tallest-on-the-Mountain, and I'm the biggest by God Injun in the state of Oregon and probly California and Idaho. Born right into it.

You're the biggest by God fool if you think that a good Christian woman takes on a name like Tee Ah Millatoona. You were born into a name, so okay, I'm born into a name. Bromden. Mary Louise Bromden.

And when we move into town, Papa says, that name makes gettin' that Social Security card a lot easier.

Guy's after somebody with a riveter's hammer, get him too, if he keeps at it. I see those lightning flashes again, colors striking.

Ting. Tingle, tingle, tremble toes, she's a good fisherman, catches hens, puts 'em inna pens...wire blier, limber lock, three geese inna flock...one flew east, one flew west, one flew over the cuckoo's nest... O-U-T spells out...goose swoops down and plucks *you* out.

My old grandma chanted this, a game we played by the hours, sitting by the fish racks scaring flies. A game called Tingle Tingle Tangle Toes. Counting each finger on my two outspread hands, one finger to a syllable as she chants.

Tingle, ting-le, tang-le toes (seven fingers) she's a good fisherman, catches hens (sixteen fingers, tapping a finger on each beat with her black crab hand, each of my fingernails looking up at her like a little face asking to be the *you* that the goose swoops down and plucks out).

I like the game and I like Grandma. I don't like Mrs. Tingle Tangle Toes, catching hens. I don't like her. I do like that goose flying over the cuckoo's nest. I like him, and I like Grandma, dust in her wrinkles.

Next time I saw her she was stone cold dead, right in the middle of The Dalles on the sidewalk, colored shirts standing around, some Indians, some cattlemen, some wheatmen. They cart her down to the city burying ground, roll red clay into her eyes.

I remember hot, still electric-storm afternoons when jack-rabbits ran under Diesel truck wheels.

Joey Fish-in-a-Barrel has twenty thousand dollars and three Cadillacs since the contract. And he can't drive none of 'em.

I see a dice.

I see it from the inside, me at the bottom. I'm the weight, loading the dice to throw that number one up there above me. They got the dice loaded to throw a snake eyes, and I'm the load, six lumps around me like white pillows is the other side of the dice, the number six that will always be down when he throws. What's the other dice loaded for? I bet it's loaded to throw one too. Snake eyes. They're shooting with crookies against him, and I'm the load.

Look out, here comes a toss. Ay, lady, the smokehouse is empty and baby needs a new pair of opera pumps. Comin' at ya. *Faw!*

Crapped out.

Water. I'm lying in a puddle.

Snake eyes. Caught him again. I see that number one up above me: he can't whip frozen dice behind the feedstore in an alley—in Portland.

The alley is a tunnel it's cold because the sun is late afternoon. Let me...go see Grandma. Please, Mama.

What was it he said when he winked?

One flew east one flew west.

Don't stand in my way.

Damn it, nurse, don't stand in my way Way WAY!

My roll. *Faw.* Damn. Twisted again. Snake eyes.

The schoolteacher tell me you got a good head, boy, be something.. ..

Be what, Papa? A rug-weaver like Uncle R & J Wolf? A basket-weaver? Or another drunken Indian?

I say, attendant, you're an Indian, aren't you?

Yeah, that's right.

Well, I must say, you speak the language quite well.

Yeah.

Well...three dollars of regular.

They wouldn't be so cocky if they knew what me and the *moon* have going. No damned regular Indian...

He who—what was it?—walks out of step, hears another drum.

Snake eyes again. Hoo boy, these dice are *cold.*

After Grandma's funeral me and Papa and Uncle Running-and-Jumping Wolf dug her up. Mama wouldn't go with us; she never heard of such a thing. Hanging a corpse in a *tree!* It's enough to make a person sick.

Uncle R & J Wolf and Papa spent twenty days in the drunk tank at The Dalles jail, playing rummy, for Violation of the Dead.

But she's our goddanged mother!

It doesn't make the slightest difference, boys. You shoulda left her buried. I don't know when you blamed Indians will learn. Now, where is she? you'd better tell.

Ah go fuck yourself, paleface, Uncle R & J said, rolling himself a cigarette. I'll never tell.

High high high in the hills, high in a pine tree bed, she's tracing the wind with that old hand, counting the clouds with that old chant: ...three geese in a flock...

What did you say to me when you winked?

Band playing. Look—the *sky*, it's the Fourth of July.

Dice at rest.

They got to me with the machine again...I wonder...

What did he say?

...wonder how McMurphy made me big again.

He said Guts ball.

They're out there. Black boys in white suits peeing under the door on me, come in later and accuse me of soaking all six these pillows I'm lying on! Number six. I thought the room was a dice. The number one, the snake eye up there, the circle, the white *light* in the ceiling . . . is what I've been seeing . . . in this little square room . . . means it's after dark. How many hours have I been out? It's fogging a little, but I won't slip off and hide in it. NO . . . never again . . .

I stand, stood up slowly, feeling numb between the shoulders. The white pillows on the floor of the Seclusion Room were soaked from me peeing on them while I was out. I couldn't remember all of it yet, but I rubbed my eyes with the heels of my hands and tried to clear my head. I worked at it. I'd never worked at coming out of it before.

I staggered toward the little round chicken-wired window in the door of the room and tapped it with my knuckles. I saw an aide coming up the hall with a tray for me and knew this time I had them beat.

There had been times when I'd wandered around in a daze for as long as two weeks after a shock treatment, living in that foggy, jumbled blur which is a whole lot like the ragged edge of sleep, that gray zone between light and dark, or between sleeping and waking or living and dying, where you know you're not unconscious any more but don't know yet what day it is or who you are or what's the use of coming back at all—for two weeks. If you don't have a reason to wake up you can loaf around in that gray zone for a long, fuzzy time, or if you want to bad enough I found you can come fighting right out of it. This time I came fighting out of it in less than a day, less time than ever.

And when the fog was finally swept from my head it seemed like I'd just come up after a long, deep dive, breaking the surface after being under water a hundred years. It was the last treatment they gave me.

They gave McMurphy three more treatments that week. As quick as he started coming out of one, getting the click back in his wink, Miss Ratched would arrive with the doctor and they would ask him if he felt like he was ready to come around and face up to his problem and come back to the ward for a cure. And he'd swell up, aware that every one of those faces on Disturbed had turned toward him and was waiting, and he'd tell the nurse he regretted that he had but one life to give for his country and she could kiss his rosy red ass before he'd give up the goddam ship. *Yeh!*

Then stand up and take a couple of bows to those guys grinning at him while the nurse led the doctor into the station to phone over to the Main Building and authorize another treatment.

Once, as she turned to walk away, he got hold of her through the back of her uniform, gave her a pinch that turned her face red as his hair. I think if the doctor hadn't been there, hiding a grin himself, she would've slapped McMurphy's face.

I tried to talk him into playing along with her so's to get out of the treatments, but he just laughed and told me Hell, all they was doin' was chargin' his battery for him, free for nothing. "When I get out of here the first woman that takes on ol' Red McMurphy the ten-thousand-watt psychopath, she's gonna light up like a pinball machine and pay off in silver dollars! No, I ain't scared of their little battery-charger."

He insisted it wasn't hurting him. He wouldn't even take his capsules. But every time that loudspeaker called for him to forgo breakfast and prepare to walk to Building One, the muscles in his jaw went taut and his whole face drained of color, looking thin and scared—the face I had seen reflected in the windshield on the trip back from the coast.

I left Disturbed at the end of the week and went back to the ward. I had a lot of things I wanted to say to him before I went, but he'd just come back from a treatment and was sitting following the ping-pong ball with his eyes like he was wired to it. The colored aide and the blond one took me downstairs and let me onto our ward and locked the door behind me. The ward seemed awful quiet after Disturbed. I walked to our day room and for some reason stopped at the door; everybody's face turned up to me with a different look than they'd ever given me before. Their faces lighted up as if they were looking into the glare of a side-show platform. "Here, in fronta your very eyes," Harding spiels, "is the *Wildman* who broke the arm . . . of the black boy! Hey-ha, lookee, lookee." I grinned back at them, realizing how McMurphy must've felt these months with these faces screaming up at him.

All the guys came over and wanted me to tell them everything that had happened; how was he acting up there? What was he doing? Was it true, what was being rumored over at the gym, that they'd been hitting him every day with EST and he was shrugging it off like water, makin' book with the technicians on how long he could keep his eyes open after the poles touched.

I told them all I could, and nobody seemed to think a thing about me all of a sudden talking with people—a guy who'd been considered deaf and dumb as far back as they'd known him, talking, listening, just like anybody. I told them everything that they'd heard was true, and tossed in a few stories of my own. They laughed so hard about some of the things he'd said to the nurse that the two Vegetables under their wet sheets on the Chronics' side grinned and snorted along with the laughter, just like they understood.

What kinds of things happen to the Chief in shock treatment? How does McMurphy's influence affect the outcome?

As we saw in the previous episode, shock therapy has little effect on McMurphy. But his buddies are convinced that it is time for McMurphy to escape before Big Nurse thinks up a more drastic treatment for him. However, he wants to carry out one more exploit before he leaves.

In a hilarious scene, McMurphy sneaks two girls and several bottles into the ward, and the usually lifeless ward becomes the scene of a wild party. As the Chief observes:

> ... I was drunk, actually drunk, glowing and grinning and staggering drunk for the first time since the Army, drunk along with half a dozen other guys and a couple of girls—right on the Big Nurse's ward!

In a quiet moment just before dawn McMurphy, Harding, and the Chief have been discussing the plans for McMurphy's escape. In the exchange that follows, we see another side of McMurphy, and we see how far the men have come.

He asked what about us, why didn't we just up and get our clothes on and make it out with him?

"I'm not quite ready yet, Mack," Harding told him.

"Then what makes you think I am?"

Harding looked at him in silence for a time and smiled, then said, "No, you don't understand. I'll be ready in a few weeks. But I want to do it on my own, by myself, right out that front door, with all the traditional red tape and complications. I want my wife to be here in a car at a certain time to pick me up. I want them to know I was *able* to do it that way."

McMurphy nodded. "What about you, Chief?"

"I figure I'm all right. Just I don't know where I want to go yet. And somebody should stay here a few weeks after you're gone to see that things don't start sliding back."

"What about Billy and Sefelt and Frederickson and the rest?"

"I can't speak for them," Harding said. "They've still got their problems, just like all of us. They're still sick men in lots of ways. But at least there's that: they are sick *men* now. No more rabbits, Mack. Maybe they can be well men someday. I can't say."

McMurphy thought this over, looking at the backs of his hands. He looked back up to Harding.

"Harding, what is it? What happens?"

"You mean all this?"

McMurphy nodded.

Harding shook his head. "I don't think I can give you an answer. Oh, I could give you Freudian reasons with fancy talk, and that would be right as far as it went. But what you want are the reasons for the reasons, and I'm not able to give you those. Not for the others, anyway. For myself? Guilt. Shame. Fear. Self-belittlement. I discovered at an early age that I was—shall we be kind and say different? It's a better, more general word than the other one. I indulged in certain practices that our society regards as shameful. And I got sick. It wasn't the practices, I don't think, it was the feeling that the great, deadly, pointing forefinger of society was pointing at me—and the great voice of millions

chanting, 'Shame. Shame. Shame.' It's society's way of dealing with someone different."

"I'm different," McMurphy said. "Why didn't something like that
happen to me? I've had people bugging me about one thing or another
as far back as I can remember but that's not what—but it didn't drive
me crazy."

"No, you're right. That's not what drove you crazy. I wasn't giving
my reason as the sole reason. Though I used to think at one time, a few
years ago, my turtleneck years, that society's chastising was the sole force
that drove one along the road to crazy, but you've caused me to reappraise my theory. There's something else that drives people, strong
people like you, my friend, down that road."

"Yeah? Not that I'm admitting I'm down that road, but what is this
something else?"

"It is us." He swept his hand about him in a soft white circle and
repeated, "Us."

The escape plans never materialize because everybody falls asleep.
They are caught in the morning by Big Nurse, and while most of the
men are able to laugh off their embarrassment, Billy Bibbitt is not.
Overcome by humiliation and shame under the accusations of Big
Nurse, he cuts his throat. And, once again, McMurphy is trapped.
Driven by the needs of his friends, he murderously attacks Big Nurse.

McMurphy is carried off, and Big Nurse, though hospitalized for a
week, returns to make one final play.

She tried to get her ward back into shape, but it was difficult with
McMurphy's presence still tromping up and down the halls and laughing
out loud in the meetings and singing in the latrines. She couldn't rule
with her old power any more, not by writing things on pieces of paper.
She was losing her patients one after the other. After Harding signed
out and was picked up by his wife, and George transferred to a different
ward, just three of us were left out of the group that had been on the
fishing crew, myself and Martini and Scanlon.

I didn't want to leave just yet, because she seemed to be too sure;
she seemed to be waiting for one more round, and I wanted to be there
in case it came off. And one morning, after McMurphy'd been gone
three weeks, she made her last play.

The ward door opened, and the black boys wheeled in this Gurney
with a chart at the bottom that said in heavy black letters, MC MURPHY,
RANDLE P. POST-OPERATIVE. And below this was written in ink, LOBOTOMY.

They pushed it into the day room and left it standing against the
wall, along next to the Vegetables. We stood at the foot of the Gurney,
reading the chart, then looked up to the other end at the head dented
into the pillow, a swirl of red hair over a face milk-white except for the
heavy purple bruises around the eyes.

After a minute of silence Scanlon turned and spat on the floor. "Aaah,
what's the old bitch tryin' to put over on us anyhow, for crap sakes.
That ain't him."

"*Nothing* like him," Martini said.

"How stupid she think we are?"

"Oh, they done a pretty fair job, though," Martini said, moving up alongside the head and pointing as he talked. "See. They got the broken nose and that crazy scar—even the sideburns."

"Sure," Scanlon growled, "but *hell!*"

I pushed past the other patients to stand beside Martini. "Sure, they can do things like scars and broken noses," I said. "But they can't do that *look*. There's nothin' in the face. Just like one of those store dummies, ain't that right, Scanlon?"

Scanlon spat again. "Damn right. Whole thing's, you know, too *blank*. Anybody can see that."

"Look here," one of the patients said, peeling back the sheet, "tattoos."

"Sure," I said, "they can do tattoos. But the arms, huh? The arms? They couldn't do those. His arms were *big!*"

For the rest of the afternoon Scanlon and Martini and I ridiculed what Scanlon called that crummy sideshow fake lying there on the Gurney, but as the hours passed and the swelling began subsiding around the eyes I saw more and more guys strolling over to look at the figure. I watched them walk by acting like they were going to the magazine rack or the drinking fountain, so they could sneak another look at the face. I watched and tried to figure out what he would have done. I was only sure of one thing: he wouldn't have left something like that sit there in the day room with his name tacked on it for twenty or thirty years so the Big Nurse could use it as an example of what can happen if you buck the system. I was sure of that.

I waited that night until the sounds in the dorm told me everybody was asleep, and until the black boys had stopped making their rounds. Then I turned my head on the pillow so I could see the bed next to mine. I'd been listening to the breathing for hours, since they had wheeled the Gurney in and lifted the stretcher onto the bed, listening to the lungs stumbling and stopping, then starting again, hoping as I listened they would stop for good—but I hadn't turned to look yet.

There was a cold moon at the window, pouring light into the dorm like skim milk. I sat up in bed, and my shadow fell across the body, seeming to cleave it in half between the hips and the shoulders, leaving only a black space. The swelling had gone down enough in the eyes that they were open; they stared into the full light of the moon, open and undreaming, glazed from being open so long without blinking until they were like smudged fuses in a fuse box. I moved to pick up the pillow, and the eyes fastened on the movement and followed me as I stood up and crossed the few feet between the beds.

The big, hard body had a tough grip on life. It fought a long time against having it taken away, flailing and thrashing around so much I finally had to lie full length on top of it and scissor the kicking legs with mine while I mashed the pillow into the face. I lay there on top of the body for what seemed days. Until the thrashing stopped. Until it was still a while and had shuddered once and was still again. Then I rolled off. I lifted the pillow, and in the moonlight I saw the expression hadn't changed from the blank, dead-end look the least bit, even under suffocation. I took my thumbs and pushed the lids down and held them till they stayed. Then I lay back on my bed.

I lay for a while, holding the covers over my face, and thought I was being pretty quiet, but Scanlon's voice hissing from his bed let me know I wasn't.

"Take it easy, Chief," he said. "Take it easy. It's okay."

"Shut up," I whispered. "Go back to sleep."

It was quiet a while; then I heard him hiss again and ask, "Is it finished?"

I told him yeah.

"Christ," he said then, "she'll know. You realize that, don't you? Sure, nobody'll be able to prove anything—anybody coulda kicked off in post-operative like he was, happens all the time—but her, she'll know."

I didn't say anything.

"Was I you, Chief, I'd breeze my tail outa here. Yessir. I tell you what. You leave outa here, and I'll say I saw him up and moving around after you left and cover you that way. That's the best idea, don't you think?"

"Oh, yeah, just like that. Just ask 'em to unlock the door and let me out."

"No. He showed you how one time, if you think back. That very first week. You remember?"

I didn't answer him, and he didn't say anything else, and it was quiet in the dorm again. I lay there a few minutes longer and then got up and started putting on my clothes. When I finished dressing I reached into McMurphy's nightstand and got his cap and tried it on. It was too small, and I was suddenly ashamed of trying to wear it. I dropped it on Scanlon's bed as I walked out of the dorm. He said, "Take it easy, buddy," as I walked out.

The moon straining through the screen of the tub-room windows showed the hunched, heavy shape of the control panel, glinted off the chrome fixtures and glass gauges so cold I could almost hear the click of it striking. I took a deep breath and bent over and took the levers. I heaved my legs under me and felt the grind of weight at my feet. I heaved again and heard the wires and connections tearing out of the floor. I lurched it up to my knees and was able to get an arm around it and my other hand under it. The chrome was cold against my neck and the side of my head. I put my back toward the screen, then spun and let the momentum carry the panel through the screen and window with a ripping crash. The glass splashed out in the moon, like a bright cold water baptizing the sleeping earth. Panting, I thought for a second about going back and getting Scanlon and some of the others, but then I heard the running squeak of the black boys' shoes in the hall and I put my hand on the sill and vaulted after the panel, into the moonlight.

I ran across the grounds in the direction I remembered seeing the dog go, toward the highway. I remember I was taking huge strides as I ran, seeming to step and float a long ways before my next foot struck the earth. I felt like I was flying. Free. Nobody bothers coming after an

AWOL, I knew, and Scanlon could handle any questions about the dead man—no need to be running like this. But I didn't stop. I ran for miles before I stopped and walked up the embankment onto the highway.

I caught a ride with a guy, a Mexican guy, going north in a truck full of sheep, and gave him such a good story about me being a professional Indian wrestler the syndicate had tried to lock up in a nuthouse that he stopped real quick and gave me a leather jacket to cover my greens and loaned me ten bucks to eat on while I hitchhiked to Canada. I had him write his address down before he drove off and I told him I'd send him the money as soon as I got a little ahead.

I might go to Canada eventually, but I think I'll stop along the Columbia on the way. I'd like to check around Portland and Hood River and The Dalles to see if there's any of the guys I used to know back in the village who haven't drunk themselves goofy. I'd like to see what they've been doing since the government tried to buy their right to be Indians. I've even heard that some of the tribe have took to building their old ramshackle wood scaffolding all over that big million-dollar hydroelectric dam, and are spearing salmon in the spillway. I'd give something to see that. Mostly, I'd just like to look over the country around the gorge again, just to bring some of it clear in my mind again.

I been away a long time.

point of departure

Let us begin our exploration of how to go about *recognizing agents of change* and *evaluating change* by considering the following questions.

What kind of person is McMurphy? What effect does he have on the other characters?

What kind of person is Big Nurse? What effect does she have?

What is McMurphy's view of man and society?

What is Harding's? Do Harding and Big Nurse share the same view of human nature?

What finally happens to Harding, the Chief, and McMurphy?

As you ponder these questions, consider whether McMurphy is the kind of person who may serve as an agent of change. Is Big Nurse also an agent of change? And, what kind of change is a change for the better?

What, then, may we list as the characteristics of a person who is an agent of change *for the better?* How can we best pin down what we mean by "for the better"?

In the course of your thinking about these issues, it should become clear that the view of man held by McMurphy, Big Nurse, and Harding is closely related to the kind of person each is, the effect each has on other people, and the kind of environment each helps to create. Do you think this is generally true—true for all people?

A. H. Maslow is a contemporary psychologist who has devoted himself to the study of the conditions under which man develops his human capacities to their fullest degree. He believes the key to such development is in the gratification of basic needs. These needs develop in an hierarchical sequence, from "lower" to "higher," and a man must meet the demands of his lower needs before those of the higher levels can emerge. This hierarchy, from lowest to highest, includes: *physical* needs, such as the need for food and water; *safety* needs, illustrated by the quest for a milieu which is relatively free from threats to life and which fosters a sense of security; *belonging and love* needs, illustrated by the felt hunger for affectionate, accepting relationships with other persons; *esteem* needs, illustrated by the desire to be respected by others for one's accomplishments and the quest for recognition and prestige. Once a person has successfully learned to cope with these needs as they arise, his energies will then be more readily freed for *self-actualization.* Actualization of self cannot be sought as a goal in its own right, however; rather, it seems to be a *by-product* of active commitment of one's talents to some cause outside the self, such as the quest for beauty, truth, or justice. Without some such mission in life, a person is likely to experience boredom or a sense of stultification. Once he finds a purpose (or purposes), he can then dedicate his energies and talents to its fulfillment. As he meets the challenges of the tasks he will encounter his growth or actualization will be fostered.

How well does the environment on Big Nurse's ward supply "the conditions under which man develops human capacities to their fullest degree"?

Does McMurphy's presence on the ward change the environment?

Could we evaluate an agent of change in terms of how well he helps people fill these basic needs Maslow has identified?

Reprinted with permission of The Macmillan Company from *Personal Adjustment* by Sidney M. Jourard. © by The Macmillan Company 1958.

Maslow found that persons who were well along in the process of actualizing themselves shared certain traits. Read Sidney Jourard's description of the traits shared by Maslow's self-actualizing (S-A) persons. Then discuss these questions.

Which of these traits does McMurphy have? Can you find examples in the story?

What about Big Nurse? Harding?

1. A more adequate perception of reality and more comfortable relations with reality than occur in average people. His S-A cases seemed to detect the spurious, the fake, and the dishonest in interpersonal relations and to be attuned to the truth and to reality in all spheres of life. They eschewed the illusory and preferred to cope with even unpleasant reality rather than retreat to pleasant fantasies.

2. A high degree of acceptance of themselves, of others, and of the realities of human nature. They were not ashamed of being what they were, and they were not shocked or dismayed to find foibles and shortcomings in themselves or in others.

3. Spontaneity. The S-A people displayed spontaneity in their thinking, emotions, and behavior to a greater extent than average people.

4. Problem-centeredness. Maslow's subjects seemed all to be focused on problems *outside* themselves. They were not overly self-conscious; they were not problems *to* themselves, and could hence devote their attention to a task, duty, or mission that seemed peculiarly cut out for them.

5. A need for privacy. The S-A people could enjoy solitude; indeed, they would even seek it out on occasion, needing it for periods of intense concentration on subjects of interest to them.

6. A high degree of autonomy. The S-A people seemed able to remain true to themselves in the

Reprinted with permission of The Macmillan Company from *Personal Adjustment* by Sidney M. Jourard. © by the Macmillan Company 1958.

face of rejection or unpopularity; they were able to pursue their interests and projects and maintain their integrity even when it hurt to do so.

7. A continued freshness of appreciation. The S-A people showed the capacity to "appreciate again and again, freshly and naïvely, the basic goods of life . . . a sunset, a flower, a baby, a person"; it was as if they avoided merely lumping experiences into categories and then dismissing them. Rather, they could see the unique in many apparently common-place experiences.

8. Frequent "mystic experiences." The S-A people seemed subject to periodic experiences that are often called "mystic" or "oceanic"—feelings that one's boundaries as a person have suddenly evaporated and one has truly become a part of all mankind and even of all nature.

9. Gemeinschaftsgefühl. The German word *gemeinschaftsgefühl* also means "brotherly feeling," the feeling of belongingness to all mankind (related to the mystic experiences above); the attitude was found to be characteristic of S-A people. They felt a sense of identification with mankind as a whole, such that they could become concerned not only with the lot of members of their immediate family but also with the situation of persons from different cultures.

10. Close relationships with a few friends or loved ones. Maslow found that his S-A subjects, while not necessarily very popular, did have the capacity to establish truly close, loving relationships with at least one or two other people.

11. Democratic character structures. The S-A people tended to judge people and to be friendly with them, not on the basis of race, status, religion, or other group membership traits; rather, they related to others as *individuals.*

12. A strong ethical sense. The S-A subjects were found to have a highly developed sense of ethics. Though their notions of right and wrong were not always wholly conventional, their behavior was always chosen with reference to its ethical meaning.

13. Unhostile senses of humor. The S-A people had senses of humor which made common human foibles, pretensions, and foolishness the subject of laughter, rather than sadism, smut, or rebellion against authority.

14. Creativeness. The S-A people were creative and inventive in some areas of their existence, not followers of the usual ways of doing or thinking.

15. Resistance to enculturation. The S-A subjects could detach themselves somewhat from complete absorption, or "brainwashing," or imprinting by their cultures. This would permit them to adopt critical attitudes toward cultural inconsistencies or unfairness within their own society.

Truly, this is a most impressive collection of attributes! One would like to meet or to become such a person. We have dwelt at length on Maslow's composite portrait of self-actualization because it offers a detailed conception of human potentials— a concept of man at his best.

Do you agree that this is a portrait of man at his best?

Which of these traits do you think you have?

trying on your ideal self

Think of a setting in which the pressures on you to conform are inhibiting your growth as a person (e.g., home, school, job, church). Describe what would happen if you were a self-actualizing person.

Here are two ways to do this:

1. You are a conforming person. An agent of change comes into your life, and you become more self-actualizing. Show us first your conforming self, then the agent of change, and then

your changed self. (This is what the Chief does in *Cuckoo*.)
2. You are a self-actualizing person. Show us the pressures and how you cope with them.

> To be "average' 'in personality means to suffer from various "socially patterned defects," as [Erich] Fromm calls them. That is, the typical person in our society usually shows signs of premature arrest in his growth; he may carry symptoms of neurosis which are so widely shared in his society that he does not realize he is half sick. The simple fact is that in an age when space is being explored, and when man has the nuclear power to destroy his planet, average personality is just not good enough.
>
> **Sidney M. Jourard,**
> *Personal Adjustment*

ways and meanings

Harding uses a metaphor to describe his view of man. Here are metaphors used by two playwrights.

> "You know Franz Kafka? I don't mean, did you know him personally, I mean you know who he was? You know that story he write where this fella wake up one mornin' and find out he turned into a bug? You know that story? That actually happen to me....
>
> "You see, baby, what is euphemistically called life is actually just one big bug-house and you either gotta grow up to be one a them bugs or you gotta scurry. Know what I mean? Scurry. You stand still and you find yourself bein' squashed.
>
> "We are all bugs. You, me. Everybody!... Just waitin' to be squashed.... By bigger bugs."
>
> Randall in **William Hanley,**
> *Slow Dance on the Killing Ground*

What would your metaphor be to describe your view of man?

Reprinted with permission of The Macmillan Company from *Personal Adjustment* by Sidney M. Jourard. © by the Macmillan Company 1958.

. . . Just see me
As I am, me like a perambulating
Vegetable, patched with inconsequential
Hair, looking out of two small jellies for the means
Of life, balanced on folding bones, my sex
No beauty but a blemish to be hidden
Behind judicious rags, driven and scorched
By boomerang rages and lunacies which never
Touch the accommodating artichoke
Or the seraphic strawberry beaming in its bed:
I defend myself against pain and death by pain
And death, and make the world go round, they tell me,
By one of my less lethal appetites:
Half of this grotesque life I spend in a state
Of slow decomposition, using
The name of unconsidered God as a pedestal
On which I stand and bray that I'm best
Of beasts, until under some patient
Moon or other I fall to pieces, like
A cake of dung. . . .

Thomas' description of himself in **Christopher Fry**,
The Lady's Not for Burning

taking another look

One Flew Over the Cuckoo's Nest, like *Invisible Man,* or any other good novel, holds levels of meaning often only sensed on a first reading. We may sense, for example, that the characters are somehow larger than life. When we look again, we may discover that the author has given them not only particular, unique qualities, but also general, shared qualities. By depicting the qualities a character has in common with some, perhaps all, other people, the author reveals his own insights into human nature and society.

If we look closely at the episode in which the Chief undergoes shock treatment, we see him working through a crisis of identity. His need for a sense of his own worth as a unique human being is in conflict with society's insistence that he view himself with shame as "the Indian in American society." Kesey does not, however, intend the Chief to stand for the category of person called "the Indian"; rather, the Chief shares certain qualities with anyone who is robbed of his identity by being stamped with a label. Paradoxically, insisting that someone is more than he is—that is, the Indian (all Indians), rather than an Indian (one person)—can make him less than he is.

Take a look at the part of the episode dealing with the Chief's name. The similarities with *Invisible Man* are striking: both point to the depersonalizing of the individual and to the culture shock accompanying the awareness of loss of identity. The Chief, like the invisible man, found his real self at odds with his socially imposed self-structure.

In America the Indian and the Negro experience culture shock because they are aliens in the dominant culture. What could cause culture shock in the person who is identified with the dominant culture? The rise of the culture of the "thinking" machine? Of the culture of youth? Of black culture? Communication with extraterrestrial beings or with other intelligent species on our planet?

A second probe of the broader meanings of *Cuckoo* is to examine the clues Kesey gives us which suggest that McMurphy is, like Christ, a messiah and a martyr. The larger-than-life role McMurphy's friends assign to him is a threat to his identity, and he treats it as such. At one point in the story McMurphy says, "... you guys were coming to me like I was some kind of savior." McMurphy struggles to avoid the role, but ultimately, in the service of a larger social goal, he accepts it, in spite of the sacrifice of himself. The Chief describes it:

> Climbs on the table without any help and spreads his arms out to fit the shadow. . . . He don't look a bit scared. He keeps grinning at me. . . . They put a graphite salve on his temples. "What is it?" he says. "Conductant," the technician says. "Anointest my head with conductant. Do I get a crown of thorns?"

He does, of course. You may wish to explore just how far Kesey carries the messiah theme.

What does the messiah theme do to our discussion of agents of change? When we consider more carefully the role of a messiah, we discover it *is* that of an agent of change.

There is a curious paradox here. As a messiah, McMurphy led people to freedom by a supreme assertion and revelation of his own identity. But as a martyr, he sacrificed his own identity as well as life itself. (The combination is not unusual. Can you think of persons in our society who began as messiahs and ended as martyrs?) How may we resolve this paradox? Would it be true to say that *transcending* one's identity is an ultimate step in developing one's human potential? Is it a step beyond self-actualization, or is it part of self-actualization, or are the two at odds? It might be interesting to think about Jesus and other religious leaders in terms of Maslow's description of the self-actualizing person.

> Actualization of self cannot be sought as a goal in its own right...; rather, it seems to be a by-product of active commitment of one's talents to some cause outside the self, such as the quest for beauty, truth, or justice.
>
> Sidney M. Jourard,
> *Personal Adjustment*

A number of possible definitions of agents of change have been implied and perhaps should be examined here. Is an agent of change someone who helps supply our basic needs? Is an agent of change someone who is himself a self-actualizing person? Is an agent of change someone who helps break our early imprints—or who has broken through his own?

Don Fabun's discussion of imprinting in *The Dynamics of Change* would seem to suggest that the last should be at least part of the definition:

> Nearly every human we know of who has profoundly affected the way we live has somehow broken through his infantile imprints.

Fabun goes on to describe other ways in which people are changed:

> Historically we know of a number of ways, most of them related to some traumatic incident, some vast, new experience that shatters the ancient imprints and forces them into new combinations. Nearly all of our great art and music came about that way; so did most of our scientific advances.
>
> What kind of traumatic incidents? Well, among them severe emotional disturbance, such as the loss of a loved one; failure to succeed in a world of conformity; the collapse of economic or political systems; change in body chemistry through the introduction of drugs or alcohol; a religious experience so powerful it breaks earlier imprints; or intensive study (as with savants of both the Western and Eastern worlds). In all of these methods the effect is to bring about new levels of understanding that change the infantile imprint.

The Dynamics of Change, Kaiser Aluminum & Chemical Corporation, © 1967.

If we think of these ways as agents of change, we may now broaden our definition to include anything or anybody that provokes an experience profound enough to break through our imprinting—and we are back to culture/future shock.

nine

perspective amid
so much madness

> *[M]an's play-forms may even outwit human adaptation itself.* The fiction can become greater than physical reality, the struggle for survival becomes a struggle with the ideas one has inherited, and not with nature itself. Man would rather sacrifice survival than change the ideas he has learned from the group.... Yes, war too is a game, a play-form.
>
> Ernest Becker,
> *Beyond Alienation*

All over the world, boys on every side of the bomb line were laying down their lives for what they had been told was their country, and no one seemed to mind, least of all the boys who were laying down their young lives. There was no end in sight....

This passage and the following three short excerpts are from Joseph Heller's *Catch-22,* a novel about World War II flyers. Yossarian and Dunbar are pilots who have become demoralized by the fact that every time they fly enough bombing missions to qualify them to be sent home the colonel raises the necessary number of missions. Clevinger is a fellow pilot who stoutly defends the military way of doing things.

from Catch-22

Joseph Heller

The only thing going on was a war, and no one seemed to notice but Yossarian and Dunbar. And when Yossarian tried to remind people, they drew away from him and thought he was crazy. Even Clevinger, who should have known better but didn't, had told him he was crazy the last time they had seen each other, which was just before Yossarian had fled into the hospital.

Clevinger had stared at him with apoplectic rage and indignation and, clawing the table with both hands, had shouted, "You're crazy!"

"Clevinger, what do you want from people?" Dunbar had replied wearily above the noises of the officers' club.

"I'm not joking," Clevinger persisted.

"They're trying to kill me," Yossarian told him calmly.

"No one's trying to kill you," Clevinger cried.

"Then why are they shooting at me?" Yossarian asked.

"They're shooting at *everyone*," Clevinger answered. "They're trying to kill everyone."

"And what difference does that make?"

Clevinger was already on the way, half out of his chair with emotion, his eyes moist and his lips quivering and pale. As always occurred when he quarreled over principles in which he believed passionately, he would end up gasping furiously for air and blinking back bitter tears of conviction. There were many principles in which Clevinger believed passionately. He was crazy.

"Who's they?" he wanted to know. "Who, specifically, do you think is trying to murder you?"

"Every one of them," Yossarian told him.

"Every one of whom?"

"Every one of whom do you think?"

"I haven't any idea."

"Then how do you know they aren't?"

"Because . . ." Clevinger sputtered, and turned speechless with frustration.

Clevinger really thought he was right, but Yossarian had proof, because strangers he didn't know shot at him with cannons every time he flew up into the air to drop bombs on them, and it wasn't funny at all. And if that wasn't funny, there were lots of things that weren't even funnier. There was nothing funny about living like a bum in a tent in Pianosa between fat mountains behind him and a placid blue sea in front that could gulp down a person with a cramp in the twinkling of an eye and ship him back to shore three days later, all charges paid, bloated, blue and putrescent, water draining out through both cold nostrils.

There were four of them seated together at a table in the officers' club the last time he and Clevinger had called each other crazy. They were seated in back near the crap table on which Appleby always managed to win. Appleby was as good at shooting crap as he was at playing ping-pong, and he was as good at playing ping-pong as he was at everything else. Everything Appleby did, he did well. Appleby was a fair-haired boy from Iowa who believed in God, Motherhood, and the American Way of Life, without ever thinking about any of them, and everybody who knew him liked him.

"I hate that son of a bitch," Yossarian growled.

The argument with Clevinger had begun a few minutes earlier when Yossarian had been unable to find a machine gun. It was a busy night. The bar was busy, the crap table was busy, the ping-pong table was busy. The people Yossarian wanted to machine-gun were busy at the bar singing sentimental old favorites that nobody else ever tired of. Instead of machine-gunning them, he brought his heel down hard on the ping-pong ball that came rolling toward him off the paddle of one of the two officers playing.

"That Yossarian," the two officers laughed, shaking their heads, and got another ball from the box on the shelf.

"That Yossarian," Yossarian answered them.

"Yossarian," Nately whispered cautioningly.

"You see what I mean?" asked Clevinger.

The officers laughed again when they heard Yossarian mimicking them. "That Yossarian," they said more loudly.

"That Yossarian," Yossarian echoed.

"Yossarian, please," Nately pleaded.

"You see what I mean?" asked Clevinger. "He has antisocial aggressions."

"Oh, shut up," Dunbar told Clevinger. Dunbar liked Clevinger because Clevinger annoyed him and made the time go slow.

"Appleby isn't even here," Clevinger pointed out triumphantly to Yossarian.

"Who said anything about Appleby?" Yossarian wanted to know.

"Colonel Cathcart isn't here, either."

"Who said anything about Colonel Cathcart?"

"What son of a bitch *do* you hate, then?"

"What son of a bitch *is* here?"

"I'm not going to argue with you," Clevinger decided. "You don't know who you hate."

"Whoever's trying to poison me," Yossarian told him.

"Nobody's trying to poison you."

"They poisoned my food twice, didn't they? Didn't they put poison in my food during Ferrara and during the Great Big Siege of Bologna?"

"They put poison in *everybody's* food," Clevinger explained.

"And what difference does *that* make?"

"And it wasn't even poison!" Clevinger cried heatedly, growing more emphatic as he grew more confused.

As far back as Yossarian could recall, he explained to Clevinger with a patient smile, somebody was always hatching a plot to kill him. There were people who cared for him and people who didn't, and those who didn't hated him and were out to get him. They hated him because he was Assyrian. But they couldn't touch him, he told Clevinger, because he had a sound mind in a pure body and was as strong as an ox. They couldn't touch him because he was Tarzan, Mandrake, Flash Gordon. He was Bill Shakespeare. He was Cain, Ulysses, the Flying Dutchman; he was Lot in Sodom, Deirdre of the Sorrows, Sweeney in the nightingales among trees. He was miracle ingredient Z-247. He was—

"Crazy!" Clevinger interrupted, shrieking. "That's what you are! Crazy!"

"—immense. I'm a real, slam-bang, honest-to-goodness, three-fisted humdinger. I'm a bona fide supraman."

"Superman?" Clevinger cried. "Superman?"

"Supraman," Yossarian corrected.

"Hey, fellas, cut it out," Nately begged with embarrassment. "Everybody's looking at us."

"You're crazy," Clevinger shouted vehemently, his eyes filling with tears. "You've got a Jehovah complex."

"I think everyone is Nathaniel."

Clevinger arrested himself in mid-declamation, suspiciously. "Who's Nathaniel?"

"Nathaniel who?" inquired Yossarian innocently.

Clevinger skirted the trap neatly. "You think everybody is Jehovah. You're no better than Raskolnikov—"

"Who?"

"—yes, Raskolnikov, who—"

"Raskolnikov!"

"—who—I mean it—who felt he could justify killing an old woman—"

"No better than?"

"—yes, justify, that's right—with an ax! And I can prove it to you!" Gasping furiously for air, Clevinger enumerated Yossarian's symptoms: an unreasonable belief that everybody around him was crazy, a homicidal impulse to machine-gun strangers, retrospective falsification, an unfounded suspicion that people hated him and were conspiring to kill him.

But Yossarian knew he was right, because, as he explained to Clevinger, to the best of his knowledge he had never been wrong. Everywhere he looked was a nut, and it was all a sensible young gentleman like himself could do to maintain his perspective amid so much madness. And it was urgent that he did, for he knew his life was in peril.

Yossarian's arguments really annoy Clevinger. Why? Do they annoy you?

In these passages, Heller, it seems, is posing a problem: What is a rational attitude in an irrational setting?

When Yossarian comes to Doc Daneeka to plead again to be grounded, Heller shows that the rules of war are illogical and absurd.

"You're wasting your time," Doc Daneeka was forced to tell him.

"Can't you ground someone who's crazy?"

"Oh, sure. I have to. There's a rule saying I have to ground anyone who's crazy."

"Then why don't you ground me? I'm crazy. Ask Clevinger."

"Clevinger? Where is Clevinger? You find Clevinger and I'll ask him.

"Then ask any of the others. They'll tell you how crazy I am."

"They're crazy."

"Then why don't you ground them?"

"Why don't they ask me to ground them?"

"Because they're crazy, that's why."

"Of course they're crazy," Doc Daneeka replied. "I just told you they're crazy, didn't I? And you can't let crazy people decide whether you're crazy or not, can you?"

Yossarian looked at him soberly and tried another approach. "Is Orr crazy?"

"He sure is," Doc Daneeka said.

"Can you ground him?"

"I sure can. But first he has to ask me to. That's part of the rule."

"Then why doesn't he ask you to?"

"Because he's crazy," Doc Daneeka said. "He has to be crazy to keep flying combat missions after all the close calls he's had. Sure, I can ground Orr. But first he has to ask me to."

"That's all he has to do to be grounded?"

"That's all. Let him ask me."

"And then you can ground him?" Yossarian asked.

"No. Then I can't ground him."

"You mean there's a catch?"

"Sure there's a catch," Doc Daneeka replied. "Catch-22. Anyone who wants to get out of combat duty isn't really crazy."

There was only one catch and that was Catch-22, which specified that a concern for one's own safety in the face of dangers that were real and immediate was the process of a rational mind. Orr was crazy and could be grounded. All he had to do was ask; and as soon as he did, he would no longer be crazy and would have to fly more missions. Orr would be crazy to fly more missions and sane if he didn't, but if he was sane he had to fly them. If he flew them he was crazy and didn't have to; but if he didn't want to he was sane and had to. Yossarian was moved very deeply by the absolute simplicity of this clause of Catch-22 and let out a respectful whistle.

"That's some catch, that Catch-22," he observed.

"It's the best there is," Doc Daneeka agreed.

Yossarian saw it clearly in all its spinning reasonableness.

point of departure

Heller is dealing with some complex issues in *Catch-22*. They concern what Ernest Becker calls "social fictions"—commonly held ideas incorporating the beliefs, values, and experience of society. They are not facts, though they may be consistent with facts; they are ways of thinking. Remembering earlier discussions of *Invisible Man* and *One Flew Over the Cuckoo's Nest*, we may observe that, like self-structures, social fictions seem to be passed on from society to individuals by imprinting, or by an analogous process.

We are borrowing here the term social fictions from the field of sociology to help us deal with the complexities of change, just as we borrowed the terms self-actualizing person, real self, and self-structure from the field of psychology, and the term imprinting from the field of biology. There are, of course, other ways to read Ellison, Kesey, and Heller; and there is much more to be said about these terms than we have included in our discussion of change.

We should, of course, recognize that the human being is a symbol-making animal, that we *will* make mental constructs such as social fictions. Indeed, we need such constructs, if there is to be any common ground on which we can relate to each other. However, we must also be aware that a social fiction is not absolute, that it does not apply at all times and in all places. Changing circumstances may make it obsolete.

Is the idea that war is a necessary part of life a social fiction? Are there circumstances in today's world which require that we re-examine this notion?

For example, the commonly held belief that man must earn his bread by the sweat of his brow is a social fiction, and one which we need to reappraise as we move into an environment in which machines do the work. Thus, the first question that might be asked about any social fiction is whether it is appropriate to the circumstances in which it is operating—or putting the question another way, whether it serves men well in the environment in which they are operating. A second question comes hard on the heels of the first: If not, do we change the fiction or do we change the environment? Which of our beliefs and values are we willing to give up?

These are the very issues Heller is dealing with in *Catch-22*. Yossarian refuses to give up his concern for his survival merely because there's a war going on. Whether people are shooting at him personally or impersonally is, for Yossarian, a distinction without a difference. When people are shooting at him, they are trying to kill him; his life is in danger, and he must try to escape.

Heller shows us Yossarian through Clevinger's eyes, highlighting Yossarian's apparent obtuseness by contrasting it with Clevinger's apparent sensibleness. The maddening, if not mad, logic of Yossarian's position is irritating to Clevinger, whom Heller represents as holding the commonly accepted belief that in wartime it is good to be willing to lay down your life. With all the weight of society behind him, he indignantly denounces Yossarian. Yossarian, clinging to what he has always believed, is isolated; his beliefs, so sensible in peacetime, are idiosyncratic in wartime—held by him alone.

Yet each man can ask of the other, "How could a sane person doubt what I am convinced is true?" Appeal to reason is useless. There is no common ground for establishing what is rational because each view has meaning only within a given context. Clevinger and Yossarian do not share the same social fiction because Yossarian refuses to pretend that *war* is a self-justifying context.

The change expected of Yossarian is that he stop being concerned with his own safety and adopt an attitude of willingness, even eagerness, to continue risking his neck. The wartime environment, in short, demands change in the form of a complete switch in his system of values. Yossarian refuses. Rejecting Clevinger's argument that war changes values, he continues to operate within a context which gives self-preservation top priority.

Thus Heller, by setting one set of values against another, attempts to reveal the incongruity in a society's holding both. Like a game, war has rules that make sense only within its own context. Wartime values and rules of behavior are incompatible with those of peacetime.

But if one considers war itself a social fiction, as Yossarian does, has one a right to refuse to play the game? If so, on what grounds?

The conflict between peacetime and wartime morality is illuminated quite differently in the following poignant, uncompromising, and angry poem by Calvin Scott.

The Whole of My Days

Calvin Scott

The whole of my days are sick and weary
with the sight of blood unseen.
I know that they are dying,
bleeding their blood into the green earth.
And I curse the butchers who kill them,
I call them the sons of pigs
all of them.
No coloring of their worthless hides
could conceal the deeds they do,
these killers of woman and child.
I can see them sitting there

From *Pretty Black Is the Color Soul*, reprinted by permission of the author.

drinking their hot blood
and spitting out the white corpuscles
talking their mad talk
thinking their mad thoughts
their sleepless eyes searching the night
looking for something to kill.

I can see their dragons fly,
consuming the earth in their hot flames
and their pilots,
mechanized and as cold as the weapons
they themselves command,
their blank glass bubble faces
looking nowhere, seeing nothing.
These are the burners of the earth
that set the devouring flames upon beauty.
These are our brothers,
our sons and lovers, the fathers of our children.
Will not the whole of these blood-laden hands
defile the virgin force of our youth,
should they return from the fray?

And you the lover,
will you welcome this beast home to your bed
to suck at your breast
and make it hard and cold as granite?
And the mothers, what of the mothers
to see their sons come marching home,
the blood streaming
from the corners of their mouths and eyes
and the scream of death in their faces?
Will not they know then,
will not we all know then that we have failed?

For if this is the worth of manhood
the glory of this earth-god steeped in blood,
then I spit on it
and masturbate to confirm my contempt.
Call me what you will—
the foolish child
unbound to the ways of the world—
then place your hand firmly on my shoulder
and say to me (quietly of course)
that these are trials that all men must face
and weights that they must bear;
for not one civil generation has ever passed
without the fighting of wars.
And I will say to you, biting my tongue
then spitting of salty blood
to the righteous ground you stand on,

Ha! Generations past
what did they know but war
and where have all their foolish wars gotten us?
Are not we so humane,
our icy blood trundling over itself
freezing the veins
and the senses freeze—
For the sake of the bitch who bore the world,
must we walk the earth as lemmings always?

What grounds for refusing to play the game underlie Calvin Scott's poem? How does his attitude toward pilots differ from Heller's? Is Clevinger a lemming?

Another poet, Carl Sandburg, uses humor in talking about war, not to obscure the seriousness of war but to highlight it. Casting war in an unusual light, he brings its seriousness into perspective. In *The People, Yes,*

... a little girl, watching a
parade of soldiers, says: "You
know something?—Sometime they'll
give a war—and nobody will come...."

Why do we smile? Incongruity, an essential quality of the poetic and the humorous, lies in the simple, sweet wisdom of this little girl offering a solution to one of mankind's bitterest problems—a solution posed at the level of her own innocence, which at the same time transcends the level of the sophisticated adult. The solution is so simple, yet so profound. And we smile—with some chagrin, perhaps, because we have been found out; with some delight, too, because there is hope in this humor. And it serves Sandburg's purpose; Sandburg's message is clear: the little girl takes for granted that nobody *wants* to go to war; this is Sandburg's view, too. So let us listen, he says, to the natural wisdom, to the untutored wisdom of the child.

ways and meanings

Heller, Scott, and Sandburg all condemn war, but each artist expresses it differently. How would you express your attitude toward war? Would you write a poem or a story? Paint a picture? Make a collage? Do it.

In Norman Corwin's *The World of Carl Sandburg.*

Do you think Heller, Scott, and Sandburg differ from each other in their views of human nature? Does your statement reflect a view of human nature? What is it?

Is war an agent of change? In a previous discussion we said an agent of change included anything or anybody that provokes an experience profound enough to break through our imprinting. If war is an agent of change, is it one we can afford?

Change from one environment to another forces us to test our social conventions to see if they still fit. Here are some examples, from the field of education, that Don Fabun calls three "anachronisms in late twentieth-century America":

> The first of these is the year at which formal education begins. Typically in this country it is the age of five or six, and this develops not from the learning capacity of children, but from the days when schools were few and far apart, transportation was inadequate, and the child was kept home until he was big enough to walk to the schoolhouse. . . .

> The typical school day may run from 8:30 to 3:30. This is to allow Johnny to do the morning chores before leaving for school, and to get back home in the afternoon in time to bring in the firewood, slop the pigs, round-up the cows, and bring in water for the early evening supper (since there was no electric light), before dark.

> Typically students begin their school year in September and conclude it in June, with a three month hiatus, originally designed so that Johnny could help on the farm during the important part of the growing season.

There is generally a practical basis for social conventions, institutions and laws. All too often, however, the practical basis is lost sight of, and these are seen as good and necessary in and of themselves. Thus, they become difficult to change, even though they may no longer serve a practical end. Again, we see that social fictions—and we include conventions often frozen in institutions and laws—have no value in and of themselves. They are means only, not ends.

Often it is not the fundamental value that must be discarded, but the traditional means of pursuing it. In the following quotation, for example, Dr. Carl Rogers contends that preparing children for life remains an educational value, but that how this is to be accomplished must be changed.

Kaiser Aluminum NEWS, © 1967.

In the world which is already upon us, the goal of education must be to develop individuals who are open to change, who are flexible and adaptive, who have learned how to learn, and are thus able to learn continuously. Only such persons can constructively meet the perplexities of a world in which problems spawn much faster than their answers. The goal of education must be to develop a society in which people can live more comfortably with *change* than with *rigidity*. In the coming world the capacity to face the new appropriately is more important than the ability to know and repeat the old.

Don Fabun, reflecting on the need for change that Dr. Rogers points out, says:

The most pervasive (and unexamined) constant is the teacher-pupil relationship. In this an older person imparts to a younger person (or a less "educated" person) the cultural wisdom or the skills which the teacher has learned. This is the pattern of education in even the most primitive societies, and it presupposes a constancy of environment in which the cultural inheritance that is passed on is still pertinent. There are some serious questions whether most of the cultural inheritance of America's past is any longer relevant to the future in which the child will live as an adult.

catching up with environment

Can you think of some basic values, social conventions, institutions, or laws that are incongruous with our present, changing environment? Conversely, can you think of some new needs, circumstances, or practices that our conventions, institutions, or laws do not accommodate? List some.

Now choose one from your list and set yourself this problem:

How can the conflict be resolved?

To answer this, consider the following issues:

Have we a choice?

What of value would we have to give up if the solution were to change a convention, institution, or law?

Carl Rogers, quoted in *Kaiser Aluminum NEWS*, © 1967.

Is the cost worth it, or have we better alternatives?
When are we willing to compromise?

One form of future/culture shock is the moral dilemma we feel
when a new environment brings a new set of values. Janis Ian's song
"Society's Child" expresses the pain one suffers when attempting to
live by two conflicting sets of values.

Society's Child

Janis Ian

Come to my door, baby,
Face as clean and shinin'
Black as night. My mother went to answer, you
Know that you looked so fine.

Now, I could understand your tears and your shame—
She called you "boy" instead of your name!—
When she wouldn't let you inside,
When she turned and said, "But, honey, he's not our kind."

She says I can't see you anymore, baby,
Can't see you anymore.

Walk me down to school, baby.
Everybody's acting deaf and blind
Until they turn and say, "Why don't you
Stick to your own kind?"

My teachers all laugh. Their smirkin' stares
Couldn't defend our affairs.
Preachers of equality!
If they believe it, then why won't they just let us be?

They say I can't see you anymore, baby,
Can't see you anymore.

One of these days I'm gonna stop my listenin',
Gonna raise my head up high.
One of these days I'm gonna raise my glistenin'
Wings and fly.

But that day'll have to wait for awhile
Baby, I'm only society's child.
When we're older things may change,
But for now this is the way they must remain.

I say, I can't see you any more, baby,
Can't see you anymore, no,
I don't wanna see you any more, baby. . . .

Have you experienced a moral dilemma
in your own adjusting to today's changing world?

ten

on the edge
of a new world

It may seem paradoxical, but one comes best to know one's real self, and to be able to introspect honestly, as a consequence of unselected, spontaneous disclosure of self to another person.

Sidney M. Jourard,
Personal Adjustment

If we attempt to summarize in a phrase what our many probes have pointed to, we can say something like: the key to coping with change is *finding out who we are*. And the "we" is either each one of us individually or all of us collectively. Interestingly, the very process of finding out changes us. *We become who we are.*

We have seen persons who found out who they were through their experience of a changed environment. For most of them the shock of alienation became the shock of self-discovery—a positive experience grew out of a negative one. In this sense, culture/future shock can be a positive experience.

Our next author, Eldridge Cleaver, is a person whose alienation from society and from himself ran very deep. Unlike Ellison's hero, Cleaver was fully aware of his alienation before the experience shown here took place. Cleaver, Minister of Information for the Black Panther Party for Self-Defense, wrote *Soul On Ice*, or parts of it, while serving in California's Folsom State Prison on charges ranging from possession of marijuana to what Cleaver describes as "rape-on-principle."

In this most unlikely setting—a prison—with this most unlikely person —a rapist—we may observe that finding out who we are can come with one of the most powerful and positive experiences a human being can have: loving another human being.

from SOUL ON ICE

Eldridge Cleaver

PRELUDE TO LOVE:—THREE LETTERS

[*Note:* Eldridge Cleaver had been in prison in California for nearly nine years. Beverly Axelrod is a San Francisco lawyer. Prior to the time the following letters were written, Mr. Cleaver had written to Mrs. Axelrod for legal assistance. She had visited him three times before the following exchange of letters took place.]

ELDRIDGE CLEAVER
Folsom Prison
Represa, California
September 5, 1965

Dear Beverly Axelrod:

For two charged days and restless nights after you left, I loafed in the case of my skull, feeling prematurely embalmed in some magical ethered mist dispensed by the dialectic of our contact. When I left you sitting in that little glass cage, which I must somehow learn to respect because it has a special, eternal meaning now, I did not stop or pause. Including the door to that glass cage, and counting the door of my cell, I passed through twelve assorted gates and doors before collapsing on my narrow bed, staggering under the weight of the DAY. The doors and gates swung open before me as I advanced upon them, as I charged down on them, as if they were activated by photoelectric cells responding to my approach. I walked swiftly, but I felt myself to be running, stumbling, thrashing and flailing with my arms to clear a passage through dense, tangled vines. I spoke to no one, recognized no one, and I felt that no one could see or recognize me (wrong: I was accused next day of walking past a couple of henchmen as if they weren't even there. I kept telling them that, in fact, as far as I was concerned, they weren't there, but they refuse to believe in their own non-existence or invisibility).

On the third day I arose again from the damned. No, that's going too far!

What a transfusion! I don't believe I can stand you in such massive doses. It may prove lethal.

I am almost afraid to return to my manuscripts—which themselves seem to cringe from me—after talking with you. I know I shall remain immobile, transfixed, until I've gotten this letter off to you. Then....

I really have no sense of myself and I have always suffered under the compliments of others, especially my friends. I panic. I ran for an office in the Folsom Gavel Club recently. One of my boosters poured lavish praise upon me and my qualifications for the job. I squirmed in my seat and felt oppressed. Does this mean that I do not have the ego for a compliment? No, it does not. It's hypocritical of me, but whenever someone says something nice about me, it sort of knocks me for a loop. And you? The things you said sent me spinning. But don't stop, let me suffer—and overcome.

I feel impelled to express myself to you extravagantly, and words, phrases, sentences, paragraphs leap in my mind. But I beat them down, refuse to write them, because it all seems so predictable and trite. I feel humiliated by the words you inspire me to write to you. I refuse to write them. What right have you to summon my soul from its slumber? But it's all golden and I write this from a sense of the sweetness of irony, the better to marvel at the unbelievable sequence of chance events which brought us face to face in a little glass cage in the office of the Warden of Folsom Prison.

You have tossed me a lifeline. If you only knew how I'd been drowning, how I'd considered that I'd gone down for the third time long ago, how I kept thrashing around in the water simply because I still felt the impulse to fight back and the tug of a distant shore, how I sat in a rage that night with the polysyllabic burden of your name pounding in my brain—Beverly Axelrod, Beverly Axelrod—and out of what instinct did I decide to write to you? It was a gamble on an equation constructed in delirium, and it was right.

Let me say this. I was 22 when I came to prison and of course I have changed tremendously over the years. But I had always had a strong sense of myself and in the last few years I felt I was losing my identity. There was a deadness in my body that eluded me, as though I could not exactly locate its site. I would be aware of this numbness, this feeling of atrophy, and it haunted the back of my mind. Because of this numb spot, I felt peculiarly off balance, the awareness of something missing, of a blank spot, a certain intimation of emptiness. Now I know what it was. And since encountering you, I feel life strength flowing back into that spot. My step, the tread of my stride, which was becoming tentative and uncertain, has begun to recover and take on a new definiteness, a confidence, a boldness which makes me want to kick over a few tables. I may even swagger a little, and, as I read in a book somewhere, "push myself forward like a train."

NOW TURN THE RECORD OVER AND PLAY THE OTHER SIDE

I have tried to mislead you. I am not humble at all. I have no humility and I do not fear you in the least. If I pretend to be shy, if I appear to hesitate, it is only a sham to deceive. By playing the humble part, I sucker my fellow men in and seduce them of their trust. And then, if it suits my advantage, I lower the boom—mercilessly. I lied when I stated that I had no sense of myself. I am very well aware of my style. My vanity is as vast as the scope of a dream, my heart is that of a tyrant, my arm is the arm of the Executioner. It is only the failure of my plots that I fear. Whereas in the past we have had Prophets of Doom, in my vanity I wish to be the Voice of Doom itself. I am angry at the insurgents of Watts. They have pulled the covers off me and revealed to all what potential may lie behind my Tom Smile. I had planned to run for President of the United States. My slogan?

PUT A BLACK FINGER ON THE NUCLEAR TRIGGER

400 years of docility, of being calm, cool and collected under stress and strain would go to prove that I was the man for the job, that I would not panic in a crisis and push the button. I could be counted on to be cool. It was a cinch, I had it made—but then came Watts! All my plans went up in smoke! And so, with worn-out tools, I stoop to begin again.

Please take care of yourself.

Until something happens, I shall remain, because I have no other choice—and even if I had another choice I would still remain—

Most Emphatically Yours,
Eldridge

BEVERLY AXELROD
Attorney-at-Law
San Francisco, Calif.
September 10, 1965

Dear Eldridge Cleaver:

... The need for expression is now upon me, having finished the legal matters, and I'm getting panicky. I'm not strong enough to take the safest course, which would be to not widen the subject matter of our correspondence, and I'm having a terrible time trying to say what I want knowing it will be read by the censors.

Your letter, which I keep rereading, shows you're going through the same turmoil I am; but I bear the onus of having allowed it. You talk about it being lethal, and then about life coming back—and I know that both are true.

I'm going purely on instinct now, which is not usual for me, but somehow I know I'm right, or maybe it's just that it's so important that I don't care about the risk of being wrong. Am I coming through to you? I'm writing I know in an obscure kind of way because of the damnable lack of privacy in our communications.

Believe this: I accept you. I know you little and I know you much, but whichever way it goes, I accept you. Your manhood comes through in a thousand ways, rare and wonderful. I'm out in the world, with an infinity of choices. You don't have to wonder if I'm grasping at something because I have no real measuring stick. I accept you.

About that other side of the record: Did you really think I didn't know? Another facet of the crystal might be an apter term; I have a few facets myself. I do not fear you, I know you will not hurt me. Your hatred is large, but not nearly so vast as you sometimes imagine; it can be used, but it can also be soothed and softened.

What an enormous amount of exploring we have to do! I feel as though I'm on the edge of a new world.

Memo to me: Be rational. It cannot be resolved. The choices: 1. He believes everything he says, but he cannot know, he has no choice; or 2. It's a beautiful put-on because he doesn't know that you would do exactly what you are doing for him anyway; or 3. It's a game to relieve the monotony, conscious or not. Answer: It doesn't make a damn bit of difference, because I can't find out, he can't find out, and it's too late anyway. The only important thing is to get him out, and that was obvious from the first letter, with all lawyerlike objectivity.

What an awesome thing it is to feel oneself on the verge of the possibility of really knowing another person. Can it ever happen? I'm not sure. I don't know that any two people can really strip themselves that naked in front of each other. We're so filled with fears of rejection and pretenses that we scarcely know whether we're being fraudulent or real ourselves.

Of all the dangers we share, probably the greatest comes from our fantasizing about each other. Are we making each other up? We have no way of testing the reality of it.

I can't write any more. I'm thunderstruck at having written this much. I'm afraid to read it over, because it's likely I would tear it up, so I'll send it as is. Can you imagine how much I haven't said?

Sincerely yours,
Beverly Axelrod

Eldridge Cleaver
Folsom Prison
Represa, California
September 15, 1965

Dear Beverly Axelrod:

Your letters to me are living pieces—chunks!—of you, and are the most important things in my life. This is fantastic. It only happens in books —or in the dreams of inmates of insane asylums—and with people who are for real. I share with you the awesome feeling of being on the verge of really knowing another person.

I place a great deal of emphasis on people really listening to each other, to what the person has to say, because one seldom encounters a person capable of taking either you or themselves seriously. But I was not *really* like this when I was out of prison—although the seeds were there, but there was too much confusion and madness mixed in. I was not too interested in communicating with other people—that is not true. What I mean is, I had a profound desire for communicating with and getting to know other people, but I was incapable of doing so, I didn't know how.

Do you know what shameless thought just bullied its way into my consciousness? That I deserve you, that I deserve to know you and to communicate with you, that I deserve to have all this happening. What have I done to merit this? I don't believe in the merit system. I Am That I Am. No, I will not hurt you.

Memo to us: 1. He believes everything he says and knows what he is saying; 2. Put-ons are cruel, and how could I be cruel to you? 3. He does not play games, and he does not find life monotonous, conscious or not. He has plans and dreams, and he is deadly serious. Answer: It makes every bit of difference, and I hope to help you find out, he is already finding out; taking it like you find it is a burn, it sells yourself short: be discerning and take only after you spot what you like—but I'm hoping that it is too late for you to flip over on me because it is certainly much too late for me.

Your thought, "Of all the dangers we share, probably the greatest comes from our fantasizing about each other. Are we making each other up?" bothers me. It would be very simple if that were the case: I could arrange (and how easy it would be!) to spend the rest of my life in prison and we could live happily ever after. But it is not that easy, is it? I seek a lasting relationship, something permanent in a world of change, in which all is transitory, ephemeral, and full of pain. We humans, we are too frail creatures to handle such titanic emotions and deep magnetic yearnings, strivings and impulses.

The reason two people are reluctant to really strip themselves naked in front of each other is because in doing so they make themselves vulnerable and give enormous power over themselves one to the other. How awful, how deadly, how catastrophically they can hurt each other, wreck and ruin each other forever! How often, indeed, they end by inflicting pain and torment upon each other. Better to maintain shallow, superficial affairs; that way the scars are not too deep, no blood is hacked from the soul. You beautifully—O, how beautifully!!—spoke, in your letter, of "What an awesome thing it is to feel oneself on the verge of the possibility of really knowing another person..." and "I feel as though I am on the edge of a new world." Getting to know someone, entering that new world, is an ultimate, irretrievable leap into the unknown. The prospect is terrifying. The stakes are high. The emotions are overwhelming. In human experience, only the perennial themes can move us to such an extent. Death. Birth. The Grave. Love. Hate.

I do not believe that a beautiful relationship has to always end in carnage. I do not believe that we have to be fraudulent and pretentious, because that is the source of future difficulties and ultimate failure. If we project fraudulent, pretentious images, or if we fantasize each other into distorted caricatures of what we really are, then, when we awake from the trance and see beyond the sham and front, all will dissolve, all will die and transform into bitterness and hate. I know that sometimes people fake on each other out of genuine motives to hold onto the object of their tenderest feelings. They see themselves as so inadequate that they feel forced to wear a mask in order to continuously impress the other. I do not want to "hold" you, I want you to "stay" out of your own need for me.

I seek the profound. Contrary to the advice of the Prophet, I'll take the credit and let the cash go. What I feel for you is profound. Beverly, there is something happening between us that is way out of the ordinary. Ours is one for the books, for the poets to draw new inspiration from, one to silence the cynics, and one to humble us by reminding us of how little we know about human beings, about ourselves. I did not know that I had all these feelings inside me. They have never been aroused before. Now they cascade down upon my head and threaten to beat me down to the ground, into the dust. But because of the strength of the magnetic pull I feel toward you, I am not fazed and I know that I can stand against the tide.

I even respect you behind your back. I have a bad habit, when speaking of women while only men are present, of referring to women as bitches. This bitch this and this bitch that, you know. A while back I was speaking of you to a couple of cutthroats and I said, "this bitch . . ." And I felt very ashamed of myself about that. I passed judgment upon myself and suffered spiritually for days afterward. This may seem insignificant, but I attach great importance to it because of the chain of thought kicked off by it. I care about you, I am concerned about you, which is all very new for, and a sharp departure from, Eldridge X.

Your persistent query, "How can he tell? He has no choices," deserves an answer. But it is not the type of question that can be answered by words. It takes time and deeds, and this involves trust, it involves making ourselves vulnerable to each other, to strip ourselves naked, to become sitting ducks for each other—and if one of the ducks is shamming, then the sincere duck will pay in pain—but the deceitful duck, I feel, will be the loser. (If both ducks are shamming, what a lark, what a fiasco, what a put-on, what a despicable thought! I laugh at it because it has no power over me, I do not feel vulnerable to it, I feel protected by the flashing eyes of Portia. I extended my trust to you. I am vulnerable and defenseless and I make myself a duck for you.)

Listen: Your letter is very beautiful, and you came through with rockets on. You came through and landed on your feet, with spiked shoes on, right on my heart. It is not that we are making each other up and it is not ourselves alone who are involved in what is happening to us. It is really a complex movement taking place of which we are mere parts. We represent historical forces and it is really these forces that are coalescing and moving toward each other. And it is not a fraud, forced out of desperation. We live in a disoriented, deranged social structure, and we have transcended its barriers in our own ways and have stepped psychologically outside its madness and repressions. It is lonely out here. We recognize each other. And, having recognized each other, is it any wonder that our souls hold hands and cling together even while our minds equivocate, hesitate, vacillate, and tremble?

Peace. Don't panic, and don't wake up.
Dream on. I am
Yours,

Eldridge

point of departure

If our probes have any bearing on real life, they should be helpful in any situation in which we are attempting to understand and evaluate change. As we move on to speculate on alternative futures, we should be able to test any change with the criteria these probes help to develop. Let us review them now by applying them to the Cleaver letters, recognizing that the letters do not show the whole picture and that your responses will be based, in part, on inferences.

---

finding out who we are

How did Cleaver change? Did he find out who he was?

How did he cope with changes in himself?

What insights into himself did he have? Can you distinguish between his real self and his self-structure?

What was the agent of change? How did it function? Was the change good for him?

Was he more self-actualizing after the experience?

---

finding out where we are

What imprints did he break?

Were there any social fictions he rejected? Accepted?

Did his view of the nature of man change?

Did his values change?

Did the way in which he viewed his relationship to society change?

> We represent historical forces and it is really these forces that are coalescing and moving toward each other.

What historical forces do you think he means?

Does this represent a change from conventional belief?

If he is right, what conflict might there be between old conventions, institutions, or laws and new needs, circumstances, or practices? (Is Janis Ian's song "Society's Child" an example of this conflict?)

How would you resolve such a conflict?

Consider again the following issues:

Have we a choice?

What of value would we have to give up if the solution were to change a convention, institution, or law?

Is the cost worth it, or have we better alternatives?

When are we willing to compromise?

breaking with the past

Apply the questions under "Finding Out Who We Are" and "Finding Out Where We Are" to any character in any of the selections in Part Two, or to yourself. If you apply them to yourself, consider changes over the last three months.

> [A]t the rate things are moving today, our criterion should not be the immediate past. Our immediate future is as different from anything we have known as the nineteenth century was from the Maya civilization. We must therefore proceed by projecting ourselves farther and farther into space and time instead of making trivial comparisons within an infinitely small period where the past we have just been living in bears no resemblance to the future, and where the present has no sooner come into being than it is swallowed up by this unusable past.
> **Louis Pauwels and Jacques Bergier,**
> *The Morning of the Magicians*

> We are living at a time when history is holding its breath, and the present is detaching itself from the past like an iceberg that has broken away from its icy moorings to sail across the boundless ocean.
> **Arthur C. Clarke,**
> *The Children of Icarus*

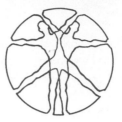

For at least 2,000,000 years, men have been reproducing and multiplying on a little automated spaceship called Earth, in an automated universe in which
the entire process is so successfully predesigned that
men did not even know that they were automated,
regenerative passengers on a spaceship and were so
naïve as to think they had invented their own success
as they lived egocentrically on a seemingly static earth.

R. Buckminster Fuller,
"The Prospect for Humanity"

PART III

exploring
spaceship earth

man — an endangered species?

We cannot alter the past. At current speeds, the present becomes the past even as we set hand to it. At such speeds, our options for today are drastically narrowed. Only tomorrow can be dealt with.

Man . . . an Endangered Species?

Earth. Air. Fire. Water. For the ancient Greeks, these were the elements of the environment. And so they are for us today, but with what a difference! Earth we have burrowed under–and built on–and cemented over; yet we have extended its capacity to support and sustain human life in untold measure. Air we have filled with noise, fumes, and flying bodies; yet we have cracked the shell of our atmosphere and broken out into space. The resources of our planet to make fire, the provider of heat and light, we have been consuming at a catastrophic rate; but we have found new sources of "fire" in atomic energy and the laser beam. And water. On the one hand we have polluted every major river in the nation; on the other hand, we have found the sea.

Our exploration of spaceship Earth begins with our physical environment. What is happening to it? What is happening to us in it? How is it changing? What controls do we have? What controls should we use?

Our task is three-fold:

First, we must get the key facts.

Second, we must identify major alternatives.

Third, we must critically examine the values at stake.

At each stage, we must speculate. The world will not sit still and wait for us. No matter where we look, it will be changing before our eyes. So, the "facts" are in the form of processes, of trends, of patterns, and we will speculate about where they are taking us. We will speculate about alternatives when we consider and, in fact, design some

Pollution Peril
For Caviar

Earth's Oceans

Colonizing

New Choking Menace That Covers the Land

The City of the Future

Japan Answers

Garbage Crisis

Our Polluted Air

Fertilizers

Pollution

To Attack

An Institute

A Sea City

Plan to Ease

Population

The Population
Time Bomb

Beneath the Sea

Gloomy Report on

Population Boom

Our Vanishing Wildlife

MAN'S EXTINCTION
HELD REAL PERIL

Bad air causes accidents

Hopes dim for noise reductions

City

For the Starving

Millions, Seeds of Hope

Some Unpopular

'200 N

A Month in Air Population Curbs

Here (and on pp. 160, 213, and 238) are some 1968 headlines. To get a notion of the rapidity of change—or the durability of problems—collect some headlines from your own newspaper, for comparison.

possible environments. And we will speculate about values by asking ourselves two questions: What is the best environment for man? Must we develop a new image for man?

> Western philosophers have always gone on the assumption that fact is something cut and dried, precise, immobile, very convenient, and ready for examination. The Chinese deny this. The Chinese believe that a fact is something crawling and alive, a little furry and cool to the touch, that crawls down the back of your neck.
>
> **Lin Yutang,**
> *Chinese scholar*

from # Man . . .
An Endangered Species?

Man is a threatened species. The twin specters facing him are over-population and unbridled technology —both self-induced.

The double threat is aimed most directly at man's environment. As the United States strives to accommodate more human beings than it has ever had to serve before, increased demands are placed on our natural resource bank. Our surroundings become increasingly crowded, noisy, and soiled.

The environmental squeeze from technology and population pressures is more than the mere loss of mineral reserves, air and water quality, and forest resources. These are losses that can be measured—in used tons of ore, in coliform bacteria count, in felled board feet—and these measurements suffice to describe what is happening to the parts of our world we must breathe and drink and feed on.

But we have yet to devise a satisfactory index to measure the diminishing quality, the creeping vulgarity and ugliness, of those environmental components which man must look at, listen to, work with, and play in.

Searching back into prehistory, we find that almost every loss of a life form or species has been caused by one or a combination of three things: Intensive specialization leading to an evolutionary deadend, geological or climatic forces which proved catastrophic, or some other species of fatally inimical life.

It is remarkable that throughout millions of years of evolutionary struggle toward humanity, the life form which was to become man es-

"Man . . . An Endangered Species?," *U.S. Department of the Interior Conservation Yearbook No. 4* (Washington, D.C.: U.S. Government Printing Office, 1968), pp. 7, 9, 10, 11, 13, and 14.

caped the trap of specialization. This changing, adapting species with its human destiny managed to maintain its options. It also survived the elements.

The third threat—from a strain of hostile life—remains a force to be reckoned with. That threat is man himself.

Having avoided the fatal turn of the evolutionary road which led other life forms to an overdeveloped hide, a wing, or a fin, man has used his grasping hand and his creative brain to build himself another kind of trap—a technological trap—and he is crowding it with ever-increasing numbers of his own kind.

The question becomes, most urgently: Is man *still* exercising free choice—that one absolute necessity if he is to avoid the fate of the dinosaurs and the dodos?

Buffeted by the elements and beset by other life forms, man has always stubbornly insisted on exercising every option open to him. Does he still run his own show today: Or has he finally stumbled upon two forces—population and technology—that he considers too sacred to tamper with: Is he still convinced that the roaring crescendo from babies and bulldozers is the sweet music of progress?

Does he confuse technology with science? Will he continue to accord to the jackhammer the same revered status as the test tube? Or will he recognize in time that the tools he uses to rip up mountains and destroy estuaries must be extensions of his mind as well as his muscle? Will he see that science must remain free, since it is the *search* for truth, but that technology is only a means of *applying* truth—and that these applications need the control and balance of wisdom and a concern for posterity?

Man stands at a fork in his environmental road to the future.

The two arms of the signpost do not state categorically, "Man—Master of Himself" and "Man—An Extinct Species," but it is increasingly apparent that the direction he takes now will move him rapidly along the path toward one or the other destination.

Let us look closely for a moment at this creature who pauses at the crossroads and clamors for attention with our own voice. Who is he? Where has he come from and how has he made the journey this far?

Anthropologists tell us he is the product of millions of years of evolution—his being literally shaped by the environment without and the life force within. During all these eons he fought a pitched battle for survival. His attitude toward nature was understandably ambivalent, for nature was his best friend and his worst enemy.

In the beginning, his progress was agonizingly slow, his survival often in doubt. But with the passage of the ages and with a cunning constantly sharpened by the struggle for survival, man established himself at the top of the totem pole of life. He went from flint and flame to rocket-powered flight, with ever increasing speed, until he had created a veritable juggernaut against nature and, in so doing, against himself. Now that he has forced the lock on Pandora's nuclear tool box, his capacity to tamper with his environment and his destiny is virtually limitless.

Today, the most significant thing about change is the speed at which it is occurring. The acceleration rate of tooled tampering with our environment is in the nature of a nearly vertical line on the chart of time. Its path is almost straight up—its destination out of sight.

We are in desperate need of guidelines, but too often our steering apparatus is geared to a tomorrow projected off on a horizontal time-line from today. In reality, when tomorrow becomes today, it will probably be breaking somewhere far over our heads instead of off to one side.

We cannot alter the past. At current speeds, the present becomes the past even as we set hand to it. At such speeds, our options for today are drastically narrowed. Only tomorrow can be dealt with.

The technology to shape tomorrow is in our hands. What is still needed, and urgently, are the social and political means of giving intelligent direction to the awesome tools we have fashioned.

The speed of change has introduced a new danger—the increasing role that chance plays in our human society and its interactions with the natural environment. Man's adaptability, which allowed him to make the dangerous passage from the world of the merely organic into the world of thought, "shorn of fangs and fur and claws," as the poetic anthropologist Loren Eiseley puts it, is today being sorely taxed as it tries to cover the expanding range of choice.

Says Professor Eiseley: "Choice, even intelligent choice, becomes increasingly hard to make among an infinite number of diverging pathways some of which show signs of leading into new and dangerous corners."

The late Robert Oppenheimer, physicist, wrote: "One thing that is new is the prevalence of newness, the changing scale and scope of change itself, so that the world alters as we walk in it, so that the years of a man's life measure not some small growth or rearrangement or moderation of what he learned in childhood, but a great upheaval."

Professor Eiseley put the same idea this way: "I myself, like many of you, have been born in an age which has already perished . . . I will not be merely old; I will be a genuine fossil embedded in onrushing man-made time before my actual death."

The warning is clear. While we indulge in worthy, earnest, but nevertheless limited enterprises such as saving the whooping cranes, we fail to notice our own growing eligibility for the title "endangered species."

The terrible urgency of accelerated change as a focus for intensive applica-

tion of human brains is summed up in the phrase "technological momentum." Admiral Hyman Rickover told a 1966 meeting of the Royal National Foundation in Athens, Greece: "If people understood that technology is the creation of man, therefore subject to human control, they would demand that it be used to produce maximum benefit and do minimum harm to individuals and to the values that make for civilized living."

"Unfortunately," Rickover continued, "there is a tendency in contemporary thinking to ascribe to technology a momentum of its own, placing it beyond human direction or restraint— a tendency more pronounced in some countries but observable wherever there is rapid technological progress."

We have, no matter how dimly we perceive it, a moral obligation to the future. Kenneth Boulding, the economist, has observed that it is always hard to find a convincing answer to the man who says, "What has posterity ever done for me?"

"The whole problem," Boulding maintains, "is linked up with the much larger one of the determinants of the morale, legitimacy, and 'nerve' of a society, and there is much historical evidence to suggest that a society which loses its identity with posterity and which loses its positive image of the future loses also its capacity to deal with present problems, and soon falls apart."

In a world which is essentially (with the important exception of solar energy) a "closed system," our primary considerations are those of extraction and waste disposal. As we extract our natural resources we diminish them. As we dispose of waste products, we contribute to pollution. Ironically, it is the waste rather than the supply problem that demands our prior attention.

With air and water in many places exhibiting signs of intolerable overload, this question of waste disposal has become one of the prime threats to human survival. The attempts being made today to remove man from the endangered list are aimed in large measure at this threat.

Economist Boulding is hopeful that "as a succession of mounting crises, especially in pollution, arouse public opinion and mobilize support for the solution of the immediate problems, a learning process will be set in motion which will eventually lead to an appreciation of and perhaps solutions for the larger ones."

The earth has been likened to a spaceship on which man must carry all his needs and live with all his waste products. It is within this closed-system context of our predicament that we must consider our pollution problems. Again, we find science a mixed blessing. For while we can be fairly sure of discoveries that will lead to new ways of supplying needed materials and energy, these new supplies lead to new waste problems, such as the insidious and inadequately charted contamination from man-released radioactive materials.

As we crowd more and more people into the spacecraft (and population growth becomes "exponential" when it is significantly freed from such checks as disease) then we face an eventually impossible situation, but one that carries some tragic possibilities on the way to the ultimate impossibility. An example:

Rene Debos, in an essay on "Environmental Quality in a Growing Economy," says that "the problems posed by adaptation to crowding bid fair to change in character and to become of increasing importance in the near future . . . Furthermore, experimental studies with various animal species have revealed that excessive crowding results in many forms of behavioral disturbances, ranging from sexual aberrations to cannibalism or . . . more interestingly to complete social unresponsiveness."

Thus the question of whether we are to survive on this planet at all becomes not just one of controlling the birthrate but of whether, along the way to the critical mass of humanity, we create conditions that will make existence well-nigh intolerable.

It has been noted, and fairly, that the only question with relation to the future of world population is whether the inevitable decline in rate of growth will come about through a tremendous upsurge in the death rate or through a drastic fall in the birth rate. Over the long haul, these two solutions represent our only choice. The former will mean unprecedented human misery; the latter, unprecedented human wisdom.

The problems created by thoughtless growth in some areas of technology are sometimes compounded by lags in other areas. There has been, for instance, a regrettable lack of technological activity in solving air pollution, where our problems are chronically aggravated by an automobile whose internal combustion system has hardly progressed since it was adopted. A true pursuit of technological improvement might well have solved the exhaust pollution problem long before it became the near tragedy it is today.

It is generally conceded that we have now, or know how to acquire, the technical capability to do nearly anything we want to do. Possessing such capability (and here it is well to draw a parallel distinction to that between science and technology—the distinction between capability and wisdom) , we have a duty to shift the emphasis far more heavily from "how can we do it?" to "*should* we do it?"

This is the central question facing modern conservation. With so many humans inhabiting the environs, and with such powerful tools for shaping the environment, where should we move ahead, where should we hold back, and what directions should we take?

We must start by rejecting what we *cannot* do. Walter Sullivan, science columnist for *The New York Times*, wrote on March 25, 1967: "In a world of proliferation—proliferation of human beings, of nuclear weapons, of food additives—unplanned, uncontrolled technological growth can no longer be tolerated. . . . The world has become too dangerous for anything less than utopias."

We are not likely to find many utopias lying around, tied up in neat packages of total solutions. Our main hope is that we are beginning to understand the totality of the problem of survival. The threats to this survival are woven in a skull and crossbones pattern into the fabric of our entire world; it crisscrosses the boundaries between the social and the natural. We cannot continue to exist if we do not take care of our natural world, and we cannot exercise the life-or-death brand of stewardship required without massive exercise of wisdom at the social level.

The time span remaining for constructive action is short. The future slips into the past at a blurred clip and our hope lies with those whose vision is as wide as the problem and whose courage is a match for the corrective measures so urgently needed.

IT TOOK FROM	FOR EARTH'S POPULATION TO REACH
the beginning of man to the Neolithic age	7,990,000 years to reach 10 million
Neolithic to the Birth of Christ	10,000 years to reach 300 million
Birth of Christ to the days of Columbus	1,500 years to reach 500 million
Columbus to 1850 A.D.	350 years to reach 1 BILLION
1850 to 1925 A.D.	75 years to reach 2 BILLION
1925 to 1962 A.D.	37 years to reach 3 BILLION
and will take to 1975	13 years to reach 4 BILLION
and from there to 1982	7 years to reach 5 BILLION

Don Fabun, *The Dynamics of Change*, Kaiser Aluminum & Chemical Corporation, © 1967.

[T]he inevitable decline in rate of growth will come about through a tremendous upsurge in the death rate or through a drastic fall in the birth rate."

Man . . . an Endangered Species?

"Are you kidding?"

"Listen to this. A writer way back in 1966 predicted that our generation would have one person to every square foot."

"It is obvious that the best qualities in man must atrophy in a standing-room-only environment. Therefore, if the fulfillment of the individual is our ultimate goal, we must soon determine the proper man-land ratio for our continent."

Stewart L. Udall,
U.S. Secretary of the Interior

...By 1985," says John G. Wells, head of the University of Denver Research Institute, "we shall be asking some new questions. Among them, how many people should there be in the U.S.? In my state? In my community? And some old ones.... Who should be allowed to breed, with whom, and how fast? The educated classes? The physically healthy? And should it be discovered that the poorer classes and the unhealthy are breeding faster than the rest of the nation—is the quality of the human race being downgraded?...

Quoted in Don Fabun,
The Dynamics of Change

What is the true end of Man? Is it to populate the Earth with the maximum number of human beings...or is it to enable human beings to lead the best kind of life that the spiritual limitations of human nature allow?

Arnold Toynbee,
quoted in Don Fabun,
The Dynamics of Change

Some Unpopular Population Curbs

David Perlman,
Science Correspondent

If Professor Paul R. Ehrlich of Stanford University is hanged in effigy by parents and politicians, he may figure the price worthwhile.

For Dr. Ehrlich is convinced that this over-populated planet is entering a period of inevitable and increasing worldwide famine right now—and that only the most drastic, ruthless measures for population control can hope to give the human race a second chance for survival.

So Dr. Ehrlich proposed a few such measures yesterday, and thereby risked outraging a major segment of the population he hopes to save.

PROPOSALS

A distinguished zoologist and specialist in problems of population biology, Dr. Ehrlich spoke at a scientific symposium at the University of Texas in Austin.

He was offering his highly controversial proposals, he said, because only through debate about future measures can a consensus be reached in time to make the measures work.

Dr. Ehrlich's proposals for the United States, offered "in the full knowledge that they are socially unpalatable and politically unrealistic," included:

Federal laws to make birth control instruction mandatory in all public schools, and a Federal ban on State laws limiting the right of women to undergo abortions.

An end to all income tax deductions for children, addition of new taxes on large families, and heavy luxury taxes on diapers, baby bottles and baby foods.

A major increase in Federal funds for research into birth control and population regulation—"rather than into short-sighted programs on death control."

Establishment of a powerful Federal Population Commission with a "large budget for propaganda which supports reproductive responsibility."

Dr. Ehrlich based his program on the supposition that an ideal population for the United States would be 150 million. This is far short of the U.S. Census Bureau, that America's population now at about 200 million will reach 300 million by 1999.

Said the Census Bureau earlier this week: America can produce "plenty of food and then some" for all its growing population. "Our productive capacity is more than keeping up, despite the fears of overcrowding."

This is nonsense, declared Dr. Ehrlich. The quality of American life is becoming disastrously ugly because of the burden of numbers, he said.

And besides, he added, "Saying that the population explosion is a problem of underdeveloped countries is like telling a fellow passenger 'your end of the boat is sinking.'

"A great many people are going to starve to death, and soon. There is nothing that can be done to prevent it."

American foodstuffs can't possibly avert famine elsewhere, Ehrlich said, and so he proposed tough measures:

He suggested announcing to the world that "we will no longer ship food to countries (like India) where dispassionate analysis indicates that the food-population unbalance is hopeless.

AID

He urged withholding all foreign aid from any country with a rising birth rate "until that country convinces us that it is doing everything within its power to limit its population."

He called for massive American aid in the technology of birth control, and massive technical aid for increasing the yield of cultivated land abroad.

And finally, he proposed that America frankly employ its political power and economic pressure to force the world's birth rate down—just as it uses its military power for other ends.

"A good place to start," said Dr. Ehrlich, "would be breaking off diplomatic relations with the Vatican until that organization brings its policies into line with the desires of the majority of American Catholics.

"Much of the world will be horrified at our stand, but as a nation we're clearly willing to go against world opinion on other issues—why not on the most important issue?"

Pollution

Tom Lehrer

(Time was when an American about to go abroad would be warned by his friends or the guide books not to drink the water. But times have changed and now, a foreigner coming to this country might be offered the following advice:)

If you visit American city
You will find it very pretty.
Just two things of which you must beware:
Don't drink the water and don't breathe the air!

Pollution, pollution, they got
Smog and sewage and mud;
Turn on your tap and get
Hot and cold running crud.

See the halibuts and the sturgeons
Being wiped out by detergents.
Fish gotta swim and birds gotta fly—
But they don't last long if they try.

Pollution, pollution, you can
Use the latest toothpaste,
And then rinse your mouth
With industrial waste.

Just go out for a breath of air
And you'll be ready for medicare.
The city streets are really quite a thrill:
If the hoods don't get you, the monoxide will.

Pollution, pollution, wear
A gasmask and a veil;
Then you can breathe,
Long as you don't inhale.

Lots of things there that you can drink,
But stay away from the kitchen sink;
The breakfast garbage that you throw into the Bay,
They drink at lunch in San Jose.

Pollution, pollution, see the crazy people there.
Like lambs to the slaughter,
They're drinking the water
And breathing the air.

Air. Dr. Philip A. Leighton, professor emeritus of chemistry at Stanford, has made the following ominous calculation:

The undesirable effects of nitrogen oxides begin to appear at concentrations of about .05 parts per million. Cruising at 60 miles per hour, the average "full sized" American automobile emits about three liters of nitrogen oxides per minute. To dilute these below .05 requires, for the one automobile, more than 60,000,000 liters of air per minute, a rate which is enough to supply the average breathing requirements, over the same period of time, of 5,000,000 to 10,000,000 people.

There is only so much air on this planet. The generous rate at which we now dump pollutants into it causes Dr. Leighton to wonder if the resource which eventually will force man to adopt population control will be not land, food, or water, but *air.*

Water. Every major river in the country is now grossly polluted by both industrial wastes and municipal sewage. Lake Erie is becoming a dead sea, on its way to cesspool status. Even without the shortage due to pollution, there is not enough water for some cities in time of drought. New York City is in a very critical period. Tap the polluted Hudson; tap Niagara Falls; tap underground rivers; inaugurate a great nuclear desalinization project with the help of the federal government! The headlines reflect the current crisis and the growing shortage. Like air, there is only so much fresh water on the planet.

City Living. Survey after survey shows American cities rotting at the core, surrounded by widening areas of urban blight. One of every eight New Yorkers lives in almost incredible squalor. Some tenements are packed with as many as ten persons to a rat-infested room. Much of the city is a jungle where no one is safe after dark. Even inside some public schools, teen-age girls walk in pairs as protection against rape. Urban renewal and public housing are unable to offset the galloping deterioration. Great sums must be invested if cities are to be made fit to live in. Fortunately, here is a field for workers displaced by automation.

The raw materials of civilization, as of life itself, are matter and energy, which we now know to be two sides of the same coin. For most of human history, and all of prehistory, only the most modest quantities of either were used by man. During the course of a year, one of our remote ancestors consumed about a quarter of a ton of food, half a ton of water, and negligible quantities of hide, sticks, stones, and clay. The energy he expended was that created by his own muscles, plus an occasional small contribution in the form of wood fires.

With the rise of technology, that simple picture has changed beyond recognition. The yearly consumption of the average American citizen is more than half a ton of steel, seven tons of coal, and hundreds of pounds of metals and chemicals whose very existence was unknown to science a

Reprinted from Stuart Chase, "Can We Stay Prosperous?" by permission of the publisher. Copyright 1967 Saturday Review, Inc.

From p. 141 *Profiles of the Future* by Arthur C. Clarke. Copyright © 1959, 1960, 1962 by Arthur C. Clarke. Copyright © 1961 by H.M.H. Publishing Company. Reprinted by permission of Harper & Row, Publishers.

century ago. Every year, over *twenty tons* of raw materials are dug from the earth to provide a modern man with the necessities—and luxuries—of life. No wonder we hear warnings from time to time of critical shortages, and are told that within a few generations copper or lead may be added to the list of rare metals.

Consider the questions raised in the article, "Man . . . An Endangered Species?" Are they answered in the article? How would you answer them?

If we continue in our present course, what is the likeliest outlook for man? Do you believe that man is an endangered species? After atrophy, what? Try to imagine what human life in the year 2000 would be like if current trends continue. Record your impressions in a story, drawing, poem, cartoon, etc.

If we change our course, what of value would we have to give up? Though overpopulation would limit our freedom, population control could also limit our freedom. If freedom is a value, how can it best be preserved?

Which of Ehrlich's proposals can you accept? Can you suggest others?

Decide how you would answer the questions on p. 122. Then, using any medium you choose (film, videotape, speech, collage, story, poem, persuasive paper, etc.), try to persuade others to your point of view.

---

getting the facts

Collect materials which suggest that your city, county, state, or federal government is taking positive steps to meet the threats of technology and overpopulation discussed in this section.

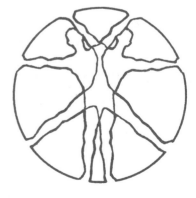

What agencies or organizations in your area should you actively support if you feel that pollution (both air and water) and overpopulation pose threats to your survival? Collect as much data on these organizations as you can. Invite speakers if they are available or arrange a field trip for your group if that is possible. Evaluate the efforts of these agencies. Are they doing enough? Are they taking radical enough action? Have they the insight and power to make the changes you consider necessary?

Arrange a debate on Ehrlich's proposals for population control.

twelve

designing
environments
for man

Our environment today is an eccentrically tailored cloak which enfolds all—but fits few. It binds here and chafes there, impairing the circulation and causing widespread irritation. The seams are frayed. Threadbare patches need reweaving, stains need removing. But the fabric of this universal cloak still has plenty of wear in it, which is a good thing because it is the only one we have. It won't last forever in a conscionable state, however, unless it stops being torn, trampled, and cast into the corner. Our environment urgently needs restyling, mending, sprucing up. This we know because our senses and sensibilities tell us so. But how do we go about evaluating the work to be done? To achieve what ends? To preserve which values? To create which new ones? These are questions for anyone and everyone to ponder, for each man is his own expert in conceiving the kind of world he wishes to experience.

31 Minds Explore Our Environment,
National Association of Home
Builders—1965

On the following pages several conceptions of future environments are presented. Some are more likely, some more immediate than others. They are divided into three groups, according to the natural medium within which they would be developed: *land, sea* and *space.* As you consider these alternatives, ask yourself: How would this environment affect the development of human beings? What would it be like to live there? How adequately does each deal with the problems of overpopulation, pollution, and the depletion of natural resources?

These conceptions are a jumping off point for your own speculation and further study. Here is a way to go more deeply into the problem.

designing environments

First, consider these questions. Which medium—land, sea, space—would you most like to live in? Work in? Play in? In other words, do you see yourself as a land person, a sea person, a space person?

Next, choose one and design an environment. Then prepare to describe and defend it. (The following article describes five *shapers of man:* nature, man himself, his society, his structures, and his networks. Consider these as you develop your design.) You might do this individually or in a group. You might build a model, simulate the environment in class, or make a drawing or a film or a videotape. You might present a debate or write a dialogue.

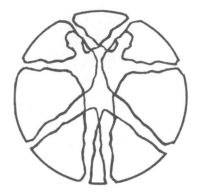

In planning your presentation, set yourself this problem: If I were the person to decide whether this environment would be developed, what arguments would I use to persuade my friends of its value? What objections might be raised, and how would I respond? (Bear in mind the two pivotal questions posed earlier: What is the best environment for man? Must we develop a new image for man?)

designing environments on land

Within the next century, 30 billion people may live in a universal city that covers the earth. Will we build wisely?

C. A. Doxiadis,
"The Coming Era of Ecumenopolis"

THE COMING ERA OF ECUMENOPOLIS

We must face the fact that modern man has failed to build adequate cities. In the past his problems were simpler, and he solved them by trial and error. Now human forces and mechanical ones are mixed

"The environ-
ment is
always the
brainwasher,
so that the
well-adjusted
person, by
definition,
has been
brainwashed.
He is
adjusted.
He's had it."
Marshall
McLuhan,
"Our
Dawning
Electric Age"

and man is confused. He tries and fails. We say he will become adapted. Yes, he is running the danger of becoming adapted, since adaptation is only meaningful if it means the welfare of man. Prisoners, too, become adapted to conditions! For man to adapt to our present cities would be a mistake, since he is the great prisoner. Not only is man unsafe in his prison, but he is facing a great crisis and heading for disaster.

Confused by the danger, man behaves unwisely. He takes the new conditions of a hostile habitat for granted, and, for example, builds new cities in the image of those that failed or, in the countryside, builds air-conditioned schools with no windows because he is accustomed to doing it in industrial areas. Sometimes he attempts to turn to the past, or dreams of Utopias which have no place in our world. What man needs is an Entopia, an "in-place" which he *can* build, a place which satisfies the dreamer and is acceptable to the scientist, a place where the projections of the artist and the builder merge.

How can man achieve this?

Man and the space surrounding him are connected in many ways within a very complex system. Man's space is just a thin layer on the crust of the earth, consisting of the five elements which shape man and are shaped by him: nature, in which he lives; man himself; society, which he has formed; the shells (or structures) which he builds; and the networks he constructs. This is the real world of man, the *anthropocosmos* halfway between the electron and the universe. But only one subject is of primary importance: man as an individual. The subjects of secondary importance are nature and society. Shells and networks come last. Every element of the anthropocosmos has to serve man; otherwise our endeavor would have no justification.

So how can we best serve our basic subject, man? What is our goal? At this point we have to admit that we have no goals. We are developing a technology that is changing our life, yet we have set no goal for it. No businessman would buy machinery at random when building a factory, no housewife would collect furniture at random for her home. Yet this is exactly what we are doing in the case of our cities, the physical expressions of our life. For them we are producing and collecting at random.

". . . average
personality
is just not
good
enough."
(p. 85)
Sidney M.
Jourard

shapers of
man:

nature
man himself
his society
his structures
his networks

"I seek . . . to
reform the
environment
instead of
trying to
reform men."
(p. 18)
R. Buckminster
Fuller

What will our goal be? Aristotle said that the aim of the city is to make man happy and safe. I can find no better definition. So if, in the chaos of our present situation, we can accept this, then we have something firm to stand on, provided we can define what we mean by man, happiness, safety, and city.

I shall begin with man, so close to us and still "man the unknown." But which man are we talking about? Which one is it who best represents the nature of man? Is it primitive man, to whom some romantics want us to return, or the ancient Greek? The medieval or Renaissance man, or the modern technocrat? The only possible answer is the contemporary man. He is our starting point.

Which man, then, is our ideal? To answer we have to look at man from every possible angle. We have to look at the body, and, when we see people stretching or youngsters rock 'n' rolling, realize that their bodies are revolting against the inactivity we have condemned them to. We have to realize how ignorant we are as to whether the taller, larger people which our children are becoming are more resistant to the hardships of life than are their shorter, smaller forebears. And we must look be-

yond the body. Man transcends this sphere by many other concentric ones defined by his senses. No sensation can be overlooked: a sweet or bitter taste, the caressing of a marble carving or a loved one, walking on sand with bare feet, the smells, the sounds, the sights—all physical sensations, and then all metaphysical ones such as faith and religion.

The mind of man carries him into areas which cannot be reached through the senses. So does his soul, by way of sentiments, for sentiments, too, are shaping factors. Body, senses, mind, and soul are only partial aspects of man, but they cannot be separated; they all operate together in health and in sickness. A dancer may find his motivation through stimulation of his senses, or mind, or sentiments. The mind can be stimulated through the rhythmical movement of the body walking or swimming. We must not forget the example of the peripatetic philosophers.

Science is beginning to merge the separate images of man that it had set up and see him again as a whole. Common man finds perfection in the *complete* man. When, for example, one is contemplating marriage, not one aspect of the prospective mate is overlooked. And history demonstrates how in his great eras man believed in developing all his capacities harmoniously.

At present we are at a disadvantage since we have not been studying man properly and have formed no concept of our ideal man. Because of this, man's body and soul are developing in a nonharmonious way, according to the mind rather than the senses. And even the mind is not developing harmoniously in all its areas, but only in some, which are expanding much more than before, while others become atrophic. What kind of creature is this man going to be? The risks we are running by allowing the present trends to continue are very great. We may be turning out monsters without proper balance between their different parts, monsters who may annihilate one another or mankind.

Confronted with such a threat, I think we have a twofold obligation: first, to study man as a whole, without rejecting anything that he has learned throughout his history unless we can prove scientifically that it is harmful. This we can achieve not by coordinating existing sciences—man does not consist of externally coordinated parts, since he forms a whole—but by Anthropics, the Science of Man. Second, in the absence of any proof that we can produce a better man by changing the relationship between the body, the senses, the mind, and the soul, we should work toward a complete man with a harmonious development of all his elements, a total man whom I cannot name anything but *human man*.

defining happiness

Now I turn to the second term in Aristotle's definition, happiness. I beg the skeptics to forgive me, but I cannot omit dealing with this aspect of life. Happiness cannot be measured, but it is still happiness that the common man dreams of and which represents the fulfillment of his goals, the satisfaction of his interests.

One can be unhappy if one's trousers are too tight, the ceiling too low, or the temperature uncomfortable—also because of other similar physiological reasons. But one can be equally unhappy if the senses suffer—in a room painted red, for example, since one's eyes are not used to it, or through noise, smell, coarse clothes, or bad food. Also through stresses on his mind or soul. Man's happiness depends on the alleviation of the stresses he is subject to within his social environment or within himself.

These stresses can be relieved. There is, for example, the story about the man who always wore tight shoes so that when he'd take them off at home the physical relief would help him put up with an unhappy home life. But man can also learn to enjoy these stresses. As the balance between man and his environment changes continuously, his chances for happiness change, too. So what is of major importance is man's capacity for happiness. This capacity man is either born with—we could perhaps express it by an HQ, or Happiness Quotient—or he acquires or loses it by training. A proper science of Anthropics can develop a scientific HQ which will be of the greatest importance to man.

By such approaches man can hope not only to alleviate or enjoy stresses, as the case might be, but also to work toward his further betterment by drawing from within himself something better than himself. This can be gradually achieved when he begins to understand how to coordinate his internal rhythm with that of his environment by changing one or the other. He will have a variety of choices, ranging from harmony with the physical world (matching his footsteps to the pavement slabs) to harmony with nature (swimming along with the waves) to harmony with others (in the rhythmical marching of parades or in work for the amelioration of his society) to harmony with external influences (dancing to a certain tune) to the complete freedom of climbing a mountain or lying on its slopes as it pleases his internal personal rhythm.

The next term in Aristotle's definition—safety— is a concept just as difficult to understand as is happiness, and just as indispensable. Civilization started when man first felt safe within his city. Today, for the first time in history since then, he is no longer safe, and this constitutes the greatest problem to be faced by him and his civilization.

defining safety

How can the city be made safe once more? This question has to be answered through an analysis of all five elements of the anthropocosmos, since the neglect of any one would upset the whole system. Nature has to be preserved, since without the proper development of all its resources there can be no hope for man's safety. The survival of man depends on his evolutionary resources and on his inborn diversity; consequently, he needs a free democratic society which will allow for the survival of the greatest variety of individuals, since we don't yet know which type is going to lead to a better total human man.

Every individual must feel and be safe, which means that personal safety within a safe society can regulate personal and group conflicts. The question is, at what cost can this be achieved? A man would be much safer if he never left his home, but he wouldn't be happy and he wouldn't develop further. We cannot sacrifice happiness and evolution in the cause of safety, nor safety in the cause of happiness. So we come to the conclusion that what we need is a safety which can guarantee a basis from which to begin our endeavors toward happiness and the fulfillment of our duties to society. This leads to the concept of a system which will allow for different environments offering all degrees of safety, ranging from the absolute one, if possible, for newborn babies and invalids, to a completely natural environment which young people will have to conquer; ranging from sterilized rooms to jungles. In such a habitat we can hope for the best balance between controlled and uncontrolled environment that will offer man the maximum safety and allow the dynamic balance of man and environment which is indispensable for lasting happiness, which is the only goal.

setting
criteria
for the
human city

We can now turn to the city of man, but not with preconceived notions about limiting the operation of forces which are independent of man, as people very often do. We must understand that, unlike Utopia, our Entopia depends on forces which are dynamic and which are either uncontrollable or controllable only in the long run. It is these forces which create a new frame for the city to come.

The dynamic forces of developing humanity show that we must be prepared for a continuing increase of population which may well reach 20 to 30 billion people by the end of the next century, at which time it may level off. This will mean a universal city, Ecumenopolis, which will cover the earth with a continuous network of minor and major urban concentrations of different forms. This means that urbanization will continue and that eventually farming may be carried out from urban settlements. This also means that the pressure of population on resources will be such that important measures will have to be taken so that a balance can be retained between the five elements of the anthropocosmos in a universal scale.

But, more than with all separate phenomena, we should be concerned with the survival of man, who, long before the earth has exhausted its capacity for production, will be subjected to great forces pressing him to the point of extinction—forces caused by the elimination of human values in his settlements. If we realize only that at that point the average urban area will have twenty to thirty times more people and a hundred times more machines, and that difficulties grow much faster than the forces causing them, we will understand that this new frame is going to be inhuman in dimensions. If we understand how far the dynamic forces reach, we will see that our real challenge lies not in changing these historical trends—something we cannot do anyway—but in using them for the benefit of man by shaping this universal city in such a way that not only will it not crush man, but so that it will provide him with a human settlement much better than those of today. In order to do this we have to build the city of inhuman dimensions on the measure of man. We don't have to invent the human solutions, since they already exist—we have to understand them and use them within the new frame.

As an example, a careful study of the cities of the past proves that the maximum distance from their centers was ten minutes, and the average one six minutes meaning that people walking for a total of thirty minutes a day could visit the center or other places two or three times. This shows that there was a human dimension influencing social and other contacts, and it also gives one example of how it may be possible to measure a fundamental aspect of the human city—on the basis of the time dimension and not that of physical dimensions, since we now have new means of transportation and communications.

Up to now, measurements in cities have been based on economic criteria, but these define feasibility more than goals. It is time for man to define goals and their feasibility at the same time. Man's most precious commodity, the one which cannot be replaced and which we don't yet know how to expand, is his own life, which is expressed by its length, or lifetime. This is the basic commodity as qualified by the satisfaction and safety man enjoys and as limited by economic considerations, upon which our formula for the city will have to be based.

Man, in this case the average American citizen,

spends 76 per cent of his lifetime at home (males 69 per cent and females 83 per cent), and 24 per cent away from it. He spends 36 per cent sleeping, 20 per cent working, and 10 per cent eating, dressing, and bathing. He is left with 34 per cent, or one-third of his life, for leisure, pleasure, thought, etc. It is this one-third which constitutes the basic difference between man and animal. But males ages twenty to fifty-nine have only 20 per cent of free time, of which one-third is spent in commuting. This means ninety minutes; but for some people it means three hours, or two-thirds of their free time.

On the basis of such calculations we can develop a time budget which is more important than any other budget for man, and estimate how much time each man can afford to spend on each of his activities. We can then qualify the satisfaction that man gets at every time-length. Is it better for him, for example, to walk for twenty minutes, drive in a Volkswagen for ten, or in a Cadillac for two hours? We can also try to measure the degree of safety at every time length. In principle, then, total satisfaction would be the product of time multiplied by satisfaction. A happy life would be the product of time multiplied by satisfaction multiplied by safety. If we now insert into the picture the factor of economic feasibility for satisfaction, we have the formula of feasible happiness, which is leading to the human city that we can build, our common Entopia which should include all our personal Entopias in a balanced whole, the Entopia which is the common denominator of our feasible dreams.

a description of the city of the future

If we have managed to define human man, natural happiness, and reasonable safety, and measure them, we can define the human city. It will be very big, but it will consist of two categories of parts, the cells and the networks. The cells are going to be the size of the cities of the past—no larger than 50,000 inhabitants, no larger than 2000 by 2000 yards, no larger than a ten-minute average walk. They will be built on a human scale on the basis of human experience. The networks are going to be absolutely mechanical and automatic, interconnecting the cells by transportation and communications, forming enormous organisms with the cells as basic units. Their vehicles will reach speeds of many hundreds of miles an hour; their arteries will be underground, not highways but deepways, as they are in the bodies of all mammals. The higher the speed the deeper they will go. In the cells man will be offered all choices, from isolation and solitude to very intense participation in social and political life. (The fact that we need TV should not lead us to the elimination of the marketplace. We don't need only one-way communications, we need a natural human dialogue as well.)

The surface of the city will allow the flora to spread again, beginning from small gardens within the cells, to major zones of forests above the tunnels of the networks, to big farming areas and natural reserves where man will find the rough conditions which he also needs. Society will operate much more efficiently, and people will come together in a multitude of both natural and artificial ways.

Houses will be the natural environment, not formally specified, since there the individual will want to express himself. Normal multistory residence buildings will need much greater areas per floor so that a whole community will be able to operate at each level—a community with its shopping center, playgrounds, and public squares. Automated factories will be placed within the earth, especially in hills and mountains.

Man will be free to move over the surface of the whole city, and even though the buildings will be as pleasant as possible, he will have many chances of walking or staying out without shelter or protection, since his whole organism must be kept fit for all sorts of adjustments that the future may necessitate. In this city we can hope that man, relieved of all stresses that arise from his conflict with the machine, will allow his body to dance, his senses to express themselves through the arts, his mind to dedicate itself to philosophy or mathematics, and his soul to love and to dream.

It has often been said that man may exterminate himself through science. What we must also say is that man's hopes for a much better evolution lie in science, which, after all, is the only acquisition of a proved universal value that he can transmit from generation to generation. The whole difference between extermination and evolution lies in the goal that science will set.

The task is hard. People must learn to recognize that they must be very conservative when dealing with man, and very revolutionary when dealing with new systems and networks. The task is also hard because many expect magical solutions overnight, or formulas for the immediate solution of the problems. They actually like to talk about suffer-

one possible solution:

THE MEGASTRUCTURE

One possible solution to the problem of space and time in our cities is the megastructure. Essentially a city in one vast, continuous building, the megastructure would encompass dwellings, stores, service facilities, offices and recreation centers within one concentrated urban structure. Everything would be within walking or easy driving distance— including the countryside, which would surround the city, not be broken into fragments within it. This concentration would provide a richer, more diverse life than that of suburbia, while preserving the countryside from suburban sprawl. In addition, it would reduce the size of today's metropolis to the more workable, cohesive political unit of under 50,000 population that environmental planners suggest. The plan for one such megastructure is shown here, a "contour-rise" urban core designed for the Santa Monica mountains of southern California by Cesar Pelli and A. J. Lumsden, Director of Design, Daniel, Mann, Johnson and Mendenhall.

ings, and they do not understand that cities face such acute problems because man does not have a system of values with which to define what a good life is. Personally, I am convinced that the root of all problems in our cities lies in our minds, in our loss of belief in man and in his ability to set goals and to implement them.

We can never solve problems and tackle diseases unless we conceive the whole. We cannot build a cathedral by carving stones but only by dreaming of it, conceiving it as a whole, developing a systematic approach, and only then working out the details. But dreaming and conceiving are not enough. We have to carve the stones and lift them.

THE CITY OF THE FUTURE

The power and utility lines will be installed underground, before the city is built. Solid wastes, water, and snow will be carried off by underground pipelines. All deliveries will be made underground, and there will be no vehicles on ground-level streets. Buildings will be put together and come apart like erector sets, to be dismantled and the parts reused every thirty years or so. Public transportation will be free.

These are some of the features of the Experimental City, now being planned in all its details at the University of Minnesota. But representatives from business and industry, scholars, and the federal Departments of Housing and Urban Development, Health, Education, and Welfare, and Commerce are not resting with a mere paper program. They are organizing and financing just such a city from scratch. So reports committee member Athelstan Spilhaus of the Franklin Institute in Philadelphia. (*Science*, Feb. 16, 1968.)

The members of the Minnesota group believe that, in the most basic sense, "the prime pollutant on earth is too many people." If the 200 million people now living in this country were grouped in 800 cities—with a population of 250,000 each, spaced evenly across the country—then the water and air pollution, the traffic congestion, and many of the other ills that plague our cities now would be ended.

The Experimental City will be a densely populated center, surrounded by open land and separated by at least 100 miles from any other major city. Industries that want to operate in the Experimental City will have to abide by the city's extraordinary building regulations and waste-disposal methods. Spilhaus believes they *will* be willing— because of the tremendous advantages of the city's central waste-processing facilities, smoke sewers, and other underground-disposal facilities. As for people, they will come to the city because it will offer the benefits of urban life without the burdens of conventional cities. The makeup of the population can be balanced by carefully selecting the type of industry invited to join the city, since the industry will influence the work force that comes to live there. The city could be managed, Spilhaus suggests, by a city corporation with professional management.

An Experimental City of this size, the planners calculate, might cost about $4 billion to build. With an average family group of 2.5 people, the 250,000 residents will need 100,000 housing units. These units will cost $20,000 each, and the resulting estimate of $2 billion has been doubled to provide for the substructure this city will have. These costs are not impossibly high.

A strong case can be made for building an entire Experimental City rather than trying out one or more of its elements separately. Everything that happens in a city has an impact on everything else. For example, in a city that is clean and quiet and where factories do not cause pollution, separate industrial and residential zoning is not necessary. When factories, schools, and houses are built in the same neighborhood, there is less need for transportation; when transportation is reduced, air pollution is further diminished. In a city with little pollution, disease is reduced and health-care programs are affected.

The planners of the Experimental City believe that other approaches to ameliorating big-city life are bound to be unsuccessful. Urban renewal in cities already too large, and the building of special communities like Reston, Va. (which can only become dormitories for their big-city neighbors), have not grappled with the main problems. The solution for our polluted cities, then, is to get rid of them; to harness modern technology to build a radically different kind of city for the future.

A one-hundred-foot diameter geodesic sphere weighing three tons encloses seven tons of air. The air to structural weight ratio is 2/1. When we double the size so that geodesic sphere is 200 feet in diameter the weight of the structure

Photo and description courtesy R. Buckminster Fuller.

goes up to seven tons while the weight of the air goes up to 56 tons—the air to structure ratio changes to 8/1. When we double the size again to a 400 feet geodesic sphere—the size of several geodesic domes now operating—the weight of the air inside goes to about 500 tons while the weight of the structure goes up to fifteen tons. Air weight to structure weight ratio is now 33/1. When we get to a geodesic sphere one-half mile in diameter, the weight of the air enclosed is so great that the weight of the structure itself becomes of relatively negligible magnitude for the ratio is 1000/1. When the sun shines on an open frame aluminum geodesic sphere of one-half mile diameter the sun penetrating through the frame and reflected from the concave far side, bounces back into the sphere and gradually heats the interior atmosphere to a mild degree. When the interior temperature of the sphere rises only one degree Fahrenheit, the weight of air pushed out of the sphere is greater than the weight of the spherical frame geodesic structure. This means that the total weight of the interior air, plus the weight of the structure, is much less than the surrounding atmosphere. This means that the total assemblage, of the geodesic sphere and its contained air, will have to float outwardly, into the sky, being displaced by the heavy atmosphere around it. When a great bank of mist lies in a valley in the morning and the sun shines upon it, the sun heats the air inside the bank of mist. The heated air expands and therefore pushes some of itself outside the mist bank. The total assembly of the mist bank weighs less than the atmosphere surrounding it and the mist bank floats aloft into the sky. Thus are clouds manufactured. As geodesic spheres get larger than one-half mile in diameter they become floatable cloud structures. If their surfaces were draped with outwardly hung polyethylene curtains to retard the rate at which air would come back in at night, the sphere and its internal atmosphere would continue to be so light as to remain aloft. Such sky-floating geodesic spheres may be designed to float at preferred altitudes of thousands of feet. The weight of human beings added to such prefabricated "cloud nines" would be relatively negligible. Many thousands of passengers could be housed aboard one mile diameter and larger cloud structures. The passengers could come and go from cloud to cloud, or cloud to ground, as the clouds float around the earth or are anchored to mountain tops. While the building of such floating clouds is several decades hence, we may foresee that along with the floating tetrahedronal cities, air-deliverable skyscrapers, submarine islands, sub-dry surface dwellings, domed-over cities, flyable dwelling machines, rentable, autonomous-living, black boxes, that man may be able to converge and deploy around earth without its depletion.

CITIES WILL MOVE UNDERGROUND

The twenty-first century will see man burrowing underground. A hundred years from today, most of mankind will still be living above ground, but every city will already have its underground portion. Many newer suburbs will be entirely underground.

"The underground city will have as its chief advantage an utter freedom from weather vicissitudes or day-night changes. Temperature will be equable the year round and there will be neither wind nor rain nor snow. Well lighted and well ventilated, the underground cities will be computer-designed from the start for rationality and comfort. With the day-night cycle gone, the entire planet can eventually be put on a single 'planet-time'.

"Nor will the underground dweller be deprived of the touch of nature. Quite the contrary. Where the modern city dweller may have to travel twenty miles to get 'in the country', the underground dweller will merely have to rise a few hundred feet in an elevator, for once a city is completely underground, the area above can be made into parkland."

Isaac Asimov in
The Futurist

from THE CITY AND THE STARS

Arthur C. Clarke

Like a glowing jewel, the city lay upon the breast of the desert. Once it had known change and alteration, but now Time passed it by. Night and day fled across the desert's face, but in the streets of Diaspar it was always afternoon, and darkness never came. The long winter nights might dust the desert with frost, as the last moisture left in the thin air of Earth congealed—but the city knew neither heat nor cold. It had no contact with the outer world; it was a universe itself.

Men had built cities before, but never a city such as this. Some had lasted for centuries, some for millenniums, before Time had swept away even their names. Diaspar alone had challenged Eternity, defending itself and all it sheltered against the slow attrition of the ages, the ravages of decay, and the corruption of rust.

Since the city was built, the oceans of Earth had passed away and the desert had encompassed all the globe. The last mountains had been ground to dust by the winds and the rain, and the world was too weary to bring forth more. The city did not care; Earth itself could crumble and Diaspar would still protect the children of its makers, bearing them and their treasures safely down the stream of Time.

They had forgotten much, but they did not know it. They were as perfectly fitted to their environment as it was to them—for both had been designed together. What was beyond the walls of the city was no concern of theirs; it was something that had been shut out of their minds. Diaspar was all that existed, all that they needed, all that they could imagine. It mattered nothing to them that Man had once possessed the stars.

Yet sometimes the ancient myths rose up to haunt them, and they stirred uneasily as they remembered the legends of the Empire, when Diaspar was young and drew its lifeblood from the commerce of many suns. They did not wish to bring back the old days, for they were content in their eternal autumn. The glories of the Empire belonged to the past, and could remain there—for they remembered how the Empire had met its end, and at the thought of the Invaders the chill of space itself came seeping into their bones.

Then they would turn once more to the life and warmth of the city, to the long golden age whose beginning was already lost and whose end was yet more distant. Other men had dreamed of such an age, but they alone had achieved it.

They had lived in the same city, had walked the same miraculously unchanging streets, while more than a billion years had worn away....

The wall flickered partially out of existence as he stepped through to the corridor, and its polarized molecules resisted his passage like a feeble wind blowing against his face. There were many ways in which he could be carried effortlessly to his goal, but he preferred to walk. His room was almost at the main city level, and a short passage brought him out onto a spiral ramp which led down to the street. He ignored the moving way, and kept to the narrow sidewalk—an eccentric thing to do, since he had several miles to travel. But Alvin liked the exercise, for it soothed his mind. Besides, there was so much to see that it seemed a pity to race past the latest marvels of Diaspar when you had eternity ahead of you.

It was the custom of the city's artists—and everyone in Diaspar was an artist at some time or another—to display their current productions along the side of the moving ways, so that the passers-by could admire their work. In this manner, it was usually only a few days before the entire population had critically examined any noteworthy creation, and also expressed its views upon it. The resulting verdict, recorded automatically by opinion-sampling devices which no one had ever been able to suborn or deceive—and there had been enough attempts—decided the fate of the masterpiece. If there was a sufficiently affirmative vote, its matrix would go into the memory of the city so that anyone who wished, at any future date, could possess a reproduction utterly indistinguishable from the original.

The less successful pieces went the way of all such works. They were either dissolved back into their original elements or ended in the homes of the artists' friends.

Alvin saw only one *objet d'art* on his journey that had any appeal to him. It was a creation of pure light, vaguely reminiscent of an unfolding flower. Slowly growing from a minute core of color, it would expand into complex spirals and curtains, then suddenly collapse and begin the cycle over again. Yet not precisely, for no two cycles were identical. Though Alvin watched through a score of pulsations, each time there were subtle and indefinable differences, even though the basic pattern remained the same. . . .

All the roads, both moving and stationary, came to an end when they reached the park that was the green heart of the city. Here, in a circular space over three miles across, was a memory of what Earth had been in the days before the desert swallowed all but Diaspar. First there was a wide belt of grass, then low trees which grew thicker and thicker as one walked forward beneath their shade. At the same time the ground sloped gently downward, so that when at last one emerged from the narrow forest all sign of the city had vanished, hidden by the screen of trees.

The wide stream that lay ahead of Alvin was called, simply, the River. It possessed, and it needed, no other name. At intervals it was spanned by narrow bridges, and it flowed around the park in a complete, closed circle, broken by occasional lagoons. That a swiftly moving river could return upon itself after a course of less than six miles had never struck Alvin as at all unusual; indeed, he would not have thought twice about the matter if at some point in its circuit the River had flowed uphill. There were far stranger things than this in Diaspar. . . .

From this central vantage point, Alvin could look clear across the park, above the screening trees, and out to the city itself. The nearest buildings were almost two miles away, and formed a low belt completely surrounding the park. Beyond them, rank after rank in ascending height, were the towers and terraces that made up the main bulk of the city. They stretched for mile upon mile, slowly climbing up the sky, becoming even more complex and monumentally impressive. Diaspar had been planned as an entity; it was a single mighty machine. Yet though its outward appearance was almost overwhelming in its complexity, it merely hinted at the hidden marvels of technology without which all these great buildings would be lifeless sepulchers.

Alvin stared out toward the limits of his world. Ten—twenty miles away, their details lost in distance, were the outer ramparts of the city, upon which seemed to rest the roof of the sky. There was nothing beyond them—nothing at all except the aching emptiness of the desert in which a man would soon go mad.

designing environments: the sea

With minerals resting on it, nutrients sinking into it, geologic history locked in its sedimentary layers, and petroleum beneath it, the sea's bottom is at least as interesting and certainly more useful to mankind than the moon's backside.

Dean A. Spilhaus,
Institute of Technology,
Minnesota University

COLONIZING
EARTH'S OCEANS

In the next few decades the cycle of earth life will come full circle: man will return to the all-encompassing seas from which life first emerged 300 million years ago. Divers will farm the shallow shelves that surround the continents, turning the ocean floor into an aquaculture where selectively bred fish are raised from fertilized eggs to maturity, kept in pens and fed on concentrated foods. Oil men deploying from pressurized chambers will top off well heads or repair machinery at depths of more than 1000 feet. Mining engineers will prospect for new mineral wealth using deep-diving submersibles. Oceanographic scientists will live on the bottom in anchored habitats while they study marine topography and life. But living in the sea won't be all work. Families may vacation quite literally *in* the Caribbean, swimming out from pressurized dwellings for a day of spear fishing, photography, or underwater sightseeing.

The motives that propel man back into the sea are various. Some are as misty and mythic as the origins of unicellular life itself in the primitive sea; earth, after all, is the "blue planet" in the solar system: fully 70 per cent of its surface is covered with water, and the blood in human veins is similar in composition to the oceans. But such deep matters aside, the seas also offer adventure—an underseascape as unknown as the moon is only three miles below the ocean's surface. It remains unsettled by man—a perilous situation as the Thresher and Scorpion tragedies make abundantly clear. "It is technologically feasible to send men to the moon and get them back again within six days," remarks an oceanographer, "but it takes us months to find an object under the ocean."

Economic motives also force man back to the sea. Declining land-based reserves, rising consumption, and economic pressure are forcing the oil industry to move out to sea. Some $10 billion has been invested by U.S. oil companies in offshore operations to exploit an estimated two-billion-barrel reserve in the continental shelves and slopes. The ocean floor in many areas is literally carpeted with nodules of manganese (used in making steel) and tin.

The ocean of course is vast, and man's colonizing efforts are still tentative and puny. There are only nine research submarines in use, and man's most determined efforts to live on the sea bottom—the Conshelf experiments of explorer Jacques-Yves Cousteau and the U.S. Sea Lab projects involving astronaut Scott Carpenter—have lasted no longer than a few weeks. Even in the U.S., government investment has been relatively small by defense or aerospace standards—only about $500 million a year. But the technology has been growing fast. . . . Some of the newest efforts:

GETTING THERE

Early next year Jacques Piccard, the Swiss engineer who has made the deepest dive on record, a 35,800-foot plunge to the bottom of the Marianas Trench, will embark on a six-week undersea voyage from West Palm Beach, Fla., up the Gulf Stream in his specially designed mesoscaph, the Ben Franklin. Built with funds provided by the Grumman Aircraft Engineering Corp., the Ben Franklin (also known as PX-15) is a research submarine powered by electrical engines. But the engines will not be turned on except in an emergency, to prevent their noise from interfering with delicate acoustical experiments. Throughout the 1500-mile voyage the crew of six will drift silently, carried north by the Gulf Stream, rising to depths of 500 feet, or sinking to the vessel's lower operating limit of 2000 feet.

Inside the steel pressure hull, wood-patterned decals and orange paint on the bulkheads will give the craft a "homey" atmosphere. There any resemblance to human habitation on land ends. The crew will eat freeze-dried food, reconstituted with hot water. No waste will be thrown overboard. A weight loss would cause the

ship to rise, making her unstable as an experimental platform.

The mission of the Ben Franklin touches on almost every area of interest to contemporary oceanography. As the Franklin drifts north, her crew will make temperature and salinity measurements and a complete acoustical record of the Gulf Stream. The Ben Franklin will study the ocean's deep scattering layer at close range. The DSL is not a layer but rather swarms of minute plankton that rise toward the surface at night and sink during the day. Today's submariners and tomorrow's colonizers need to know about the DSL because it reflects sonar signals, giving false depth readings. . . .

The next generation of submersibles may include nuclear-powered craft with clear glass-bubble observation domes and pressure hulls. The Navy's Deep Submergence Systems Project already has a nuclear-powered research sub under construction. Navy engineers are also testing a glass pressure hull for the Hikino sub, which will be able to reach depths of 20,000 feet, and a glass nose section for Deep View (operating depth: 5000 feet). A glass sphere or hemisphere several inches thick, engineers have found, can withstand compressive loads of more than 400,000 pounds per square inch. Furthermore, glass is much lighter than steel. Consequently, according to Edwin Lusk of the Corning Glass Works, whose company is building the Hikino and Deep View glasswork, glass could greatly increase the payload of submersibles.

LIVING THERE

Before the development of saturation-diving techniques in the past few years, the idea of men living on the ocean floor or working there for extended periods seemed hopeless. A diver working at depths of a few hundred feet can stay there only a short time because of the intense cold. And on returning to the surface he must spend long hours in a decompression chamber to rid his tissues and blood of excess amounts of gases forced into his bloodstream by the high pressures of deep water. If a diver returns to atmospheric pressure too soon, these gases form bubbles that produce painful and sometimes fatal "bends."

Now diving systems like the Navy's Mark II or Westinghouse's Cachalot allow divers to avoid the decompression penalty of short work periods. These systems consist of a pressure chamber on board the mother ship and a diving bell to take the men to and from the work site. Before going down the diver enters the deck chamber, which is held at the pressure of the work site below. When his tissues have become saturated with gas he rides down in the diving bell to the work site. When he needs to rest he returns to the pressure chamber on deck. Because the chamber keeps him at the same pressure as that on the ocean bottom where he works, he does not have to decompress. That tedious process can be postponed until the whole job has been finished.

Sea Lab III and Tektite I, two U.S. "bottom habitats," also work on the saturation-diving principle. In the 45-day Sea Lab experiment to begin this fall, five teams of eight divers under the command of former astronaut Scott Carpenter will spend twelve days each living in a cylindrical habitat, 620 feet down, off San Clemente Island, Calif. The divers, who will be pressurized in the Navy's Mark II apparatus before they go down, will be able to enter and leave the Sea Lab through a floor hatch. No water can enter the open hatch because the air pressure inside will equal the water pressure outside. No decompression will be necessary while the divers are below because they will be living at the same pressure whether in the water or out.

During the Sea Lab III experiment the divers will test three kinds of wet suits designed to stave off the numbing cold. One suit resembles a form-fitting electric blanket heated by resistance wires. Another, called a tube suit, circulates warm water over the aquanaut's body. Both are powered by an umbilical line to the habitat. The third suit will carry a radio-isotope heating device.

The Sea Lab III aquanauts will also test the possibilities of human-sea animal dialogue. During Sea Lab II, Tuffy, a bottle-nose dolphin (like man, a mammal), distinguished himself by being able to track down a "lost" diver by homing in on a signaling device the man carried. In Sea Lab III, dolphins may be used to deliver messages directly through the hatch in the bottom of the habitat. Sea Lab divers will also experiment with seals. Seals are not as intelligent as dolphins, which have brains that are 20 to 40 per cent larger than man's and can communicate with each other and even with man. But seals can stay underwater more than four times as long as a dolphin.

Tektite I is a joint NASA, Navy, and Department of the Interior project that will get under way early in 1969. Four divers, all marine biologists, will live for two months in a twin-tower habitat, resting at a depth of fifty feet on the bottom of Greater Lameshur Bay, St. John's Island in the Virgin Islands. While the divers study spiny lobsters and other creatures living in the biologically rich tropical waters, psychologists will study them via closed-circuit TV. The psychologists want to observe how tensions—and patterns of cooperation—develop among members of isolated, small groups.

Physiologist Johannes Kylstra has "designed" mice that can walk in water —rambling about the bottom of a water tank filled with highly oxygenated saline solution. The mice breathe the solution instead of air because, Kylstra has discovered, the lung is physically able to handle fluids as well as gases. If the concentration of oxygen in the water is high enough, he explained, a mammal can extract enough from the fluid to stay alive.

Kylstra has demonstrated that men, too, can breathe water. A volunteer human subject in Kylstra's laboratory at Duke University breathed water in one lung, fed through a tube inserted through an incision in his trachea. The man, who was under local anesthetic, said he did not feel that his breathing was labored or strained.

Kylstra believes that fluid breathing could eliminate the bends completely. A fluid such as liquid helium, Kylstra reasons, would resist the pressure at great depths so that no gases would go into the bloodstream except the oxygen which the man breathes. Therefore the diver could return to the surface after a dive to depths of thousands of feet without decompressing.

Kylstra's mice experiments show that this concept works. Fluid-breathing mice have been decompressed from thirty atmospheres of pressure to one atmosphere without harm. Before man can breathe fluids safely, however, Kylstra must overcome some serious problems, including the fact that most fluids do not absorb carbon dioxide rapidly enough to clear it from the blood adequately.

FOOD FROM THE SEA

By the year 2000 the world's population will have doubled to 6 billion people. Some of the increased demand for protein and energy will undoubtedly be met from the sea. In fact, the demand could be so great that man will have to raise his current fishing operations—essentially a form of hunting—to the status of systematic raising and harvesting of fish.

The University of Hawaii's Institute of Marine Biology has several programs under way aimed at increasing the yield from the ocean. In one project Vernon Brock has been studying the giant clam. He believes that these creatures, which are sometimes four feet across, could make good food sources. The reason, according to Brock, is that the giant clam grows a garden right in its own shell—plant cells growing in its tissues which produce carbohydrates. The clam can use these in its own metabolism, and men could eat the clams.

In another project Brock has been attempting to raise fish from the egg stage through maturity in tanks at a research station on Coconut Island. According to Brock, more than 99 per cent of newly-hatched fish perish. If the causes of death can be identified and controlled it should be possible to increase the harvest of fish substantially by raising them in the protective environment of a fish farm. Brock would also like to apply the principles of selective breeding to aquaculture so that only superior specimens that convert food to protein with great efficiency would be raised.

At Scripps Institution of Oceanography in La Jolla, Calif., Theodore Tutschulte dives down fifty to seventy feet off the coast of Catalina Island to tag abalone with tiny lights. At night, time-lapse cameras record the movements of the shellfish as they feed on algae, kelp, and other bottom vegetation. Scripps, together with Westinghouse, wants to find out if abalone could someday be raised in bottom cages that would restrict their movement and protect them from predators. Before such habitats can be devised, however, the feeding movements, breeding habits, and other traits of the creatures must be carefully studied.

LAND-SEA RELATIONS

Even men who never actually leave the land must understand the sea, Dr. John Isaacs of Scripps believes. He points out that temperature changes and current flows in the oceans produce profound effects on the weather and climate.

To decipher this relationship Isaacs plans to study a four-million-square-mile area in the North Pacific, using arrays of buoys that will record information on conditions under the sea and in the atmosphere concurrently. Isaacs has started off on a modest scale with a pilot project consisting of two clusters of catamaran-like buoys, grouped around a 100-ton, forty-foot-diameter monster buoy, developed by General Dynamics.

Deep-diving submersibles, habitats for men on the ocean floor, and fish farms are only as far away as the next technological innovation. However, oceanography has encountered some rough sailing recently. The war in Vietnam and the austere Federal budget have not spared oceanography. "Everyone wants to cut basic research first," says J. Lamar Worzel of Lamont Geological Observatory, "because they can't see what it does."

Yet these setbacks will probably prove temporary. The U.S. has not been the only nation to recognize the potential of the sea. The U.S.S.R. also has an ambitious, well-financed program. And last year in the U.N., Malta called for an international agency that would grant concessions for minerals and other resources and give the revenues to poor nations to finance economic development.

U.S. officials, however, point out that it would be many years before such concessions begin to yield profits. Instead, the U.S. has proposed an "International Decade of Ocean Exploration" involving all interested nations. The plan calls for a survey of ocean resources and expeditions. The return to the sea is under way.

FORMULA FOR A FLOATING CITY

R. Buckminster Fuller

To Buckminster Fuller's previous ingenious shelter concepts such as the Dymaxion House and the Geodesic Dome now must be added an even more ambitious design—a floating tetrahedronal city.

"We have learned that the most stable structure is the tetrahedron," he says. "Following this design-science clue, we find that a tetrahedronal city, to house a million people, is both economically and technologically feasible. Such a vertical tetrahedronal city can be constructed so that all of its 300,000 families have balconied 'outside' apartments. All of the organic operative machinery can be housed within the tetrahedron.

"Programed for 1,000,000 occupants, a tetrahedronal floating city would measure two miles long for each of its base edges. Such a city is so structurally efficient and therefore so relatively light that, together with its hollow box-sectioned reinforced concrete foundations, it can float. The city could be anchored in triangularly patterned canals or floated out into the ocean at any point and anchored. It would be earthquake-proof and, because the depth of the tetrahedron's foundation would be below the turbulence level of the seas, it would be a floating triangular atoll with a harbor that is always calm and protected. The cities will generate their own energy requirements using atomic reactors. The by-product of heat from these reactors will be used to desalinate water supplies."

Tetrahedrons are unique geometrically, he explains, in that they may be added to on every one of their four equilateral triangle faces and increased symmetrically in size by additions to any one of the faces. Thus the cities can begin with a program for a thousand occupants and grow to hold millions without changing their shape.

"Salvage of materials from obsolete buildings on the land can produce enough of these floating cities to have relays of them in various sizes around the oceans of the earth, at distances negotiable by relatively small boats such as those that operate between the Florida coast and the Bahamas. This will allow new habitation possibilities on that three-fourths of the earth's surface that is covered by water. It also will permit mid-ocean cargo transfer within the cities' calm harbors, extraordinarily increasing the efficiency of distribution of the world's raw and finished materials as well as aiding passenger traffic."

Is a tetrahedronal city, like many other Buckminster Fuller concepts, too advanced to win adherents in our time? The Japanese, he reports, already are interested in trying the concept, and a pilot-scale model may be built in Japan.

Buckminster Fuller's design for a floating tetrahedronal city (shown superimposed on San Francisco Bay)—In sizes up to two-and-a-half miles high, it could make possible habitation of the earth's water surfaces.

Courtesy R. Buckminster Fuller.

designing environments: space

WHY I'M FOR
SPACE EXPLORATION

Louis J. Halle

There has been life on earth for over 2000 million years now, and man himself goes back at least a million. Yet it is less than a dozen years since this life, developing and proliferating for so long, has at last emerged from our planet's atmospheric envelope into outer space. A scholar of a million years hence, wherever in the universe he is, may well regard the middle of our century as the turning point in the career of earthly life and, specifically, of our own species. I am, therefore, puzzled to find a marked lack of enthusiasm among my acquaintances at the prospect of man's liberation from this earthly prison.

What is the explanation?

There are those who want the resources now allocated to the exploration of space to be used for the support of more immediate and mundane causes. It is hard to argue with them except to the extent that there are grounds for doubting that what was saved on the space programs would in fact become available to feed, say, the hungry of India. (Since the vast governmental spending that goes with a war economy has proved to be an essential element in our economic prosperity, a more practical proposal might be that we should reduce the occasions for war spending and allocate what was saved to space exploration.) My impression, however, is that many are moved by a spiritual horror, deep-seated but unacknowledged, at the notion of even looking beyond our familiar planet, let alone leaving it. Traditional religious beliefs are threatened by any vivid recognition of how small our planet is in a cosmos of thousands of millions of galaxies, each with thousands of millions of suns, many of which must have planets like ours, the whole spread over distances that a beam of light, traveling at 186,000 miles per second, would take several thousand million years to traverse. For some there is simply the child's fear of leaving, even in imagination, what is after all home—be it ever so humble. But I myself do not feel as attached as they do to this increasingly cluttered and polluted planet. I regard it as too small, and its prospects as a habitable environment for the long future worry me. Sometimes, when I have horrors of what may be, I find relief as Logan Pearsall Smith did when the world was too much with him:

> I . . . think of Space, and the unimportance in its unmeasured vastness of our toy solar system; I lose myself in speculations on Eternity, reflecting how, at the best, human life on this minute and perishable planet is but a mock episode, as brief as a dream.

However, my enthusiasm for man's historic emergence into space has a more solid foundation. I suffer from intellectual claustrophobia. I feel like Chuang-tzu's frog in a well, denied knowledge of the great world outside.

To change the figure, imagine some creature of lively intelligence confined to the lowest depths of the oceans, where the light of the sun never penetrates. Although it combined the curiosity of a Socrates with the mind of an Einstein, its confinement to an environment so limited would exclude it from the possibility of gaining the least notion of the real universe to which it belonged. It could not know as we know that there is more to that universe than salt water and a darkness relieved, at best, by phosphorescent gleams. It could not know that miles above there was sunlight and air, mountains tipped with snow, days alternating with starry nights. It could not know that the ocean was, together with land, merely the surface of one among countless spheres errant in space. From the remains of organic decay that sink to its level it might hypothecate the existence of life far above, as we have in the past drawn conclusions from the cosmic rays that penetrate our atmosphere to reach us. Still, the ontological speculations of even the most brilliantly endowed philosophical mind, confined to such an environment, would be fruitless and absurd. Any logical order that it formulated to explain being would be so pitiful in the limitations of its scope that such creatures as ourselves, relatively godlike by virtue of our larger world, might properly be moved to tears or laughter.

Imagine this submarine species, now, beginning to make technological progress that enables it to explore ever higher reaches of its environment in craft that maintain the pressure of its native deeps. Eventually it rises to the surface of the sea and begins the discovery of a world that it could not even have begun to imagine in the confines from which it has at last been released. Surely we men are in that position. Until recently we thought our earth constituted virtually the whole of the cosmos, of which it was the center. In the last 300 years, how-

ever, we have begun the discovery of a universe that earlier hominoids had not even imagined. Of course this process has been upsetting of traditional convictions. We can no longer believe that God sits "up there" in the sky, as the deep-sea philosopher might find he could no longer believe in a God who dwells in eternal darkness, breathing salt water, after he had seen what a universe there was above the surface of the sea. But loss of the certainty that goes with ignorance is the price that must be paid for progress toward whatever the ultimate truth may be. The loss of darkness is the price of light. If we had not been willing to pay this price in the past we might still be offering human sacrifices to this or that Baal.

Now that we know there must be millions of millions of other planets like ours circling other suns in the far realms of space, it has at last become implausible that we men are the only self-consciously intelligent creatures in the cosmos. Think what possibilities this alone implies as we extend our knowledge into these realms! . . .

Life, as we know it within the terms of our earthly prison, makes no ultimate sense that we can discover; but I cannot, myself, escape the conviction that, in terms of a larger knowledge than is accessible to us today, it does make such sense. Our position is simply that of the intelligent creatures confined to the ocean deeps. Now, however, that we are at last beginning to escape from our native confines, there is no telling what light we may find in the larger universe to dissipate the darkness of our minds. There is also the possibility that we may begin to populate new planets as, after 1492, we began to populate a new continent. Suddenly man's future seems boundless.

Of course we don't know what space exploration might lead to, or even whether it can come to anything at all. Would such uncertainty, however, provide a sufficient argument to justify the fish in remaining at the bottom of the ocean, once they had acquired the means to rise above it? I can imagine the debate that might go on in a deep-sea society between the traditionalists and the adventurous, but to me it is clear which side would represent progress and the hope of the future. . . .

from PROFILES
OF THE FUTURE

Arthur C. Clarke

ROCKET TO THE RENAISSANCE

Four and a half centuries ago, European civilization started expanding into the unknown, in a slow but irresistible explosion fueled by the energies of the Renaissance. After a thousand years of huddling round the Mediterranean, Western man had discovered a new frontier beyond the sea. We know the very day when he found it—and the day when he lost it. The American frontier opened on October 12, 1492; it closed on May 10, 1869, when the last spike was driven in the transcontinental railroad.

In all the long history of man, ours is the first age with no new frontiers on land or sea, and many of our troubles stem from this fact. It is true that, even now, there are vast areas of the Earth still unexploited and even unexplored, but dealing with them will only be a mopping-up operation. Though the oceans will keep us busy for centuries to come, the countdown started even for them, when the bathyscaphe *Trieste* descended into the ultimate deep of the Marianas Trench.

There are no more undiscovered continents; set out toward any horizon, and on its other side you will find someone already waiting to check your visa and your vaccination certificate. . . .

The road to the stars has been discovered none too soon. Civilization cannot exist without new frontiers; it needs them both physically and spiritually. The physical need is obvious—new lands, new resources, new materials. The spiritual need is less apparent, but in the long run it is more important. We do not live by bread alone; we need adventure, variety, novelty, romance. As the psychologists have shown by their sensory deprivation experiments, a man goes swiftly mad if he is isolated in a silent, darkened room, cut off completely from the external world. What is true of individuals is also true of societies; they too can become insane without sufficient stimulus.

It may seem overoptimistic to claim that man's forthcoming escape from Earth, and the crossing of interplanetary space, will trigger a new renaissance and break the patterns into which our society, and our arts, must otherwise freeze. Yet this is exactly what I propose to do; first, however, it is necessary to demolish some common misconceptions.

The space frontier is infinite, beyond all possibility of exhaustion; but the opportunity and the challenge it presents are both totally different from any that we have met in our own world in the past. All the moons and planets of this solar system are strange, hostile places that may never harbor more than a few thousand human inhabitants, who will be at least as carefully handpicked as the population of Los Alamos. The age of mass colonization has gone forever. Space has room for many things, but not for "your tired, your poor, your huddled masses yearning to breathe free. . . ." Any statue of liberty on Martian soil will have inscribed upon its base "Give me your nuclear physicists, your chemical engineers, your biologists and mathematicians." The immigrants of the twenty-first century will have much more in common with those of the seventeenth century than the nineteenth. For the *Mayflower*, it is worth remembering, was loaded to the scuppers with eggheads.

The often-expressed idea that the planets can solve the problem of overpopulation is thus a complete fallacy. Humanity is now increasing at the rate of some 100,000 *a day*, and no conceivable "space-lift" could make serious inroads in this appalling figure.

With present techniques, the combined military budgets of all nations might just about suffice to land ten men on the Moon every day. Yet even if space transportation were free, instead of being fabulously expensive, that would scarcely help matters—for there is not a single planet upon which men could live and work without elaborate mechanical aids. On all of them we shall need the paraphernalia of space suits, synthetic air factories, pressure domes, totally enclosed hydroponic farms. One day our lunar and Martian colonies will be self-supporting, but if we are looking for living room for our surplus population, it would be far cheaper to find it in the Antarctic—or even on the bottom of the Atlantic Ocean.

No, the population battle must be fought and won here on Earth, and the longer we postpone the inevitable conflict the more horrifying the weapons that will be needed for victory. (Compulsory abortion and infanticide, and antiheterosexual legislation—with its reverse—may be some of the milder expedients.) Yet though the planets cannot save us, this is a matter in which logic may not count. The weight of increasing numbers—the suffocating sense of pressure as the walls of the ant-heap crowd ever closer—will help to power man's drive into space, even if no more than a millionth of humanity can ever go there.

Perhaps the battle is already lost, here on this planet. As Sir George Darwin has suggested in his depressing little book, *The Next Million Years*, ours may be a golden age, compared with the endless vistas of famine and poverty that must follow when the billions of the future fight over Earth's waning resources. If this is true, it is all the more vital that we establish self-sustaining colonies on the planets. They may have a chance of surviving and preserving something of our culture, even if civilization breaks down completely on the mother world.

Though the planets can give no physical relief to the congested and impoverished Earth, their intellectual and emotional contribution may be enormous. The discoveries of the first expeditions, the struggles of the pioneers to establish themselves on other worlds—these will inspire a feeling of purpose and achievement among the stay-at-homes. They will know, as they watch their TV screens, that History with a capital H is starting again. The sense of wonder, which we have almost lost, will return to life; and so will the spirit of adventure.

It is difficult to overrate the importance of this—though it is easy to poke fun at it by making cynical remarks about "escapism." Only a few people can be pioneers or discoverers, but everyone who is even half alive occasionally feels the need for adventure and excitement. If you require proof of this, look at the countless horse operas now galloping across the ether. The myth of a West that never was has been created to fill the vacuum in our modern lives, and it fills it well. Sooner or later, however, one tires of myths (many of us have long since tired of *this* one) and then it is time to seek new territory. There is a poignant symbolism in the fact that the giant rockets now stand poised on the edge of the Pacific, where the covered wagons halted only two lifetimes ago.

from THE FUTURE

Theodore J. Gordon

What happens after the United States and Russia land men on the moon? Where do we go from there? There is little doubt that we will set up semipermanent research stations on the moon. At first, these will be buried huts, isolated and struggling for survival. They will grow in size and complexity until at last, a hundred years from now, a true city will exist on the moon.

The early landings which we will make in the next few years will provide little more than a glimpse of what the moon really has to tell us; the astronauts will have spent less than a day there. Only after the establishment of scientific bases, will the astronaut-scientists be able to study the moon at their leisure.

Potentially, these stations can tell us how the earth was formed through geological studies of the moon's surface.

These stations can provide the world with its best astronomical observatories, since there will be no obscuring atmosphere.

The stations will certainly have the assignment of looking for life, or at least rudimentary life-like molecules trapped in the lunar rock, or in the bits of interplanetary dust impacting on the moon. Part of the look-for-life assignment might be a continuation of Project Ozma, listening for high-frequency radio signals coming from beyond our solar system.

Reprinted from Theodore J. Gordon, *The Future* (New York: St. Martin's Press, Incorporated, 1965), by permission of the publisher.

On the moon, the listeners would not be bothered by man-made interference.

The moon bases could serve as communication repeater stations, picking up broadcasts from various points on earth and re-broadcasting them to other sites on earth beyond the range of the original transmitters.

The scientists on the moon could conduct experiments in an environment which can be only imperfectly simulated on earth: high vacuum, low gravity, full solar radiation.

One of the first, most important jobs at the moon landing site will be engineering and constructing the permanent moon base itself; expanding the station from a hastily buried aluminum shell to a self-sufficient port, the earth's terminal for all points in the solar system. The moon base will some day be a city, a major research center, bustling with commerce and resort traffic. The reason why the moon may become a port is simply this: very much less energy is required for a trip in the solar system if it originates on the moon rather than on the earth. The moon's lower gravity is responsible for this. Now if it turns out that propellants can be manufactured on the moon, then it is quite possible that our big interplanetary missions will use the moon as their launching pad by the end of the century. It has been estimated that launching from the moon to Mars requires a vehicle less than one-tenth the size of the equivalent earth-launch vehicle. . . .

Food can be produced on the moon by hydroponic gardening. So, in the end, the lunar base may well manufacture many of the products necessary to equip our interplanetary voyages.

Viewing the moon as a grand launching base, as a research center, and as a supplier of space vehicle products, gives rise to the concept of frequent commercial traffic between the earth and moon. This kind of trip will become old hat, even to the point of extending into the tourist trade. . . .

Who knows? Maybe our children will consider the moon, with its environment tailored to human needs, a far more desirable place to spend the summer than Cape Cod. Its low gravity may make it an ideal sanitarium for heart patients.

Beyond the moon lies Mars. We will go there to see for ourselves a foreign planet, to study its ecology, and, in so doing, to learn about ourselves. . . .

But why put a colony on this cold, dry, dusty planet? What possible reasons could there be for the establishment of a colony of human beings on a remote piece of matter never closer to earth than 35 million miles? Why struggle for this kind of existence when the air for every breath may depend on the ingenuity, the resourcefulness of the immigrants? Let us assess some possibilities.

First, the day may come when the human race needs some living room, simply because its own population explosion has crowded its people off the face of the earth. Mars will probably be the most hospitable planet open to our overflow. I don't really believe this will happen; I mention it only as a possibility.

Second, and this is an area of almost complete conjecture, it is possible that the solar system planets may have raw materials which will prove valuable to earth. While this must remain a doubtful motivation at present, simply because of the tremendous cost of space transportation, the possibility exists nevertheless. We won't know for another fifty years.

Third, the time may come when the earth will be very happy to have a remote site on which to practice some of its more obnoxious habits. For example, perhaps a remote planet or asteroid could become a dumping ground for our radioactive wastes, the wornout fuels of our nuclear reactors. Or, perhaps Mars could become the site of the world's penal institutions.

Fourth, in the days to come when space transportation is cheap and the world's population is clamoring for foods and raw materials, a planet such as Mars could become our granary, producing food for earth on a commercial basis. This is a long time off, of course. Tremendous problems will have to be solved in extraterrestrial agronomy and logistics of transportation, to name only two, but someday it may not only be feasible, but necessary.

There will also be that motivation which has been with us since the Jews left Egypt, the search for freedom. The time may come when the environmental problems of a strange planet are simpler to face than inhospitable tyranny on mother earth. But again, the day when someone can flee to Mars is a long time off.

Dr. Wernher von Braun's Future Projects Office at the George C. Marshall Space Flight Center in Huntsville, Alabama, has said,

> The year 2000 should find humanity well along the road toward utilizing all the resources of the solar system, and traveling within the solar system should become fairly routine. To put man on the moon, on the planets, or anywhere within the solar system wherever his environment can be controlled: this is the goal. This can be done. More is not feasible now, but nothing less will suffice.*

And what comes after the solar system? Can we travel beyond? I would like to answer that that's beyond the scope of this book, but that would be unfair. The problem here is, of course, the enormous distances involved in traveling to the stars. Although we believe many stars have planetary systems, we have yet to identify a single planet outside of our solar system. Einstein's equations tell us that matter cannot travel faster than the speed of light, and even at that speed, the time required for transit to a likely star is great, perhaps a thousand years to a star with a planetary system that now bears a civilization. Clearly, we are dealing here with a problem for another era, an era that can perhaps straighten out the interrelationship between time, space, and distance. As the speed of a body approaches that of light, time slows. This we know. As the speed of a body approaches that of light, mass converts to energy. This we know. But can the speed of light be exceeded?

*Brochure titled, "Future Projects Office," George C. Marshall Space Flight Center, Huntsville, Alabama, March, 1963.

Remember this: At one time, twenty miles an hour was thought to be a lethal speed. More recently, our equations predicted the speed of sound as the maximum speed which any aircraft could achieve. Today, our equations say the speed of light is the limit. Intuitively, I reject this absolute.

The future may hold the solution to traveling to the stars. Today we cannot even guess at its form. . . .

A.D. 2267

John Frederick Nims

Once on the gritty moon (burnt earth hung far
In the black, rhinestone sky—lopsided star),
Two gadgets, with great fishbowls for a head,
Feet clubbed, hips loaded, shoulders bent. She said,
"Fantasies haunt me. A green garden. Two
Lovers aglow in flesh. The pools so blue!"
He whirrs with masculine pity, "Can't forget
Old superstitions? The earth-legend yet?"

Reprinted from John Nims, *Of Flesh and Bone* (New Brunswick, N.J.: Rutgers University Press, 1967), by permission of the publisher.

Technology has two faces: one that is full of promise, and one that can discourage and defeat us. The freedom that our power implies from the traditional tyranny of matter—from the evil we have known—carries with it the added responsibility and burden of learning to deal with matter and to blunt the evil, along with all the other problems we have always had to deal with. That is another way of saying that more power and more choice and more freedom require more wisdom if they are to add up to more humanity.

E. G. Mesthene,
Technology and Social Change

PART IV

the machine— enemy or ally?

thirteen

the threat

To many people, automation means robots and robots mean big, clanking mechanical monsters answering the commands of their mad inventors. Robots exist today and they are ambivalent monsters, indeed, devouring our concepts of work and leisure while creating a world of plenty where every man has not only the right to exist, but the right to subsist. . . .

The sophisicated age of automation will witness intelligent, decision-making machines, infinitely gentle or brutal, with the ability to sense their own input data to a level which equals or surpasses their biological sensing counterpart. What are we in for?

Theodore J. Gordon,
The Future

Technology—science's favorite but undisciplined child—has changed man's relationship to the planet so profoundly that his continued existence is in doubt. Yet instead of combatting the anxiety we feel by understanding and guiding change, we cling ever more closely to our familiar ways. We are deeply suspicious of change and often refuse to have anything to do with it.

Not yet able fully to understand or control the new technologies, we tend to focus our distrust on the cybernated computer—symbol of the end of the life we have known. Perhaps our greatest fear, more immediate than that of nuclear holocaust, is fear of The Machine. Why? Let us explore some of the reasons.

From THE FUTURE by Theodore J. Gordon, reprinted by permission of St. Martin's Press, Inc.

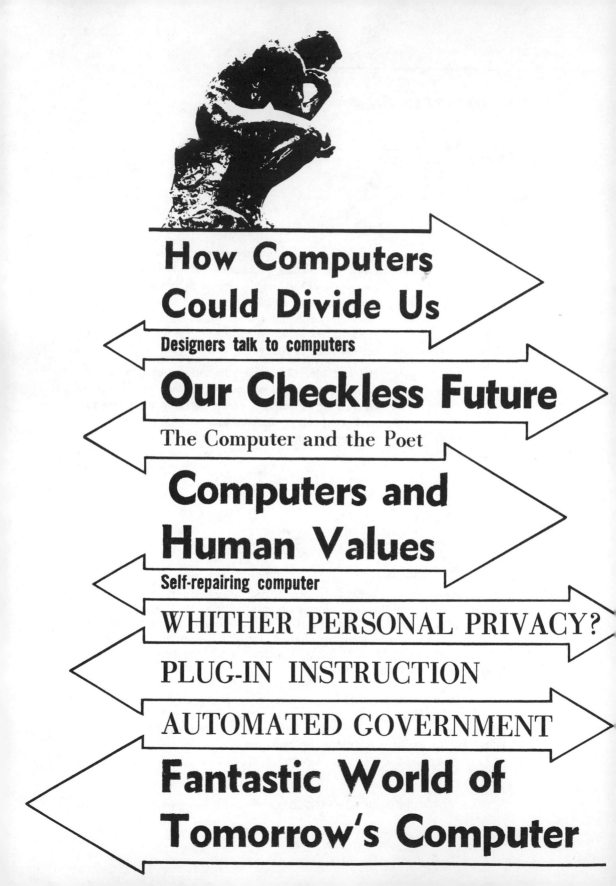

How Computers Could Divide Us

Designers talk to computers

Our Checkless Future

The Computer and the Poet

Computers and Human Values

Self-repairing computer

WHITHER PERSONAL PRIVACY?

PLUG-IN INSTRUCTION

AUTOMATED GOVERNMENT

Fantastic World of Tomorrow's Computer

To understand the benefits and dangers of automation, it is essential to understand that these machines are composed of two basic elements: brains and muscle. The jobs which the machines are to perform determine the mixture of these elements. Some machines are almost pure brain, like the automated computers; others are almost all muscle, like an automatic screwcutting lathe.

We are in for machines that will accomplish more and more of our production. We are in for machines that will increasingly take over more and more of the routine decision-making of middle management. We are in for machines that will augment natural ability on all levels of human achievement that require action or thought. We are in for machines that may become colleagues rather than slaves; machines that can make creative decisions. These machines will not only augment, but will replace man in many fields, and do a better job of his work.

Theodore J. Gordon,
The Future

MAN AS WORKER: "I am afraid a machine will take over my job. Then what will happen to me?"

from DEATH OF A SALESMAN

Arthur Miller

Linda: (to Biff and Happy) When he brought them business, when he was young, they were glad to see him. But now his old friends, the old buyers that loved him so and always found some order to hand him in a pinch—they're all dead, retired. He used to be able to make six, seven calls a day in Boston. Now he takes his valises out of the car and puts them back and takes them out again and he's exhausted. Instead of walking he talks now. He drives seven hundred miles, and when he gets there no one knows him any more, no one welcomes him. And what goes through a man's mind, driving seven hundred miles home without having earned a cent? Why shouldn't he talk to himself? Why? When he has to go to Charley and borrow fifty dollars a week and pretend to me that it's his pay? How long can that go on? How long? You see what I'm sitting here and waiting for? And you tell me he has no character? The man who never worked a day but for your benefit? When does he get the medal for that?

. . . I don't say he's a great man. Willy Loman never made a lot of money. His name was never in the paper. He's not the finest character that ever lived. But he's a human being, and a terrible thing is happening to him. So attention must be paid. He's not to be allowed to fall into his grave like an old dog. Attention, attention must be finally paid to such a person.

In a sense, when work is reduced, as it almost certainly will be, there is a very real crisis of values for people generally. Great groups of people have been trained by nothing in their whole culture, background, religion, and philosophic conceptions for anything other than work as a meaningful activity.

Leo Cherne,
Nation's Business

The Powerhouse

May Swenson

Close to my place is the powerhouse.
I knew there wouldn't be anybody in it.
It's beautiful
like a church. It works
all by itself. And with almost no sound.

All glass. And a tall square tower on it.
Colored lights shine from within. They
color the glass. Pink. Pale green.
Not stained. Not that kind.
And not fragile. Just light. Light weight.

A red rod erect from the tower
blinking on top red. Behind it gray
wings of motion. A fan of light
opening and folding somewhere in the west of town.
Periodic as a metronome.

The crickets were talking like electricity.
A white spitz barked at me
though my sneakers made no noise.
I walked up the slight slope—it's wide—
to the powerhouse

went past the doorway
big as a barn door squared. Big horse I thought.
The stars were far away. Small dim points.
I saw through the doorway gray metal coils.
All the clean machinery and engines.

I don't know what to call it all.
I don't know the names.
Painted pretty colors slick and clean.
I knew there wouldn't be anybody there.
Nobody needs to work there I thought.

And walked past that door farther on.
White lights icy and clean.
Not blazing. Cool. Gossamer. The pink and green
like-sherbet-colors bathing the gray machines.
Came to a place where vapor

cooled my skin. A breeze made by waterspray
up high. And there was white steam unfurling
evaporating against the dark.
Down lower a red transparent ball
on a pedestal. Incandescent. Big

—a balloon mystery. Inside
through another doorway I saw a hook
painted yellow. Huge and high enough
to lift a freight car. I stood looking in
—my shadow so long

and black from the streaming lights.
And I was wrong. Somebody moved
in the powerhouse. Came from between the coils
and giant tubes. Down off the balcony
on the steel stairway

smooth and slow. Like floating.
Like not having to look or think.
I thought he'd be a Negro but he wasn't.
He didn't see me. Didn't need to see anything.
He had a red face and a blue uniform.

"And any questions requiring a strictly intuitive answer we feed into our Mr. McAndrews here."

PERSON TO PERSON: **"Machines get between me and other people. They make me feel less human. I send a letter and receive an IBM card."**

Dear Computer: After the three dates you matched me with, I have decided to give up and let my mother find a nice boy for me after all.

May B.

I LOVE YOU—
THIS IS A RECORDING

Arthur Hoppe

Herewith is another unwritten chapter from that unpublished text, "A History of the World, 1950 to 1999." Its title: "Ma Bell Saves the Day."

By the early 1970s, the old morality had crumbled. The old certitudes had vanished. Wars, riots and revolutions flourished. Neighbor mistrusted neighbor. People no longer touched each other. Conversations were icily polite.

And from the look in the eyes of mankind, it was clear that the human race was on the brink.

It was the telephone company that preserved civilization.

With people retreating inward on themselves, the number of telephone calls placed daily had dropped alarmingly. To stimulate business, it was suggested that the company provide another recorded message as a public service.

"We already give our subscribers the time and the weather," said the Board Chairman irritably. "What else do people need these days?"

"Sympathy?" suggested a vice president, half jokingly.

The new service was an instant success. At first people were hesitant to dial "S-Y-M-P-A-T-H-Y." "That's silly," they'd say, shaking their heads. Then, when they were sure no one was listening, they'd pick up the phone in embarrassed secretiveness.

"Poor dear," the recording began in a gentle voice of sweet consolation. "I'm so terribly sorry for you. Oh, the pain you must be suffering! But how brave you are not to show it. How very proud of you I am. Poor dear."

After one month, studies showed each subscriber was making an average of 3.4 calls to the number daily. The company immediately announced plans for new recorder services. Next came, "I-L-O-V-E-Y-O-U":

"Oh, dearest, how deeply I love you—with my whole soul, my whole being. You are everything on earth to me—my sun, my moon, my stars . . ."

This was quickly followed by "F-R-I-E-N-D-S-H-I-P" ("Hi, there, old buddy . . ."), "C-O-N-F-I-D-E-N-C-E" ("Gosh, you're just about the greatest . . ."), and "S-E-C-U-R-I-T-Y" ("There, now, there's absolutely nothing to worry about as long as we have each other").

Special messages were added for those with special needs, such as "M-O-T-H-E-R." ("Oh, it's so good to hear your voice, son. Are you getting enough to eat? Are you wearing your galoshes? Are you. . .").

Surprisingly, one of the most popular was "A-U-T-H-O-R-I-T-Y." ("When you hear the signal, you will have 60 seconds to state your dilemma." After 60 seconds, a stern voice came on to thunder: "You know what's right. Now, by God, do it!")

Thus humanity came to have everything that man had always wanted from his fellow man—sympathy, love, friendship, confidence, security and authority. And yet, oddly enough, deep down people were still uneasy.

Further studies were made. And at last the telephone company came up with the solution: "U-L-T-I-M-A-T-E-N-E-E-D."

"You are a singular human being, unique among all living creatures, different from all other men. You are that God-created miracle: you are, above all else, an individual.

"This is a recording."

Reprinted by permission from the *San Francisco Chronicle*.

MAN AND NATURE:

"Machines get between me and nature. Will I have to live in a man-made world and never even see a tree?"

The ordinary city-dweller knows nothing of the earth's productivity; he does not know the sunrise and rarely notices when the sun sets; ask him what phase the moon is in, or when the tide in the harbor is high, or even how high the average tide runs, and likely as not he cannot answer you. Seed time and harvest time are nothing to him. If he has never witnessed an earthquake, a great flood, or a hurricane, he probably does not feel the power of nature as a reality surrounding his life at all. His realities are the motors that run elevators, subway trains, and cars, the steady feed of water and gas through the mains and of electricity over the wires, the crates of food-stuff that arrive by night and are spread for his inspection before his day begins, the concrete and brick, bright steel and dingy woodwork that take the place of earth and waterside and sheltering roof for him. . . . Nature, as man has always known it, he knows no more.

Suzanne Langer,
Philosophy in a New Key

Drawings from *Atlas* Magazine (August 1966). Cartoon from Barbe, *Arts*, Paris.

from THE FUTURE
AS HISTORY

Robert Heilbroner

What precise form the technology of the future may take, we do not know. But we can at least observe the salient directions in which industrial development is moving. One such direction, in which we have barely begun to explore, is the widespread automation of industry. Another is the mechanization, not of factory work, but of the simplest and most traditional tasks within the home. Yet another, still further removed from the industrial base, is the refinement of the arts of communication and persuasion. These general avenues of advance, diverse as they are, nonetheless present a common aspect to the private person. In one fashion or another, they weaken his solitary capacity to cope

THE INDIVIDUAL IN SOCIETY:	"I am losing my self-sufficiency, my privacy, my individuality. I am dependent on machines and the people who control them. I have less influence on the development of my own children than the TV set."

with life, whether as a job-seeker faced with the threat of technological displacement, or as a home-owner unable to make the most elementary repairs on his personal equipment without outside assistance, or as an individual mind treated as part of a mass audience. All impel the individual to define his existence in terms of an ever wider, more demanding engagement with his society. And this effect can be demonstrated in virtually every aspect of life with which modern technology comes into contact.

To a large extent this loss of personal mastery is an inescapable—

Robert Heilbroner, *The Future as History.* New York: Harper & Row, Publishers, 1957. © 1957 by Robert Heilbroner.

*"I have less and less influence on society.
Computers calculate the results of an election
before I have even cast my vote."*

and perhaps an increasing—condition of an age in which science has progressed far beyond the reach of any but the most highly trained minds. But what is at stake is not only a loss of personal mastery, of intellectual grasp. It is a loss of social mastery, of control over our own habitat. We are in the unpleasant position of watching our "society" change under the impact of its own technology while we stand impotently by to suffer the consequences for better or worse. And this loss of social mastery cannot be blamed only on the complexity of the technological process. It also lies with the fact that the main control we exercise over the social incursion of technology is that of economics. . . .

In a word, with few exceptions, we allow the products of science and technology, like half-tamed genii from Aladdin's lamp, to work their social will without hindrance, so long as they are economically obedient. As a result our economic growth steadily adds to our social involvement in technology in a manner which is essentially capricious and haphazard. We have narrowed our control over the incursion of scientific technology into our lives to the main and often to the single criterion of its profitability. . . .

Whatever the purposes of the end products of industry, their ramification continues to refashion our lives—as workers and consumers, as economic citizens, as social beings. The products of industry may be less and less connected with the alleviation of poverty or of inhuman toil, but they are not less connected with the tempo and texture of social life. Meanwhile the processes of industry continue to socialize our existences, and only too late, when their effects have become visible in social conformity or a multiplication of the needs of government, do we object to what is "going on." But by then any possibility of intervening in the process of change is limited to a partial compensation for changes which have already been irreversibly fixed into place.

ASSASSIN CAN'T HURT COMPUTER
Olympia, Wash.

Someone sneaked into the state employment security building early Thursday and fired two shots at computer 1401, but technicians said the bullets struck a steel skullplate and did not penetrate the "brains" of the device.

The computer stores the information from which the state pays unemployment compensation claims to about 50,000 persons. "I'd hate to think what might have happened if the bullets had harmed the programmed tapes," one official said.

THE HOUSEWIVES'
BRAVE NEW WORLD

Washington

Supervised nurseries and playgrounds at hometown colleges—to allow married women to park their children safely while they attend classes—were forecast for the year 2000 yesterday.

Dr. Glenn T. Seaborg, chairman of the Atomic Energy Commission, who made the prediction, also envisioned the same college-going women, and even the stay-at-homes, having:

Small household computers linked with central-station computers, to help them with family budgeting, meal planning and the like... automated kitchens wherein mechanical devices would get out preselected foods, and cook and serve them...

In a talk to a meeting of the woman's national Democratic club, Seaborg said that by the year 2000, society "will attach more importance (than now) to education for married women."

"By the turn of the century," he added, "housewives in general should have more time for study due to automation, more money for educational expenses due to the expected rise in family incomes, and more opportunities for continuing their education due to the increased availability of local colleges and universities."

Among other forecasts for tomorrow's women by the tall Nobel prizeman who has two daughters of his own:

Low-cost disposable dresses, made from new synthetic fibers, which "could enable women never to be seen more than once in the same outfit... grocery shopping by videophone without leaving the house ... weekend vacations in Europe or Asia, thanks to hypersonic aircraft ... perhaps even anti-grouch pills for their husbands.

THE WAR ON
COMPUTERS

Nigel Muir

London

The International Society for the Abolition of Data Processing Machines, dedicated to the mammoth task of foiling computers, now has more than 500 members throughout the world. It is also collecting evidence against the machines which will include "an hor-

rific list of computer atrocities against mankind."

In the first step to break away, the society's members have been advised to demagnetize their checks—a strong magnet or bulk tape eraser is ideal—so their money gets personal attention at the bank.

But there is an even more devastatingly effective method of confusing the computers as the society's founder, journalist Harvey Matusow of New York, explained to me in London.

Using an IBM punch, he punches holes in anything from magazine subscription cards to household bills. The result is usually chaos in the computers and headaches for their operators.

"In New York, I punched six extra holes in my electricity bill and sent it back unpaid," Matusow said. "A few days later the company gave me a huge credit. When I told them this was wrong, they just wouldn't accept it because they didn't believe the computer could be wrong.

"The more holes I punch, the more often I prove computers cannot be regarded as infallible."

Why is Matusow so determined to short-circuit the world's electronic brains?

"We want to question Man's reliance upon the computer. We don't want to destroy it. Our dependence upon it today is appalling, and sooner or later someone is going to be seriously hurt because of this dependence."

Matusow claimed that computers in the Pentagon were running the military side of the Vietnam war.

"The trouble is that they are programmed for victory only. The computer's answer to a set-back in a particular zone is to send another few thousand troops. Meanwhile, another computer in Washington, geared to the political aspects of the war, is churning out entirely different ideas for the politicians. As politics and military tactics are not compatible, the computers are virtually at war with each other."

"STOP SNOOPING"

SOCIAL WORKERS
BALK AT COMPUTERS

San Francisco

State social workers protested a new departmental regulation yesterday requiring them to supply computers with intimate facts about the mental illness of their clients.

More than twenty pickets paraded at noon with signs attacking the new regulation before the regional office of the State Department of Social Welfare.

The regulation, which went into effect yesterday, requires social workers to feed information about the mental and emotional problems of their clients to department computers in Sacramento.

The data is linked for the first time to the client's social security number, and the protesting social workers feel the new rule opens the door to wholesale invasions of privacy.

And they fear the data could at some time fall into the hands of outsiders.

Reprinted by permission from *The San Francisco Chronicle.*

MAN AS MAKER:

"Computers even play games, write poems, sing songs. I thought those were things only people could do."

from COMPUTERS: THE MACHINES WE THINK WITH

D. S. Halacy, Jr.

By making the true test of intelligence something like artistic creativity, we can rule out the machine unless it can write poetry, compose music, or paint a picture. So far the computer has done the first two, and the last poses no particular problem, though debugging the machine might be a messy operation. True, the machine's poetry is only about beatnik level:

CHILDREN
Sob suddenly, the bongos are moving.
Or could we find that tall child?
And dividing honestly was like praying badly,
And while the boy is obese, all blast could climb.
First you become oblong,
To weep is unctious, to move is poor.

This masterpiece, produced by a computer in the Librascope Laboratory for Automata Research, is not as obscure as an Eliot or a Nostradamus. Computer music has not yet brought audiences to their feet in Carnegie Hall. The machine's detractors may well claim that it has produced nothing truly great; nothing worthy of an Einstein or Keats or Vermeer. But then, how many of us people have?

New Computer Football Game.
Holy smokes it's wild!

**Brand new game for football fans. Works on computer circuit.
All the thrills and excitement of a regular game. Anybody, old or
young who loves football can play. Exclusive at Abercrombie & Fitch.**

5 activator buttons. Computer works. One
of 16 lights flashes on, tells player how many
yards he gained or lost, whether he fumbled,
was intercepted, etc. All the excitement and
chance of football. Hours of fun. Perfect for
everyone who loves football. Wood frame
board is 17"x22". Batteries not included.
Only at Abercrombie. $24.50. 4 batteries .80.
Also in our Short Hills, Chicago, San Francisco, Bal Harbour and Palm Beach Stores.
Phone orders accepted—CALL (212) 261-4900.

Madison Ave. at 45th St., 10017

Two fine men from North Carolina, who are
in the electronic computer field, came to us
with their great new football game.

Holy smokes, it's wild. The berry patch. The
just plain football fans dream. With this computer football two people actually play a full
game of football. Children who are football
fans can play too. Don't have to be a football
expert, just a fan who sometimes thinks he
could do better than the coach. Here's how
it works: offensive player picks play he thinks
will work best—pushes two of his activator
buttons. Defensive player pushes one of his

Reprinted by permission of Abercrombie and Fitch Co.

from THE ADMIRATION
OF TECHNIQUE

Edward McIrvine

[M]y viewing of the television golf match was interrupted by my friend, Cy Bernation, who dropped in unexpectedly. When my wife ushered him in, I quieted him with a wave of my arm until Arnold Palmer had chipped from the edge of the rough to within a few feet of the seventeenth pin.

"Isn't that remarkable?" I said to my learned friend. Professor Bernation sniffed in disgust.

"An operational definition of a game of golf is easily formulated," said he. "It consists of conveying a ball of known size and mass sequentially from eighteen tees to eighteen holes, all 36 locations being definable by coordinates in three-dimensional space. Any sensible mechanical engineer could tell you, faced with that problem, that the *last* means of conveyance that would occur to him would be a man with a club!"

"And you propose?" I queried.

"To eliminate the human operator, of course," said Cy Bernation. "Now my uncle, Otto Mation, twenty years ago developed a power-driven golf club, with telescopic sights, a built-in range-finder and anemometer, and a slide-rule calibrated for windage corrections. In 1947 he played a round at Pebble Beach in 39 strokes, including two holes-in-one.

"But with the computer capabilities of today," said Professor Bernation, warming to his favorite topic, "we need no longer send a man onto the golf course. My first plan was to build a series of pipes from tee to hole, and to convey the balls with air pressure. Just think, eighteen sure holes-in-one. But the owners of golf courses insist upon compatibility with the present users, so I have had to fall back on a more mundane plan. Essentially it is a computer-controlled version of my uncle's machine. The balls have radio transmitters for easy tracking. Further transmitters in each hole and at each tee provide guidance. Robot forecaddies, equipped with surveying instruments, read the greens, and report to the central controller.

"The first few times around a given course, my automatic player may do no better than Uncle Otto," the professor said, "but the results of its actions are fed back into the central memory. After a few practice rounds, I suspect we will come within a few strokes of scoring eighteen. And we certainly will speed up the game."

I frowned at the thought of a golf-playing machine broadcasting a tape-recorded "playing through!" as it tore past me in pursuit of its 495-yard drive. I picked up one of my golf clubs for psychological support.

"But why do you want to replace men on the golf course with machines?" I asked desperately.

"Because men play the game badly," Cy Bernation replied. "You are a sentimentalist, McIrvine. People like you admire human performance without any thought of the relevance of that performance to the operational description of the task. You are the sort who admires John Henry for being an ambitious, if inefficient, pile-driver.

"Why resist progress? Within a decade," predicted Professor Bernation with a happy smile, "the golfer will be obsolete."

Swinging my mashie-niblick, I chased him from my dream.

Reprinted from *motive*, March/April 1967, by permission.

from PROFILES
OF THE FUTURE

Arthur C. Clarke

THE OBSOLESCENCE OF MAN

The old idea that man invented tools is . . . a misleading half-truth; it would be more accurate to say that *tools invented man.* They were very primitive tools, in the hands of creatures who were little more than apes. Yet they led to us—and to the eventual distinction of the ape-men who first wielded them.

MAN AS THINKER: "I feel that my world is no longer guided by human intelligence and human values. If computers can outthink us now in some ways, perhaps in a few years they will outthink us in all ways. Then what will happen to the human race?"

Now the cycle is about to begin again; but neither history nor pre-history ever exactly repeats itself, and this time there will be a fascinating twist in the plot. The tools the ape-men invented caused them to evolve into their successor, Homo sapiens. The tool we have invented *is* our successor. Biological evolution has given way to a far more rapid process—technological evolution. To put it bluntly and brutally, the machine is going to take over. . . .

Living creatures, because of their very nature, can evolve from simple to complex organisms. They may well be the only path by which intelligence can be attained, for it is a little difficult to see how a lifeless planet can progress directly from metal ores and mineral deposits to electronic computers by its own unaided efforts.

Though intelligence can arise only from life, it may then discard it. . . .

The popular idea, fostered by comic strips and the cheaper forms of science fiction, that intelligent machines must be malevolent entities hostile to man, is so absurd that it is hardly worth wasting energy to refute it. I am almost tempted to argue that only unintelligent machines can be malevolent; anyone who has tried to start a balky outboard will probably agree. Those who picture machines as active enemies are merely projecting their own aggressive instincts, inherited from the jungle, into a world where such things do not exist. The higher the intelligence, the greater the degree of cooperativeness. If there is ever a war between men and machines, it is easy to guess who will start it.

Yet however friendly and helpful the machines of the future may be, most people will feel that it is a rather bleak prospect for humanity if it ends up as a pampered specimen in some biological museum—even if that museum is the whole planet Earth.

THE FEARS, IN A NUTSHELL

MAN AS WORKER: The machine threatens man's identity as worker, as a producing member of society.

PERSON TO PERSON: The machine depersonalizes man's human relationships.

MAN AND NATURE: The machine obliterates man's natural environment.

THE INDIVIDUAL IN SOCIETY: In his personal life, the machine robs man of his self-sufficiency, of his privacy, of his individuality, of his influence in the development of his children.
Machine technology makes man feel powerless to influence his society.

MAN AS MAKER: The machine impinges more and more on personal areas of expressive activity: crafts, arts, sports.

MAN AS THINKER: The machine could make man himself, as an intelligent being, irrelevant, inadequate, or meaningless.

Do you share these fears?

Will technology actually make these feared changes? Must it? Would that be bad? Are there compensating courses of action for us, or new potentialities resulting from technological developments?

As machines substitute for human beings in more and more areas of activity, we have a tendency to personify the machine, to speak of it in human terms, as if it had purpose, values, feeling and will. At the same time, we tend to dehumanize people, to speak of them in machine terms, as, for example, "the human brain has circuitry which processes input." Do you think that this tendency is based on a genuine insight into both human and machine "nature," or that it simply blurs a necessary distinction between a man and "a thing"?

Is it computers or men we are really afraid of?

---

fourteen

the promise

The machine—enemy or ally? The fears are real. And we can probably agree that, at least in part, the dangers are real. What, then, can we do about it?

Dr. Glenn T. Seaborg, chairman of the Atomic Energy Commission, and General David Sarnoff, Chairman of the Board of the Radio Corporation of America, believe that the machine can and must be our ally, and tell why in the following articles.

NO LIFE UNTOUCHED

David Sarnoff

In our increasingly complex world, information is becoming the basic building block of society. However, at a time when the acquisition of new scientific information alone is approaching a rate of 250 million pages annually, the tide of knowledge is overwhelming the human capability for dealing with it. So man must turn to a machine if he hopes to contain the tide and channel it to beneficial ends.

The electronic computer, handling millions of facts with the swiftness of light, has given contemporary meaning to Aristotle's vision of the liberating possibilities of machines: "When looms weave by themselves, man's slavery will end." By transforming the way in which he gathers, stores, retrieves, and uses information, this versatile instrument is helping man to overcome his mental and physical limitations. It is vastly widening his intellectual horizon, enabling him better to comprehend his universe, and providing the means to master that portion of it lying within his reach.

Although we are barely in the second decade of electronic data processing, the outlines of its influence on our culture are beginning to emerge. Far from depersonalizing the individual and dehumanizing his society, the computer promises a degree of personalized service never before available to mankind.

By the end of the century, for the equivalent of a few dollars a month, the individual will have a vast complex of computer services at his command. Information utilities will make computing power available, like electricity, to thousands of users simultaneously. The computer in the home will be **communications** joined to a national and global computer system that provides services ranging from banking and travel facilities to library research and medical care. High-speed communications devices, linked to satellites in space, will transmit data to and from virtually any point on earth with the ease of a dial system. Students, businessmen, scientists, government officials, and housewives will converse with computers as readily as they now talk by telephone.

In the health field, computers will be employed to maintain a complete medical profile on every person in the country from the hour of birth. The record will be constantly updated by a regional **medicine** computer for immediate access by doctors or hospital personnel. The computer also will maintain files on every known ailment, its symptoms, diagnosis, and treatment. A doctor will communicate a patient's symptoms to the computer center and within seconds receive suggestions for treatment based both on the symptoms and the patient's history.

Computers will handle the nation's fiscal transactions from a central credit information exchange, to which all banks, business enterprises, and in-finance

dividuals will be connected. Purchases will be made, funds invested, and loans issued by transfers of credit within the computer without a dollar or penny physically exchanging hands. Even the soil will be computerized. The long-range outlook for agriculture includes new sensing devices that will be placed on larger farms, feeding information to the computer on soil moisture, temperature, weather outlook, and other details. The computer will calculate the best crops to plant, the best seeding times, the amount of fertilizer, and even the correct harvesting time for maximum yield.

education

Some of the most profound changes wrought by the computer will be in education. Here, the machine will do more than assist students to solve problems and to locate up-to-date information: It will fundamentally improve and enrich the entire learning process. The student's educational experience will be analyzed by the computer from the primary grades through university. Computer-based teaching machines, programed and operated by teachers thoroughly trained in electronic data processing techniques, will instruct students at the rate best suited to each individual. The concept of mass education will give way to the concept of personal tutoring, with the teacher and the computer working as a team. Computers will bring many new learning dimensions to the classroom. For example, they will simulate nuclear reactors and other complex, dangerous, or remote systems, enabling students to learn through a form of experience what could formerly be taught only in theory.

The computer's participation in the field of learning will continue long after the end of formal education. The government estimates that 50 per cent of the jobs to be held ten years from now do not even exist today. With this tremendous rate of occupational obsolescence, future generations of Americans may pursue two or three careers during their lifetimes. The home computer will aid in developing career mobility by providing continuing self-instruction.

printing

Just as it is recasting the educational process, the computer is also fundamentally changing the production and distribution of the printed word. Five centuries ago, Gutenberg broke words into individual letters. Electronic composition now breaks the letters into tiny patterns of dots that are stored in the computer's memory. Any character can be called up by the computer, written on the face of a cathode ray tube, and reproduced on film or paper in thousandths of a second. Nothing moves except the electrons.

When the electronic computer first appeared in composition rooms and printing shops several years ago, its job was to hyphenate words and justify text. But the computer, working at speeds of thousands of words a minute, was driving mechanical typesetting devices capable of setting only a few words per minute. Now the development of computerized composition makes it possible to set text at hundreds of lines per minute. Photographs and drawings will be set the same way. Since the printed picture is itself a dot structure, the computer can electronically scan any photograph or drawing, reduce it to dots and store it, then retrieve it and beam it on a cathode ray tube for immediate reproduction.

In the future, electronics will develop processes that will make it possible to go from final copy and illustrations to printing in one integrated electronic process. One result will be that newspapers, in the foreseeable future, will no longer be printed in a single location. Instead, they will be transmitted through computers in complete page form to regional electronic printing centers that will turn out special editions for the areas they govern. Local news and advertising will be inserted on the spot. Eventually, the newspaper can be reproduced in the home through a small copying device functioning as part of a home communications center.

Basic changes also will come to other areas of the printed word. For example, of the more than one billion books published every year, almost half are textbooks. The growth of knowledge and the factor of obsolescence mean that these texts must be supplemented by a professor's mimeographed notes. Today, these notes have a small distribution of only a few hundred copies. Computers will make it possible to catalogue this information and thus broaden its availability.

At the turn of the century, most large universities will not only have electronic composition systems that allow them to reprint original research, theses, or course notes upon demand; they will also have a computerized information retrieval library. This process of information retrieval can be dupli-

research

law

business

cated in almost any other field. The scientist will have the latest technical papers culled by the computer and reproduced in the laboratory or home. The computer will bring to the attorney all the pertinent laws, decisions, and precedents on any case that concerns him. The business executive need not rush to the office every morning; most of the information he will need to conduct his business will be run off for him at home, and he will have two-way national and global closed-circuit television, via satellites, for meetings and conferences.

Some of these developments are probabilities, some of them are certainties, and all of them are or soon will be within the capabilities of the computer art. But one fact is absolute: the incredible growth of the computer in numbers, power and availability.

In just ten years, the typical electronic data processor has become ten times smaller, 100 times faster and 1000 times less expensive to operate. These trends will continue, and our national computing power, which is doubling every year, will soon be sufficient to make the computer a genuinely universal tool.

In 1956, there were fewer than 1000 computers in the United States. Today, there are 30,000, or more than $11 billion worth; and by 1976 the machine population may reach 100,000. And these figures will, of course, be greatly increased through the growth of data processing in other nations.

A decade ago, our machines were capable of 12 billion computations per hour; today, they can do more than 20 trillion, and by 1976—a decade from now—they will attain 400 trillion—or about two billion computations per hour for every man, woman and child. Quite evidently, the threshold of the computer age has barely been crossed.

Nevertheless, for all its potential to stretch the mind a thousandfold, it is perhaps necessary to point out that the computer is still a thing—that it cannot see, feel, or act unless first acted upon. Its value depends upon man's ability to use it with purpose and intelligence. If his postulates are wrong, the computerized future can only be a massive enlargement of human error.

Ramsay MacDonald once warned against "an attempt to clothe unreality in the garb of mathematical reality." Computers echo this warning. For they cannot usurp man's unique ability to blend intuition with fact, to feel as well as to think. In the end, this remains the basis of human progress.

The task ahead will be to assign to the machine those things which it can best do, and reserve for man those things which he must provide and control. It is my conviction that society will adjust itself to the computer and work in harmony with it for the genuine betterment of life.

from THE CYBERNETIC AGE: AN OPTIMIST'S VIEW

Glenn T. Seaborg

[T]he ultimate potential of the computer puts us to the test as human beings. It brings up questions we have lived with for centuries, but never have been asked to answer fully or act upon if we believed we knew the answers. It gives us new freedom and yet tremendous responsibilities which, if not acted upon, could result in a loss of almost all freedom. It presents us with choices and decisions of enormous consequences. It offers man a remarkable new chance to shape his own destiny, but asks him to be God-like enough to select that destiny without much margin for error.

Let me project a few thoughts on how the computer may forge our future—and, more important, on some of the ideas and alternatives with which we must come to grips if we are going to control the direction of that future.

To begin with, I believe that cybernation—the complete adaptation of computer-like equipment to industrial, economic, and social activity—will represent a quantum jump in the extension of man. The Industrial Revolution amplified (and to a large extent replaced) man's muscle as a productive force. Still, a large percentage of our production resulted from the energies of man and beast. Today in the United States, only a fraction of 1 per cent of our productive power results from the physical energy of human beings or animals.

Springing from our Scientific Revolution of re-

Reprinted by permission of the author and Saturday Review, Inc. Copyright 1967 Saturday Review, Inc.

cent decades is what is being called a "Cybernetic Revolution." This revolution, which, comparatively speaking, is only in its infancy, amplifies (and will to a large extent replace) man's nervous system. Actually, this is an understatement because computers amplify the collective intelligence of men—the intelligence of society—and, while the effect of the sum of men's physical energies may be calculated, a totally different and compounded effect results from combining facts and ideas—the knowledge generated within a society or civilization. Add this effect to the productive capacity of the machine driven by an almost limitless energy source like the nucleus of the atom, and the resulting system can perform feats almost staggering to our imagination. With the fullest development of cybernation we could be faced with prospects that challenge our very relationships to such basic concepts as freedom and the nature of work and leisure. . . .

Depersonalization, a separation of man and product, a collapse of time, a further reduction of human work, and a shift of needs and skills—all of these offer both threats and promises. I believe that the promises will eventually override the threats, but not before they have made us face and solve a great many problems we have not had to face before. This in itself is going to account for a great deal of human growth.

There is no doubt that the Cybernetic Revolution is going to make us reexamine the relationship between our freedoms and our responsibilities within the framework of society and find ways to guarantee a maximum of freedom for the individual within a highly organized society.

Another way in which the Cybernetic Revolution is going to force considerable human growth is in making us take a more rational, long-range approach in handling our affairs—our relationships with our fellow man and with nature. We are beginning to learn that the crisis-to-crisis approach that we have been using to carry on will no longer work. Science and technology have shrunk time by increasing the rate of change and have forged the world into a global civilization capable of exerting tremendous forces in a highly interrelated sphere of activity. We must make the fullest use of tools like the computer to help us prevent chaos and self-annihilation in such a complex world.

Looking at the most positive aspects of the computer, and projecting how its growing applications might control and multiply the forces of science and technology, one can foresee some remarkable "alternative futures." The most promising among these would be an era of abundance for all mankind—one in which most goods and services are provided by cybernated systems. And this brings us to the most striking aspect of human growth that could take place as a result of the Cybernetic Revolution—the change in our relationship to labor and leisure.

For a good part of our history we have been shaping through the manipulation of wealth what Peter Drucker calls "economic man." Perhaps the Cybernetic Revolution will carry us to a new level of man—a higher level—at which we will enjoy different values. On this subject it is interesting to recall what the great economist John Maynard Keynes wrote in 1932 in his *Essays in Persuasion:*

> When the accumulation of wealth is no longer of high social importance there will be great changes in the code of morals. We shall be able to rid ourselves of many of the pseudo-moral principles which have hag-ridden us for 200 years, by which we have exalted some of the most distasteful of human qualities into the position of highest values.

work-play

If the Cybernetic Revolution produces such a social millennium, a radical change in man's relationship to work would take place and the growth of leisure time would pose new problems to be solved.

As a result, our ideas on leisure would change drastically. Most people today do not recognize the true value of leisure. A little leisure has always been treasured, and there have been societies in which certain men and women lived in almost complete leisure, though at the expense of others' labor. But the idea of almost an entire civilization living in even relative leisure is beyond the comprehension of many of us and still frowned upon by most others.

A civilization equipped and educated to live in an era of relative leisure can bring about a new Golden Age—one without a slave base, other than those mechanical and cybernetic slaves produced by the ingenuity of a higher level of man. Such an age does not have to be, as a few predict, a civilization of drugged, purposeless people controlled by a small elite. But it could tragically become that, if we did nothing but let ourselves be swept along by some of the forces in motion today.

There are indications that some of these forces are just that overwhelming. There are also indications, however, that society is reacting to the "feedback" of certain personal and social effects of technology. This feedback is coming from more and more people in all levels of society and all walks of life. It is expressing an increasing uneasiness about the state of our personal and community lives in a highly materialistic society, a concern over the individual's role in the growing complexity and impersonalization of that society, a groping for "national purpose," and a feeling that the unity of man, referred to by poets and philosophers throughout the ages, is becoming a reality with immense psychological and physical implications.

To me, these feelings forecast the need for a huge re-evaluation of our goals and values, and it will be in our universities where such a re-evaluation will take place. Perhaps its seeds have already been sown in the current unrest on the campuses of many of our universities. From this re-evaluation, from the debates and soul-searching that take place, will evolve both a new understanding and reinforcement of those old ideals which are still valid, and new ideals and goals. Together they may provide us with something like a comprehensive philosophy of life to match the physical unity of mankind rapidly being fostered by today's science and technology.

If we can use this new philosophy to guide the great scientific and technological forces we have created, we could witness, possibly within a few decades, the equivalent of a new "human breakthrough"—an advance to a new stage of social development—one that was initiated by our reactions to today's trends.

education-evolution   In such a development the university, the greatest depository and dispenser of man's knowledge, should play a major role. In fact, I can see no other institution more logically equipped to be the central force in this evolutionary process, to develop, refine, and pass on to the new generations a new heritage of a higher level of mankind.

But if we are to carry out such a monumental

task, many changes will probably have to take place in the universities and our educational system in general. One such change will involve reconciling the continuing importance of specialization with a growing need for interdisciplinary thinking —not only in science and technology, but in all areas of our economic, social, and human development. Specialization has been giving us increasing amounts of knowledge, but the world cries out today for more of something beyond knowledge— for *wisdom*.

All of this demands a new role of leadership from our educational system. Most of today's schools are involved to a great degree in serving the requirements of an industrial age, in fulfilling the needs of a society which has been only partly and indirectly of their making. In the future, this role will shift to one in which the nature of society is determined more by the thinking of the university, and in which the industrial community will tend to serve goals created by that thinking.

What we must look for from the universities is the development of an education that turns out individuals of the highest intellect and broadest outlook, able to understand man and machine, and live creatively with both. Such an education could not be expected in a four-year curriculum or even a six- or eight-year one. It would start as early as the beginning of school or sooner and involve continuing education of one type or another throughout a person's lifetime. And, as Robert Theobald indicates, education in the age of the Cybernetic Revolution would not be directed toward "earning a living" but toward "total living."

This is a big order involving imagination, energy, and bold leadership from the academic world. But the time is certainly ripe for this kind of leadership.

The coming Cybernetic Revolution which calls forth these new goals for education will also give education valuable new tools and technologies for pursuing them. The computer will make knowledge more accessible. It will perform miracles in compiling, organizing, and analyzing information. It should link the knowledge of the world's libraries and depositories of information into networks responding like a giant brain. And it should put at the fingertips of anyone who wishes to be a modern-day Faust all the knowledge he desires without selling his soul to the Devil.

Some believe that, in a cybernated utopia, human

incentives will diminish and we will completely stagnate. I don't believe this will happen at all. New incentives will arise as man moves up to higher levels of needs. The quest for new knowledge will always grow. The domain of science is practically boundless. We are only beginning our adventures in space, and we still have a long way to go in understanding many things about this planet and the life on it.

Much has been said about the impersonalization caused by the growth of machines, but as a result of this growth I can see a new and better relationship arising among men. If in the past we have spent most of our time working with machines, serving and being served by them, naturally we feel a sense of isolation and alienation among them. But when machines have truly freed us from the necessity of physical work, perhaps we can better accept them for what they are and have the time to see and relate to other people in a different light. **communication-transportation** When we have more time to be with other people —not accidentally, on crowded buses, in elevators, in markets and offices, but in places of our own choosing at our own leisure—we may feel differently toward one another.

When we are less likely to be in competition with one another, much of the hypocrisy of society will vanish and more honest relationships will be formed. And, finally, when we can walk down the street—anywhere in the world—in a community free from want, where every human being has a sense of dignity not gained at the expense of others, we might not only walk free from fear but with a great feeling of exaltation.

If we can make the transition of living with and using the complex machines of the future in a *human-oriented* society, the rewards will be worth any effort we can make. As everyone knows, such a transition will not be easy, because it involves so much of what Eric Hoffer has called "The Ordeal of Change." But I think we will have to make such a transition eventually. We may have already begun to do so.

R. Buckminster Fuller—engineer, architect, and social planner—points out that we spend billions for **weaponry**; he proposes that we can and must turn now to **livingry**. Our technology and science must, he believes, be turned toward "design science," toward the living as opposed to the killing arts.

John R. Platt, a physicist and chemist turned biologist, argues that not only technology but science as well must be guided by a concern for what might make living more worthwhile and the planet we live on richer and more diverse.

from DIVERSITY

John R. Platt

[W]e develop some things well and other things not at all. We send men into orbit and we can fly faster than sound, but our clothes are inferior to those of a bird in many ways. The technical design of clothes is still prehistoric, in spite of synthetic fibers and sewing machines. The fibers must still be drawn out like animal or plant fibers, then spun, then woven or knitted, and then cut and sewn more or less to fit, just as fibers and cloth have been spun and sewn for thousands of years. And then these threads do not protect us against rain or cold, or ventilate or shade us in the hot sun, unless we put on and take off many layers which we must carry around in a suitcase. Why should someone not make us a single suit that would shed rain and that we could ruffle up for comfort in any weather, as a bird ruffles its feathers? A bird needs no suitcase. The reason is that no one—not even the Army, which might be expected to have the greatest interest in it—has put a task force on the problem of designing clothing material of variable porosity and variable thermal conductivity that could be molded to the body. Not everybody would want a single universal suit, but it would be nice to have the option. It might not even be very hard to in-

vent. But we still have prehistoric patterns of thought in what touches us most closely. Helicopters, *si*; clothes, *no*.

It is the same story with shoes, which are still sewn of pieces of leather or plastic. And again with housing, which lags far behind automobiles in technology and still has piece-by-piece assembly and leaking roofs and windows and no standard modular connection to the needed city services.

It is as though we had collective taboos against certain types of development, like the taboo against work on oral contraceptives before about 1950, or the refusal to consider or finance Buckminster Fuller's geodesic dome buildings until the Army used the principle for radomes, or the reluctance of psychologists and physiologists to study sleep before the work of Nathaniel Kleitman and his coworkers made it respectable. Scientists are not really innovators, and neither are industrial companies and government agencies and their research-and-development teams. They all shrink, like other men, from unheard-of projects for which there is no precedent, even obvious and important projects, because they are afraid they will be laughed at or cut off from support....

I think we neglect many important

Reprinted from John R. Platt, "Diversity," in *Science*, Vol. 154, 1132–1139 (2 December 1966), by permission of the author and the publisher. Copyright 1966 by the American Association for the Advancement of Science.

alternatives in our patterns of housing and living. We have automobiles in plenty—and I am no longer one of those who complain about their design; they are remarkably functional and economical and satisfying, and some day they may even be safe! But why should not our magnificent economic and social system be able to give us a similar level of technological skill and competitive cost in the construction of our houses? And why should we not be able to have more diversity and choice in our patterns of houses and lots? Again, there is a coupling of money to conventional patterns of tradition and taboo. If we were to put our houses at the edge of the streets, facing inward on the block, the houses could all look onto a sizable little park in the middle of the block, with trees and a fountain and swings and a place for oldsters to sit and for children to play safely away from the street. Given the pleasure of facing your very own park, who would prefer all these separate private lots with their wasteful driveways and unused areas? Very few, perhaps; but most of us will never know, because our system is focused on a different image and is not flexible enough to give us the option.

It would also be useful to try animal-copying with the nucleus taken from one species and the egg in which it was implanted taken from another. Donkey and horse can be mated; will a donkey nucleus in a horse egg cell give a donkey—or something more like a mule? This might teach us something about the developmental embryonic differences between species. If it would work, we might be able to save some vanishing species by transplanting their cell nuclei into the egg cells of foster species. Is the DNA that carries heredity destroyed immediately when an animal dies? If the meat of woolly mammoths locked for thousands of years in the Arctic ice is still edible, perhaps their DNA is still viable and might be injected, say, into elephant egg cells to give baby mammoths again. By some such methods, perhaps we

might achieve "paleo-reconstruction" of the ancient Mexican corn, or of "mummy wheat," or even of the flies that are sometimes found preserved in amber. One man has devoted his life to reconstructing creatures like the ancient aurochs, by backcrossing modern cattle. May not these other genetic methods of paleostudy also be worth trying? Success is uncertain, but the rewards would be great.

There must be dozens of other areas of study that contain such families of unconventional experiments just waiting to be tried. In biological technology alone there are the experiments required for the selective breeding and herding of sea animals and "farming the oceans"; experiments on animal development, in which our new knowledge of embryonic growth would be used in attempts to develop larger brains or stronger muscles; experiments on the closer shaping of animal behavior, not just to make trick animals for the movies, but to make more versatile pets or better dogs for the blind; and experiments on electronic transducers to bring animal sounds into our range of hearing and our sounds into their range of hearing, so as to learn whether dolphins or chimpanzees or Siamese cats might learn to use signals and symbols more as we do if we made it easier for them. This might give us a better understanding of the origins of our own communication and linguistic development over the last few hundred thousand years.

Finally there is an important set of experiments and developments needed for devising more sophisticated machines that would serve biological functions. Not just artificial kidneys, and pacemakers, and artificial hearts, which are all now under study, but things like balancing machines, to help the paralyzed to walk, with motors as compact and powerful and fast as our own muscles, and with feedback circuits as clever as our own balancing. Should these be so hard to devise, for men whose electronic circuits have flown past Mars transmitting pictures? Perhaps not; but the amount of scientific and engineering effort devoted by the nation to such problems is probably less than a ten-thousandth of the space effort.

The balancing problem is part of the interesting problem of making self-guiding automata—artificial cybernetic organisms, or "Cyborgs" as someone has called them—with pattern-perceiving sensory systems, communication systems, and control programs, and with self-contained power sources and motor motions. Such devices will be needed by exploring the hostile surface of the moon and Mars and sending back data, but they would also be useful for exploring sea bottoms and volcanoes and for fire-fighting and other dangerous operations. We are on the edge of understanding how to make such automata, but the problem is still being studied at only a half-dozen centers, and still does not enlist the hundreds of trained and inventive minds that will be needed to make such devices work cheaply and well. . . .

It is time for more scientific diversity. The question to be asked is no longer, what does physics have the apparatus and the equations for? It is, rather, what are the curious things in the world? And what are the needs of man?

catching up with technology

Fulfilling the Promise. Develop a list of functions (including new ones you can think of) which computers could perform to fulfill the promise of technology:

in the physical environment (for example, regulating traffic, forecasting the weather)
in the cultural environment—school, work, play, etc. (for example, playing word games with English students)
Can you think of any tasks requiring brains and/or muscle that computers could not be built to perform?

Visit a data processing center and/or a computer company (Xerox, IBM, Syntex, etc.). Consult with computer experts about possible new uses of computers and the practical and cultural consequences of increasing reliance on technology. With the help of a programmer, design a computer program. Play a game of checkers, chess, tic tac toe, etc., with a computer.

Averting the Threat. What kinds of control or planning are necessary to assure that the new technologies serve rather than dictate social ends? A Federal agency? New laws? Self-policing by industry? List and rank some alternatives.

Those who study the impact of the new technologies agree that man must invent his future if his future is to have any meaning. But while this reality is increasingly accepted, the amount of effort devoted to this necessary task remains minimal. Almost all of our study, our planning, our actions, continue to be based on the assumption that the future will resemble the past.

What are the reasons for our failure to re-examine social systems and institutions in the light of new requirements? The primary reason is well-known: Every viable social system must ensure that the vast majority of its members accept its assumptions about the nature of reality, about events, and about right and wrong. This result is achieved through the process of education by inculcating values in each child. Thus, each culture and institution tends to perpetuate itself.

Today, however, the perpetuation of the industrial age culture is inappropriate. But the recognition of inappropriateness by itself is not enough. Existing structures tend to limit, if not prevent, any attempt at fundamental change in the culture. It is for this reason that Arnold Toynbee, the noted historian, has argued that fundamental change in a culture is impossible. The historical record appears to confirm his judgment, and it therefore becomes essential to imagine, devise, and apply new methods of causing change if the modern world is to be able to deal creatively with new realities.

To what extent are our fears of the machine based on assumptions and values we have learned from the industrial age culture? What might some of these assumptions and values be? Which ones are social fictions? Which still seem valid, and which outdated and no longer an accurate reflection of our real needs and concerns?

Toynbee's pessimism about the possibility of fundamental change in a culture underlines the importance of agents of change, and the urgency of our need to break through our imprinting and become aware of our social fictions.

How can we best prepare ourselves "to deal creatively with new realities"?

These are questions we may continue to ponder as the probes in the following pages take us deeper into our uncharted future.

Robert Theobald, *Dialogue on Technology*. Indianapolis, Ind.: Bobbs-Merrill Company, Inc., 1967.

One of the most dynamic characteristics of man, distinguishing him from other species and giving him pretensions to be more than merely a machine, is that, faced with an environment which threatens his self-development, his instinct is to change it. This instinct is sustained by his ability to sense—as he meshes the logic of his past with his intuitions of the present—the future implications of his actions. Expression of this instinct has brought the word *revolution* into currency.

Richard Kean,
Preface to
Dialogue on Education

PART V

evolution or
revolution?

fifteen

world enough,
and time

Just as we explored three natural media within which new environments can be designed, we will now explore three cultural media within which existing structures can be changed and more fulfilling life styles envisioned.

We will be looking at three media—three realms of activity—and each may be viewed as a whole comprising two parts: "Work-Play," "Communication-Transportation," and "Education-Evolution." Devising new relationships between the parts will be the task before us.

The new technologies are playing fast and loose with three precious, though invisible, resources: our time, our space, and our energies. Regaining command over our self-development requires that we regain control over how these are spent.

EACH REALM IS A PIE, WITH
TIME AND ENERGY AS INGREDIENTS.

Work / Play

Transportation / Communication

Evolution / Education

HOW SHOULD WE CUT EACH PIE?

If we work for
pleasure rather
than profit, how
does work differ
from play?

If war, business,
and government
are games, how
does play differ
from work?

If we send our mind
and our senses though
not our bodies from
one place to another,
how does transportation
differ from communication?

If we learn by
direct stimulation
of the brain, or
by growing new
brain tracks rather
than by studying,
how does education
differ from evolution?

If changes in our
species only makes
us more human, how
does evolution differ
from education?

THERE IS A SENSE IN WHICH EACH ACTIVITY IS
ITS OPPOSITE.

trying on a new life

Here is a list of "labels" of persons who could be profoundly affected by change in our patterns of work-
play, communication-transportation, and education-
evolution. Some may be affected so greatly that they
will cease to exist, or at least to be identifiable by
these labels. Can you extend this list to include others
whose future you might be curious about?

After each section you will be asked to imagine what
life would be like for one or more of these persons,
if some or all of the proposed changes came about.
You will be asked to decide which changes *should*
occur and to design a life style for the person or
persons you choose.

a twenty-year-old business man
a computer programmer
a film maker
a thirty-year-old retired welder
a nine-year-old child
a mother of two
an instructor in a community college
an artist (painter, sculptor, etc.)
a trainer of dolphins
a construction engineer
a mystic
a nature lover
an adventure lover
a white Anglo-Saxon Protestant
a professional football player
a department store clerk
a nurse
an ecologist
a mechanic
a technologist
a scientist
a doctor
a lawyer
any of the characters in Part II
your son or daughter
your grandchild
yourself
a ??

sixteen

work — play

In the automated future, the term "leisure" will be increasingly inadequate to express the revolution in time itself that is taking place, a revolution in which time is no longer a by-product of the machine, but a basic form of wealth.

**Phyllis Daignault,
"New Markets in Time"**

As we move from an industrial to a cybernated society, where more and more work is done by machines, we seem to be facing four crises.

The first is an *economic crisis*. If a human being has no role as productive worker, how does he feed his family, clothe his children, and provide for the other necessities and the luxuries of a full life?

The second is a *crisis of identity*. If a human being in our society can no longer identify himself by his job ("I am a teacher," "I am a printer," etc.), who is he? How *does* he define himself?

The third is a *moral crisis*. Of what worth is a man, if he cannot earn his place in society by working?

The fourth is a *crisis of meaning*. If a man can no longer work, what can he strive for? What makes life itself worthwhile? What can he do instead of working?

Let us look at each in turn, beginning with the economic crisis. How strong is the likelihood that people will not be able to work at jobs of their choice in the near future?
Three men who believe we must give up the goal of full employment, discuss the question in the following conversation. The men are Robert Theobald, author and socioeconomist; Ralph Helstein, president of the United Packinghouse Workers of America; and Gerald Piel, publisher of the magazine *Scientific American*.

from JOBS, MACHINES, AND PEOPLE

PIEL: The general hypothesis of our system is that people displaced in employment in one sector will find it in others, and we are assured that retraining and other such programs will fit them to get jobs in that part of the labor force which is engaged in distribution, the service trades, and so on. But these sectors, which have been growing rapidly in the past fifty years and have been soaking up the disemployed from productive and extractive functions, are beginning to fail to soak them up. New jobs are *not* being created in these fields.

HELSTEIN: Retraining has some meaning in that it may well raise the total level of skills, and to the extent that knowledge is never entirely wasted this is useful. But it would be much better if we could create a system under which the industrial jobs would be available on an area-wide basis, say, instead of on a one-plant basis and thus create mobility between jobs. For example, in a city like Chicago a man might work one week in a packing house, another week in a steel mill, and another week in an automobile plant, or whatever other available work there was. This would make for a diversity of skills, and as long as the mobility was kept within a particular geographical area there would be no problem of families having to move.

THEOBALD: Isn't one of the big problems with retraining that planning hasn't caught up with the immense flexibility of automated and cybernated machinery? There is a tendency to assume that the traditional jobs will still need to be filled; whereas, when you calculate what is going to be taken over by the machine in the next five years, you realize that most of the occupations for which people are being retrained are going to vanish within this period. Machines will take over most of the repetitive mental *and* physical tasks within the foreseeable future.

PIEL: The very possibility of training a man so that he can work one week in a packing house and another week in a steel mill is in itself an indication of the degree to which the human being is being disengaged from the production process. The actual productive work is done by the machine; the man's role is that of a machine tender. The new development in our technology is the replacement of the human nervous system by automatic controls and by the computer that ultimately integrates the functions of the automatic control units at each point in the production process. The human muscle began to be disengaged from the productive process at least a hundred years ago. Now the human nervous system is being disengaged.

THEOBALD: The difference between the industrial age of the nineteenth and the first half of the twentieth centuries and the cybernated age today is that the first combined human skill and machine power and the second combines *machine* skill and machine power. The human being has been pushed right out of the productive process. It is just a question of how long it will take us to recognize that he has been pushed out.

HELSTEIN: The trouble is that so many people today continue to believe in the myth that if a man wants to work, he can work. It is not really a question of not being "worth it." It is that a state of mind is created at some point in which the man becomes aware that he is no longer a part of any meaningful strains in our society. . . .

PIEL: We are really confronted with having to make the political and social decision that full employment is no longer a feasible economic and political goal. . . .

"The actual productive work is done by the machine; the man's role is that of machine tender."

Is May Swenson saying the same thing in her poem "The Power-house"? (p. 162)

Why does the person in the poem expect the man to be a Negro? Why isn't he?

What does a man *do* as a machine tender? What does this role do to *him*?

What kind of jobs have already been taken over by a machine?

What kinds of jobs can be taken over by a machine?

Will your job (the one you are planning for yourself) be taken over by a machine?

If we assume that Piel's appraisal that full employment is no longer a feasible economic and political goal is correct, what solutions are there to the economic crisis individuals will have to face?

The conversation continues.

THEOBALD: Knowing how long it takes to change political attitudes, knowing what public opinion, economic opinion, administration opinion is on these issues, I would agree that the chances of reaching full employment in the context of today's world are pretty slim and that one should be realistic and admit that the goal of full employment is dead. Therefore, we should be talking about how to provide income for people when there are no jobs for them. As I understand it, the whole Western world has a fundamental commitment to the principle that every individual should have enough income to live with dignity.

HELSTEIN: I certainly agree. It seems to me that work and income are the result of an ethic that has long since lost its viability because it has never been brought up to date. If we want to give meaning to the Protestant ethic, we had better start revising our concept of what we mean by work. Work and income are the product of what society said had to be done under the circumstances of our one-time economy of scarcity. . . . Now this no longer has any meaning because there isn't scarcity if we don't want it to be there.

PIEL: So, in the first place, the fundamental premise of our economic system and of all our economic thought is overturned. In the second place, when the electronic nervous system replaces the human nervous system, then, clearly, in the technological sense, the job is disjoined from income. In other words, the notion that a job is required to qualify and certify a person for income becomes obsolete.

Buckminster Fuller has pointed out that in the future we may serve our society better by consuming than by producing.

In that case, science fiction writer Frederick Pohl suggests in "The Midas Plague," the "poor" would be those who had to consume the most.

HELSTEIN: This is not such a revolutionary proposition. It may sound so to people who don't want to look at it, but the fact is that either as a result of work done by their ancestors or work done by themselves in earlier years there are already millions of people in America who have income without work. People on relief are another group. The difference with them is that our society pieces them off in order to sweep the guilt away, without making it possible for them to live socially creative lives.

I would like, if I may, though, to go back to one other point. I accept the fact that full employment at this juncture in time is a misleading goal if by full employment is meant the traditional kind of jobs in the private market—a market that has failed in the last five years to produce the kind and number of jobs necessary. A revision of our concept of work is required. After all, work is only what society says it is. There is no reason why we cannot start redefining our notions of what work is and in this way provide full employment, but not all of it at the kind of work that we have always called work.

PIEL: We certainly ought to do some redefinition, because the kind of work made available by the market economy is increasingly work that is not fit for human beings to do precisely because it has been redesigned for machines.

HELSTEIN: Not only the jobs that are better done by machines, but a job like working on the killing floor of a packing house—human beings shouldn't have to do this.

THEOBALD: One of the worst stories I've ever heard was about one of the automobile companies where if a person dies while the assembly line is operating and he is in a place where he can't be got at, he lies there until the line breaks down. . . .

The point is this: The machine system now requires such efficiency that no human being ought to be tied into it any longer. Another kind of system can be developed so that human beings don't have to be involved, and they shouldn't be. They should be taken out just as soon as they can be. I would like to put this another way, which may be less shocking: If we have a productive system in which we can turn out all the goods we require without human beings involved in it, it is obviously ludicrous to say that only the people who are working specifically in the production of the goods are entitled to live. This is the situation we are approaching. This is the other way of saying that we have to split up jobs and income.

Is the belief that jobs and income must be linked a social fiction?

The notion that a person's right to income is not inevitably linked to his productivity was propounded in 1887 by Edward Bellamy in *Looking Backward*. Even though society's need for productive workers was not questioned in Bellamy's time, Bellamy believed that income was a basic human right. His novel is a projection. The narrator fell asleep on the thirtieth day of May, 1887; he awoke on the tenth day of September in the year 2000. In the following conversation the narrator's benefactor acquaints him with some of the features of the new society to which he has awakened.

from LOOKING BACKWARD

Edward Bellamy

"A credit corresponding to his share of the annual product of the nation is given to every citizen on the public books at the beginning of each year, and a credit card issued him with which he procures at the public storehouses, found in every community, whatever he desires whenever he desires it. This arrangement, you will see, totally obviates the neces-

Edward Bellamy, *Looking Backward, 2000–1887*, first published in 1887.

sity for business transactions of any sort between individuals and consumers." . . .

"What if you have to spend more than your card in any one year?" I asked.

"The provision is so ample that we are more likely not to spend it all," replied Dr. Leete. "But if extraordinary expenses should exhaust it, we can obtain a limited advance on the next year's credit, though this practice is not encouraged, and a heavy discount is charged to check it. Of course if a man showed himself a reckless spendthrift he would receive his allowance monthly or weekly instead of yearly, or if necessary not be permitted to handle it all."

"If you don't spend your allowance, I suppose it accumulates?"

"That is also permitted to a certain extent when a special outlay is anticipated. But unless notice to the contrary is given, it is presumed that the citizen who does not fully expend his credit did not have occasion to do so, and the balance is turned into the general surplus."

"Such a system does not encourage saving habits on the part of citizens," I said.

"It is not intended to," was the reply. "The nation is rich, and does not wish the people to deprive themselves of any good thing. In your day, men were bound to lay up goods and money against coming failure of the means of support and for their children. This necessity made parsimony a virtue. But now it would have no such laudable object, and, having lost its utility, it has ceased to be regarded as a virtue. No man any more has any care for the morrow, either for himself or his children, for the nation guarantees the nurture, education, and comfortable maintenance of every citizen from the cradle to the grave."

"That is a sweeping guarantee!" I said. "What certainty can there be that the value of man's labor will recompense the nation for its outlay on him? On the whole, society may be able to support all its members, but some must earn less than enough for their support, and others more; and that brings us back once more to the wages question, on which you have hitherto said nothing. It was at just this point, if you remember, that our talk ended last evening; and I say again, as I did then, that here I should suppose a national industrial system like yours would find its main difficulty. How, I ask once more, can you adjust satisfactorily the comparative wages or remuneration of the multitude of avocations, so unlike and so incommensurable, which are necessary for the service of society? In our day the market rate determined the price of labor of all sorts, as well as of goods. The employer paid as little as he could, and the worker got as much. It was not a pretty system ethically, I admit; but it did, at least, furnish us a rough and ready formula for settling a question which must be settled ten thousand times a day if the world was ever going to get forward. There seemed to us no other practicable way of doing it."

"Yes," replied Dr. Leete, "it was the only practicable way under a system which made the interests of every individual antagonistic to those of every other; but it would have been a pity if humanity could never have devised a better plan, for yours was simply the application to the mutual relations of men of the devil's maxim, 'Your necessity is my opportunity.' The reward of any service depended not upon its difficulty, danger, or hardship, for throughout the world it seems that the most perilous, severe, and repulsive labor was done by the worst paid classes; but solely upon the strait of those who needed the service." . . .

"How is the amount of the credit given respectively to the workers in different lines determined? By what title does the individual claim his particular share? What is the basis of allotment?"

"His title," replied Dr. Leete, "is his humanity. The basis of his claim is the fact that he is a man."

"The fact that he is a man!" I repeated, incredulously. "Do you possibly mean that all have the same share?"

This notion seemed Utopian in 1887 when Bellamy proposed it—and for many decades thereafter. Today, however, some social planners hold that providing a basic income for all is both feasible and just.

> Our key problem stems from the fact that we have made the value of a man synonymous with the economic value of the toil he performs: we fail to recognize that people should have a claim on resources even if they do not toil. The measure of destruction of our values is, I believe, shown in the fact that those living in an industrial society find it natural that people do not receive an adequate amount of food, clothing, and shelter even though there is surplus food in storage and the possibility of producing more housing and more clothing if we gave people the money to buy them. We can contrast this view with that of the so-called primitive societies; in many of these it was literally impossible to starve unless the whole community was starving. George Peter Murdoch, the celebrated anthropologist, described the reaction of one group of natives when he tried to explain the problem of the poor in Western countries. There was stark disbelief: "How can he have no food? Does he have no friends? How can he have no house? Does he have no neighbors?"
>
> **Robert Theobald,**
> *An Alternative Future for America*

Reprinted from Robert Theobald, *An Alternative Future for America* (Chicago: Swallow Press, Inc., 1968), pp. 25–27 and 82, by permission of the author.

Robert Theobald believes that the transition to a cybernated economy can be accomplished by establishing a guaranteed annual income (GAI), based on the concept of an absolute constitutional right to an income. But he also has come to realize that a change in social and psychological attitudes is essential to the recognition that the guaranteed income is a necessity.

Those who would like to study a model for a guaranteed income system might wish to read Theobald's Basic Economic Security plan (BES) in *An Alternative Future for America*

What might some of these attitudes be? Some people might object on moral grounds: "Why should all, whether working or not, be supported by society?" Others might object on practical grounds: "Why would anyone work if he didn't have to?" Still others might object on the basis of individual rights: "What happens to people who feel they have a right and a need to work?"

All of these objections grow out of particular beliefs about human nature. Do you hold any of these attitudes? What are the arguments for and against these objections, and what are some underlying beliefs about human nature and the purposes of society?

In his essay "Programs: Present and Future" in *Dialogue on Poverty*, Theobald addresses these issues. Do you find his arguments persuasive?

My goal ... is to create a situation of full *unemployment*, a world in which people do not have to hold a job, and I believe that this kind of world can actually be achieved. But clearly there are a number of people, particularly older people, for whom society will still have an obligation to provide structured work, because these people will need structured work. Therefore, the key becomes: give an income to everybody and give some sort of structured work to those who will need it.

But such a program is only possible if you have some faith in yourself and your fellow man. If you have a pessimistic view of human nature, you may as well forget everything I am saying, because it is irrelevant as far as you are concerned. There are a lot of people like this. They feel

Reprinted from Robert Theobald, "Programs: Present and Future" in Robert Theobald, ed., *Dialogue on Poverty* (Indianapolis: The Bobbs-Merrill Company, Inc., 1967), by permission of the author.

that, "Well, it would be nice if human beings were good people, but they aren't, you know. They are lazy, dishonest, unloving, irresponsible and proud; so forget it." Now, I would claim that if you really are discouraged enough to say something of this sort you are not far, logically, from the position that we are not going to survive much longer anyway. The guaranteed income, like so many other policies designed for a free society, is intended to help men work out their human destinies. It is based on the optimistic assumption that men actually *want to* develop themselves and their society and that they are capable of it. . . .

I am not just arguing that the guaranteed income is a way to abolish poverty. We all know it does this. The guaranteed income, at a reasonable level, will abolish poverty tomorrow, and this is a good reason for it. But the real reason for a guaranteed income is beyond this. It is a change in the structure of society. I don't believe our problem is that people are evil as some would suggest, but that people are trapped. The guaranteed income is a way for people to get out of the traps they are in and overcome their poverty of spirit. There is no reason why a man should have to hold a job in order to survive today, and, if what you want to do is important enough, you can say, "I don't require a very big income because I am doing what I want to do." And I believe that the result would be to set free enormous social energy to do the things that need to be done.

The net result of guaranteed income would be a decentralizing effect on society running counter to the present intense centralization. When people can get an income without having to hold an income producing job, they can begin to go away from the places where incomes are produced. They can create new kinds of communities and new kinds of colleges which suit their human needs. It will be harder for highly centralized institutions of government, business and education to hold on to people. Moreover, we can expect the creation of what I call "consentives." Consentives are enterprises at which people work together because they want to, rather than because they need a job.

It should be understood that a guaranteed income, as Theobald sees it, would not make one rich. It would however, provide for the necessities of life and free the individual to work (or not) at some low-paying or non-paying activity which he chose because he wanted to do it.

If work were a luxury and a privilege rather than an economic necessity, would you choose to work? For what rewards other than money would you be working?

Theobald continues:

I believe the computer can set us free. To me this is the exciting thing. But far too many people want to keep us constrained. . . . Most people want to tie us down. You go back to the average debate, and you are told that this is a perfectly good society which doesn't need to be changed. Sometimes you are told, "Well, maybe it isn't such a good society, but there's nothing you can do about it."

> It was not a pretty system, ethically, I admit;
> but it did furnish us with a rough and
> ready formula. . . .
> Bellamy,
> p. 201

I believe we can create a better society. I believe that man can abolish toil and abolish it well before the end of this century, that he can develop, instead, *work*. I see man working in four areas: first, self-development—both mental and physical; second, the human care of human beings; third, the whole area of human relationships. It takes a lifetime to get to know somebody, and if you don't like to call it "work," I don't care. It's still something to do, and that's what worries a lot of people: what will man do next? Fourth, politics—the creation of a good community.

Perhaps a redefinition of work, to distinguish it from toil, can be based on a distinction between what machines appropriately can do and what men appropriately can do. Theobald seems to be suggesting that activities which help fulfill the human being are man's appropriate work.

How would you redefine work?
Do you agree with Theobald?

To deal further with this question, let us now turn to the other three crises mentioned at the beginning of our probe of work-play. Even if we can envision a society in which work is separated from income and income is guaranteed to all, how do we determine our identity, our worth, and our function as social beings?

You may have begun to perceive that the crises all derive from conventional beliefs about human value that are based on a work economy. And as we look into the bases for these beliefs and consider some alternatives we may find that they will not be "resolved" so much as "dissolved." The moral crisis, the crisis of identity, and the crisis of meaning all derive from social fictions developed at a time when work was deemed a social good because it was a social necessity. As we saw in our consideration of social fictions (p. 95), society tends to convert a relative into an absolute good. Thus, though it may no longer be necessary for a man to work, nevertheless we continue to feel that it is right or good for him to do so.

from THE ADMIRATION OF TECHNIQUE

Edward McIrvine

The classical economists were convinced of the necessity for man to participate in productive processes. "A man must always live by his work," says Adam Smith in *The Wealth of Nations*. Robert Owen postulates that "...manual labour, properly directed, is the source of all wealth, and of national prosperity." Thomas Carlyle sees an inevitability in the system of wages-for-added-value: "A fair day's-wages for a fair day's-work: it is as just a demand as governed men ever made of governing. It is the everlasting right of man. Indisputable as Gospels, as arithmetical multiplication-tables. ..." Carlyle carries his argument even further, in a later chapter of *Past and Present*, when he states categorically: "All True Work is sacred; in all true work, were it but true hard labor, there is something of divineness."

Nor did the nineteenth-century socialists doubt man's role as the practitioner of technique. The Fourieristic socialist Parke Godwin (in *Democracy, Constructive and Pacific*) states that "Society owes [human beings] a guarantee of life and work. They possess a right to labor, which is the most sacred of all rights." The Christian socialist George D. Herron (in *The New Redemption*) carries the admiration of technique to an extreme with his apotheosis: "This is a world of work. God works and man works. Work is the manifestation of life. Work is communion with God. There is no righteous work that is not sacred and divine."

Our economic system, built to fan the flames of productivity during the nineteenth century, continues to emphasize productive capacity despite the advent of affluence.

Thus, a man was defined and learned to define himself by the function he performed in society.

Upon meeting a stranger, ask a third party "Who is he?" and the reply is likely to be "He is an attorney," or "He works for the railroad"; seldom are you told "He is a camper," or "He reads poetry," although the latter activities may indicate the identity of the man more closely and may involve more of his conscious thoughts than does his productive occupation. The identification of man by his productive function extends to the choice of surnames such as Butcher, Barbero, Baumeister, and Bouvier.

So ingrained has this attitude become that, as Sebastian DeGrazia points out,

> One is not appalled or indignant on learning that another doesn't work; one simply does not understand, doesn't know where next to turn for conversation, cannot size up the ostensibly human object standing there.

If we can accept the notion that society has less and less need of workers, in the traditional sense, may we not now discard this basis for estimating a man's identity and worth?

This leaves us with the crisis of meaning: the problem of what to put in the place of "productive" work. "We are faced," says R. J. Havighurst, "with the fundamental question—Can men be happy in any other way than in work?" Julian Huxley puts it this way:

> The leisure problem is fundamental. Having to decide what we shall do with our leisure is inevitably forcing us to re-examine the purpose of human existence, and to ask what fulfillment really means.

Lewis Mumford, in *The Myth of the Machine*, argues that unless we pry ourselves loose from the very limiting view that man is essentially a tool-making, tool-using animal, we will be reduced by our own technology to being nothing more than that. He contends that tool-making, far from being the defining quality of man, is shared by other creatures and cannot begin to account for the development of the human brain. Rather, Mumford believes the pursuit of culture is the truly distinguishing activity of man.

> Ritual, art, poesy, drama, music, dance, philosophy, science, myth, religion are all as essential to man as his daily bread: man's true life consists not alone in the work activities that directly sustain him, but in the symbolic activities which give significance both to the processes of work and their ultimate products and consummations.

"What is specially and uniquely human," Mumford writes in the Prologue to *The Myth of the Machine*, "is man's capacity to combine a wide variety of animal propensities into an emergent cultural entity: a human personality." And, with J. R. Huizinga, Ernest Becker, and others, he holds that all cultural activities are play-forms.

From Lewis Mumford, *The Condition of Man*.

from THE MYTH OF THE MACHINE

Lewis Mumford

Only a little while ago the Dutch historian, J. Huizinga, in "Homo Ludens," brought forth a mass of evidence to suggest that play, rather than work, was the formative element in human culture: that man's most serious activity belonged to the realm of make-believe. . . . Long before he had achieved the power to transform the natural environment, man had created a miniature environment, the symbolic field of play, in which every function of life might be refashioned in a strictly human style, as in a game.

So startling was the thesis of "Homo Ludens" that his shocked translator deliberately altered Huizinga's express statement, that all culture was a form of play, into the more obvious conventional notion that play is an element in culture. But the notion that man is neither *Homo sapiens* nor *Homo ludens*, but above all *Homo faber*, man the maker, had taken such firm possession of present-day Western thinkers that even Henri Bergson held it. So certain were nineteenth-century archaeologists about the primacy of stone tools and weapons in the "struggle for existence" that when the first paleolithic cave paintings were discovered in Spain in 1879, they were denounced, out of hand, as an outrageous hoax, by "competent authorities" on the ground that Ice Age hunters could not have had the leisure or the mind to produce the elegant art of Altamira.

But mind was exactly what *Homo sapiens* possessed in a singular degree: mind based on the fullest use of all his bodily organs, not just his hands. In this revision of obsolete technological stereotypes, I would go even further: for I submit that at every stage man's inventions and transformations were less for the purpose of increasing the food supply or controlling nature than for utilizing his own immense organic resources and expressing his latent potentialities. . . .

When not curbed by hostile environmental pressures, man's elaboration of symbolic culture answered a more imperative need than that for control over environment. . . .

On this reading, the evolution of language—a culmination of man's more elementary forms of expressing and transmitting meaning—was incomparably more important to further human development than the chipping of a mountain of handaxes. Besides the relatively simple coordinations required for tool-using, the delicate interplay of the many organs needed for the creation of articulate speech was a far more striking advance. This effort must have occupied a greater part of early man's time, energy, and mental activity, since the ultimate collective product, spoken language, was infinitely more complex and sophisticated at the dawn of civilization than the Egyptian or Mesopotamian kit of tools.

To consider man, then, as primarily a tool-using animal is to overlook the main chapters of human history. Opposed to this petrified notion, I shall develop the view that man is pre-eminently a mind-making, self-mastering, and self-designing animal; and the primary locus of all his activities lies first in his own organism, and in the social organization through which it finds fuller expression. . . .

Mumford's description of the true nature and purpose of man begins to sound much like Maslow's description of the self-actualizing person. And, indeed, W. A. Weisskopf, in his article "The Psychology of Abundance," builds on Maslow's distinction between lower and higher needs. He argues that in an age of automated abundance, where basic needs for food, clothing, and shelter can be easily met, we are at last free to pursue the goal of self-actualization—*if* we use our time and energies wisely. He, too, believes that cultural activities, conceived as play on a high level, are the means by which self-actualization can be achieved.

Those human needs which I call non-economic and nontechnical because they cannot be satisfied through automated machine production are clearly envisaged in Maslow's scheme. Robots cannot produce mental security or develop a harmonizing interpretive world philosophy; they cannot arrange warm, close, affectionate primary human relations; neither can they satisfy the needs for love and belongingness. All these (and other higher) needs will have to be taken care of even in an economy of technical abundance and will require time and energy to be saved from the unlimited consumption of machine-produced goods. . . .

Bertrand de Jouvenel has defined play as "the activity which procures satisfaction in such a way that the goal is merely the final point of such activity; labor is the activity which is only justified by the end." His definition of play reads like a description and prescription of what human life should be: it should be lived joyfully, even in suffering, until the end. The end should merely be the final point; what counts is how it is lived until then. If this is recognized, play should become more important, and work more satisfying in itself, regardless of its result, thereby assuming more characteristics of "play." . . .

Is it possible to visualize at least dimly a civilization in which "playful," artistic, and contemplative pursuits satisfy the higher needs, games and circuses all sorts of lower needs, fishing and sheer loafing the lowest needs, and where necessities and means of survival are of little importance because they are produced routinely by cybernetically controlled robots? There are still a multitude of experiences that machines cannot procure. I have still to hear about a robot producing a mystical union. . . . And how can friendship, love, worship, and expressive behavior (art, dance, etc.) possibly be performed by machines?

But will we as a society indeed develop enough understanding of our own nature to fulfill our highest potentialities, or will we continue to spend our time and energies on maximizing production and consumption? "The problem may be put in this way," writes R. N. Iyer, in "The Social Structure of the Future":

The wealthiest and most powerful nation in the world is the poorest in what was supremely precious to the highest cultures of classical antiquity and the renaissances of world history —the availability of time for thought and contemplation, for relaxation and creative (time-taking) work, for conversation and study, for love and friendship, for the enjoyment of the arts and the beauties of nature, for solitude and communion, for doubts and dreams, and for much else—for indolence and excellence, for salons and coffee-houses and the marketplace, for laughter and tears, for poetry and philosophy, for song and dance and worship, for birds and beasts, for sleep and convalescence, for birth and death, time to live and enough time to dwell on eternity. Can the mere availability of more time teach the most time-saving society in history how to spend time and how to transcend it and how to appreciate timelessness?

Robert Theobald is optimistic. He holds that there are many hopeful indications in our society today.

from AN ALTERNATIVE FUTURE FOR AMERICA

Robert Theobald

THE PROMISE

It is now quite clear that a new view of the nature of man is developing, as many people re-examine the emerging data. This view can be briefly expressed in Abraham Maslow's thesis that human beings begin to drive toward self-actualization as soon as their basic needs for food, clothing and shelter are satisfied.* Indeed, there are some suggestions that this insight should be perceived as part of a wider reality—that the universe itself can only be understood in terms of "self-actualization."

Two major implications would appear to stem from the new insight. First, this convergence among leading thinkers in many disciplines should make it possible to reverse the present, apparently irreversible, trend toward greater specialization.

Second, if it is indeed true that man can only be healthy when he is self-actualizing, it becomes possible to understand many of the developments presently occurring throughout the world which now appear to threaten our survival. Perhaps the most critical of these issues is the

*See Abraham Maslow, *Toward a Psychology of Being* (New York, D. Van Nostrand, Inc., 1962), especially chapters 3, 4, and 14.

demand for power, using slogans such as "black power" and "student power." At the present time these slogans are widely understood to mean that the groups using them want power without responsibility. In the light of man's absolute necessity to be able to strive for self-development, they take on a different meaning. They state essentially that each man must be provided with the potential to control the conditions of his own life and that the failure to develop this potential leaves him with no choice but to fall into anomie and apathy on the one hand or violence on the other.

It is in this context that today's potential abundance takes on its full meaning: man now has the material ability to provide all human beings with the goods and services required to serve as the basis for full human development. Today, national and international poverty results from a failure of will rather than a failure of productive ability; those who are powerless sense or know this and naturally consider it intolerable.

We have no choice, therefore, but to create a new social order, one where powerlessness has been abolished. For only then will man's drive toward self-actualization be capable of fulfillment and his self-destructive tendencies, generated through failure to honor the fundamental necessity for self-actualization, be eliminated.

designing life styles: 1

Do you think that the four crises are real? Can you think of others? Do you think that any or all of them can be averted?

Pick a person from the list on p. 195 and design a life style for him. Perhaps show him on a typical day. You might want to incorporate your design of a life style into your design of an environment (p. 128). Let your design reveal how you think we should deal with the four crises.

Consider carefully the meanings you attribute to the words "work" and "play." Make these meanings clear in the way you present your design.

seventeen

communication —
transportation

As a sight and sound experience, there is nothing to choose between sending a man to New York, or sending New York to him.

Already the car in the garage and the television set in the living room—both of them tools for communication—are in direct competition for man's time and energy, and this is but the beginning of the beginning.

... Where experience can be brought to the human sensory system with the speed of light, what is the point of transporting the nervous system to the experience at earth-bound speeds at all?

Don Fabun,
The Dynamics of Change

We hear so much these days about people's inability to communicate. If people can't communicate, the least they can do, says Tom Lehrer, is shut up about it!

The failure of communication, like so many of our failures, is often attributed to technology. The machine comes between person and person. It is becoming increasingly easy to spend a day conducting business—shopping, paying bills, taking in a lecture, concert, or play—without directly encountering a single human being. Because so many of our communications functions are most efficiently performed by machines—the extensions of man—we are in danger of allowing our own personal capacity for communicating to fall into disuse, and perhaps eventually to wither away. This is a lonely prospect, and one of the more frightening aspects of the new age. What can we do about it?

We can begin by looking more closely at what communication *is* and what it is *for*. Here are two descriptions of people trying to communicate. Both involve the use of the machine, but with quite a difference, as we shall see.

from THE MACHINE STOPS

E. M. Forster

Imagine, if you can, a small room, hexagonal in shape, like the cell of a bee. It is lighted neither by window nor by lamp, yet it is filled with a soft radiance. There are no apertures for ventilation, yet the air is fresh. There are no musical instruments, and yet, at the moment that my meditation opens, this room is throbbing with melodious sounds. An arm-chair is in the center, by its side a reading-desk—that is all the furniture. And in the arm-chair there sits a swaddled lump of flesh—a woman, about five feet high, with a face as white as a fungus. It is to her that the little room belongs.

An electric bell rang.

The woman touched a switch and the music was silent.

"I suppose I must see who it is," she thought, and set her chair in motion. The chair, like the music, was worked by machinery, and it rolled her to the other side of the room, where the bell still rang importunately.

"Who is it?" she called. Her voice was irritable, for she had been interrupted often since the music began. She knew several thousand people; in certain directions human intercourse had advanced enormously.

But when she listened into the receiver, her white face wrinkled into smiles, and she said:

"Very well. Let us talk, I will isolate myself. I do not expect anything important will happen for the next five minutes—for I can give you fully five minutes, Kuno. Then I must deliver my lecture on 'Music during the Australian Period'."

She touched the isolation knob, so that no one else could speak to her. Then she touched the lighting apparatus, and the little room was plunged into darkness.

"Be quick!" she called, her irritation returning. "Be quick, Kuno; here I am in the dark wasting my time."

But it was fully fifteen seconds before the round plate that she held in her hands began to glow. A faint blue light shot across it, darkening to purple, and presently she could see the image of her son, who lived on the other side of the earth, and he could see her.

"Kuno, how slow you are."

He smiled gravely.

"I really believe you enjoy dawdling."

"I have called you before, mother, but you were always busy or isolated. I have something particular to say."

"What is it, dearest boy? Be quick. Why could you not send it by pneumatic post?"

"Because I prefer saying such a thing. I want——"

"Well?"

"I want you to come and see me."

Vashti watched his face in the blue plate.

"But I can see you!" she exclaimed. "What more do you want?"

"I want to see you not through the Machine," said Kuno. "I want to speak to you not through the wearisome Machine."

"Oh, hush!" said his mother, vaguely shocked. "You musn't say anything against the Machine."

"Why not?"

"One musn't."

"You talk as if a god had made the Machine," cried the other. "I believe that you pray to it when you are unhappy. Men made it, do not forget that. Great men, but men. The Machine is much, but it is not everything. I see something like you in this plate, but I do not see you. I hear something like you through this telephone, but I do not hear you. That is why I want you to come. Come and stop with me. Pay me a visit, so that we can meet face to face, and talk about the hopes that are in my mind."

She replied that she could scarcely spare the time for a visit. . . .

For a moment Vashti felt lonely.

Then she generated the light, and the sight of her room, flooded with radiance and studded with electric buttons, revived her. There were buttons and switches everywhere—buttons to call for food, for music, for clothing. There was the hot-bath button, by pressure of which a basin of (imitation) marble rose out of the floor, filled to the brim with a warm deodorised liquid. There was the cold-bath button. There was the button that produced literature. And there were of course the buttons by which she communicated with her friends. The room, though it contained nothing, was in touch with all that she cared for in the world.

Vashti's next move was to turn off the isolation-switch, and all the accumulations of the last three minutes burst upon her. The room was filled with the noise of bells, and speaking-tubes. What was the new food like? Could she recommend it? Had she had any ideas lately? Might one tell her one's own ideas? Would she make an engagement to visit the public nurseries at an early date?—say this day month.

To most of these questions she replied with irritation—a growing quality in that accelerated age. She said that the new food was horrible. That she could not visit the public nurseries through press of engagements. That she had no ideas of her own but had just been told one—that four stars and three in the middle were like a man: she doubted there was much in it. Then she switched off her correspondents, for it was time to deliver her lecture on Australian music.

The clumsy system of public gatherings had been long since abandoned; neither Vashti nor her audience stirred from their rooms. Seated in her arm-chair she spoke, while they in their armchairs heard her, fairly well, and saw her, fairly well. She opened with a humorous account of music in the pre-Mongolian epoch, and went on to describe the great outburst of song that followed the Chinese conquest. Remote and primeval as were the methods of I-San-So and the Brisbane school, she yet felt (she said) that study of them might repay the musician of today: they had freshness; they had, above all, ideas.

Her lecture, which lasted ten minutes, was well received, and at its conclusion she and many of her audience listened to a lecture on the sea; there were ideas to be got from the sea; the speaker had donned a respirator and visited it lately. Then she fed, talked to many friends, had a bath, talked again, and summoned her bed.

The bed was not to her liking. It was too large, and she had a feeling for a small bed. Complaint was useless, for beds were of the same dimension all over the world, and to have had an alternative size would have involved vast alterations in the Machine. Vashti isolated herself—it was necessary, for neither day nor night existed under the ground—and reviewed all that had happened since she had summoned the bed last. Ideas? Scarcely any. Events—was Kuno's invitation an event?

By her side, on the little reading-desk, was a survival from the ages of litter—one book. This was the Book of the Machine. In it were instructions against every possible contingency. If she was hot or cold or dyspeptic or at loss for a word, she went to the book, and it told her which button to press. The Central Committee published it. In accordance with a growing habit, it was richly bound.

Sitting up in the bed, she took it reverently in her hands. She glanced round the glowing room as if some one might be watching her. Then, half ashamed, half joyful, she murmured "O Machine! O Machine!" and raised the volume to her lips. Thrice she kissed it, thrice inclined her head, thrice she felt the delirium of acquiescence. Her ritual performed, she turned to page 1367, which gave the times of the departure of the air-ships from the island in the southern hemisphere, under whose soil she lived, to the island in the northern hemisphere, whereunder lived her son.

She thought, "I have not the time."

She made the room dark and slept; she awoke and made the room light; she ate and exchanged ideas with her friends, and listened to music and attended lectures; she made the room dark and slept. Above her, beneath her, and around her, the Machine hummed eternally; she did not notice the noise, for she had been born with it in her ears. The earth, carrying her, hummed as it sped through silence, turning her now to the invisible sun, now to the invisible stars. She awoke and made the room light.

"Kuno!"

"I will not talk to you," he answered, "until you come."

"Have you been on the surface of the earth since we spoke last?"

His image faded.

Again she consulted the book. She became very nervous and lay back in her chair palpitating. Think of her as without teeth or hair. Presently she directed the chair to the wall, and pressed an unfamiliar button. The wall swung apart slowly. Through the opening she saw a tunnel that curved slightly, so that its goal was not visible. Should she go to see her son, here was the beginning of the journey.

Of course she knew all about the communication-system. There was nothing mysterious in it. She would summon a car and it would fly with her down the tunnel until it reached the lift that communicated with the air-ship station: the system had been in use for many, many years, long before the universal establishment of the Machine. And of course she had studied the civilization that had immediately preceded her own—the civilization that had mistaken the functions of the system, and had used it for bringing people to things, instead of for bringing things to people. Those funny old days, when men went for change of air instead of changing the air in their rooms! And yet—she was frightened of the tunnel: she had not seen it since her last child was born. It curved —but not quite as she remembered; it was brilliant—but not quite as brilliant as a lecturer had suggested. Vashti was seized with the terrors of direct experience. She shrank back into the room, and the wall closed up again.

"Kuno," she said, "I cannot come to see you. I am not well."

Immediately an enormous apparatus fell on to her out of the ceiling, a thermometer was automatically inserted between her lips, a stethoscope was automatically laid upon her heart. She lay powerless. Cool pads soothed her forehead. Kuno had telegraphed to her doctor.

So the human passions still blundered up and down in the Machine. Vashti drank the medicine that the doctor projected into her mouth, and the machinery retired into the ceiling.

One of the most important ends to be served by technology is to conserve for man a resource which is severely limited: time. But what is time for? To spend, naturally. There is little profit and less pleasure in saving time by failing to do those very things which make life worthwhile.

What makes life worthwhile for Vashti? Do you share her values? Is this the direction in which we are moving?

Consider, now, the following episode, from *The Sand Pebbles*, a novel about a tough young American sailor and his adventures as engineer aboard a Yangtze River gunboat in 1925 during the Chinese revolution.

When Jake Holman first joins the ship's crew, he is shocked to learn that the ship, though staffed by American seamen, is run by Chinese coolies. In particular, he is aghast at the condition of the engines and the fact that none of the crew has any knowledge or concern about how they run. He finds that an eager young coolie named Po-han has been assuming almost total responsibility for the engines.

Jake Holman loved machinery in the way some other men loved God, women, and their country. He loved main engines most of all, because they were the deep heart and power center of any ship and all the rest was trimming, much of it useless.

Resolving to make a complete study and overhaul of the engines, he is encouraged to discover that Po-han's respect and concern for them equals his own.

from THE SAND PEBBLES

Richard McKenna

After supper he went below again, in clean dungarees, to check some of his sketches. Po-han followed him and he would point to one of Holman's sketched crosses and then to a particular valve and ask, "Same? B'long same?" Po-han was always wrong, but he knew that there was something very wonderful about those marks on paper, if he could only grasp the secret. He worked his lips and screwed up his features and he looked about to cry. Holman could read that expression and he had often known in himself the painful, tantalizing feeling behind it. Something in Holman answered to the young bilge coolie.

He tried to explain, but the pidgin English they shared was not enough. Po-han could not get the idea of breaking down the great mass of piping into separate systems. He could not say what was moving in what direction through any of the pipes that Holman pointed out. He did not even have the idea of stuff moving through pipes. All of Holman's doubts came back. How could these bilge coolies ever tend machinery?

"Come over here," he told Po-han.

Po-han followed him over to the feed pumps. Holman choked the throttle on the duty pump and dropped the pressure fifty pounds.

"You fix," he told Po-han.

Po-han eased open the steam inlet and restored the pressure. The hot well stood just aft of the pumps. Holman knelt and opened the rundown valve. Po-han watched the water level drop in the gauge glass with his Chinese eyes as wide and round as he could get them. Just as the water went out of sight, Holman closed the rundown valve.

"You fix," he said.

Po-han practically flew to the make-up feed pump and set it clacking. He watched tensely until the water level built up again and then secured the pump. Holman tried him on several other operations and questioned him on them all. Po-han knew what to do, but he did not know what it was that he did. He knew in a vague way that steam and water moved through pumps and valves, but when he twisted a valve he did not realize that he was opening or closing it. To Po-han, all that he did was isolated little magics that moved a pressure gauge pointer or a water level back to the right place. What he had glimpsed in Holman's sketches, what his eager, wistful eyes were reaching out for, was the big magic that would make a living whole out of all the little magics. Well, some navy engineers he had known were not much better off than Po-han, Holman thought. He decided to try to show Po-han the steam cycle. He started at the boiler.

"Inside b'long steam. Live steam," he said, thumping the boiler shell. "Strong steam."

Po-han nodded. They traced the steam from the boiler shell to the feed pump throttle, and Po-han could not understand the difference between live steam going in and exhaust steam coming out. He just did not have the basic words and saying "exhaust" to him did not give him the idea behind the word. It was no good showing him pressure gauges. Po-han thought fifteen pounds on the exhaust gauge was "moh plashah" than one hundred thirty pounds on the steam gauge, because the exhaust gauge and its numerals were physically the larger. He could not read the numerals and he did not know the meaning of "pressure."

"Jesus. I don't know how to tell you, Po-han," Holman said.

Disappointment began dulling the eager pain on Po-han's face.

"We'll try a different way," Holman said.

This time Holman acted it out. He was live steam, coming along the line snorting and bulging his muscles, and the live steam did work in the feed pump, Holman reaching in to the crosshead with both arms, grunting heavily, pretending to lift the piston rod up and down as it stroked, and then the steam came out the exhaust valve wheezing, drooping, muscles slack, staggered over to the condenser and went to sleep, Holman's folded hands beside his head.

Po-han went through the same act. His eyes never left Holman's face. He understood that the steam got tired in the pump, but he thought it died in the condenser.

"Maskee. This side steam makee dead," Holman said, slapping the condenser shell. He knelt and bled water from a cock on the air pump discharge. "Before steam, just now water," he told Po-han. "Water belong dead steam."

"Stim dead! Stim dead!"

Po-han knelt with the water flowing over his fingers and his eyes sparkled. He knew fire turned water to steam in the boiler, but apparently he had never realized that a flow of river water through the condenser turned steam back into water. The thought excited him. Holman became water and made undulating motions along the condensate discharge line to the hot well. Po-han followed, undulating too. At the hot well he pointed to the water in the gauge glass.

"Stim dead!"

Holman nodded and grinned. He undulated from the hot well along the feed suction line into the water end of the feed pump. Po-han followed. Holman came out of the feed pump still undulating silently, but stiffly, fists clenched and muscles bulging to indicate increase in pressure. Po-han followed suit, but he looked puzzled. He did not understand pressure. Holman undulated stiffly through the feed heater and began making a sizzling noise.

"This side makee hot," he told Po-han.

He had Po-han feel the temperature difference between inlet and outlet. Po-han understood. Holman sizzled and undulated along the feed line to the feed check on the boiler shell, pushed open an imaginary trap door, clacked and went into the boiler. Po-han clacked and went in too.

His face was like a searchlight. He looked at Holman and tapped the bottom of the boiler gauge glass. "Stim dead!" Then he tapped the steam space above the water in the glass. "Stim live! Stim live!" It was wonderful to see his face. He was just realizing in his own fashion the life-and-death cycle of the steam, endlessly repeated, and how it tied together pumps, piping and heat exchangers into the big magic. He looked like Columbus discovering America.

Suddenly, his Chinese face alive with joy, he began acting out the steam cycle again, as Holman had done it. Holman followed, grinning. When Po-han came back as water to the feed pump, his face shadowed and he stopped.

"This side . . . how fashion . . ."

He didn't know how to ask and Holman didn't know how to tell him.

"Pressure," Holman said. "Makee pressure."

"Plashah." It was just a noise in the air to Po-han.

"Push. Workee," Holman said. "Inside boiler live steam have got too much pressure. Suppose water wanchee go inside boiler, no have got pressure, no can open door."

He imitated the clack of the feed-check valve. Po-han was trying very hard, almost crying, but he couldn't get it. Holman dropped the feed pressure by fifty pounds and tapped the gauge.

"You belong water. Just now no have got pressure," he told Po-han.

He motioned Po-han to come along the feed line and Po-han did, undulating stiffly and doubtfully.

"My belong live steam, have got too much pressure," Holman said.

He began snorting and grasped Po-han's bare, sweaty shoulders and pushed him backward, sliding on the oily floorplates, to beside the feed pump. Then he stopped and raised the feed pressures back to normal and tapped the gauge. The feed check on the boiler began clacking again.

"*Now* you have got pressure!" Holman put Po-han's hands against his shoulders. "Now push me, pushee live steam!" he said. Po-han pushed weakly. "Workee! Have got too much plashah!" Holman said. Po-han pushed harder and Holman's feet began to slide. He slid backward, his hands resting lightly on Po-han's shoulders, and he saw the pure light of joyful learning come back into Po-han's face. This time he really had the idea, with no dark spots left in it anywhere.

"Plashah! Plashah!" Po-han cried.

"Pressure!" Holman echoed him, grinning happily too.

Jake Holman's task would have been simpler and shorter if he could have shown Po-han an animated cartoon film strip. Better still, the engine might have been fully automated and cybernated. Or, better even than that, the gunboat might have been replaced by a Sabre Jet. Too bad Holman did not have the benefits of modern technology. Or is it?

What is communication? Communication is the exchange of information. We may include anything from art to data processing under that broad umbrella.

The exchange of information requires a sender and a receiver. For example, as John Dewey pointed out many decades ago, a "concert" includes both musicians and audience. Of course, it is possible for a musician to be his own audience; he is then both sender and receiver.

There are many communications systems, each with at least one language, medium, and purpose, and, most importantly, each with at least one mind or brain participating in the exchange.

The *medium* may be any "conductor"—whether paint, wood, stone, paper, print, metal, electricity, the human body, the human voice, or these and others in combination.

The *language* may be any ordered arrangement of symbols—whether verbal, numerical, pictorial, rhythmical, etc. Wherever mind can order a pattern which can be distinguished by one or more of our senses, there is the possibility of language.

The *message* may be anything from the most delicate indication of a feeling-tone (bleegh!) to a highly complex and abstract formula ($E = mc^2$).

The exchange may take place within a person, between or among persons, with or without the intervention of machines, between machines—in fact, wherever there is *mind* to process the information. Ants, bees, dolphins, extraterrestrial intelligences are all, at least potentially, communicators among themselves and with man.

And the *purpose* of a communications system? If we can determine that, we may be in a position to decide when to let our machines do our communicating and when to do it ourselves. The problem is comparable to the problem raised by McIrvine in his account of his dream about cybernated golf. As he later explains,

Clearly the response to the professor's suggestion of a golf-playing machine is this: Why would we want to replace men on golf courses with machines? So long as our operational definition concentrates on the physical process of moving the ball, the answer is simply that men play an inferior game. Only if the game's definition is enlarged to include the human values of our personal involvement is there any logical reason to impede the cybernation of golf.

"The human values of our personal involvement"—is this perhaps the key? When the value to be gained by the exchange of information is the value of personal involvement, of the experience itself—as, for example, in love-making—shall we reserve this communication for ourselves? And when the value of the exchange is not in the process

> "The task ahead will be to assign to the machine those things it can best do, and reserve for man those things which he must provide and control."
>
> David Sarnoff,
> p. 181

of exchange but rather accrues merely to some end served by the exchange—as, for example, getting our groceries delivered—shall we leave that communication to the machines?

Does this touchstone help us understand our reactions to the episodes from "The Machine Stops" and *The Sand Pebbles?* Let us try it out by applying it to the following article. At the same time we may get a glimmering of what is in store for us in the rapidly spreading communications revolution.

In 1968 the future of television looked like this to one writer. From your vantage point, a little further into the future, how good do his guesses seem? Are there factors this author did not anticipate which have influenced or changed the trend?

LOOKING AHEAD

David Lachenbruch

America's most celebrated child prodigy—television—is now 21 years old. Among its accomplishments in that time have been the manufacture of more than 140 million television sets (of which 85 million are still in use and nearly 60 million have already been junked) and the launching of close to 800 TV stations and one flying nun.

In 21 years, America's TV stations have broadcast a total of some 50 million hours of programs (and com-

mercials). This would take more than 6000 years to watch, on a 24-hour-a-day basis, if you could stand it. Among television's major technical achievements have been nation-wide and world-wide interconnections for instantaneous programming, and a color-transmission system which has been in use for fourteen years. No other institution or industry in our history has achieved so much growth or so much influence in so short a time.

But that's just the beginning.

In this year of 21 A.T., remarkable and revolutionary changes already are starting—changes which will transform television from a passive to an active member of the family, or, as some critics might say, from idiot box to genius box.

Today, your TV set is just a piece of furniture full of thingamabobs. It shows pictures when you turn it on, closes its eye and becomes a sleeping monster when you turn it off. It's easy to think of it as an appliance, like a refrigerator, a vacuum cleaner, or a stove. But there's a big difference: An appliance is capable of performing one basic function—a refrigerator just stands there and gets cold, a stove gets hot, a vacuum cleaner draws in dirt.

There are three reasons why the sleeping monster in your living room is something else: It's already a bundle of sophisticated electronics, and these same electronics—with modifications and additions—can be taught many new tricks. It can communicate, convey intelligence (broadly speaking, this includes deodorant commercials). It's plugged in to the world.

The big changes which are about to occur will convert your TV link with the world from an "appliance" to a "system," as new functions are added, a few at a time. The result will be an electronic-communication center that touches on almost every phase of your daily life.

Many of the elements that will go into your TV communication system are already in limited use or test stages—such as two-way Picturephone service, wired television services to the home, transmission of printed matter by TV, home video recorders.

While it's difficult to put technology on a timetable, let's look into the future at bench marks in television's next 21 years as they might occur, based on the forecasts of many scientists, engineers and marketing men.

IN FIVE YEARS (1973)

Your television set will sprout several exciting new uses, and already it will start making like an all-purpose communication center. A new triple-threat accessory (less than $500) or built-in feature (adding perhaps $300 to the cost of the set) is the home video recorder, or HVR.

The HVR is sort of a picture-and-sound storage closet. When ready for the mass market, it will be as easy to use as a record changer and will broaden your TV set's horizon in three main ways: (1) It will record any TV show for playback in color any time you want to see it. With a built-in automatic timer, you can set the HVR to record a program you don't want to miss, even if you won't be home, for viewing at your leisure. (2) It will show color picture-and-sound "video records"—plays, movies, telecourses—which you can buy at the store, borrow from the library or perhaps rent through a Show-of-the-Month Club. (3) It will include a midget TV camera for "instant home sound movies" which you can make yourself, starring your family and friends, for showing on your TV set.

Your selection of channels will be considerably broadened as the result of the beginning of a new "communication pipe" between your set and the outside world. This is a television service which comes to your home by wire in the same manner as electricity and telephone, and is an outgrowth of cable systems now in use which already serve well over 2 million homes.

By 1973, your wired TV system should provide you with 20 or 25 channels, including the regular on-the-air stations. The extra wired channels, in the early years at least, will specialize in local services—such as continuous weather forecasts (already featured by some 500 cable TV systems), news-ticker service (more than fifty systems now have this feature), live coverage of city-council meetings, at-home school-room telecasts for your children to watch when they're sick. One of the most interesting new services may be "Teleshop," which will show, in color, items on sale at local stores. To shop for groceries, toys or a new dress, you'll simply watch the appropriate channel and place your order by phone. The price of the things you buy will be added to the regular monthly bill you receive from the wired-TV system.

By 1973, most homes will have at least one color set. Large-screen sets will lose some of their bulk, as a result of a one-third reduction in the depth of the color tube. The innards will also shrink because of extensive use of tiny integrated circuits in place of conventional parts. Picture brightness will be nearly double that of 1968 sets. You'll rarely have to touch a knob, because all color adjustments will be automatic. A new tuner, with virtually no moving parts, will make chair-side remote tuning less expensive and more popular.

IN TEN YEARS (1978)

Would you believe that your television set will learn to write? By 1978, it's quite possible that facsimile service —"fax" for short—will be added to your home TV communications system. From impulses sent over the air or through your wire-communication pipe, fax will provide you with an almost unlimited variety of reading material —newspapers, magazines, books, pictures. By pre-setting a dial on your TV set before going to bed you'll be able to choose your reading matter for the next day. The high-speed electronic printing will be done while you sleep, and your day's reading will be waiting for you when you arise.

There'll be changes in the appearance of your television set. The color tube will be now so thin that it can be hung on the wall in an attractive furniture frame. The controls and works (including the fax printer) will be housed in a compact table-style cabinet alongside your favorite easy chair.

Every room in the house will be equipped with its own TV screen, not only for programs but for your home closed-circuit system. Tiny cameras will be mounted wherever you wish about the house. Push the proper

button in any room and the screen will show you who's at the door, whether baby's asleep and what the kids are up to out in the yard.

There'll be other, more portable, home TV cameras. A battery-operated color camera, about the size of today's 8mm. film cameras, will be designed for making home video recordings. Since it will contain its own low-power transmitter, the camera no longer will be tied by cable to your TV set or video recorder.

While almost all home sets will be in color, there'll also be pocket black-and-white portables. Some of these may operate without batteries or line cords, "stealing" power through the air from near-by TV or radio stations. Some slightly larger portables will have built-in video players to provide up to an hour's canned sight-and-sound entertainment from a slide-in, graham-cracker-sized program cartridge.

And 1978 could go down in history as the year the world saw and heard the first live colorcast from the moon. It's not clear whether the commentary will be in English or Russian.

IN FIFTEEN YEARS (1983)

Your communication pipe by this time will be two-way and your TV picture will be "hi-vi" (the video equivalent of hi-fi). A change in aspect ratio (width vs. height) will give the TV screen the proportions of a Cinema-Scope picture—but the image will be even sharper than today's motion picture or glossy magazine photos as the result of a switch from the present 525 horizontal TV lines to 1000 or more, vastly increasing the resolution of the picture.

And at long last, you'll be able to talk back to your TV screen. Your communication center will now have a group of numbered push buttons for use with its wired TV service. There'll be a new, more sophisticated multichannel shopping service, in which purchases will be made by pressing buttons in the proper sequence, the cost of the purchase being deducted directly from your bank account, if you wish. You'll be able to register your opinion on any issue—or even your approval or disapproval of a TV show—and see it tallied almost immediately on the screen. When you take telecourses, you'll answer quiz and exam questions by using the button keyboard. Some day—but probably later than 1983—you may vote in local and national elections via TV, without leaving your home. The computerized tally board will flash up-to-the-minute election returns on the screen almost instantaneously.

Home Picturephone service could be a reality by 1983, adding sight to everyday telephone conversations. For private tête-a-têtes, there'll be a small screen built into the telephone instrument. But entire families will be able to have living-room-to-living-room visits by switching the Picturephone image to the big-screen set.

IN 21 YEARS OR SO (1989—?)

By the end of television's second 21 years, true three-dimensional video could be a reality. A new type of flat screen, replacing the thin picture tube, will display pictures virtually life-size

and in realistic depth, without the need for special viewing eye-glasses.

Your communication pipe will be computerized by connection to a nation-wide grid of electronic brains. Using your now-expanded home push-button keyboard, you'll be able to dial virtually any TV program, play, book, movie, concert or telecourse you wish from a huge catalog and have it delivered immediately—or any time you want it—to your 3-D screen or colorfax printer.

The computer grid will be at your service 24 hours a day to solve math problems, tell you your bank balance, help junior with his homework, look up recipes, make travel reservations, map out auto routes (and supply you with instructions for the exact setting of your autopilot) and perform a wide variety of other services.

Some of the services which may be available are almost beyond our imagination today. Take one possible example—let's call it "Dial-a-View." As the Nation's population multiplies, an ever-increasing number of people may live in huge apartment cities—many of them completely windowless. The giant 3-D color screen in every

> "The earth carrying her, hummed as it sped through silence, turning her now to the invisible sun, now to the invisible stars."
>
> "The Machine Stops"
> p. 216

room may literally become your "window on the world." At the push of a button, you may be able to choose your own environment—your TV-screen "window" would look out on mountains, pasture, seascape, city skyline, or some exotic foreign vista—in utmost realism, depth, and motion, with changing light patterns, according to the time of day or night, and

even sounds (the roll of the waves, temple bells of India, the city's roar). Or, if you prefer, you may be able to dial exact reproductions of art masterpieces electronically "hung" on your wall from the world's great museums.

Your TV communications system will also be an active companion. It may be your Telegame board—from chess to football—with the central computer as your opponent. In football, for example, you may take the quarterback's role, calling the plays by means of the keyboard. The computer constructs the actual game on the basis of these plays—and you watch "your" game on the screen.

Another possible future service might be kiddy radar. To locate the children, Mother uses her trusty keyboard. A map of the neighborhood appears on the screen, with each of her children identified by a special color or symbol. An almost microscopic "identification transponder," sewn into the children's clothes, identifies them immediately on the radar screen.

Despite the almost incredible complexity of the future TV set, repairs will be less of a problem than they are today. Breakthroughs in ultra-

reliable circuits and the virtual elimination of individual components will make serious trouble extremely infrequent. When one part of the set does fail, just dial your friend the central computer for complete repair-it-yourself instructions—usually which plug-in circuit module to replace.

No one can swear it's going to work out exactly like this. But the experts are reasonably sure that there are some things about television which will remain pretty much the same. In spite of its future as a complete communications system, it will continue to be the family's main provider of entertainment. What kind of entertainment? Well, for example, on Sunday evenings there'll be *The Ed Sullivan Show* . . .

from A "COMMIE" IN EVERY HOME

Robert Russel

. . . There's a great deal of talk about machines dehumanizing and alienating the individual. I think it's only true if we let it be. The great thing about the new computerized technology is its potentiality to serve the individual personally, privately, patiently, unquestioningly. The intrinsic element in the system making this personal attention possible is the feedback loop. This permits the machine to care about us as individuals (if it is so programmed). Combining the feedback loop with the larger memories and time-sharing possibilities of the newer machines, each of us will soon be able to use the machine or the system of machines, as though it or they were personally programmed for our exclusive use. . . .

. . . Cyrus Levinthal, MIT's brilliant young geneticist, has created a most

elegant and beautiful program for Project MAC which points the way to new art forms. He has analyzed the structure of a long molecule of genetic material into mathematical terms. Programmed into the time-sharing computer, a model of the molecule appears on the TV-like display of the Project MAC console: a white latticework on a black background. Levinthal is then able to rotate the molecule, head over heels or spinning side to side, so that it appears to have a three-dimensional form, like a simple animated film. In addition, he is able to make the molecule model change its shape and structure as it would on the addition of other chemicals. Not only is the display extremely beautiful to behold, as it moves and evolves; but one's admiration grows as one's understanding increases. Imagine a teacher conducting

Robert Russel, "A 'Commie' in Every Home," from *Take One Magazine*. Feb. 1967. Reprinted by permission of the author.

a chemical experiment with his class, while at the same time the commie display shows exactly what is happening in model form. What might take years to teach at the college level can become clear to a six-year-old. In this sense, I think of the programmer as the artist of the new medium. Just as Keats's Grecian urn has yielded the secrets of its beauty to mathematical analysis, now the mathematician has an instrument to express the elegance of his ideas in compelling and enlightening visual form.

Let us consider briefly the effects of this new medium on one of our more traditional and expensive institutions: education. The great things happening in the world of science are beyond the range of our senses: electronics, chemistry, atomic energy, biology, and many other sciences demand a theoretical understanding of what we will never directly see. The teaching film can show us what happens in one of the invisible zones of science, but it is a cold cumbersome device alongside a program like Levinthal's displayed on the commie screen. For, with the feedback loop, Levinthal's model changes as the student adds a chemical, turns up the temperature of the experiment or shakes the test-tube, showing him exactly what happens when he does this or that. Thus, each student has a personal relationship, through the com-

"Po-han knew what to do, but he didn't know what it was that he did."
From *The Sand Pebbles*,
p. 218

mie, with the process or idea he is studying. This is of vital importance to the educational process. Give each student a commie, access to a series of programs like Levinthal's, a room of his own to study in, and a teacher to guide him occasionally and to steer him into new explorations, and in one generation we can "turn on" the country to knowledge, fulfilment, and power. We can escape from the incredible burden of schoolrooms, the stupidity of organizing growing minds into rigid groups of twenty or thirty, the insufferable inefficiency of curricula and exams which prevent us from learning what we happen to be interested in, and from the greatest burden of all, the ignorance and incompetence of the average teacher, attempting to do an impossible job. . . .

Does the future of communication depicted in "Looking Ahead" strike you more favorably than that in "The Machine Stops," written some forty years earlier?

One way in which the two accounts differ is that Forster gives us a picture of a human being, while the author of "Looking Ahead" shows us the capabilities of a system.

What verbal picture might we draw of a human being who uses this system?

A Member of Parliament wrote: "Television has within its power to decide what kind of people we become. Nothing less."

Do you think that if the system described in "Looking Ahead" is actually developed we will become like Vashti?

"Looking Ahead" and "A 'Commie' in Every Home" seem to suggest that we will not only use machines to relieve us of chores, and to do our pragmatic communicating, but also to involve us in communications experiences which are rewarding in themselves. The new computerized communications systems can overcome one of the main drawbacks of earlier systems. In earlier systems we have found ourselves cast exclusively either in the role of receiver (watching TV) or in the role of sender (paying bills with IBM cards). Either of these roles pursued without the other quickly palls. Our frustration comes from the lack of feedback.

When, however, we are dealing with machines which permit genuine interaction through their feedback mechanisms, we may find that they do not impoverish us, but rather enhance and extend our experiences.

Russel, in "A 'Commie' in Every Home," suggests that the feedback mechanism makes it possible to "personalize" or "individualize" our transactions with machines. Is this literally true, or is it an illusion or metaphor?

Is there any reason why we should feel more pleasurably involved when we "commune" with nature than when we "commune" with machines?

In "I Wish I Was a Fish," we raised some questions about man's relationship to nature. If this issue interests you, take a look at pp. 30–31. You might also look ahead to p. 325.

Many people who are infatuated with "thinking machines," and many who are not are fascinated by the analogue between the human brain, with its neural system, and the machine brain, with its electronic system. If you would like to know more about this processor of information—what is going on in that invisible realm between input and output—take a look at these writings:

"Automation," in
Dynamics of Change

"The Computer and the Brain,"
by John Von Neumann

Cybernetics, by Norbert Wiener

Still, if we turn over to machines both the pleasurable and the practical communications activities which have formerly linked us with other persons, will not our occasions for relating personally to others be drastically reduced? Many people believe that they will, and in fact already are. They argue that we must create new modes and new occasions for communicating.

We explore some possible new modes of communication in the next probe, when we look at the future of education.

Let us now see if we can close the circle within which communication and transportation may be seen as different ways of accomplishing many of the same functions.

To understand how the development of the new communications technologies can help overcome the disadvantages of our transportation systems, we must examine what those disadvantages are. There are three:

They waste our time.
They waste our space.
They waste our energies.

How can a communications system help? Arthur C. Clarke puts it this way:

> As communications improve, so the need for transportation will decrease. Our grandchildren will scarcely believe that millions once spent hours of every day fighting their way into city offices—where, as often as not, they did nothing that could not have been achieved over telecommunication links.

Quite simply, crossing space physically (transportation) takes longer and is more harrowing than crossing it electronically (communication). Can you think of other situations in which communication can eliminate the need for transportation and thus save us time and energy?

How many of our vehicles—with all the space-cluttering paraphernalia of highways, tracks, docks, garages, airports, traffic jams, gas stations, noise, crashes, pollution—could we dispense with if we made full use of our communications technology?

How much of our traveling is for the purpose of communicating? Consider this suggestion of Arthur Clarke:

> The business of the future may be run by executives who are scarcely ever in each other's physical presence. It will not even have an address of a central office—only the equivalent of a telephone number. For its files and records will be space rented in the memory units of computers that could be located anywhere on Earth: the information

stored in them could read off on high-speed printers whenever any of the firm's offices needed it.

The time may come when half of the world's business will be transacted through vast memory banks beneath the Arizona desert, the Mongolian steppes, the Labrador muskeg, or wherever land is cheap and useless for any other purpose. For all spots on Earth, of course, would be equally accessible to the beams of the relay satellites: To sweep from pole to pole would mean merely turning the directional antennas through seventeen degrees.

And so the captains of industry of the twenty-first century may live where they please, running their affairs through computer keyboards and information-handling machines in their homes. Only on rare occasions would there be any need for more of the personal touch than could be obtained via wide-screen full-color TV. The business lunch of the future could be conducted perfectly well with the two halves of the table ten thousand miles apart; all that would be missing would be the handshakes and exchange of cigars.

We might mention, parenthetically, that there may very well be fewer lunching captains; machine captains will work right through lunch.

If we reserve traveling for those occasions when we need to communicate face to face or to experience something in the flesh, then we have a chance of developing transportation systems which serve that purpose, without wasting our time, energies, and space.

It is important to note that the United States has never had a transportation system. We have had bits and pieces. A system of transportation for people is people-oriented in the sense that to be effective it must minimize time loss, energy loss, and psychological and emotional strain. For a system to be developed, the gaps between the different elements of transportation must be filled without sacrificing human values.

from TRANSPORTATION IN THE WORLD
OF THE FUTURE

Hal Hellman

On his way into the kitchen, Andrew Mann touched the "Car" button on the electronic communications panel in the living room. By the time he had finished breakfast a rented Electra-car, delivered automatically from the town depot, was waiting for him at the door.

Andrew slid into the sleek two-seater, inserted his All-Credit card (which acted as both ignition key and accounting agent), stepped on the accelerator, and was on his way.

Taken from *Transportation in the World of the Future* by Hal Hellman, copyright © 1968 by Hal Hellman and reprinted by permission of M. Evans and Company, Inc.

A short, two-mile drive brought him to the electronic highway. As he approached the entrance, he punched out his destination on the dashboard console, which automatically beamed the information, plus the car code, to the highway control computer.

Immediately, the computer announced via his car radio, "Sorry, Mr. Mann, but you will have to wait about two minutes before you can get onto the Autoway. We have just reached critical density. However, if you will drive onto the ramp at your right, you can relinquish manual control; the automatic system will take over and will check out your car at the same time.

"I see," continued Highway Control, "that you are going to the Long Distance Transportation Terminal in New York. Since traffic is particularly heavy this morning, some of the vehicles are being routed through the new Hudson Tunnel. Your distance to the terminal is therefore 28 miles; the trip will take 17 minutes. We will inform you when you are approaching your destination. Please switch to automatic now."

Andrew Mann flicked the proper switch and relaxed. "Now for an important decision," he chuckled. "Shall I read, sleep, or watch the news . . . ?"

Andrew opened his eyes. He could feel the car decelerating smoothly but perceptibly. His car radio came on and a gentle voice said, "Mr. Mann, you are approaching the terminal. We hope you enjoyed your ride. Thank you."

Andrew shook himself slightly and mumbled, "So soon?" He checked his cathode ray tube map display. Sure enough, the little white dot showed that he was entering the midtown New York area. "Hm. Must have slept right through the ride."

The Electra-car, still moving at a rapid clip, entered the new Hudson Tunnel and a moment later came to a smooth halt in the basement of the giant Long Distance Terminal. Andrew got out, punched the "Park" button, and watched the car glide off—to be used by someone else. He mused, "Seems to me I read somewhere that people had to park their own cars a hundred years ago. Seems hard to believe."

A few steps brought him to the glidewalk. He stepped on and a lovely female voice sounded in his ear. "Welcome, traveler, to the first fully integrated public transportation system on earth. Where are you bound?"

"Area 303, Oakland, California."

"Oh, I'm sorry, but the hypersonic transport has just left, and there won't be another one for two hours."

"That's all right. I'm in no rush and I would like to use the 'Tube' anyway. I've never used it before."

"Fine. The next train comes through from Boston in 25 minutes. A pod is waiting, however, in the subterminal. Unless you have some other need, I suggest you get off the glidewalk at Exit 2, which you will reach in a few moments. You will see the pod off to the right of the Exit sign. How much luggage do you have with you?"

"Just a hand case. I can handle it."

"Good. Do you have your All-Credit card with you?"

"Yes."

"Would you please show it to the accounting machine on your right?"

Andrew flashed his card, and the computer's voice continued, "Thank you. We'll charge your travel account at the end of the month. Will that be satisfactory?"

"Yes, that's fine."

"As you probably know, the main train does not stop as it comes through. The pod will be accelerated to the same speed as the main section and will then hook onto it. The train travels at roughly 1,000 miles per hour. Therefore, your trip will take just under three hours, and will bring you into the San Francisco terminal at 9:17 A.M. local time."

Andrew grinned and glanced at his watch. It read 9:25.

"At the terminal," his guide continued, "you have a choice of transportation modes. Are you perhaps going to the new two-mile-high building in Oakland?"

"Why, yes. I am."

"Well, in that case you could use the new Ele-Car, which would take you directly from the terminal to the building and then up to the floor of your choice. Or, since you are not in a great hurry and might like to get up above ground for a while, we would suggest that you take the Air-Cushion Vehicle. It leaves directly from the terminal, crosses the bay and continues right into Oakland. It's a beautiful ride. The ACV then connects with a mini-bus that will take you to your destination. However, the total trip may be lengthened by ten minutes or so."

"That's all right. The air-cushion mode sounds like a good idea."

"Very well, then. When you get off at the San Francisco terminal, take the escalator marked 'ACV'. Incidentally, don't worry about the details. You will receive printed instructions on the train. All right, step off here, please."

Andrew stepped off sideways onto a belt that was moving in the same direction as he was, but more slowly, and then finally onto solid ground. He walked toward the pod, a sleek silver train-car—without windows.

His unseen companion anticipated his question. "Although there are no windows in the train, a large 3-D screen will show highlights of the areas through which you will be passing on your cross-country trip. There are also small screens and earpieces which will provide a wide choice of private entertainment; they may be used for long-distance calls, if you wish. For your further convenience, an autobarber, a snack bar, and a dictatyper are also available. If you need anything else, please ring. There is a hostess on board who will be happy to serve you. Good-by now."

Does the last third of the twentieth century hold the key to a system of transportation, or is Hellman's projection a pipe dream? Here are some attempts to improve on our present approach. How satisfactory are they? Can we do better?

DREAM COMBINATION

A 5-WAY TRANSIT SYSTEM

Elmont Waite

The dream of an ideal urban transit system in the 1980's really should include five different systems, from moving sidewalks to super-speed trains, Stanford Research Institute reported yesterday.

And for a city like San Francisco, it might cost $720 million to install the quintuplet system, according to SRI estimates.

SRI made a year-long study for the U.S. Urban Transportation Administration to predict future urban transit needs and to suggest feasible systems.

SYSTEMS

Some fifty transportation concepts of the future were reviewed by the SRI team before it settled on five "families" of systems as the best combination to meet big-city needs. The new systems would supplement, not replace the private automobile.

The team noted that already nearly half of all city residents have inadequate mobility—and that the situation is getting worse. By the year 2000, urban travel demands are expected to triple.

"Existing transportation systems are simply not meeting the needs," said Clark Henderson, leader of the SRI team.

SOCIETY

"As a result, we have generated an auto-dominated society which is causing serious problems of traffic congestion, environmental pollution and freeway disruption. Meanwhile, many nondriving citizens are left relatively immobile."

FIVE

The five recommended systems:

For short trips (stations one or two blocks apart), moving sidewalks that could carry passengers at 6 to 15 miles per hour for 5 or 10 cents per ride.

For longer trips within local areas, little electric automobiles, driven by the customers, stored at stands no more than a couple of blocks apart. They would be picked up at one stand, returned to another near the driver's destination. Cost: 10 to 15 cents per ride.

For similar-length trips for nondrivers, a Dial-a-Bus system, dispatching mini-buses by radio to pick up passengers at or near their homes, rather than running on regular routes. Cost, 35 cents per ride.

TRIPS

For medium and long trips throughout the urban area, a network of small automated (driverless) vehicles controlled by computers. The passengers would simply get in and push a button to indicate his destination, and get there at speeds up to 70 miles per hour at a cost of 3 to 6 cents per mile.

For long trips, of up to fifty miles, with stations four to eight miles apart, electric trains that could reach a maximum speed of 160 miles per hour, at a cost of 3 to 5 cents per mile. (This "fast transit link," as the SRI team called it, corresponds roughly with inter-city systems like BART, although faster.)

The SRI scientists said all of these new systems could be developed within six to thirteen years at a cost of ap-

Reprinted by permission from *The San Francisco Chronicle.*

proximately $1 billion, and that installation of them in a typical city would cost about $1000 per person. For San Francisco, that would be something over $720 million. SRI, however, said the systems should repay their construction costs and pay their operating costs from fares.

THE PEOPLE-TAINER

... [W]e might begin to find, in the next twenty years, the application of some of the already advanced technologies we have for the movement of goods to the movement of people. No manufacturer would put up with a system in which his product has to be repackaged at each change of carriers. One might look at the camper-back or the travel trailer, with their compact comfort, and ask if they could not be adapted to a system of "people-tainers." When the family wants to go on a long, involved trip, the transport service provides the "people-tainer," complete with its fold down beds, toilet facilities, closet space, view windows, etc., whose dimensions have been standardized for handling over the whole system. The "people-tainer" is pulled up to the family's front door, the kids, bedding, food for snacks, toys, etc. are stored in it, and away they go to the closest terminal, to be picked up by forklift and placed, with similar units on a flat bed railroad car, a highway rig, or a super-air transport. Luggage would be about as necessary as high-button shoes. The "people-tainer" could be handled—just as containerized cargo is today—on all parts of the system; and when it arrives at its destination, it would simply be lifted by elevator into open compartments in hotel or apartment house frames, where the "people-tainer" becomes one of a complex of rooms connecting with eating, recreational and other facilities.

It might not happen, and most likely it won't, but it is an example of what we have been trying to say here: even in a wheel-dominated technology, there is no reason why we should not live better than we do.

Don Fabun,
The Dynamics of Change

The Dynamics of Change, Kaiser Aluminum & Chemical Corporation, © 1967.

How satisfactory does each system described seem to you?
How adequately does each deal with:

Wear and tear on people
Pollution and congestion
Destruction of the natural environment
Wasted time

To what extent would we need to redesign our cities to accommodate these systems?

Could you expand on Don Fabun's suggestion of "people-tainers"? Design a "people-tainer." Or write a short account—"A Day in the Life of a People-Tainer."

Here are some components of a transportation system. Using these components and/or others you could suggest, develop a plan for a transportation system which would serve the needs of people in your lifetime.

Electric vehicles
Hydrafoils
VTOL (vertical takeoff and landing craft)
Automatic highways
Mini buses
SST (supersonic transport)

What forces and pressures in society would work for changes your system demands? Which would work against such changes? Can you think of ways in which companies, corporations, industries and governmental agencies with a vested interest in current practices could be induced to accept your system?

designing life styles: 2

To what extent do you believe communication should substitute for transportation? Pick a person from the list on page 195 and design a life style for him. Let your design reveal your thinking on these questions:

Do you believe that we should retain many systems of communication: e.g., between persons, between persons and machines, between machines, between persons and other living beings? What purposes should each system serve?

For what purposes should we travel in the future; and how?

Consider carefully the meanings you attribute to the words "communication" and "transportation." Make these meanings clear in the way you present your design. (Note: perhaps you will want to revise or extend your work-play design, rather than develop a new one.)

eighteen

education —
evolution

The most controversial issues of the twenty-first century will pertain to the ends and means of modifying human behavior and who shall determine them. The first educational question will not be "What knowledge is of most worth?" but "What kinds of human beings do we wish to produce?" The possibilities defy our imagination.

The nerve cells of the brain, far more than muscles or any other organs, are highly sensitive to small electric currents, to a variety of chemicals, and to changes in blood supply. Sedatives, barbiturates, tranquilizers, and various psychedelics provide powerful ways of controlling behavior by direct action on the brain. Similarly, we can manipulate behavior by applying electric currents to regions of the brain. Experiments are now under way with drugs and brain extracts designed to enhance learning or memory.

Aldous Huxley long ago introduced us to the possibilities of genetic selectivity through the availability of sperm and ovum banks. The means of drastically altering the course of human development through artificial insemination, chemical treatment, and electric manipulation are with us. We are already tampering with human evolution.

John I. Goodlad,
"Learning and Teaching in the Future"

What will the people of the future be like?
In what ways will we be different; what will bring about change; how shall we direct and control it?

Reprinted from John I. Goodlad, "Learning and Teaching in the Future," *NEA Journal*, pp. 50–51, by permission of the National Education Association of the United States.

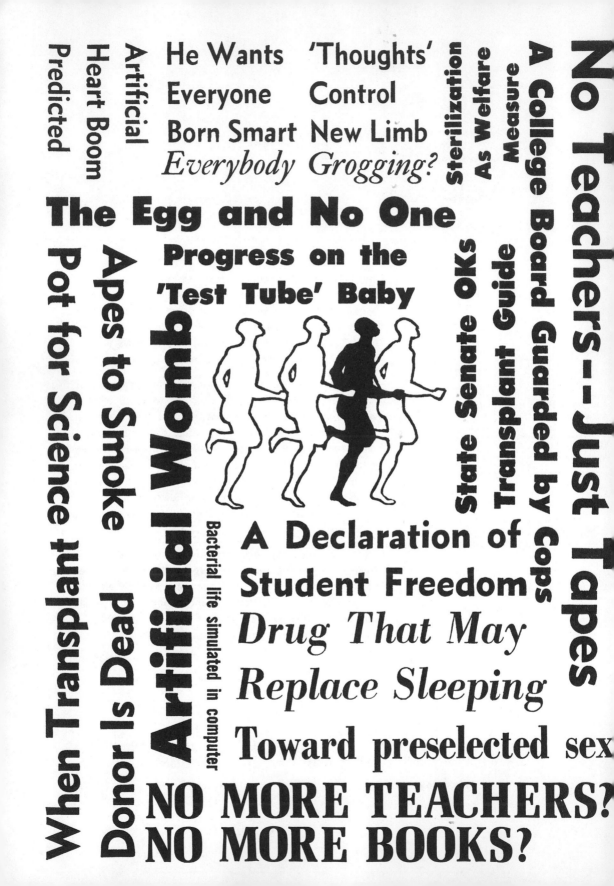

In "Work-Play" and "Communication-Transportation" we have examined some of the adjustments technology is both forcing and facilitating in the ways we use our time, our space, and our energies. We have looked at some of the changes we must make in our social attitudes and values if we wish to develop new life styles. And we have considered some of the ways in which the purpose of human existence itself may be understood and enhanced. These adjustments are, of course, changing us as individuals and as a society. However, they are less the result of direct manipulation of the human personality than the result of both planned and unplanned changes in the cultural environment.

In "Education-Evolution" we will look at ways of changing the human personality and the human organism by human engineering. The notion of actually taking hold of and molding the human being is somehow more awesome than simply "letting it happen." But is it more dangerous?

We will look first at the branch of human engineering with which we are probably most familiar: education. The educational establishment is perhaps the most conservative business in America, in part because its members have seen its role as just that: one of conserving the values, wisdom, skills, and traditions of society.

Don Fabun describes these conserving aims:

> In America, the first aim of education was to prepare children to read the Scripture and its intent was religious. Later on the purpose was to enable people to read and write, and thus participate in a democratic process which required an understanding of the issues and candidates involved. Still later, the purpose increasingly became to prepare young people for jobs in an industrial society. At no time was the aim of education to prepare students to become individuals or complete human beings.

Because people are stuck at each of the various stages along this spectrum of changing purposes, the battle still rages over the true aims of education. Yet, as Fabun argues,

> in a society that can easily be foreseen, one in which cybernation and mechanization will minimize the human factor in industrial production, the purpose of education must once again change. It must begin to educate people to live full and meaningful lives in which "jobs" are at best only incidental; or at least for jobs that are oriented toward human service rather than physical productivity.

Among persons who are analyzing current educational practices from the vantage point of future goods and goals, a few key concepts are shared. Terms conveying these concepts appear again and again in their writings:

Kaiser Aluminum NEWS © 1967.

Participation, not regimentation
Problems, not answers
Change, not fixity
Self-actualization, not adjustment
Integration, not fragmentation
Creativity, not conformity
Pattern-recognition, not fact-gathering
Imagination, not objective intellectualizing and, above all,
Dialogue, Discovery, and Diversity

In the following pages are some of the insights of future-oriented thinkers into what we are doing wrong and what our alternatives are. Try them on; mull them over. What *should* the people of the future be like?

H. G. Wells said a generation ago that history is a race between education and catastrophe. The statement is truer now than it ever was because we are faced with a situation for which there is no parallel in history: an opportunity for mankind to be happy in an easy and permissive society. The achievements of science and technology allow him to satisfy his basic needs with ease, leaving a large portion of his time free to pursue the larger goals of man.

Dennis Gabor,
"Education for a Future
World of Leisure"

life-long education:
for awareness and delight

"Teachers are overworked and underpaid. True. It is an exhausting business, this damming up the flood of human potentialities. What energy it takes to turn a torrent into a trickle, to train that trickle along narrow, well-marked channels!...
Do not blame teachers if they fail to educate. The task of *preventing* children from changing in any significant way is precisely what most societies require."

George B. Leonard,
Education and Ecstasy

Institutions established to prepare students for goals by specialist courses and credits are being rejected and even defied by their clients. The TV generation wants participation in the educational process. It does not want packages. The students want problems, not answers. They want probes, not exams. They want making, not matching. They want struggle, not goals. They want new images of identity, not careers. They want insights, not classified data.

Marshall McLuhan,
"The Reversal of the Overheated Image"

from EDUCATION AND ECSTASY

George B. Leonard

A boy sits on the floor of the hall next to a classroom door, his back against the wall, his head between his knees. He is a cliché—sweaty, tousled black hair, loose shirttail, a tennis shoe untied. As we pass, one big, luminous eye appears between his knuckles and aims an accusation at me. Why has he been expelled from the company of his peers? I am drawn to the left. "On the right here is our new teachers' lounge." I go right. "I want you to feel free to use this room anytime you want. There's always coffee here, or you can just chew the rag with members of our staff."

We go on, into a classroom at last. It is a fifth grade, presided over by a stout maiden with glasses and reddish hair. Upon our appearance, the electricity within the room changes in a flash; the voltage of tension drops, the amperage of interest rises. Every face turns to us. "Excuse us, Miss Brown. I want our visitor to see one of our new classrooms." At the second seat of the second row, a boy's eyes drop from us to a notebook propped up on his desk. As the principal talks, I drift around to see what the boy is reading. Ah, a copy of *Popular Mechanics* hidden behind the notebook. He glances resentfully at me, then goes on reading, his eyes stubborn and dreamy. An aura of rare intelligence encircles him. I look away. He will need to keep all his stubbornness and all his dreams.

"If you'll notice the placement of the skylight, here, on the side of the room away from the windows, you'll see that the illumination is perfectly balanced at every desk." The principal is happy, and I rejoice with him about the delicious, perfectly balanced flow of outdoor light into a room filled with beautiful children. But something disturbs me, a vinegary tingle at the back of my neck. *There is a witch in this room.* I see her near the back of the fourth row—milk-white skin, black hair falling onto a faded blue blouse, a band of freckles across the bridge of a small, sharp nose. Dark eyes with dilated pupils are fixed on me now, bold and direct, telling me that she knows, without words, everything that needs to be known about me. I return her stare, feeling that this girl, with an education she is not likely to get, might foretell the future, read signs, converse with spirits. In Salem, she eventually would suffer the ordeal of fire and water. In our society, she will be adjusted.

"When it gets dark outside," the principal is saying, "an electric-eye device—here—automatically compensates by turning up the lights." The girl's eyes never leave mine. She is a sorceress, too, for already she has created a whole new world inhabited only by the two of us. It is not a sexual world. What she has in mind—she could never put it into words— bypasses the erotic entirely. But later, when those talents of hers that do not fit the scientific-rationalist frame are finally extinguished, she may turn to sex. And she may become promiscuous, always seeking the shadow of an ecstasy and knowledge that by then she will remember only as a distant vibration, an inexplicable urge toward communion.

"You see, a classroom such as this can never become dark. The illumination will always be even." The principal, I realize, is telling Miss Brown that we are leaving. The girl has no intention of releasing my eyes. The principal is moving toward the door. For a moment, I grow dizzy, then break the connection and follow my host out of the door, quickly reassuming the disguise we all must wear to travel safely in the world that I and the principal and most of us customarily pretend is real.

Of course. The only way it could be explained is that snow is a cloud lying down. The ocean breathes a cloud into the air and it becomes tired as it ripples up and down across the desert. When it must rest, it will lie down on a mountain. Maybe it's making love to the mountain. Oh, if it is, I wish I were a mountain. If it stops too long, it can't leave the way it came. The mountains bleed their cloud away and it becomes soiled. But what beautiful punishment ...it can escape out of the inside of an aspen tree to get back into the air...but only a little at a time. That's what it costs to be too tired. Maybe though, it could...

"Kari!" Damn you! It was silent, but she thought it. Aloud, she said, "Yes, Mr. Clyde?"

"Have you solved the problem yet?"

"Oh,...no; I'll need more time."

The teacher's voice rang with bitterness, "You're the only one who needs more time. Have it here by 8 in the morning."

If you saw her running between classes with too many books in her arms and a little bit late, you would never notice that she was different. When she sat in class engrossed in the patterns the window light made on the floor, she seemed commonly inattentive. But once you got to know her, you fully realized that she was different. She flushed with a kind of awareness. Kari was handicapped. But her handicap wasn't a limp or a distorted speech pattern. Her handicap was creativity.

Robert E. Samples,
"Kari's Handicap:
The Impediment of Creativity".

What is wrong with these pictures?
What is happening to these children?
What are their concerns?
What are the concerns of the principal and the teachers?

"Education is a process of living and not a preparation for living."
Therefore, something is being learned, even when nothing is being
taught—unfortunately, Leonard believes.

[T]here our children sit, counting out a few seconds of learning for
every hour of waiting for a bell to ring, waiting for a kind of teacher they
may never have known, waiting for *something to happen*. If only their
waiting could be merely neutral, we wish. If only they could sit there,
learning *nothing*, without ill effects! . . . But not one can be rescued from
learning; learning is what human life is. . . .

There are no neutral moments. Even in those classrooms where the
education some of us might hope for is impossible, a kind of shadowy,
negative learning is going on. Some pupils learn how to daydream;
others, how to take tests. Some learn the petty deceptions involved in
cheating; others, the larger deceptions of playing the school game absolutely straight (the well-kept notebook, the right answer, the senior
who majors in good grades). Most learn that the symbolic tricks their
keepers attempt to teach them have little to do with their own deeper
feelings or anything in the here and now. The activity that masquerades
under the ancient and noble name of "education" actually seems to
serve as a sort of ransom to the future, a down payment toward "getting
ahead"—or at least toward not falling behind. Lifetime-earnings figures
are pressed upon potential high school dropouts. These figures seem to
show that giving an acceptable interpretation of *Ode on a Grecian Urn*
means you will live in a better suburb and drive a bigger car. A vision
of Florida retirement superimposes itself on every diagram in plane
geometry. Some students refuse to pay the ransom, and you should not
be surprised that these students may be what society calls the "brighter"
ones. But dropouts and graduates alike have had plenty of practice in
fragmenting their lives—segregating senses from emotions, from intellect,
building boxes for art and abstractions, divorcing the self from the reality
and the joy of the present moment. No need to look for obscure psychological explanations for modern man's fragmentation; that is what
his schools teach. . . .

Schools and colleges, until now, have served a society that needed
reliable, predictable human components. Appropriately, they have spent
overwhelming amounts of time and energy ironing out those human impulses and capabilities that seemed errant. Since learning involves behavioral change, lifelong learning becomes the most errant of behaviors
and is not to be countenanced. Educational institutions, therefore, have
been geared to *stop* learning. Perhaps half of all learning ability is
squelched in the earliest grades, where children find that there exist
predetermined, unyielding "right answers" for everything, that following
instructions is what counts and, surprisingly, that the whole business of
education is mostly dull and painful.

With the bulk of learning ability wiped out in early childhood, the
schools can proceed at their own leisure to slow and then still what is left
of each human component's capacity to change. The process moves at
different rates for different types of components. The simpler ones (un-

**does any of
this describe
you?**

skilled workers, for example) are finished off after only a few years of schooling. More complex components take longer to shape. Schooling's most elegant maneuver consists of braking learning ability so that, for all practical purposes, it will reach zero speed just at the point of graduation. Exceptions are made. Art can be set aside as a sanctuary for lifelong learning. Another activity, generally termed "the life of the mind," has been found to be generally harmless and inconsequential; so it, too, is sanctioned by society even after graduation. Thus, the illusion of lifelong learning can be maintained while the organism changes hardly at all beyond its ability to verbalize "concepts."

What is to be done about education? Leonard believes we must redefine its goals.

... Our definition of education's root purpose remains shortsightedly utilitarian. Our map of the territory of learning remains antiquated: vocational training, homemaking, driving, and other "fringe" subjects—themselves limiting and fragmenting—have invaded the curriculum, but are generally considered outside the central domain of "education." This domain, this venerable bastion, is still a place where people are trained to split their world into separate symbolic systems, the better to cope with and manipulate it. Such "education," suprarationalistic and analytical to the extreme, has made possible colonialism, the production line, space voyaging, and the H-bomb. But it has not made people happy or whole, nor does it now offer them ways to change, deep down, in an age that cries out with the urgency of a rocket's flight, "Change or die." ...

If education in the coming age is to be not just a part of life but the main purpose of life, then education's purpose will, at last, be viewed as central. What, then, is the purpose, the goal of education? A large part of the answer may well be what men of this civilization have longest feared and most desired: *the achievement of moments of ecstasy*. Not fun, not simply pleasure, as in the equation of Bentham and Mill, not the libido pleasure of Freud, but ecstasy, *ananda*, the ultimate delight.

Western civilization, for well-known historical reasons, has traditionally eschewed ecstasy as a threat to goal-oriented control of men, matter, and energy—and has suffered massive human unhappiness. Other civilizations, notably that of India, have turned their best energies toward the attainment of ecstasy while neglecting practical goals—and have suffered massive human unhappiness. Now, modern science and technology seem to be preparing a situation in which the successful control of practical matters and the attainment of ecstasy can safely coexist; in which each reinforces the other; and in which, quite possibly, neither can long exist *without* the other. Abundance and population control already are logically and technologically feasible. At the same time, cybernation, pervasive and instantaneous communication, and other feedback devices of increasing speed, range, and sensitivity extend and enhance man's sensory apparatus, multiplying the possibilities for understanding and ecstasy as well as for misunderstanding and destruction. The times demand that we choose delight.

Do discipline and mastery of technique stand in opposition to freedom, self-expression, and the ecstatic moment? Most Western educators have acted as if they did. Strange, when there exist so many models of the marriage between the two. Take the artistic endeavor: The composer discovers that the soul of creation transcends the body of form only when form is his completely. The violinist arrives at the sublime only through utter mastery of technique. The instruments of living that are now coming into our hands—rich, responsive, and diverse—require mastery. The process of mastery itself can be ecstatic, leading to delight that transcends mastery.

The new revolutionaires of education must soothe those who fear techniques no less than those who fear delight. Many a liberal educational reform has foundered on lack of specific tools for accomplishing its purposes—even if a tool may be something as simple as knowing *precisely when* to leave the learner entirely alone. Education must use its most powerful servant, technique, in teaching skills that go far beyond those that submit to academic achievement tests. Even today, as will be seen, specific, systematic ways are being worked out to help people learn to love, to feel deeply, to expand their inner selves, to create, to enter new realms of being.

. . . The new educator will seek out the possibility of delight in every form of learning. He will realize that solving an elegant mathematical problem and making love are different classes in the same order of things, sharing common ecstasy. He will find that even education now considered nothing more than present drudgery for future payoff—learning the multiplication tables, for example—can become joyful when a skillfully designed learning environment (a programmed game, perhaps) makes the learning quick and easy. Indeed, the skillful pursuit of ecstasy will make the pursuit of excellence, not for the few, but for the many, what it never has been—successful. And yet, make no mistake about it, excellence, as we speak of it today, will be only a by-product of a greater unity, a deeper delight. . . .

. . . A world in which everyone will be in touch needs people in touch with themselves. Where the actions of one can drastically affect the lives of others far distant, it will be crucially important that each person master the skill of feeling what others feel. This skill, more than new laws or new politics, will soon become crucial to the survival of the race. Such empathy is possible only in one deeply aware of his own feelings. The future will very likely judge nothing less appropriate than detached, fragmented, unfeeling men. . . .

The emerging mode of life promises to be so challenging, so vivid, so intense as to render the old life extremely dull. The end of "job" means the end of the eight-hour day and the beginning of the 24-hour day. Lifelong learning, lifelong creative change, is an exhilarating and dangerous endeavor that will require far more human intensity and courage than the old modes.

Freed from the hunter's struggle for survival, freed from the Civilized man's incumbency as specialized component, the human race can explore for the first time what it really means to be human. This quest will not be restricted to a small minority of seekers or holy men; it will be a pilgrimage by the millions, a search for the billion manifestations of increased human capacity. It will not be easy, this journey into *terra incognita*. Without clear maps, without safe travel instructions, without comforting exhortations, we can only follow delight like a hound on a trail.

We cannot guess what the distant future will ask of its schools, but perhaps we can step far enough into the future to see what our children *already* need. Schools for what?

• To learn the commonly agreed-upon skills and knowledge of the ongoing culture (reading, writing, figuring, history and the like), to learn joyfully and to learn that all of it, even the most sacred "fact," is strictly tentative.

• To learn how to ring creative changes on all that is currently agreed upon.

• To learn delight, not aggression; sharing, not eager acquisition; uniqueness, not narrow competition.

• To learn heightened awareness and control of emotional, sensory and bodily states and, through them, increased empathy for other people, perhaps the most common form of ecstasy.

• To learn how to learn, for learning—one word that includes singing, dancing, interacting and much more—is already becoming the main purpose of life.

Are any of these kinds of learning taking place in you now?
Would you like them to?

What is education? Leonard's response to this question is three-fold:

To learn is to change. Education is a process that changes the learner.

Learning involves interaction between the learner and his environment, and its effectiveness relates to the frequency, variety and intensity of the interaction.

Education, at best, is ecstatic.

Thinking of your own schooling, from kindergarten on, can you recall an experience of this kind of education? What happened? That is, how did you change, what was your interaction with your environment, what was the ecstatic moment like?

Does Leonard's definition apply to kindergarten? What would happen if college were modeled on kindergarten? Describe a day.

Does Leonard's definition apply to your current education? How would you change your present school to make it more conducive to this kind of learning? Describe an ideal learning situation.

Many articles and books on education are written for teachers, very few for students. What would you put in a handbook for students which would help them learn, even given the present educational system?

What kind of learning environment would you design specifically to encourage creativity? Do you believe that all persons are potentially creative? Or, is Kari, the child described earlier, a special kind of person? Consider these further thoughts from Robert Sample's article.

Kari has too many classmates. But the high numbers are only one excuse for the response of the teachers. Actually, if there were only ten students in each class, Kari would still be mistreated. The school reflects the society from which Kari comes. The school's compartmental treatment of intellectualism is a microcosm of society's patterns. Words, numbers, and activities are separated by fences labeled LANGUAGE, MATH, and GYM.

Kari tries to synthesize all the elements of her world into relevance. In doing so, *she* makes the choices—an act which gives her the plague mark of individuality. She sees an algebraic solution as symbolic poetry that rhymes in the symmetry of logic. The logic doesn't matter, but the meter she perceives does. Her teacher is disgusted by her lack of effort to please him. He makes his requirements clear and is piqued by her apparently intentional effort to ignore *his* needs. . . .

Her attendance to nature reflects her rejection of mediated sources of experience. Kari sees within the commonplace elements of the natural world a source of elements that are infinitely repatternable. The realm of the commonplace in the world of society is filled with already mediated devices. She is not content with the reassembling of other people's ideas or products. She instead prefers to deal with the source—nature.

In a line of poetry she once wrote, Kari claimed that "Before you can love you must know how to walk in the snow leaving no tracks." She knew the thrill of dashing chaotically through a virgin field of snow. In addition, she knew the excited fulfillment of willing abstinence. Both of these ideas were synthesized into the beautiful statement that applied to all love.

Kari is sixteen and growing up. She and her generation will soon be ours.

Try out how Goodman's idea would work for an individual by thinking of a person (yourself, or someone you know) in childhood, adolescence, or of college age. Describe him in terms of his needs, desires, curiosity, or fantasies. What kind of learning environment would you provide for him? What would happen to him?

Robert E. Samples, "Kari's Handicap: The Impediment of Creativity"

from
FREEDOM AND LEARNING:
THE NEED FOR CHOICE

Paul Goodman

We can, I believe, educate the young entirely in terms of their free choice, with no processing whatever. Nothing can be efficiently learned, or, indeed, learned at all—other than through parroting or brute training, when acquired knowledge is promptly forgotten after the examination—unless it meets need, desire, curiosity, or fantasy. Unless there is a reaching from within, the learning cannot become "second nature," as Aristotle called true learning. It seems stupid to decide a priori what the young ought to know and then to try to motivate them, instead of letting the initiative come from them and putting information and relevant equipment at their service.

Up to age twelve, there is no point to formal subjects or a prearranged curriculum. With guidance, whatever a child experiences is educational. Dewey's idea is a good one: It makes no difference *what* is learned at this age, so long as the child goes on wanting to learn something further. Teachers for this age are those who like children, pay attention to them, answer their questions, enjoy taking them around the city and helping them explore, imitate, try out, and who sing songs with them and teach them games. Any benevolent grownup— literate or illiterate—has plenty to teach an eight-year-old; the only profitable training for teachers is a group therapy and, perhaps, a course in child development.

We see that infants learn to speak in their own way in an environment where there is speaking and where they are addressed and take part. If we tried to teach children to speak according to our own theories and methods and schedules, as we try to teach reading, there would be as many stammerers as there are bad readers. Besides, it has been shown that whatever is useful in the present eight-year elementary curriculum can be learned in four months by a normal child of twelve. If let alone, in fact, he will have learned most of it by himself.

learning as creative change

Dialogue, encounter, and discovery are ways of learning. They are also ways of living. We are discovering that to live well and fully in the coming world we must view ourselves not merely as fact-gatherers or task-performers but as inventors and creators.

The idea underlying the dialogue, encounter, and discovery approaches to learning is that a person learns best when he is free to discover and perhaps even to invent his own view of the world and of himself in relationship to it. But, as George Leonard has pointed out, freedom to create does not imply absence of technique, of knowledge, or of skill. Rather, mastery of these is part of the process of creative change instead of an end in itself.

Interest in the technique of dialogue has led to the development of a document called the *dialogue-focuser*, the purpose of which is to make explicit the areas of agreement and disagreement on a particular subject. A dialogue-focuser has two parts, as Robert Theobald, the editor of the Dialogue Series, explains in his introduction to *Dialogue on Education:*

1. A statement of the body of knowledge now generally agreed upon by those at the leading edge of the debate on any particular subject....

2. A clear-cut delineation of the areas of disagreement and the causes of disagreement. It would appear appropriate to distinguish at least five reasons: disagreement about the facts and the interpretations of the facts; disagreement about trends and the interpretation of trends; disagreement about the constraints imposed by the environment; disagreement about the nature of man; disagreement about a desirable world in which to live.

Following are short excerpts from the *dialogue-focuser* in *Dialogue on Education* which you may wish to challenge or discuss.

It is now generally recognized that the education which people receive must be appropriate to the environment in which they will grow up and spend their adult lives. It is only if people understand the conditions in which they live that they can develop the ability to act intelligently and creatively.

The basic disagreement on educational issues today, ... is about the methods which can be used to help people identify the necessary changes in patterns of thinking. It is generally recognized that this task must be accomplished because a culture will always pass on to its children its own present understanding of the appropriate social frameworks. If we fail to understand the necessity for change we will provide the next generation with a set of attitudes which were appropriate for the past but which will not be appropriate for the future. . . .

Those involved in developing the theory of dialogue attempt to discover new ways in which the "reality" of the outside world and the "subjective" views of the individual can be brought into, and kept in, creative tension. It appears that to be effective, dialogue must be based on a study of problems rather than disciplines, on a recognition that authoritarian relationships cannot exist in real education and a belief that students, faculty, and citizens must cooperate in the creation of new knowledge. This creation of new knowledge will necessarily involve not only the reasoning abilities but also the emotions of those involved in the process. Important new understandings cannot be achieved without fundamental change in the view of each person about the nature of the universe in which he lives and this will necessarily involve disruption of his existing views about himself.

Two consequences, therefore, follow from any genuine dialogue experience. First, the views of the individual about the realities of the outside world and his own purposes will inevitably change. Second, new insights will be developed about the problems which have been studied. This new knowledge, however, will be recognized as being dependent upon certain views about the nature of man, the nature of the universe, the desirable world. Such knowledge must therefore be expressed in contingent terms: *if* one accepts certain premises, then certain conclusions follow inevitably. . . .

Most of those advancing the dialogue view of education appear to be optimistic about the long-run prospects of the human race if it should be allowed to develop to the full. It is suggested that life would become essentially synonymous with education and with the ability to communicate effectively. It is argued that man uses only a small fragment of his brain today and that almost unlimited development is possible. It is this view which leads to a belief that the present generation of children could be educated to understand and guide the universe which has been created by those who have provided man with the power totally to destroy the earth or to create a new order.

encounter as dialogue

from CONFESSIONS OF A
NEW ACADEMIC MAN

Stuart Miller

We know that sensory awareness must be integrated with intellect and social purpose—theory tells us that; but can we teach our theory if we are half-men and don't understand sensory awareness to begin with? . . .

The entire psychedelic culture and much of the marijuana phenomenon are a reaction to the hundreds of years in which western man progressively narrowed his conception of reality and knowledge. . . .

The younger generation is putting a vital way of knowing back into currency, but it needs help in determining the relation between the mystical and the analytical. How can the university give that help if none of its professors has any respect for or any experience of non-rational ways of knowing? . . .

Clearly, we need to follow the example of the young and put more room into the research-oriented university for the parts of the human we have excluded: there must be institutional support for learning to love, for enhancing sensory awareness, for exploring nonrational ways of knowing, and so forth. These subjects must have a place in the curriculum, and they must be integrated with the present highly rational and analytic course of study. . . .

I had been for a day at the Esalen Institute, an adult education school in Big Sur, California. For a day a miscellaneous group of adults, men and women, old and young, intellectual and not, academic and not, had been trying to carry on a seminar about the future of our society. The results had been typical of those at most academic conferences. Fear of making a mistake had made people reticent, fear of exposing themselves had made them hostile, fear of coming too close to another person had made each fall back on whatever disciplinary credentials he could offer. In the second day, one of the leaders of the seminar, George Leonard, senior editor of *Look Magazine,* suggested that we experiment with a technique that he thought would be part of the future—the future of education at least—and that might enhance our own dialogue about the future.

He asked the group of forty assembled in one large room to break up into groups of six or seven. Each of us should sit with strangers, and the group should form a circle. When we had done that, George asked that we spend five minutes talking, the only rules being that (1) we speak of feelings rather than thoughts, (2) the here and now rather than the past, and (3) that we be honest. The results in my group were immediately astonishing. One seventy-year-old woman, Miriam, a thirties' radical, tough and beautiful, thought the whole experience an utter sham and did her best to disrupt it. What she couldn't endure, above all, was the fact that the Esalen recorder, who happened to be in our group, was trying to tape our session. A meek woman in the group was driven to tears by Miriam's hostility; another, younger woman, was driven to wrestling with Miriam.

After five minutes, George called time. He observed, with a grin, that we had not opened ourselves to one another, though we were beginning. He asked that in the next five minutes each of us go around the group and tell every other person what he felt about him at that moment, and that each of us should touch the other in some way. For many of us this was an incredibly rare moment of personal confrontation. I recall, in my odyssey around that group of strangers, stopping before one sloppily sexual wreck of a suburban housewife. Full of a mixture of contempt and lust, I was unable for thirty seconds to express the complexity of my feelings, unable to let her know or myself know how this stranger was a part of myself. When I burst and told her how I hated and loved her, I had learned that she really existed. She was pleased and hurt by what I said, finally grateful for my candor—my attempt to fully en- counter her as a human being. I had come in touch with her personal reality and, in the process, my own. A technique for what the embarrass- ing jargon calls "interpersonal communication" had resulted in an en- hanced sense of what reality was. I would suggest in passing that most of our education, by ignoring such encounter, by focusing on purely intellectual ways of knowing, has blinded us to reality, made us narrow, killed a part of our spirits.

After these five minutes had passed, George asked that we return to our seats and try to communicate without words. Though I had felt such joy in learning during the previous ten minutes, I was terrified now. Months later a psychologist friend told me what had happened— I feared that after I had exposed myself to the group the silence would allow them to reject me. For a minute I sat and tried to communicate, silently, my terror. I discovered that somehow I had succeeded—a hand clasped mine and very nearly crushed it with reassurance. In the last five minutes, George asked us to return to our seats and then try to come together as a group.

By now, for attempting to record such experiences, my audience of academics will have rejected me to the point of not even believing what I record as fact, but the truth remains that these seven strangers, seven- teen minutes after meeting, were standing in the middle of a group of chairs, their arms round one another, smiling and swaying. Their en- counter with each other had issued in ecstasy.

. . . By the time George told us the final five-minute period was over, I felt as though I could do anything, that the world and I were both lovable, and that new dimensions of reality had opened to me.

I believe that most people in our generation need experiences like this. We need to shed our embarrassment at human feeling and involvement. We need experiences that will enhance our powers of communication and love and self-awareness. We need experiences that call on our deepest emotions. It is not that such experiences are the only valid ones, it is rather that they must be set beside our ordinary, alienated, subject-object, symbol-manipulating experiences so that we may integrate the emotional and the intellectual as they should be integrated. We are emotionally illiterate, John Seelye told a meeting of consultants on a new college. He is right, and we must pass beyond breast beating to affective education. Naturally, I would recommend such experiences as the basic encounter group and would even suggest that we might encounter our own students this way.

The T-Group is only one example of the kind of education we need. I think we need more experience with contemplation and mysticism. I think we need more experience with exercises in sensory awareness, inner imagery, and visual process training. I think we also need more experience with the practical world. If college professors and deans are urging students to go into the Peace Corps and VISTA, to cross cultural lines, to help other kinds of people, and to learn from them, then we must do these things too. We must, in short, work up a whole program of affective and psychomotor education ranging from purely personal development (sensory awareness) to training in communicating with other people (T-Groups and other devices for enhancing the human potential on the interpersonal level) to training in dealing with society as a whole (Peace Corps activities, radical politics, study of the change process).

The "third force" in psychology, as Maslow puts it, is probably right in thinking that people are naturally disposed to grow, to develop themselves in all ways. But the older force, the Freudians and their friends, is also right in thinking that a maladjustment is still an adjustment, a way of coping with reality. Will maladjusted human beings risk their maladjustment for the hope of becoming fuller, self-actualizing people?

education by contagion

It is time to try out on a large scale the new discoveries and methods of this new educational psychology, discoveries such as the remarkable effect of early enrichment at ages one to four, and methods such as use of the new phonetic alphabets and the programmed learning and teaching machines and programmed texts that promise to make

From "Diversity," by John R. Platt, *Science*, Vol. 154, p. 1132, 2 December 1966. Copyright 1966 by The American Association for the Advancement of Science.

spelling and geography and physics and anatomy and many other subjects easier and more quickly mastered. The new ideas have already made a revolution across the nation in the teaching of high-school science courses, and efforts are well under way to create science programs with the same exciting immediacy all the way down to the kindergarten level. In fact it now appears that the whole difficulty with many subjects is that we have been teaching them too late. A seven-year-old can learn reading and writing more easily than an 18-year-old can, and we are now finding that he may also learn about sets and binary arithmetic and rates-of-change and the difference between mass and weight more easily than many college sophomores. . . .

. . . The subjects we now teach children might be mastered in a much shorter school day, perhaps no more than three or four hours. There would be less boredom and resistance in school and more time for creative leisure outside. Some parents may shudder at this, because they do not want the children home half the day. But, with the new trends of productivity and automation in our adult life, perhaps creative leisure is one of the things we need to teach children earliest. And, if we let the adult's leisure enrich the children's leisure, homework might even become home play. The interaction between the generations might make for better relations than we have had for years. In fact the children, with their shorter hours, going home from school may soon meet the adults, with their new leisure, going back, hoping to learn in a more voluntary and serious way the subjects they missed in all their years of report-card education.

All this would change our stereotyped pattern of education in a remarkable way. The intense program of work now imposed across a few years in the late teens—where we have to study all day and all night because the earlier grades have taught us so little—might be replaced by an easier longitudinal pattern that would start with easy and fast learning methods at age one or two and would then go on all our lives for two or three or four hours a day.

The children and the college students and the leisured adults might acquire a new attitude toward education. Formal teaching might blend inseparably into more individual and creative leisure-time activities, such as building boats together or learning music or ballet or skiing—or studying embryos and catching striped bass before dawn. Education would be by contagion and long discussion, and the generations might learn to talk to each other again.

> A lifetime ago we made the transformation to education for living. It is time now to make the transformation to education for wholeness, for delight, and for diversity.
>
> John R. Platt,
> "Diversity"

We teach children how to spend money. Can we teach people how to spend time?

the underpaid student

> Students are probably the most overworked and underpaid class in our society. Their training has now been shown by many studies to be the most important element in the economic development and prosperity of a country, and yet they are not paid as well as their brothers who became plumbers' apprentices. The 18-year-old brother or sister who works in a factory or a store gets off at five o'clock and has enough income to have an apartment and a car and books and records and recreation and a paid vacation. He can have guests in and can come in or go out at any hour. But the student is treated, not like his brothers or parents or teachers, but like a monk with a vow of poverty, austerity, and overwork—a vow which is not even his own vow but has been taken for him. He often works until midnight or later at subjects his brothers might never master, and he is supposed to get money from his family, or borrow it, or be grateful for a fellowship that still leaves him below the poverty level. He is frequently locked in at night and forbidden to have a car or an apartment, and has little money for his own books or for good meals or concerts. He is given cafeteria fare in cinder-block buildings and never learns to live like a human being.
>
> John R. Platt,
> "Diversity"

If the Guaranteed Annual Income were to be adopted, at what age should one qualify?

learning by teaching

One of the oldest maxims of teaching is that no one ever really understands a subject until he is faced with the necessity of teaching it to others. Now if this is true, it follows that students never really understand anything. Note that we did not say learn, but rather, understand. For we know that students really do learn things. They acquire information, great masses of it, and often quite readily. But it is not information as such that constitutes knowledge, much less, understanding. Indeed, information alone—mere facts and figures—is of little use or significance unless we know what it means, that is, until we have acquired understanding. And according to our maxim, the elements of understanding and significance are acquired most readily in the process of teaching. It follows that if we wish to produce a situation in which several people may engage in the search for understanding it must be one in which all participate as teachers, but not as teachers to others who are students, for we have already seen that this is what we must avoid if we wish to produce understanding. Ideally, then, there must be a community in which each member respects the duty, as well as the right, of all others to acquire wisdom and understanding, and therefore salutes the immanent teachers in all other human beings. But the only way we know of honoring this commitment is through the participational dialogue that Plato termed *dialectical*.

Harvey Wheeler,
"The Civilization
of the Dialogue"

Do you agree that no one "really understands a subject until he is faced with the necessity of teaching it to others"?
Would Richard McKenna (*The Sand Pebbles*) agree?
Do you teach? Think of an occasion when you learned by teaching.

skills and beyond

from LEARNING AND TEACHING
IN THE FUTURE

John I. Goodlad

The era of instruction that will supersede the era of human-based instruction is to be one of man-machine interaction—and the machine is the computer. Although we have lived in the shadow of the computer for a long while, we have used it so little in teaching that we may be inclined to believe its future and our own to be things apart. Nothing could be further from the truth. Computers are already demonstrating their usefulness in teaching spelling, mathematics, reading, and a host of other cognitive skills. Tapes, screens, records, and other audiovisual devices, coupled with the computer, make possible a unique instructional system of sight, sound, and touch.

The computer will continue to march relentlessly into our instructional lives, and there is no reason to believe that it will not come right into the school building. To put a computer terminal into every elementary school classroom in the United States would cost, at current prices, about $1 billion; however, if we were to decide to do such a thing, competition within the industry would undoubtedly cut this figure in half. There are problems involved, especially in hooking up terminals to the computer-instructional system at some remote point, but this can be solved by improving communications connections or by having small computers closer to the schools they serve.

Providing programed sequences by way of computers offers us an efficient means of communicating educational lore. What the teaching profession must do is to *legitimatize* the computer as instructor in those basic areas that can be carefully programed. Then we must explore the question of how computers and people are to live together productively in education.

An important goal for the teaching profession now is to humanize the means of instruction. By this I mean emphasizing our very best human values in the substance of the curriculum, and showing concern for both the individual and mankind in the teaching-learning environment. I believe these tasks to be at once so formidable and so important that I welcome the computer and charge it with teaching some of those basic skills and concepts that are only the beginning of educating the compassionate, rational man. . . .

When we try to envision the school of tomorrow, we must not be limited by our concept of the school of today. Education is not a static process, and the school of today cannot be considered a sacred or unchangeable institution. After all, every decision governing schools was at one time or another made by man. At the time the decisions governing today's schools were made, fewer data were available.

The men who made those decisions were no brighter than schoolmen today, and they were less well-educated. Therefore, it behooves us to reexamine every decision about schooling: size of building and whether we want one

From "Learning and Teaching in the Future" by John I. Goodlad. Reprinted by permission of the National Education Association of the United States.

at all, numbers of teachers and whether we need a fully certificated teacher for every 28.5 children, whether the library is to be one that houses real books or computerized microfiche. (A fully automated library with no books but only microfiche is now out of the realm of science fiction into the actuality of college and university planning in the United States.)

We must not continue to assume that tomorrow's school will have X number of qualified teachers for Y number of children or that we will construct a school building large enough for all of the children to be housed. There is no reason at all why we could not employ half the usual quota of fully qualified teachers, using the balance of our money for part-time specialists and a host of instructional aids. And there is no reason at all why we could not plan an educational program that requires a school building only half the usual size, with the balance of the money going for trips, special projects, and individualized activities supervised by the staff or even programed by a computer.

A school is not necessary to teaching and learning. We do not need a school to guide children and youth in grasping their culture. And, certainly, we do not need a school to teach the fundamentals of reading, writing, and arithmetic. But we do need a formal process of instruction with the most able members of our society giving their time to it in planning and programing instructional materials, in computerizing varied programs for learning, and in interacting with other humans in the delightful business of learning from one another.

The computer, which we must legitimatize for learning and teaching in an imminent era, probably will contribute significantly in a still later era to the demise of what we now call school. We shall regard this as undesirable only if we lack faith in the ability of man to fashion a better world.

In viewing learning and teaching for the year 2000 and beyond, it is easier to predict what will *not* be than

what will be. A prescribed age for starting school will be meaningless. The computer console with an array of devices for stimuli and feedback will be as natural for the child of the twenty-first century as television is for today's two-year-old. Teaching and learning will not be marked by a standard 9 to 3 day, or a standard September to June year, or a year for a grade of carefully packaged material. The child's age will not be a criterion for determining what he is to learn.

Will learning be any less because there will be no periods, no Carnegie units, no bells, no jostling of pupils from class to class? I think not. The student will be free to concentrate exclusively on a given field for weeks or months or to divide his time among several fields. The variability and comprehensiveness of programed learning sequences will be such that the student, unaided by human teachers, will control a significant portion of his curriculum.

Clearly, the role of teachers will change markedly. Hundreds of hours of their time will go into what will occupy each student for an hour or two. But because thousands or even millions of students might eventually select this hour, the teachers' preparation time will be well spent. And the quality of education will be vastly improved.

School as we now know it—whether egg crate or flexible space—will have been replaced by a diversified learning environment including homes, parks, public buildings, museums, and guidance centers. It is quite conceivable that each community will have a learning center and that homes will contain electronic consoles connected to it. This learning center will provide not only a computer-controlled videotape, microfiche, and record library, but also access to state and national educational television networks. It is even possible that advanced technology will return the family to center stage as the basic learning unit.

As to ends, let me put them as questions to ask about the educational enterprise:

1. To what extent are our young people coming into possession of their culture?

2. To what extent is each child being provided with unique opportunities to develop his potentialities to the maximum?

3. To what extent is each child developing a deep sense of personal worth, the sense of selfhood that is a prerequisite for self-transcendence?

4. To what extent are our people developing universal values, values that transcend all men in all times and in all places?

A fifth question is the most important, challenging, and frightening of all, now that men possess such manipulative powers: *What kinds of human beings do we wish to produce?* As a citizen and an educator, I cherish the right to participate in the dialogue about it.

the classroom without walls

Many walls will crumble, if education takes the direction indicated by these theorists—walls separating child from adult, learning from living, emotion from thought, self from other, man from machine, theory from practice. The "classroom without walls" will become a reality in more than a physical sense.

Robert Bickner, in *Inventing Education for the Future*, carries the implications of life-long education a step further: if adults learn, why should not children work?

A Word About Forecasting. **In a discussion of the difficulties and pitfalls of forecasting, Bickner points out that, on the basis of the current trend, we would expect child labor to be becoming a thing of the past. Yet, with the meaning of both "education" and "labor" changing, the trend might well be reversed. In view of the expanding range of choice and uncertainty about the future, he argues, such reversals can occur and can even be arranged—if we know what we want. Therefore, he argues, let us use the crystal ball as well as the slide rule when we look ahead.**

from AFTER THE FUTURE, WHAT?

Robert Bickner

By the end of the twentieth century, my crystal ball says, a typical parent will no more think of giving his nine-year-old son an allowance than he will his twenty-nine-year-old son. Both will be in school, incidentally, but both will also be gainfully employed. Both will buy their own clothes and pay for their own medical insurance. The twenty-nine-year-old will be doing work or research selected in part to help prepare him for more difficult assignments. So will the nine-year-old. Neither of them will be guaranteed interesting assignments, however, and their scholastic standing and past performance will determine their eligibility for the better opportunities. The nine-year-old son, of course, will choose employment only in carefully administered programs approved and monitored by his school.

Education will suffer perhaps, with children tending the IBM 7090 computer as they once tended the loom, or minding infant children as they did a century ago, or wearing candy-striped dresses in the neighborhood hospital as they do today, or guiding adults through the complexities of the latest automated public library. Opportunities will be varied, but all students will be working—and in earnest. Both the children and their parents will be concerned almost as much about their progress toward more interesting and challenging and rewarding employment experiences as about their progress in classroom studies. The two will be closely interrelated. Certain classes will be requisite to certain employment activities, and vice versa. Performance in both areas will be part of the student's personal record.

Would you like a more specific impression of the vision in the crystal ball? Let's look for a moment at your nine-year-old granddaughter in the candy-striped dress. She earns money, and experience, and school credits, and occasional gratitude, and self-confidence in a work program jointly organized and supervised by a group which includes school teachers, physicians, nurses, professional educators, hospital administrators, and child psychologists. Though some of her work is drudgery, much of it is interesting; and a well-planned training and educational program is an integral part of her work. She is learning something about medicine, biology and chemistry, the practical art of first aid and caring for the sick, the nature of the large bureaucratic organizations typical of her society, and many other things about herself and others and the world she lives in. She has regular interviews with highly qualified counselors whose task is not only to help her individually but to monitor and evaluate the over-all program continuously. At the risk of shocking you altogether, I'll mention that toward the end of her year in this program, she will be given an opportunity to assist one of the more experienced nurses during an actual surgical operation. She has no career plans in the medical field, however, and this program is neither on-the-job training nor an introductory survey of the nursing profession. It is simply work and education. Next year, depending upon her qualifications and interests, she may be earning money and school credits in some entirely different field, such as architecture or law enforcement.

What will cause this reappearance of child labor? Will it be economic necessity? No. But society has disinherited youth long enough. Our refusal to let them participate in society, responsibly and productively, is no more civilized than our custom of dispossessing the older generations and turning them out to barren pastures.

With each passing decade the age level for admission to our society has been raised. How far will the trend go? I suggest the trend will reverse, dramatically, and with considerable consequences for education. It will reverse not just because the rumblings of teen-age revolt have long been audible, nor even because experience as well as the classroom can teach a person a great deal—both right and wrong. It will reverse simply because children deserve and need the right to participate.

The crystal ball still hasn't answered the question: "When will a man leave school and become gainfully employed?" It has suggested that a youth will be gainfully employed even during his school years. But when will the youth leave school? The answer: "When he becomes senile, or tired, or lazy, or when he dies."

Now you see why the crystal ball couldn't answer our question. It was a meaningless question. Work and education are interrelated and life-long activities in the society of the future, just as they were two or three hundred years ago. Who could imagine it otherwise? Who would want it otherwise?

Is Bickner's picture incompatible with that drawn in "Work-Play"?

---

from STATEMENT ON THE FIRST PROGRAM
OF THE NEW COLLEGE OF
THE STATE UNIVERSITY OF NEW YORK
AT OLD WESTBURY

The tragedy of the world is that those who are imaginative have but slight experience, and those who are experienced have feeble imaginations. Fools act on imagination without knowledge; pedants act on knowledge without imagination. The task of the university is to weld together imagination and experience.

Alfred N. Whitehead,
The Aims of Education

MANDATE FOR A NEW COLLEGE

The State University will establish in Nassau County a college that pays heed to the individual student and his concern with the modern world. . . . Specifically, this college will:

1. End the lock-step march in which one semester follows on another until four of youth's most energetic years have been consumed; to this purpose qualified students will be admitted to college without high school graduation, and those who attain competency will be granted degrees without regard to length of collegiate study.

2. Admit students to full partnership in the academic world and grant them the right to determine, in large measure, their own areas of study and research.

3. Use mechanical devices to free faculty scholars from the academic drudgery of repeated lectures, conducting classes devoted to drill, and marking many examinations, thus allowing faculty scholars to turn their full creative powers to meaningful exchange with students, to research, and to artistry.

Since the campus is to be built literally from the ground up, the president and the faculty members the president recruits will have an almost unrestricted opportunity for innovation and creativity.

INTRODUCTION

In 1968 the new State University College at Old Westbury will begin its first liberal arts program—a work-study curriculum emphasizing the humanities and social sciences—with 75 students and a faculty of about 15. This will be the first of a variety of programs to be offered in subsequent years, as the college grows to 5,000 undergraduates and a number of master's degree graduate students. By 1970, when the new campus is ready for 1000 students, a wide offering of liberal arts studies will be available including programs in the natural sciences and other important traditional academic subjects.

The 1968 pilot opening will be for students interested in a curriculum involving a substantial amount of time living and learning off-campus in teaching, community action and other public service assignments at home and abroad. Such education-in-action will be combined with on-campus seminars, workshops, and independent study designed to make the search for knowledge as vivid and challenging as the cross-cultural work experience. This welding of theory and practice—imagination and experience—will be the central theme for a "school of the world" in which everyone can learn to become his own teacher. Responsibility for one's own learning, in college as in life, will be the operating principle.

This first program is designed to meet the needs of many students for more relevant studies and for direct experience dealing with public problems. The pressing public problems of urban development and education directly affecting the two-thirds of the American people living in metropolitan counties call for the attention and assistance of higher education. "The Urban Condition" is a universal question requiring the application of many academic disciplines, especially in the social sciences and humanities. By studying and working on these problems, students and faculty can advance their own education while contributing to the community beyond the college gates.

Within this initial focus on urban problems, there will be unusual opportunities for students and faculty to choose particular questions for study and field work; to follow these questions where they lead; to initiate new seminars and workshops; to teach each other; to engage in independent study; and to participate in the continuing development of curriculum and the governance of the college. Individual independence and responsibility will be cultivated in an environment of maximum challenge—in a curriculum with demands on everyone to engage in a common search for understanding of the world; by a college committed to being a community.

As part of the effort to make the State University of New York "the most ambitious laboratory in the world for innovation in higher education," State University Chancellor Samuel B. Gould has asked the new college "to review all the conventional ingredients such as admissions policies, grades, course systems, and academic divisions, and break whatever barriers may stand in the way." . . .

In creating this new college, the State University sees the restlessness, curiosity and questioning of youth not as a spectre, but an opportunity. It is saying that the turbulent, critical mood of today's students is a great occasion for education; that their complaints against the multiversity, their concern for relevance, their search for individual identity, and their questioning of everything can lead to better teaching, more relevant courses, more disciplined and serious study, deeper personal understanding, and greater involvement with public problems. Old Westbury is being designed to test the possibilities for such a renewal of liberal education and of the liberal arts college in the center of the university.
. . .

For both students and faculty, the curriculum and the community of learning at Old Westbury will be demanding. Taking responsibility for one's own education and accepting partnership in a common venture will put pressure on each participant. The excitement of making a new college will not substitute for the attention required to master difficult arts or sciences. There will be disappointments for any who think they can change the world without understanding it, or understand it without study, or study without books. Contemporary studies will not substitute for the classics. Education-in-action, whether in the inner-city ghetto or suburbs of America, or on the other side of the globe, should leave the actors thirsty for knowledge and theories to make sense of the experience.

Which of the proposals for change put forward in the writings from *Education and Ecstasy, Dialogue on Education, Learning and Teaching in the Future,* and *After the Future, What?* are incorporated in the plans for Old Westbury?
What kinds of person should go to such a college?
Do you know of other experimental schools?
What approaches are they using?

If you would like to read an imaginative account of a future educational environment which uses both computerized and live interaction, try "Visiting Day: 2001" in *Education and Ecstasy* by George Leonard.

We have been looking at the proposals of theorists who share the conviction that learning is based on a union of thinking with feeling, and that students should engage in meaningful interaction with their total environment.

There is an opposing view, however. Very broadly, this is the view that learning is primarily intellectual, and that students should make transactions in the marketplace of ideas but not in society at large. One exponent of this view is the semanticist S. I. Hayakawa, President of San Francisco State College.

> Hayakawa has undertaken what amounts to a religious crusade for what he feels is the right of this campus—or any college campus—to be a sanctuary for debate and scholarship uninterrupted by secular problems.
>
> "I think many of our curricula are pretty stodgy and tradition-bound," he said. "But I'm a conservative in that I want to preserve the fundamental idea that a university should be kept distinct.
>
> "Every civilization needs a place where study is preserved. In the Middle Ages this was the Church." . . .
>
> "Colleges today are very much what the medieval Church was—all of that to which the hopes of human salvation are entrusted." . . .
>
> "I believe profoundly in academic freedom," he said. "But I also want to emphasize the academic part of it—that is, their freedom to debate and discuss and weigh the merits of any body of ideas. . . .
>
> "But to try the ideas out in action is the function of businesses, trade unions, city councils and churches."

What do you think?

Look again at Marshall McLuhan's statement (p. 241) about what students want. Do you agree? Is this what you want?

What do you think might be some of the consequences for students and for society, if students not only participate increasingly in the educational process but also try their ideas out in society at large?

Debate about the appropriate role in society of students and teachers involves many of the same issues as debate about two other social institutions: the church and the scientific laboratory. For churchmen,

From an interview of S. I. Hayakawa by Donovan Bess, *San Francisco Chronicle,* Jan. 2, 1969.

the issue is whether their calling requires or forbids participation in such "secular" affairs as the Civil Rights struggle. For scientists, the issue is whether they have a moral responsibility for the potential social and political uses of their discoveries, or whether as scientists they should remain objective and uninvolved. For teachers and students, the question is whether they have a right (and/or an obligation) to participate in or remain detached from the educational, political, and social decision-making process.

One might argue, on the one hand, that persons engaged in the pursuit of virtue, knowledge, and wisdom (i.e., those in the church, the laboratory, and the school) are perhaps best qualified to shape society's values and goals. On the other hand, if these persons do not maintain their detachment, how can they function with the objectivity and the freedom necessary to the unfettered development of the human potential?

Can you think of a way out of this dilemma?

---

education as evolutionary change

Let us back away from *education* a few steps to see it again in context with *evolution*. At the beginning of Part V we put education and evolution together in a pie, and suggested that there was a sense in which each was its opposite. Let us examine that possibility now, as we did with "Work-Play" and with "Communication-Transportation."

We have proposed that education and evolution are both forms of human engineering; that is to say, they are ways in which human beings are adapted to the environment. What, then, is the difference between them?

We might want to say that whereas education makes changes within individuals through personal learning, evolution makes changes in the species (for example, the human race appears to be losing its wisdom teeth through evolutionary change). We might then argue that learning is short range and reversible, whereas evolutionary change is long range (that is, taking place over generations) and irreversible.

We might instead propose that education makes changes in the personality, mind, or psyche, whereas evolution makes physical changes, or that education adapts us to the cultural environment, whereas evolution adapts us to the physical or natural environment. Perhaps we could propose that learning is voluntary, but that evolution is involuntary, or that education takes place by human design, whereas evolution is a "natural" occurrence.

However, these distinctions are becoming increasingly difficult to maintain, as more and more lights are switched on in the once dark areas of our physical and chemical make-up. To take one example, we are now discovering that personal learning can be transferred from one organism to another, not only through education or imprinting, but also through injecting chemicals from the brain of one organism into another organism. Flatworms and rats have been the learners so far. But the possibility of passing on learned information through the body rather than through the mind could make the transfer of learning involuntary, species-wide, and enduring. No longer would we wait for generations of time to work fundamental changes.

Perhaps it would be more fruitful to think of learning through education as one part of the process of evolutionary change. Very broadly, evolutionary change can occur in the nature and functioning of three phases of human life: in the process of birth, with its attendant genetic inheritance; in the process of growth, with its multitude of physical, chemical, mental, emotional, cultural, ethical, and other developments and changes; and in the process of decline and death. Learning through education, then, is part of the process of growth.

But the extent to which we can or should rely upon education both to adapt us to our environment and to keep us adaptable must be weighed against other agents of change. Wherein lies the greatest danger and the greatest promise? What if we make a mistake? *Unlearning* is more difficult than *learning*, though, as we have seen, it can be done. But what of changes through the alteration of the DNA molecule, the electrical linking of the human being and the machine, the chemical manipulation of states of consciousness, the abolition of physical death? Are these reversible? And if they are not, are we clear enough about who we are to dare to make these changes?

Let us look now at some of the possibilities ahead of us. And let us approach them with the question: How far do we wish to go? How fundamentally can we or should we change man himself?

Man, the sentient species of a small planet circling a small sun in a dim backwater of the galaxy, is about to undertake the breath-taking adventure of re-creating himself. By tinkering with the mechanisms of his heredity, he plans to improve on nature's designs. He believes he can learn to change any part of his body's engineering: his susceptibility to disease, his height and intelligence and beauty, the very span of his life. After two billion years of evolution by trial and error, we now stand at the beginning of human-kind's next phase: the Second Genesis.

"How will you choose to intervene in the ancient designs of nature for man?" asked biophysicist Robert Sinsheimer last year in the *Bulletin of the Atomic Scientists*. "Would you like to control the sex of your offspring? It will be as you wish. Would you like your son to be six feet tall? Seven feet? Eight feet? What troubles you? Allergy? Obesity? . . . These will be easily handled. . . . Even the timeless patterns of growth and maturity and aging will be subject to our design. We know of no intrinsic limits to the life span. How long would you like to live?

Max Gunther,
"Second Genesis"

changing nature's ancient designs

from WILL MAN DIRECT HIS OWN EVOLUTION?

Albert Rosenfeld

The following account is not a comprehensive survey of present-day investigations in biology and medicine. Its intent is rather to give some advance notice of what may be in store as a consequence of current research, discovery, and achievement in a number of different scientific fields—all of them related to man's new abilities to tamper with his body, and therefore with his psyche. Tampering after birth is nothing new. In fact, that is what the whole history of medicine and psychiatry is about. But the latest ways of tampering constitute radical departures from the ways we have known. They involve such procedures as the wholesale replacement of failing body parts with transplanted or artificial organs . . . ; the control of the body, brain, and behavior through electronics, drugs, and cybernetics; the freezing of "dead" bodies for possible earthly resurrection by the even more sophisticated science of the future.

Tampering before birth . . . covers not only prenatal medicine—improving the health of the fetus while it is still in the womb. Far more than this, it covers the variety of new methods of conceiving and growing babies—inside or outside the womb, with or without sex. And it deals with the further possibility of modifying future generations through eugenics or through the actual molecular manipulation of the genes.

As scientists daily edge closer to the solution of some of nature's deepest mysteries, no idea seems too wild to contemplate. Would you like education by injection? A larger, more efficient brain? A cure for old age? Parentless babies? Body size and skin color to order? Name it, and somebody is seriously proposing it. . . .

. . . In sober scientific circles today

there is hardly a subject more commonly discussed than man's control of his own heredity and evolution. And the discussions seldom leave much doubt that men will acquire this control. It is a matter of when, not if.

Scientists tend to agree that some of the most exciting future developments will come out of insights and discoveries yet to be made, with implications we cannot now foresee or imagine. So we live in an era where not only anything that we can imagine seems possible, but where the possibilities range beyond what we can imagine. In such an era it is hard to tell physics from metaphysics, to distinguish the mad scientists from the real ones, to judge what is a true possibility and what is sheer rot. But there is no resolving this kind of uncertainty. Even the scientists cannot give us sure guidance on what is really going to happen. . . .

. . . As man's knowledge takes on new dimensions, hardly any human concept or value will remain sacrosanct. Health and disease, youth and age, male and female, good and evil all these will take on transformed meanings. Life and death will have to be redefined. Family relationships will be quite different. Even individual identity may be hard to ascertain. Nothing can be taken for granted. . . .

when you've seen one, you've seen 'em all

**reproduction
by
replication?**

Recently Dr. E. S. E. Hafez, an Egyptian-born experimental biologist at Washington State University, commissioned a scientist friend from Germany to bring him a hundred head of prize sheep. The entire herd is to be delivered to Dr. Hafez in a neat package he can carry in one hand. It will be a ventilated box and inside will be a female rabbit. Inside the rabbit will be 100 incipient rams and ewes, all of them embryos only a few days old, growing as if still in their natural mother. Then, following a procedure already well established in Europe, he will implant each embryo in a ewe where it will gestate and, in a few months, be born.

Dr. Hafez, whose research support includes over $160,000 supplied by the National Institutes of Health alone, sees no reason why his method would not work just as well with people.

He speculates that, only ten or fifteen years hence, it could be possible for a housewife to walk into a new kind of commissary, look down a row of packets not unlike flower-seed packages, and pick her baby by label. Each packet would contain a frozen one-day-old embryo, and the label would tell the shopper what color of hair and eyes to expect as well as the probable size and I.Q. of the child. It would also offer assurance of freedom from genetic defects. After making her selection, the lady could take the packet to her doctor and have the embryo implanted in herself, where it would grow for nine months, like any baby of her own. . . .

Already it is commonplace to keep alive various kinds of human cells in tissue culture for extended periods of time, growing whole colonies from single cells again and again. It has been seriously suggested that it may be possible eventually to grow an entire organ, like a kidney or a liver, in tissue culture. Some years ago the eminent French biologist Jean Rostand even predicted that a man might one day be able to have a culture of his own cells —cells from almost anywhere in his body—stashed away somewhere so that a complete new replica of himself could be grown in case he met with an untimely accident.

Far-fetched? Certainly. Yet Cornell

University's Dr. Frederick C. Steward ... has been achieving exactly this sort of asexual reproduction with the lowly carrot. It is, of course, a very long way from carrots to people, and Steward cautions that animal and human cells may behave differently. Here again, a series of breakthroughs are required to overcome the formidable technical barriers that still lie ahead before any definitive answers can be expected. Nevertheless, as a result of recent work, Dr. Rostand now believes more firmly than ever that tissue-culture tech-niques "would in theory enable us to create as many identical individuals as might be desired. A living creature would be printed in hundreds, in thousands of copies, all of them real twins. This would, in short, be human propagation by cuttings, capable of assuring the indefinite reproduction of the same individual—of a great man, for example!"

Would anyone like to name the great man he would care to see duplicated by the hundreds, by the thousands—or even by the dozen?

better people for better living— through chemistry

genetic manipulation

Of all the variations that might be played upon the theme of human procreation, the ultimate—at least, the "ultimate" we can now project—will be the production of beings whose specifications can be drawn in advance. This could come about, scientists predict, through the manipulation of the genetic material itself, though the estimates of when this might come to pass vary considerably.

The basic genetic material, the stuff of which chromosomes are made, is deoxyribonucleic acid or DNA.... In the coiled structure of the DNA molecule and the complex arrangement of its atoms lie the final secrets of heredity. DNA's genetic messages are written out in a four-letter code, each "letter" being a specific chemical substance. Scientists have begun to be able to read the genetic code—but only in a halting, incipient way, and it may take a long time before they become really fluent readers. But once we can read, we may then learn to "write"— i.e., to give genetic instructions in the DNA code.

When that time comes, man's powers will be truly godlike. He may bring into being creatures never before seen or imagined in the universe. He may even choose to create new forms of humanity—beings that might be bet-ter adapted to survive on the surface of Jupiter, or on the bottom of the Atlantic Ocean.

Even without going that far, man presumably will be able to write out any set of specifications he might desire for his ideal human being. This is what many scientists mean when they talk about man controlling his own evolution. And who can find fault with that? Is there anyone not in favor of emphasizing man's good qualities and eliminating the bad ones? The rub, of course, is that "good" and "bad" are words that are easier to say than to apply.

There is at least one area of consensus as to what is good for man— the medical area. Most people would agree that it is good to reduce infant mortality, to make it possible for infertile parents to have children, to eradicate cancer and heart disease.

But consensus is not unanimity. Dissident voices are even now insisting that many of our so-called medical advances actually militate against human progress by aggravating the population problem, thus assuring an overcrowded planet where more people will die of war and starvation. Others warn of the deterioration of the human race because so many people with hereditary defects—people who formerly would have died at an early age—are often now being kept alive, to marry and pass on their defects. A majority undoubtedly would choose—at least for themselves and those they love—the benefits of health and longevity, and worry later about problems like overpopulation and the possible deterioration of the race.

Beyond getting rid of diseases and defects, there is the prospect that we can actually improve human beings—making them more intelligent, more talented, more virtuous—by manipulating genetic material. No one would argue that man couldn't stand some improvement, but having the actual power to do so presents some sticky choices. Who is it that we will appoint to play God for us? Which scientist, which statesman, artist, judge, poet, theologian, philosopher, educator—of which nation, race or creed—will you trust to write the specifications, to decide which characteristics are desirable and which not? . . .

Writers and artists already devote much articulate worry to the subject of how alienated they are, and psychiatrists' couches are full of people who say, in effect: Doctor, I don't know who I am. So, even before the new age of biology has set in, modern man has begun to face a crisis of identity.

If people today have such troubles, what of a child turned out "in vitro"?

What is *his* status and identity as a human being? Will city hall record his existence? Who is his father, and who is his mother? Can he have any brothers or sisters? What are his citizenship and voting rights? Can the scientist who produced him simply keep him as an experimental animal? . . .

We are . . . entering an era where children may be born of geographically separated or even long-dead parents, where virgin births may become relatively common, where women may give birth to other women's children, where romance and genetics may be separated, where some few favored men may father thousands of babies, where a permit may be required in order to have a baby. Can the traditional family—already a shaky institution—survive in the midst of all this? Do we want it to survive? If so, how will we insure its survival? If not, what will we substitute for it?

If a new being is grown from the cell of a man still living, does it, too, have a soul? If he has none, is he human? Can he be saved? And suppose 100 people are grown from the cells of a dead man. Do they all have souls? Where were they meanwhile? Perhaps in the DNA of the cell nucleus? Could the present concept of the soul become barren of meaning, and would some other theological concept have to be substituted for it? . . .

we are not alone

transplants and cyborgs

Even you and I—in 1965, already here and beyond the reach of prenatal modification—could live to face curious and unfamiliar problems in identity as a result of man's increasing ability to control his own mortality after birth. As organ transplants and artificial body parts become even more available, it is not totally absurd to envision any one of us walking around one day with, say, a plastic cornea, a few metal bones, and Dacron arteries; with donated glands, kidney, and liver from some other person, from an animal, from

an organ bank, or even from an assembly line; with an artificial heart, and computerized electronic devices to substitute for muscular, neural, or metabolic functions that may have gone wrong. It has been suggested—though it will almost certainly not happen in our lifetime—that brains, too, might be replaceable, either by a brain transplanted from someone else, by a new one grown in tissue culture, or an electronic or mechanical one of some sort. . . .

Dr. Seymour Kety, an outstanding

psychiatric authority now with the National Institutes of Health, points out that fairly radical personality changes already have been wrought by existing techniques like brainwashing, electroshock therapy, and prefrontal lobotomy, without raising serious questions of identity. But would it be the same if alien parts and substances were substituted for the person's own, resulting in a new biochemistry and a new personality with new tastes, new talents, new political views—perhaps even a different memory of different experiences? Might such a man's wife decide she no longer recognized him as her husband and that he was, in fact, not? Or might he decide that his old home, job, and family situation were not to his liking and feel free to chuck the whole setup that may have been quite congenial to the old person?

Not that acute problems of identity need await the day when wholesale replacement of vital organs is a reality. Very small changes in the brain could result in astounding metamorphoses. Scientists who specialize in the electrical probing of the brain have, in the past few years, been exploring a small segment of the brain's limbic system called the amygdala—and discovering that it is the seat of many of our basic passions and drives, including the drives that lead to uncontrolled sexual extremes such as satyriasis and nymphomania. . . .

a switch in time saves mind

brain manipulation   Improved brain capacity is one innovation that appears likely. An actual physical enlargement of the brain might be brought about by genetic or prenatal manipulation. Even without that, we can do infinitely more with the gray matter we presently possess. A variety of experiments in hypnosis, drug therapy, electric brain stimulation, and molecular biology point to the probability that specific memories including all of experience and education are stored at specific sites in the brain, and that they are stored electrochemically.

Several years ago Dr. Wilder Penfield, the eminent Canadian brain surgeon, discovered that when a certain spot in a patient's brain was electrically stimulated, it called up, in vivid detail, an incident the patient thought he had altogether forgotten. The stimulation of the same spot brought forth the same memory every time. Similar feats have been performed under hypnosis and under the influence of certain drugs. The long-range promise is that these powers of recall, instead of being sporadic and conditional, could be permanent and constant, and that our own conscious minds could replace the outside experimenter. Think what our intellects might be like if we could really remember everything, and have it all efficiently stored away for instant retrieval.

No one really knows what the capacity of the human brain might be, used to its limit. But this limit, whatever it is, may one day be overcome by hooking up the human brain to a computer. When this kind of brain-computer hook-up is imagined, it is usually to envision the computer as remotely controlling and directing the brain or a dozen brains, or a hundred. There is no reason why it could not work the other way around, as Dr. Simon Ramo suggests, with the computer serving as a vast storehouse of readily accessible information for the brain's use.

But we need not stop here. Some of the same experiments revealed that a man may be made to remember things that never happened to him at all. If memory does indeed consist of electrochemical changes in the structure of certain molecules in the brain cells, there is no theoretical reason why,

D.O.M., A.D. 2167

John Frederick Nims

When I've outlived three plastic
    hearts, or four,
Another's kidneys, corneas (*beep!*),
    with more
Unmentionable rubber, nylon, such—
And when (*beep!*) in a steel drawer
    (DO NOT TOUCH!),
Mere brain cells in a saline wash, I
    thrive
With thousands, taped to quaver out,
    "Alive!"—
God grant that steel two wee (*beep!*)
    eyes of glass
To glitter wicked when the nurses pass.

IT'S A WHOLE NEW WORLD

Mrs. Gordon Needham of Pleasant Hill donated a kidney to Howard Smith of Lafayette in a highly successful transplant at UC Medical Center— but that's not all. Smith was fired from his job the first of the month, and Mrs. Needham is trying to find him a new one. "After all," she says spunkily, "I have a vested interest in him—he's wearing my kidney." "She's a wonderful woman," says Smith. "You might say I have her under my skin."

Herb Caen

John Nims, *Of Flesh and Bone* (New Brunswick, N.J.: Rutgers University Press, 1967), p. 36.
Reprinted by permission from the *San Francisco Chronicle.*

when it becomes possible to alter these structures, experiences of any kind cannot be implanted at will. The brain thus influenced would never know the difference.

Dr. Holger Hyden in Sweden has performed experiments indicating that when mice are trained in certain skills, the training permanently changes the structure of nucleic-acid molecules in their brain cells. The learning seems to reside in these structural changes. Still-controversial experiments with flat-worms suggest that "training" can be passed on simply by passing on the changed molecules themselves from one flatworm to another. This kind of research has bred speculation that subject matter of any sort might be taught merely by injecting the subject with what could in effect be an artificial virus containing nucleic acids of the appropriate molecular structure.

A virus of the future, then, might give us algebra or French instead of the flu. In his recent book *Profiles of the Future,* Arthur C. Clarke expresses his conviction that the famous "mechanical educator" of science fiction is no longer necessarily relegated to fiction. He believes information might be fed into the brain almost as sounds are recorded on a magnetic tape, to be stored there for playback on command.

If true information could be recorded and stored this way, why not false information? And if information is recordable as on a magnetic tape, might it not be erasable as well? Any knowledge no longer useful, any memory of an experience a man would rather forget, could be wiped out as if it had never been there at all. And artificial experiences could be supplied at will.

by the time it's news, it's old hat

CHEMISTS' NEW EVIDENCE

TRANSFERRING MEMORIES

Dallas

New and significant evidence that the mystery of memory may be encoded in the changing chemistry and structure of the brain was presented here yesterday by an enthusiastic band of scientific pioneers.

The scientists—whose controversial research was once viewed with scepticism, if not downright derision, by their conservative colleagues—reported that no fewer than fifteen laboratories throughout the world have now achieved the intriguing feat of "memory transfer" in mammals.

By memory transfer they mean this: training an animal to perform a specific task; extracting chemicals from the animal's brain; injecting the

chemicals into an untrained animal, and observing in the recipient an ability to perform a task the animal had never been trained to do before.

The new studies in memory transfer were reported here to the American Association of Science by Dr. Georges Ungar of Baylor University and Dr. Ejnar J. Fjerdingstad of the University of Copenhagen, who is also working at Baylor.

Dr. Ungar described experiments in which he trained more than 2800 rats to avoid the kind of cozy dark boxes that rats normally like to skulk in. He trained them to prefer lighted boxes by giving their feet an electric shock when they entered the dark boxes.

Then he prepared extracts of the

Reprinted by permission from the *San Francisco Chronicle.*

brains of the trained rats and injected various types of "brain soup" into 638 untrained mice, who responded by promptly and overwhelmingly avoiding the dark boxes.

CODE

Ungar said that in similar experiments, different types of brain extracts have proven to be specifically related to different types of learning: one set of brain chemicals, for example, seems to govern the transfer of light-dark discrimination; another relates to the acceptance of fear-inducing noises.

Ungar said his experiments indicate "an overwhelming probability that learned information can be transferred chemically." It is also highly probable, he said, that "the extracts injected into the recipients contain some highly specific information encoded in molecular structure."

KEY

Dr. Ungar said his research colleagues are now trying to pinpoint the specific chemical responsible for one specific type of memory—perhaps protein-like molecules.

"Identification of this substance would be the first step in the formidable task of deciphering the code in which learned information is handled by the brain," he said.

Dr. Fjerdingstad reported positive results from memory-transfer experiments in which rats were trained over a three-week period to perform extremely difficult tasks involving the use of two levers to receive a reward.

WORMS

Achievements like these in memory-transfer were first tentatively described more than six years ago by experimenters who fed "trained" flatworms to other flatworms and thereby "educated" the cannibals.

Since then, the research has generated explosive excitement among psychologists because of the light it may shed on the basic biochemical processes of learning—and because of the possibility that chemistry may one day be used to enhance human education.

The day of the "get-smart-pill" may be closer than we think.

REVOLUTIONARY STUDIES

BRAIN IS MOLDED
BY THE AGE OF 12

Dallas

A revolution is going on in knowledge of how the brain works.

It tells us that a child's brain has been physically set into a firm culture-bound mold by age twelve, and after that it is very hard to make changes in it.

It tells us that a Russian's brain, once he has reached the age of twelve, is physically different from an American's, a white man's from a black man's, a hippie's from a square's. The molecules and atoms of these different brains actually become set in different patterns from every other, but between cultures there may be vaster differences still.

Also, it is not only the brain that is physiologically different. Each brain's receptors—eyes, ears, and nerve endings—and the relays on the way to the

Reprinted by permission of Los Angeles Times/Washington Post News Service.

brain come to differ in how they receive sights, sounds and experiences. So one person, seeing or hearing something, may actually see or hear different things than the next person.

The revolution in understanding all this has occurred in the last ten or twelve years and in the last few years has come to a sudden head, according to Dr. Robert B. Livingston, professor of neurosciences at the University of California in Los Angeles.

People have always known, he told the American Association for the Advancement of Science Sunday that two individuals often tell different stories about the same event—as did young people and policemen, for example, after the street riots in Chicago.

OBJECTIVE

But now, he said, "We know that the other guy is not necessarily lying," nor does he "lack the moral fibre to be objective"—his ears may have simply not heard the same words or his eyes seen certain relevant events, all depending on his past experience and the way the molecules of his brain and receptor organs have learned to function.

All this has been shown, he said in "thousands" of experiments in animals and human beings in the United States, Europe, and the Soviet Union.

And our ideas, concepts, and images are modified by our "experiences, expectations and purposes, with much data either shielded out or distorted so it may never reach two of us in just the same form.

It is in the childhood years, Professor Livingston reported—when the brain is doubling in size in the first six months and doubling again by age four—that "people become embedded in language and culture, so that what we consider 'common sense' in any culture is actually what we experience before age twelve."

MOON

For example: "There are youngsters now growing up who will take man's capacity to go to the moon quite for granted because it happened before they were twelve."

Does all this mean we can never change or learn after twelve?

No, said Livingston, though it becomes harder and harder and even "increasingly hopeless." Maturation, however, is "learning not to be strictly bound by past experience" and to take a larger view. In fact, he said, "If we learn to understand these mechanisms better," we could be far "more capable of tolerance of the other man's perception of the world."

The truth is, he said, that "there may be much less son-of-bitchery in the world than we suppose," just different degrees of perception.

In effect each culture provides individuals with a set of filters which enables them to perceive order in a universe where an infinite number of discrete events occurs. These filters determine which events an individual will perceive as unimportant, as important and as critical. Thus the education which each individual receives essentially determines which issues will be examined and which will be ignored: the areas in which the society will take action and the areas where it will fail to act. Recent research shows that the culture determines not only patterns of analysis, but also perception itself. In other words, selective perception is not limited to the brain but also occurs in the operation of the primary sense organs: ear, eye, nose, etc.

From Dialogue on Education.

THEY CAN BE DIVIDED

WE ALL HAVE A "PAIR OF BRAINS"

Gobind Behari Lal

Two California scientists have demonstrated conclusively that every human has not one but two brains—each with its own mind or consciousness.

Dr. Roger W. Sperry Hixon, professor of psychobiology at the California Institute of Technology, Pasadena, and Dr. Michael S. Gazzaniga, now assistant professor of psychology at the University of California at Santa Barbara, have led the researches which show that man has a "pair of brains" and a "pair of independent minds."

Medical scientists heretofore have regarded the two hemispheres, half globes, inside the head as halves of a single global brain, and mind or consciousness as a unified mental experience. But, studying the brains of cats, Doctor Sperry discovered the two hemispheres really serve as separate but connected brains.

TISSUE BRIDGE

Normally in man, as in cats or other mammals, the two hemispheres are principally connected by a nervous tissue bridge, and appear to operate as a single organ. Actually, the two brains are Siamese twins and can be divided by surgery, apparently without damage.

"Bisection" of the two brains has been done in ten patients of severe, otherwise uncontrollable epilepsy.

The first operation was performed on a 48-year-old epileptic in 1962 at the White Memorial Hospital, Los Angeles. Doctor Hixon theorized that epileptic fits could be reduced by separating the hemispheres of the brain.

FITS ENDED

Surprisingly, the fits ceased altogether.

Next patient was an eleven-year-old schoolboy whose frequent fits left him unable to study. Separating his left and right brain surgically made him normal.

As a psychologist, Gazzaniga made many tests to determine how the brain separation affects performance of the senses, muscular organs, emotional and intellectual activities.

All tests showed, as this psychologist reports in *Scientific American*, that each brain hemisphere behaved quite independently.

Following the operation on an epileptic man, it was observed that the two brains, now parted, showed "opposite" wills. When this man was pulling on his trousers, his left hand sometimes worked against the right. One hand pulled up, the other down.

HELP EACH OTHER

While his right hand pulled his wife toward him, his left hand pushed her away aggressively. But eventually the two independent brains began to help each other.

As far as emotions are concerned, the two brains seem to behave almost equally but in different styles.

When Doctor Gazzaniga presented a picture of a nude woman to a woman patient with freshly separated brains, her right and left brains reacted emotionally, but differently. Perceived by the left brain, the picture made the patient burst into a laugh, and she said that she saw a nude woman. But the right brain's perception resulted in a sly smile, and she was unable to say the words "nude woman."

LANGUAGE POWER

In language capacity, particularly, in all patients the left brain was defi-

Reprinted from the *San Francisco Examiner*.

nitely superior to the right brain. However, according to Doctor Gazzaniga, in a two- to three-year-old child, the two brains are equally proficient even in language capacity. As development takes place, the capacity of the right brain becomes somehow inhibited, thwarted.

On the whole, in grownups, one brain, usually the left, is dominant, while the right one behaves as a minority brain.

However, suppose the brains were separated at an early age, when both had equal capacities. Then a person might grow up with two fully efficient brains, working in agreement established by education. Such a person would be twice-brained, double-minded —a superior mental being.

Following the operation, the epileptic patient can carry on two utterly different tasks with eyes or hands as fast as the normal person performs just one task.

from WILL MAN DIRECT HIS OWN EVOLUTION?

Albert Rosenfeld

WHO WILL CREATE A NEW IMAGE FOR MAN?

It is fitting that doctors and scientists, who are most closely involved with the new developments, are the first to express their concern. But everyone will have to be concerned. It would be hard to exaggerate either the challenges or the opportunities for educators, for business leaders, for legislators and jurists, for artists and writers, for theologians and philosophers—and for you and me, personally.

One of the weightiest burdens is bound to fall on the statesmen and leaders of men at all levels of national and international life. They are, of course, already confronted with enormous problems brought on by science and technology. Nuclear weaponry, supplemented by chemical and biological warfare, threatens everyone re-

gardless of race, color, or creed. As space gets increasingly cluttered with hardware, including licensed communications satellites, a body of space law becomes imperative. Worldwide weather control, too, may be in the offing, and the accelerated exploitation of the oceans' resources. Now, with the biological bomb ready to explode, the need to face this complexity of problems takes on more acute, do-it-now urgency.

The most tempting solution is to let things ride and pay as little attention as possible to these mind-boggling developments. But a decision to ignore them is simply a decision to turn them over to any unscrupulous opportunist who chooses to employ them for his own ends. To appreciate the consequences, we need only imagine some totalitarian nation of the future, led by a man sure he knows what is best for everybody. He has at his command all the new means of controlling reproduction and the human brain and behavior. In addition to being able to raise entire populations in vitro or in tissue culture, he could implant electrodes or begin administering drugs to people at a very early age, maintaining his subjects in a constant state of hardworking subservience and at the same time in a constant state of euphoria by stimulating the pleasure centers of their brains. Practically no one in such a society would have any true choice in any area of life which we now consider important. But everybody would be "happy."

Who cares about the pursuit of happiness if everybody already has it? If everybody is happy, can anything be wrong?

If we think so, says Sir Julian Huxley, we must ascertain once again that we know what answers we would give to some basic questions: What are people for? What human values are we eager to hang onto? Without answers to such questions we remain helpless to use scientific advance as it should be used—as a tool to serve human values in a society that can still be called democratic.

The overriding political predicament, then, is this: how to plan and organize—intelligently, efficiently, flexibly—and at the same time safeguard the individual from intolerably restrictive state controls. Can there be real planning without real control? Some breakthroughs in political science, and in the other behavioral sciences, may be necessary to handle the problems created by breakthroughs in physics and biology. Obviously the professional political types, though they will ultimately be responsible for making the laws and administering them, cannot do it all themselves. They will need all the help they can get.

Artists and writers, for instance,

can make a major contribution. There will be much more for them in the new age than new themes and new plots for plays, poems, novels, and paintings. With a vast, opened-up universe of new possibilities and relationships to explore and portray, with unparalleled human powers and dimensions, they can help create an already badly needed new image of man. . . .

Many biologists are hopeful that the revelations of biology itself will give us new and profound insights into the true nature of man, allowing us to draw up laws and ethical systems that are consistent with that nature. The New Man science helps create may also be much better equipped to deal with problems that now look insoluble, and the new powers we get may give us answers we cannot now predict—or may even render some of the problems obsolete. So, even at a time when the daily newspapers are full of wars and riots and murders, and we despair that "human nature" can never be different, let us not give up hope yet. "Can the Ethiopian change his skin," asked Jeremiah, "or the leopard his spots? Then may ye also do good, that are accustomed to do evil." If it suddenly turns out that the Ethiopian and the leopard and you and I can change anything it pleases us to change, then it follows—does it not?—that even we may also do good.

It may be comforting to know that the statesmen and the theologians and the philosophers and the scientists are worrying about all these things, but we cannot let them do all the worrying for us, or make all the decisions for us. The time ahead is wild and uncharted. No one has been there, so there are no experts. Each of us, whose body and brain may be modified or whose descendants' characteristics may be predetermined, has a vast personal stake in the outcome. We can guarantee that good will be done only by looking to it ourselves.

> Since man is a primate with weaker instincts than the reindeer, the horse, and the goat, he may be a readier subject for domestication. We cannot be sure. Human slavery has represented man's only persistent attempt to tame his fellow man. The slave as a rule, however, was cheaper to buy or to capture than to breed; and so we cannot interpret the collapse of slavery as the failure of controlled human breeding. We and our greater philosophers must grant, I believe, that the masters of a universal society with the aid of a captive science might just possibly succeed in producing, over a long enough period, a lasting answer to the problem of our animal nature: a universal human slave inherently obedient to other people's reason. Whether through sentimental attachment or rational choice, I find myself moved to prefer the wild creatures among whom I was born to the more literal *Homo sapiens* that science and tyranny might unite to produce. I may in my preference be a victim of a new self-delusion, and be looking at human affairs through another transparent curtain. But I find that I cannot disbelieve in nature. I cannot but believe in the pure wild gene, in natural selection as opposed to human, and in the strength and balance of our natural endowment as sufficient foundation for our species' ambitions.
>
> Robert Ardrey,
> *African Genesis*

onward to paradise:
postponing aging—and death

from SECOND GENESIS

Max Gunther

It may be possible, some scientists think, to design a life-span-lengthening virus. Each species on earth has its characteristic span: A man is allotted some seventy years; a dog, up to eighteen; a sea turtle, 150. Yet nobody knows precisely why this should be. By con-tinual replication of DNA molecules, life itself has existed on earth for some two billion years; and there seems to be no built-in reason why each individual creature should not live almost eternally through continual regeneration of its own cells. A DNA molecule doesn't "wear out" in the sense that a machine does. Why, then, do a man's cells regenerate less and less perfectly as he passes his fortieth year? One possibility, suggests Professor Markert at Yale, is that replicaselike enzymes collect in the cells and interfere with the processing of genetic instructions. Another possibility is that the system for switching genes on and off breaks down—perhaps founders in its own complexity as too many switchings pile up. In either case, it's conceivable that a viral or direct chemical treatment can be devised for nullifying the effects of such cellular garbage.

Another possible cause of aging, some biophysicists think, is cosmic radiation. We're bombarded constantly by high-energy atomic particles from space. We don't feel them, but our DNA might. Each time such a particle hits a DNA molecule, part of the molecule may be chipped off or knocked. awry. After 75 years of living, the molecules in all our cells may have sustained so many such "aging hits" that they can't function properly anymore.

"If this is the case," says Dr. Heller, "it's conceivable we may be able to es-tablish a kind of 'youth bank.' At the age of, say, 25, you'd report to the bank and have a patch of skin or a few other cells removed. We should be able, in time, to culture these cells and obtain a significant amount of 25-year-old DNA, and we should also learn how to get DNA back into your living cells. Your 'young' DNA would be stored and protected at, say, the temperature of liquid helium. Every few years, you'd report back to the bank and have your aging DNA diluted with young material. This could retard aging for a long time—perhaps forever."

A similar vision of the future is held by James Bonner, a molecular biologist at the California Institute of Technology. He is interested in the avenue of research being explored by Professor Markert—the mysterious switching on and switching off of genes in various cells. When the mystery is solved, he says, it may be feasible to grow new organs inside the body as replacements for damaged, diseased or aging ones. If you have heart disease, for instance, your body might be induced to grow a new heart next to the the old one.

"We're not yet at the point where we dare tamper directly with human genetics," says Dr. Heller, "and some scientists think it's useless right now to begin worrying about the potential problems involved. I strongly disagree. I don't think you should wait for a problem to clobber you before you begin worrying about it."
Many scientists share this view. "Back in 1910," says Dr. Saltman in California, "Einstein enunciated the relationship between energy and matter. Nobody marched in a picket line protesting or agreeing. Yet people should have been thinking about what protest signs they were to carry in 1945 when a mushroom cloud rose over Hiroshima. This time, I say let's show more foresight."

Max Gunther,
"Second Genesis"

PROFESSOR'S TALK

"ONLY THE LAZY
EVER NEED DIE"

Dr. Robert C. W. Ettinger said the freezing of bodies shortly after all signs of life have ebbed away now offers an alternative to death as we know it.

"To die simply because you're too lazy to undertake steps to avoid it is not only ignorant, it's ignominious," he declared.

CRYOBIOLOGY

Ettinger, a Highland Park College professor, spoke before some eighty persons here at the University of California Medical Center.

He is an authority on the new science of cryobiology—the science of preserving and storing life forms at extreme low temperatures.

Ettinger reported a half a dozen people in this country have already elected to have their corpses frozen in hopes of reawakening to life at some distant point in the future.

FRESH LIFE

The Michigan scientist said there has been enough experimentation already done to indicate that human organisms can survive long periods of freezing.

Ettinger acknowledged that most scientists scoff at the concept of freezing bodies now in hopes that one day technology will breath fresh life into them.

But, he said, "we're gaining adherents in the ranks of these experts—they're slowly seeking the logic of it."

In the future, he assessed, medical science will improve men and women so much "they won't even be considered human beings by current criteria."

ONLY EVOLUTION

Ettinger acknowledged that the society of the future may have no use for any ice-cubed relics of the past.

"Instead of reviving me, they might chop me up and use me for fertilizer," he said philosophically.

He said only a "small percentage" of clergymen aware of the concept of deep-freezing bodies after death object to it on theological grounds.

"We're saving and extending life, not creating it," he declared.

He provoked the biggest laugh of the evening when he solemnly declared the "motto" of those dedicated to cryobiology. "We never say die."

bidding farewell to the flesh: immortality

from PROFILES OF THE FUTURE

Arthur C. Clarke

A safe and practical form of suspended animation—which involves no medical impossibility and may indeed be regarded as an extension of

Reprinted by permission from the *San Francisco Chronicle*.
From pp. 207–211, *Profiles of the Future* by Arthur C. Clarke. Copyright © 1959, 1960, 1962 by Arthur C. Clarke. Copyright © 1961 by H. M. H. Publishing Company. Reprinted by permission of Harper & Row, Publishers.

anesthesia—could have major effects upon society. Men suffering from incurable diseases might choose to leapfrog ten or twenty years, in the hope that medical science might have caught up with their condition. The insane, and criminals beyond our present powers of redemption, might also be sent forward in time, in the expectation that the future could salvage them. Our descendants might not appreciate this legacy, of course; but at least they could not send it back.

All this assumes—though no one has yet proved it—that the legend of Rip van Winkle is scientifically sound, and that the processes of aging would be slowed down, or even checked, during suspended animation. Thus a sleeping man could travel down the centuries, stopping from time to time and exploring the future as today we explore space. There are always misfits in every age who might prefer to do this, if they were given the opportunity, so that they could see the world that will exist far beyond their normal span of life.

And this brings us to what is, perhaps, the greatest enigma of all. *Is there a normal span of life, or do all men really die by accident?* Though we now live, on the average, far longer than our ancestors, the absolute limit does not seem to have altered since records became available. The Biblical three-score-years-and-ten is still as valid today as it was four thousand years ago.

No human being has been proved to have lived more than 115 years; the much higher figures often quoted are almost certainly due to fraud or error. Man, it seems, is the longest lived of all the mammals, but some fish and tortoises may attain their second century. And trees, of course, have incredible life-spans; the oldest known living organism is a small and unprepossessing bristlecone pine in the foothills of the Sierra Nevada. It has been growing, though hardly flourishing, for 4,600 years.

Death (though not aging) is obviously essential for progress, both social and biological. Even if it did not perish from overpopulation, a world of immortals would soon stagnate. In every sphere of human activity, one can find examples of the stultifying influence of men who have outlived their usefulness. Yet death—like sleep—does not appear to be biologically inevitable, even if it is an evolutionary necessity.

Our bodies are not like machines; they never wear out, because they are continually rebuilt from new materials. If this process were uniformly efficient, we would be immortal. Unfortunately, after a few decades something seems to go wrong in the repair-and-maintenance department; the materials are as good as ever, but the old plans get lost or ignored, and vital services are not properly restored when they break down. It is as if the cells of the body can no longer remember the jobs they once did so well.

The way of avoiding a failure of memory is to keep better records, and perhaps one day we will be able to help our bodies to do just that. The invention of the alphabet made mental forgetfulness no longer inevitable; the more sophisticated tools of future medicine may cure physical forgetfulness, by allowing us to preserve, in some suitable storage device, the ideal prototypes of our bodies. Deviations from the norm could then be checked from time to time and corrected, before they became serious.

Because biological immortality and the preservation of youth are such potent lures, men will never cease to search for them, tantalized by the examples of creatures who live for centuries and undeterred by the unfortunate experience of Dr. Faust. It would be foolish to imagine that this search will never be successful, down all the ages that lie ahead. Whether success would be desirable is quite another matter.

The body is the vehicle of the brain, and the brain is the seat of the mind. In the past, this triad has been inseparable, but it will not always be so. If we cannot prevent our bodies from disintegrating, we may replace them while there is yet time.

The replacement need not be another body of flesh and blood; it could be a machine, and this may represent the next stage in evolution. Even if the brain is not immortal, it could certainly live much longer than the body whose diseases and accidents eventually bring it low. Many years ago, in a famous series of experiments, Russian surgeons kept a dog's head alive for some days by purely mechanical means. I do not know if they have yet succeeded with men, but I shall be surprised if they have not tried.

If you think that an immobile brain would lead a very dull sort of life, you have not fully understood what has already been said about the senses. A brain connected by wire or radio links to suitable organs could participate in any conceivable experience, real or imaginary. When you touch something, are you *really* aware that your brain is not at your fingertips, but three feet away? And would you notice the difference, if that three feet were three thousand miles? Radio waves make such a journey more swiftly than the nervous impulses can travel along your arm.

One can imagine a time when men who still inhabit organic bodies are regarded with pity by those who have passed on to an infinitely richer mode of existence, capable of throwing their consciousness or sphere of attention instantaneously to any point on land, sea, or sky where there is a suitable sensing organ. In adolescence we leave childhood behind; one day there may be a second and more portentous adolescence, when we bid farewell to the flesh.

But even if we can keep the brain alive indefinitely, surely in the end it would be clogged with memories, overlaid like a palimpsest with so many impressions and experiences that there was no room for more? Eventually, perhaps yes, though I would repeat again that we have no idea of the ultimate capacity of a well-trained mind, even without the mechanical aids which will certainly become available. As a good round figure, a thousand years would seem to be about the ultimate limit for continuous human existence—though suspended animation might spread this millennium across far longer vistas of time.

Yet there may be a way past even this barrier, as I suggested in the novel *The City and the Stars*. This was an attempt to envisage a virtually eternal society, in the closed city of Diaspar a billion years from now. I would like to end by quoting the words in which my hero learns the facts of life from his old tutor, Jeserac:

A human being, like any other object, is defined by its structure—its pattern. The pattern of a man is incredibly complex; yet Nature was once able to pack that pattern into a tiny cell, too small for the eye to see.

What Nature can do, Man can do also, in his own way. We do not know how long the task took. A million years, perhaps—but what is that? In the end our ancestors learned to analyse and store the information that would define any specific human being—and to use that information to recreate the original. . . .

The way in which information is stored is of no importance; all that matters is the information itself. It may be in the form of written words on paper, of varying magnetic fields, or patterns of electric charge. Men have used all these methods of storage, and many others. Suffice to say that long ago they were able to store themselves—or, to be more precise, the disembodied patterns from which they could be called back into existence. . . .

In a little while, . . . I shall prepare to leave this life. I shall go back through my memories, editing them and cancelling those I do not wish to keep. Then I shall walk into the Hall of Creation, but through a door that you have never seen. This old body will cease to exist, and so will consciousness itself. Nothing will be left of Jeserac but a galaxy of electrons frozen in the heart of a crystal.

I shall sleep, . . . and without dreams. Then one day, perhaps a hundred thousand years from now, I shall find myself in a new body, meeting those who have been chosen to be my guardians. . . . At first I will know nothing of Diaspar and will have no memories of what I was before. Those memories will slowly return, at the end of my infancy, and I will build upon them as I move forward into my new cycle of existence.

This is the pattern of our lives. . . . We have all been here many, many times before, though as the intervals of nonexistence vary according to random laws this present population will never repeat itself. The new Jeserac will have new and different friends and interests, but the old Jeserac—as much of him as I wish to save—will still exist. . . .

At any moment only a hundredth of the citizens of Diaspar live and walk in its streets. The vast majority slumber in the memory banks, waiting for the signal that will call them forth on to the stage of existence once again. And so we have continuity, yet change—immortality, but not stagnation. . . .

Is this fantasy? I do not know; but I suspect that the truths of the far future will be stranger still.

designing life styles: 3

What changes do you believe human engineering should make in the body and mind of man? To what extent should change come about through education and/or other kinds of evolution? Do you believe that change should come about through personal learning or through chemical, genetic, physical, electronic manipulation—or in all of these ways?

Pick a person from the list on p. 195 and design a life style for him. Let your design reveal how you think we should change human beings.

> Show in what ways as a human being he is different from human beings existing today. In what ways is he the same? What enduring values (or problems) do you foresee?

> Decide whether you will project into the near future or the far future on the basis of which gives us a better insight .into the particular values you are dealing with.

(Note: again, you may want to extend or revise a design you have already made.)

"[The dialogue community] would seem uniquely suited for taking evolutionary steps which would have revolutionary consequences."
Richard Kean

"Life would become essentially synonymous with education and with the ability to communicate effectively."
Dialogue-Focuser

"Work and education are interrelated and lifelong activities in the society of the future."
Robert Bickner

Evolution is revolution.

Will there come a time when we can say: work *is* play? Communication *is* transportation? Education *is* evolution?

And more: work-play is communication-transportation is education-evolution?

Could one shining moment provide an experience of all six, all as one?

Look again at the description on p. 7 which begins: "Let us imagine a particular space and time circa 1986 . . ."

Try doing one yourself.

It is the superb paradox of our time that in a single century we have proceeded from the first iron-clad warship to the first hydrogen bomb, and from the first telegraphic communication to the beginnings of the conquest of space; yet in the understanding of our own natures, we have proceeded almost nowhere. It is an ignorance that transcends national or racial boundaries, and leaps happily over iron curtains as if they did not exist. Were a brotherhood of man to be formed today, then its only possible common bond would be ignorance of what man is.

Robert Ardrey,
African Genesis

PART VI
discovering
human nature

nineteen

defining the quest

Advances in science and technology have rewritten the very terms and conditions of the human contract with no more warning than the morning's headlines.

Robert Heilbroner,
The Future as History

In all the history of man, key elements in the human condition have remained constant. The human condition has been defined largely in terms of man's limitations: MAN, a mortal, the product of natural evolution; though possessing the distinction among creatures of having the biggest brain for his size, confined to the planet Earth, and fortunately lacking the capacity to destroy his species or his planet. Within the last decade or two, the human condition as we have known it has abruptly ended.

The harnessing of nuclear energy, the creation of cybernetic computers, the discovery of DNA, the development of the rocket—these, primary among a host of changes—have placed within man's reach the power to create life and nonhuman intelligence, to control evolution, to defer and perhaps abolish death, to destroy our species and our planet, to break out of our closed system into space.

The *need* to discover human nature is acute and urgent, because we have the capacity to alter or even extinguish it, and with it the whole baffling experiment. For a number of reasons, we are *not* going to discover human nature, at least in this brief exploration. The subject is both too well known and too mysterious for that.

Poets, painters, dramatists, composers, novelists, historians, psychologists, anthropologists, archeologists, sociologists, biologists, and philosophers—all are explorers in the field of human nature. Museums and libraries are crammed with strange and beautiful maps brought back by explorers since the beginning of man.

Secondly, inasmuch as there is something of all of these seekers in every man, each of us holds a more or less coherent personal image of human nature, in terms of which he relates himself to the world (and, it hardly need be added, in the light of which he makes choices about the future). The array of alternative views is vast.

289

WHAT IS MAN?

"A self-balancing, 28-jointed adapter-base biped; an electro-chemical reduction plant, integral with segregated stowages of special energy extracts in storage batteries for subsequent actuation of thousands of hydraulic and pneumatic pumps with motors attached; 62,000 miles of capillaries. . . .

"The whole extraordinary complex mechanism guided with exquisite precision from a turret in which are located telescopic and microscopic self-registering and recording range finders, a spectroscope, etc.; the turret control being closely allied with an air-conditioning intake-and-exhaust, and a main fuel intake. . . ."

R. BUCKMINSTER FULLER
"Nine Chains to the Moon"
J. B. Lippincott Co., 1938

The Dynamics of Change, Kaiser Aluminum & Chemical Corporation, © 1967. Drawing by Masami Miyamoto.

Man is a predator whose natural instinct is
to kill with a weapon.
Ardrey

What is specially and uniquely human is man's
capacity to combine a wide variety of animal
propensities into an emergent cultural entity:
a human personality.
Mumford

...A man is essentially no more
than a complex machine.
Wooldridge

Man is merely the most complex product of organic
evolution on earth, the only organism whose
intelligence has evolved to the point that his culture
far transcends his biological endowment.
Lederberg

...We are God in disguise, pretending
not to be himself.
Watts

Man is a zoological group of sentient rather than
sapient beings, characterized by a brain so large
that he uses rather little of it, a chin distinctive
enough to identify him among related animals, and
an overpowering enthusiasm for things that go boom.
Ardrey

...the truth is, full human consciousness has still
to be won. It is waiting to be born from a marriage
that has not yet taken place, that only *can*
take place at the deepest level of the psyche—the
marriage between thinking and feeling.
McGlashan

As compared even with other anthropoids, one
might refer without irony to man's superior
irrationality.
Mumford

A perambulating vegetable? A bug waiting to be
squashed by bigger bugs? A rabbit at the mercy
of wolves? Who are we?

A third complication is that there are three kinds of continuous change in the subject "human nature."

One is in human nature itself, or in which potentialities we actualize at a given time; for example, whether we stress the mind or the senses.

A second is in the way we look at human nature—that is, what we isolate as important; for example, whether we stress our tool-making capacity or our game-playing capacity.

A third is in what we *know* about human nature; an example of new knowledge is the discovery of the structure of the DNA molecule.

Change, then, occurs in *the thing itself* (either in its nature or its functioning), in our *interpretations*, and in our *knowledge* of facts or potential facts. Further, change in one of these areas can lead to change in the others. For example, Ardrey's description of man as by nature a weapon-carrying predator is in the realm of interpretation or conjecture; however, as we learn more about our genes or as we make more archeological discoveries, such a description could move into the realm of fact. From there, through manipulation of the genes or through conscious change in our functioning, it could lead to a change in human nature itself. (One danger, of course, is that we will skip the second step.)

Because we live in a time of accelerating change in our physical and intellectual environment, the rate of change in all three aspects of the subject "human nature" is accelerating, too. Human beings have always lived at the interface between the known past and the unknown future. One difference today is that now we are more aware of being in this position. This awareness in itself accelerates change, because certainly the way we look at ourselves and what we believe to be true about ourselves influence what we are, at least functionally.

So we cannot hope here to discover human nature. What we can do is discover some current ways of thinking about it, by focusing on issues most closely related to changes in "the terms and conditions of the human contract." And perhaps each of us can discover some portion at least of what *he* believes, by trying on alternatives.

The word "discover" means "to find out." But it has a second meaning: "to discover" is also "to make known or manifest, to reveal to others." And isn't this what our whole journey is about? Isn't discovering human nature—both in the sense of personal insight and in the sense of revealing our version of it to others, either in how we live or in what we say—isn't this the process and purpose of man's quest?

Alice B. Toklas relates that Gertrude Stein on her deathbed mused, "Ah, Alice, what is the answer?" and, receiving no response, asked, "In that case, what is the question?" As we seek to probe the meanings of change in the human condition, let us at least be aware of the questions.

Alienated from our environment and from each other, overrunning our planet and destroying its life-support systems as rapidly as we can, turning our cities into jungles and our jungles into amusement parks, displaced from our work and unable to play—how did we get into this mess? More importantly, how do we get out?

What is the condition?	What is the question?
We are rapidly increasing our capacity to destroy the planet—either by blowing it up or by using it up.	Are we violent by nature? Is war in our genes? What is the place of instinct? What is the place of reason? How can we adjust to a crowded planet?
We have created machines which could conceivably surpass us in intelligence.	Are we finished as a species? Can we get along with machines better than we have gotten along with nature? Are we a kind of machine?
We have an increasing capacity to change the human species, by genetic, social, and cultural engineering.	Who are we? What do we want to be? How can we live meaningfully together? Can we develop sufficient wisdom not only for survival but for greatness? How can we develop a safe world peopled with fulfilled human beings?
We have vastly extended our experiential arena—both outside the planet and within it. The macrocosm and the microcosm are both opening before us, and we are extending the capacities of our senses far beyond their physical limitations.	What kind of perceptual change is possible for us? What must we learn anew about time and space? How do we fit into the universe?

In the following pages, these questions are addressed from a number of viewpoints. Lewis Mumford is a cultural historian. Robert Ardrey is a dramatist-turned-anthropologist. Alan McGlashan is a psychiatrist. Alan Watts is a sort of mystic psychologist. Carl Rogers is a humanist-psychologist. Their concerns, approaches, and emphases differ sharply. Ardrey seeks answers in man's animal heritage, Mumford in man's cultural heritage. Rogers seeks them in behavior patterns, McGlashan in the unconscious, Watts in consciousness or thought habits.

They differ, too, in the strength of the evidence they bring to bear in support of their theories. While the brief passages quoted here do not give their supporting evidence, or even their supporting arguments in full, it is important to remember that there *is* evidence, and that it is subject to varied interpretation. Our purpose, however, is less to gauge the validity of their argument than to examine the usefulness of their point of view and to try on some of the hypotheses around which argument is shaped.

In "Coping with Change" we faced the question: "Who am I?" We are about to face it again. With change the only apparent constant, with much of my experience, the experience of society, and the experience of the race seemingly irrelevant—what touchstone(s) have I for choice, for value, and for judgment? On what ground(s) can I base a personal creed?

There are four questions hidden in the question "Who am I?" They concern our relatedness and our separateness.

What is unique about me?

What have I in common with all men?

How am I as a human being different from all other kinds of being?

What have I as a human being in common with other kinds of being?

Different persons (including the authors you are about to read) are primarily interested in exploring one or another of these questions. If they emphasize one to the exclusion of the others their insights and answers will be partial. If a person could answer all four of these questions, his problem of identity would be solved.

Before you read on, start some word clusters which reflect your personal response to these four questions. Later you will be asked to see if they still fit, and to develop at least a tentative personal creed.

As you finish reading each of the following authors, put the book aside and make a list of five or ten words which seem to you to catch his key ideas. Then compare your word clusters. What are the essential differences? What are the important similarities?

conquest or civilization?

from AFRICAN GENESIS

Robert Ardrey

From the time of Darwin, it had been assumed by science that man evolved from some extinct branch of happy apedom not radically different from contemporary species. No assumption could have been more reason-

Reprinted from Robert Ardrey, *African Genesis* (New York: Atheneum Publishers, 1961), by permission of the publisher.

able, since without exception every modern primate, whether gorilla or macaque, chimpanzee or vervet monkey or gibbon or baboon, is inoffensive, nonaggressive, and strays no farther from the vegetarian way than an occasional taste for insects. And so our psychology, sociology, and anthropology professors had no reason to believe that the human ancestor led a life less bland. Yet within a decade African palaeontologists would demonstrate beyond doubt the presence on that continent of a race of terrestrial, flesh-eating, killer apes who became extinct half a million years ago. Within another decade the human emergence would be demonstrated as having taken place on that continent at about that time. And the final decade of the contemporary revolution would establish the carnivorous, predatory australopithecines as the unquestioned antecedents of man and as the probable authors of man's constant companion, the lethal weapon. . . .

the enmity instinct   The territorial drive, as one ancient, animal foundation for that form of human misconduct known as war, is so obvious as to demand small attention. When Sir Arthur Keith found himself too old for any active contribution to the Second World War, his broodings produced the marvellous volume, *Essays on Human Evolution*, and the conclusion: "We have to recognize that the conditions that give rise to war—the separation of animals into social groups, the 'right' of each group to its own area, and the evolution of an enmity complex to defend such areas —were on earth long before man made his appearance." . . .

But it is the other side of the territorial coin that may provide the foundations for a philosophical revolution. It is the hidden, unread, animal cipher stamped on the metal of our nature that may resolve the dilemma of a Spencer, the doubts of a Darwin, or the despairs of contemporary man. *The command to love is as deeply buried in our nature* **the amity instinct**   *as the command to hate.*

Amity—as Darwin guessed but did not explore—is as much a product of evolutionary forces as contest and enmity. In the evolution of any social species including the human, natural selection places as heavy a penalty on failure in peace as failure in battle. The territorial instinct, so ancient in its origin that we cannot mark its beginnings, demands *of all social animals*, with equal force, the capacities for cooperation as well as competition. . . .

As a dramatist-turned-scientist, Ardrey uses the insight of the playwright to grasp and present the drama of the human genesis. His account of the drama gives new meaning to an old myth. We are, he says, Cain's children. We had a brother once, whom we slew. And long before that, our ancestors were forced out of Paradise.

The Miocene period in Kenya was our Garden of Eden, the time and setting of the first act of the drama. Here, in the lush, fruitful forests which extended over much of Africa, dwelt the forest apes and our ancestors, the terrestrial apes. Food was there for the picking, and the living was easy.

But then came the Pliocene, a period of terrible drought which lasted twelve million years, a time when the forests dwindled and the terrestrial apes had to adapt or perish. This was the time of Paradise Lost; and Abel and Cain were born. Almost nothing is known of this period; it is the unwritten second act of the drama. During this time, however, two new species developed from the terrestrial apes. Both were very intelligent; both used tools. One was *Australopithecine Robustus*, big, powerful, a vegetarian, a root-eater, who lived in the bush and grubbed for a living. The other was *Australopithecine Africanus*, lithe and small, a carnivore who lived in the savannah— and killed for a living.

During the first half of the Pliocene period, too, the big brain came into existence; the big brain did not "evolve" by gradually increasing in size from generation to generation; it was a mutation, brought about perhaps by some unusual radiation. Ardrey believes—and he wrote *African Genesis* to present his case—that it was a mutation in Africanus, his Cain. When the period of drought at last gave way to a period of plenty, a new creature had emerged on the scene: man.

Africanus and Robustus lived in different parts of Africa. But at some time they met, for the bones of both are found in the Olduvai Gorge in Tanganyika, and Ardrey had his third act.

When did they meet? We do not know. But somewhere in the storeyed archives of the Olduvai Gorge there should be a record of the meeting of brothers. There should be that moment, frozen in stone, when Cain met Abel, and slew him, and made his weapons thenceforth of quartzite and lava, and fathered the human race.

cain's children

Man is a predator whose natural instinct is to kill with a weapon. The sudden addition of the enlarged brain to the equipment of an armed already-successful predatory animal created not only the human being but also the human predicament. . . .

the romantic fallacy

. . . For generations we have been enchanted by the romantic fallacy. Assuming that man is unique, innocent in his creation, noble by nature, and good in all his potentialities when not distorted by personal or social experience, modern thought has contented itself with the question, "How can we bring an end to war?" No one making such assumptions could be impelled to ask, "How can we get along without it?" Yet today the honest observer must conclude that man is noble in his nature only

the contrary view

in the sense that he partakes of the nobility of all living things; that he is unique to no greater degree than that of any fellow species; that far from being created innocent, he originated as the most sophisticated predator the world has ever known; and that amity in his nature, while partly founded on animal values, must largely be erected as a learned response by the social conditioning of each baby born.

war? . . .   How can we get along without war? It is the only question pertaining to the future that bears the faintest reality in our times; for if we fail to get along without war, then the future will be as remarkably lacking in human problems as it will be remarkably lacking in men. Yet war has been the most natural mode of human expression since the beginning of recorded history, and the improvement of the weapon has been man's principal preoccupation since Bed Two in the Olduvai Gorge. What will happen to a species denied in the future its principal means of expression, and its only means, in last appeal, of resolving differences? What will happen to a species that has dedicated its chief energy to the improvement and contest of the weapon, and that now arrives at the end of the road where further improvement and contest is impossible?

Let us not be too hasty in our dismissal of war as an unblemished evil. Are you a Christian? Then recall that Christendom survived its darkest hour in the fury of the Battle of Tours. Do you believe in law? The rule of law became a human institution in the shelter of the Roman legions. Do you subscribe to the value of individual worth? Only by the success of the phalanx at Marathon did the Greeks repel the Persian horde and make possible the Golden Age. Are you a materialist? Do you regard as a human good the satisfaction of economic want? *The Pax Britannica*, made possible by the unchallengeable supremacy of the British fleet, gave mankind the opportunity to lay the broad foundations of the Industrial Revolution.

I am free to uphold in the pages of this account certain views challenging the orthodoxies of my time because I belong to a nation that obtained freedom for its citizens through war, and that has successfully defended my freedom, by the same means, on all occasions since. You are free to read this book, and to consider, evaluate, reject, or accept my views, because we are all members of a larger civilization that accepts the free mind as a condition of such profound if painful value that on innumerable occasions it has been willing to fight for it. Do you care about freedom? Dreams may have inspired it, and wishes promoted it, but only war and weapons have made it yours.

No man can regard the way of war as good. It has simply been our way. No man can evaluate the eternal contest of weapons as anything but the sheerest waste and the sheerest folly. It has been simply our only means of final arbitration. Any man can suggest reasonable alternatives to the judgement of arms. But we are not creatures of reason except in our own eyes.

I maintain in these pages that the superior weapon, throughout the history of our species, has been the central human dream; that the energy focused on its continual development has been the central source of human dynamics; that the contest of superior weapons has been the most profoundly absorbing of human experiences; and that the issues of such contest have maintained and protected much that I myself regard as good. Finally, I maintain that deprived of the dream, deprived of the dynamics, deprived of the contest, and deprived of the issue, *Homo sapiens* stands on a darkened threshold through which species rarely return.

The true predicament of contemporary man is not entirely unlike the Pliocene predicament of the gorilla. The bough was the focus of his experience as the weapon has been the focus of ours. It provided him with the fruit that was his nourishment, and with his means of locomotion. It dominated his existence even to the specialization of his anatomy: his hook-like thumbs, his powerful chest, his long arms, his weak and truncated legs. The bough was the focus of gorilla tradition, gorilla instinct, gorilla security, gorilla psyche, and of the only way of life the gorilla knew. Then a natural challenge deprived him of his bough. And the gorilla took to the ground. There we find him today, a depleted crew of evolutionary stragglers. Every night he builds a nest in tribute to ancestral memories. Every day he pursues the unequal struggle with extinction. His vitality sags. He defends no territory, copulates rarely. And the story of the gorilla will end, one day, not with a bang but a whimper.

Deprived of the contest of weapons that was the only bough he knew, man must descend to the cane-brakes of a new mode of existence. There he must find new dreams, new dynamics, new experiences to absorb him, new means of resolving his issues and of protecting whatever he regards as good. And he will find them; or he will find himself lost. Slowly his governments will lose their force and his societies their integration. Moral order, sheltered throughout all history by the judgement of arms, will fall away in rot and erosion. Insoluble quarrels will rend peoples once united by territorial purpose. Insoluble conflicts will split nations once allied by a common dream. Anarchy, ultimate enemy of social man, will spread its gray cancerous tissues through the social corpus of our kind. Bandit nations will hold the human will a hostage, in perfect confidence that no superior force can protect the victim. Bandit gangs will have their way along the social thoroughfare, in perfect confidence that the declining order will find no means to protect itself. Every night we shall build our nostalgic family nest in tribute to ancestral memories. Every day we shall pursue through the fearful cane-brakes our unequal struggle with extinction. It is the hard way, ending with a whimper.

How can man get along without his wars and his weapons? It is the supreme question of the contemporary predicament. Have we within our human resource the capacity to discover new dreams, new dynamisms? Or are we so burdened by our illusions of central position, our romantic fallacies, and our pathetic rationalizations of the human condition that we can acknowledge no destiny beneath the human star but to go blindly blundering into a jingo jungle towards an indeterminate, inglorious, inexorable end?

The reader must sort out for himself, according to his own inclinations and judgment, the probabilities of the human outcome. But before we pass on to certain other consequences of our total animal legacy, I add a suggestion: If man is unique, and his soul some special creation, and his future is to be determined by his innate goodness, nobility and wisdom, then he is finished. But if man is not unique, and his soul represents the product of hundreds of millions of patient years of animal evolution, and he approaches his crisis not as a lost, lonely self-deluding being but as a proud creature bearing in his veins the tide of all life and in his genes the scars of the ages, then sentient man, sapient at last, has a future beyond the stormiest contradiction. . . .

I assert first the paradox that our predatory animal origin represents for mankind its last best hope. Had we been born of a fallen angel, then the contemporary predicament would lie as far beyond solution as it would lie beyond explanation. Our wars and our atrocities, our crimes and our quarrels, our tyrannies and our injustices could be ascribed to nothing other than singular human achievement. And we should be left with a clear-cut portrait of man as a degenerate creature endowed at birth with virtue's treasury whose only notable talent has been his capacity to squander it.

But we were born of risen apes, not fallen angels, and the apes were armed killers besides. And so what shall we wonder at? Our murders and massacres and missiles, and our irreconcilable regiments? Or our treaties whatever they may be worth; our symphonies however seldom they may be played; our peaceful acres however frequently they may be converted into battlefields; our dreams however rarely they may be accomplished. The miracle of man is not how far he has sunk but how magnificently he has risen. We are known among the stars by our poems, not our corpses.

No creature who began as a mathematical improbability, who was selected through millions of years of unprecedented environmental hardship and change for ruggedness, ruthlessness, cunning, and adaptability, and who in the short ten thousand years of what we may call civilization has achieved such wonders as we find about us, may be regarded as a creature without promise.

. . . or civilization?

My second assertion, flying farther into the speculative sky, is that civilization is a normal evolutionary development in our kind, and a product of natural selection. So far as we know it lacks direct animal origin. Like the jackdaw flock our civilization is the bearer of social wisdom and the accumulated experience of our kind; but unlike the flock it carries no instinctual authority over the conduct of its members. Nevertheless, I believe that civilization has come to mankind as neither accident nor ornament. It reflects the command of the kind. It rests on the most ancient of animal laws, that commanding order, and acts as a necessary inhibition and sublimation of predatory energies that would otherwise long ago have destroyed our species. I regard it as anything but a coincidence that the rate of civilization's rise has corresponded so closely with man's ascendant capacity to kill. Civilization is a compensatory consequence of our killing imperative; the one could not exist without the other. . . .

Cain's children have their problems. It is difficult to describe the invention of the radiant weapon as anything but the consummation of a species. Our history reveals the development and contest of superior weapons as *Homo sapiens'* single, universal cultural preoccupation. Peoples may perish, nations dwindle, empires fall; one civilization may surrender its memories to another civilization's sands. But mankind as a whole, with an instinct as true as a meadow-lark's song, has never in a single instance allowed local failure to impede the progress of the weapon, its most significant cultural endowment.

Must the city of man therefore perish in a blinding moment of universal annihilation? Was the sudden union of the predatory way and the enlarged brain so ill-starred that a guarantee of sudden and magnificent disaster was written into our species' conception? Are we so far from being nature's most glorious triumph that we are in fact evolution's most tragic error, doomed to bring extinction not just to ourselves but to all life on our planet?

It may be so; or it may not. We shall brood about this in a moment. But to reach such a conclusion too easily is to oversimplify both our human future and our animal past. Cain's children have many an ancestor beyond *Australopithecus africanus*, and many a problem beyond war. And the first of our problems is to comprehend our own nature.

. . . Man is a zoological group of sentient rather than sapient beings, characterized by a brain so large that he uses rather little of it, a chin distinctive enough to identify him among related animals, and an overpowering enthusiasm for things that go boom. Aside from these attributes—and the chin merely distinguishes *Homo sapiens* from earlier members of the human family—it is difficult to say where man began and the animal left off. We have a quality of self-awareness uncommon among animals, but whether this is a consequence of the enlarged brain or was shared with our extinct fathers, we do not know.

In any event, we do have the power to be aware of self, and to visualize ourselves in a present or future situation. And the power dictates as entirely natural our curiosity concerning the human outcome. Whether self-awareness will actually influence that outcome must strike any observer of human behavior, on the basis of past performance, as dubious. When human consciousness of potential disaster has in the past come into conflict with instincts of animal origin, our record has been one of impeccable poverty. No past situation, however, can compare with the contemporary predicament of potential nuclear catastrophe. And self-awareness, generating mortal fear, may at least partially forestall an evolutionary disaster.

the role of reason How great will be the role of reason in such inhibition or diversion of the weapons instinct must be entirely of a collateral order. The human brain came too suddenly on to the evolutionary scene, and lacking animal foundation lacks the command of instinct to enforce its directives. The mind's decrees rank merely as learned responses, and we cannot expect too much of a learned power placed in opposition to instinct. We cannot expect too much from the human capacity to reason, anyway, since its most elaborate energy is channelled as a rule into self-delusion and its most imposing construction erected so far has been that fairy-tale tower, the romantic fallacy.

The human mind, nevertheless, however sorry it may seem on a basis of past performance, cannot be ignored as a potential participant in some future human resolution. Granted a fresh comprehension of human nature and casting off pretense that reason carries power, the human mind can make alliance with animal instincts profound enough in our nature to engage forces for survival larger than the mind itself. . . .

We are a transitional species, without doubt. We are a pioneer creature testing the potentialities of the enlarged brain. The first species to be blessed by such a mutational marvel, we must be forgiven if sometimes we use it badly. Lacking instinctual authority for our mind's decrees, we must not be embarrassed if all too often human thought amounts to little but a faint, fizzing sound. We are simply doing the best we can. And if we do not behave too badly, then we shall pass on the power of thought, one day, to a descendant species who may count it a part of their animal endowment. They, not we, can found kingdoms on its strength.

We can trust no such kingdoms to the fragile constructions of the unauthoritative mind. We can use human thought and its limited powers to understand our natures; to explore our avenues of conduct; to weigh our best interests; to distinguish the false from the true and the dream from the waking. Confronted by the contemporary predicament of survival or self-annihilation, we may even do quite a distinguished job of it. But if we use our intelligence to its keenest advantage, then we shall note that the mind sits without a sovereignty. Allied to an instinct, judgment may act. In conflict with instinct, human thought becomes a wish.

In the balance of forces that make up our whole nature we must place our trust. It is the debate of our instincts that will determine our final testament.

The human mind stands free, in the sense that it is the servant of no given instinct. In the debate continually raging within us, one instinct may and will act to inhibit another. The mind cannot. The mind may act as witness, at times impartial. It may act as a brilliant investigative agency, at times uncorrupted. But on every occasion it will ride with the winner, whatever be the winner's cause, and devote to that cause in full, splendid measure its loyalty, honour, and devotion.

It is the mighty paradox of human thought that incapable of imprisoning an instinct, it is at the same time imprisoned by none. And that is mentality's most massive power, and humanity's second best hope.

Robert Ardrey (*Territorial Imperative, African Genesis*), Konrad Lorenz (*On Aggression, King Solomon's Ring*), and Desmond Morris (*The Naked Ape*) are writers who seek the key to human nature in man's biological (animal) heritage. By and large, they conclude that animal instinct is the strongest determinant of human behavior. Lewis Mumford, from his studies of primitive man, also believes that instinct is a strong motive force. But he differs from these thinkers and from earlier scientists in what he holds man's instinctual drives to be.

Modern man has formed a curiously distorted picture of himself, by interpreting his early history in terms of his present interests in making machines and conquering nature. And then in turn he has justified his present concerns by calling his prehistoric self a tool-making animal, and assuming that the material instruments of production dominated all his other activities. As long as the paleoanthropologist regarded material objects—mainly bones and stones—as the only scientifically admissible evidence of early man's activities, nothing could be done to alter this stereotype.

I shall find it necessary as a generalist to challenge this narrow view. There is sound reason to believe that man's brain was from the beginning far more important than his hands, and its size could not be derived solely from his shaping or using of tools; that ritual and language and social organization which left no material traces whatever, although constantly present in every culture, were probably man's most important artifacts from the earliest stages on; and that so far from conquering nature or reshaping his environment primitive man's first concern was to utilize his overdeveloped, intensely active nervous system, and to give form to a human self, set apart from his original animal self by the fabrication of symbols—the only tools that could be constructed out of the resources provided by his own body: dreams, images, and sounds.

In *The Myth of the Machine*, a small portion of which was presented in "Work-Play," Mumford develops his hypothesis that "man is preeminently a mind-making, self-mastering, and self-designing animal."

from THE MYTH OF THE MACHINE: TECHNICS AND HUMAN DEVELOPMENT

Lewis Mumford

tools   In this process of self-discovery and self-transformation, tools, in the narrow sense, served well as subsidiary instruments, but not as the main operative agent in man's development; for technics has never till our own age dissociated itself from the larger cultural whole in which man, as man, has always functioned. The classic Greek term *"tekhne"* characteristically makes no distinction between industrial production and "fine" or symbolic art; and for the greater part of human history these aspects were inseparable, one side respecting the objective conditions and functions, the other responding to subjective needs.

At its point of origin, technics was related to the whole nature of man, and that nature played a part in every aspect of industry: thus technics, at the beginning, was broadly life-centered, not work-centered or power-centered. As in any other ecological complex, varied human interests and purposes, different organic needs, restrained the overgrowth of any single component. Though language was man's most potent symbolic expression, it flowed, I shall attempt to show, from the same common **ritual** source that finally produced the machine: the primeval repetitive order of ritual, a mode of order man was forced to develop, in self-protection, so as to control the tremendous overcharge of psychical energy that his large brain placed at his disposal.

So far from disparaging the role of technics, however, I shall rather demonstrate that once this basic internal organization was established, technics supported and enlarged the capacities for human expression. The discipline of tool-making and tool-using served as a timely correction, on this hypothesis, to the inordinate powers of invention that spoken language gave to man—powers that otherwise unduly inflated the ego and tempted man to substitute magical verbal formulae for efficacious work.

On this interpretation, the specific human achievement, which set man apart from even his nearest anthropoid relatives, was the shaping of a new self, visibly different in appearance, in behavior, and in plan of life from his primitive animal forebears. As this differentiation widened and the number of definitely human "identification marks" increased, man speeded the process of his own evolution, achieving through culture **culture** in a relatively short span of years changes that other species accomplished laboriously through organic processes, whose results, in contrast to man's cultural modes, could not be easily corrected, improved, or effaced.

Henceforth the main business of man was his own self-transformation, **self-making** group by group, region by region, culture by culture. This self-transformation not merely rescued man from permanent fixation in his original animal condition, but freed his best-developed organ, his brain, for other tasks than those of ensuring physical survival. The dominant human trait, central to all other traits, is this capacity for conscious, purposeful self-identification, self-transformation, and ultimately for self-understanding.

Every manifestation of human culture, from ritual and speech to costume and social organization, is directed ultimately to the remodelling of the human organism and the expression of the human personality. If it is only now that we belatedly recognize this distinctive feature, it is perhaps because there are widespread indications in contemporary art and politics and technics that man may be on the point of losing it—becoming not a lower animal, but a shapeless, amoeboid nonentity.

In recasting the stereotyped representations of human development, I have fortunately been able to draw upon a growing body of biological and anthropological evidence, which has not until now been correlated

re-examining
the nature
of man

or fully interpreted. Yet I am aware, of course, that despite this substantial support the large themes I am about to develop, and even more their speculative subsidiary hypotheses, may well meet with justifiable skepticism; for they have still to undergo competent critical scrutiny. Need I say that so far from starting with a desire to dispute the prevailing orthodox views, I at first respectfully accepted them, since I knew no others? It was only because I could find no clue to modern man's overwhelming commitment to his technology, even at the expense of his health, his physical safety, his mental balance, and his possible future development, that I was driven to re-examine the nature of man and the whole course of technological change.

In addition to discovering the aboriginal field of man's inventiveness, not in his making of external tools, but primarily in the refashioning of his own bodily organs, I have undertaken to follow another freshly blazed trail: to examine the broad streak of irrationality that runs all through human history, counter to man's sensible, functionally rational animal inheritance. As compared even with other anthropoids, one might refer without irony to man's superior irrationality. Certainly human development exhibits a chronic disposition to error, mischief, disordered fantasy, hallucination, "original sin," and even socially organized and sanctified misbehavior, such as the practice of human sacrifice and legalized torture. In escaping organic fixations, man forfeited the innate humility and mental stability of less adventurous species. Yet some of his most erratic departures have opened up valuable areas that purely organic evolution, over billions of years, had never explored. . . .

irrationality

One of the reasons that important clues to man's early development may have been missed is that the scientific tradition in the nineteenth century was—whatever the individual practices of some scientists—rationalist, utilitarian, and definitely skeptical about the value of any set of beliefs that tacitly denied science's own uncriticized assumptions. While magic was admitted as an early practice, perhaps interpretable, in James Frazer's terms, as an attempt to control natural forces that would, in the end, succumb to the scientific method, anything like the larger consciousness of cosmic forces that is associated with religion, was treated as negligible. That early man may have scanned the sky, and have reacted to the presence of the sun and moon, may even have identified the seemingly fixed pole star, as Zelia Nuttall suggested more than half a century ago, seemed as removed from possibility as the fact that he had produced works of art.

magic

star light,
star bright

cosmic
forces

Yet from the moment *Homo sapiens*, at least, makes his appearance, we find evidences in his attitude toward death, toward ancestral spirits, toward future existence, toward sun and sky that betray a consciousness that forces and beings, distant in space and time, unapproachable if not invisible, may nevertheless play a controlling part in man's life. This was a true intuition, although it may have taken hundreds of thousands of years before its full import and rational proof could be grasped by the human mind, which now ranges between invisible particles and equally mysterious retreating galaxies.

The possibility of other worlds close to and interwoven with our own is, after all, no longer a mere frolic of the imagination. Denys Wilkinson, Professor of Nuclear Physics at Oxford University, had this to say in a recent broadcast: "Perhaps there do indeed exist universes interpenetrating with ours; perhaps of a high complexity; perhaps containing their own forms of awareness; constructed out of other particles and other interactions than those we know now, but awaiting discovery through some common but elusive interaction that we have yet to spot. It is not the physicist's job," the Professor added, "to make this sort of speculation, but today, when we are so much less sure of the natural world than we were two decades ago, he can at least license it."
Is it not possible that the Dreamer, this mysterious Guest who lodges uninvited in the psyche of every man—and, for all we know, of every living thing—may be one of the "common but elusive" factors which link us to other and higher-dimensional forms of existence? . . . Is it not possible?

Alan McGlashan,
The Savage and Beautiful Country

While Mumford lays stress on the development of human personality as the motive force in man, and Ardrey stresses the war of the amity-enmity instincts, interestingly they arrive at the same conclusion: the use of the human organism's creative, pattern-forming, future-inventing power to build civilization is the appropriate and necessary work of mankind.

Whether man is born good and society corrupts (a view spoken of by Ardrey as *the romantic fallacy*) or whether man is born evil and civilization saves is an issue which philosophers have debated hotly and long. It is perhaps less important to resolve this debate than to be aware that both *nature* and *nurture* go into the making of a man. And until we know more about what both contribute, we would do well to keep a range of options open.

from WAR IS NOT
IN OUR GENES

Sally Garrighar

We do not know which mammals were the nearest ancestors of primates, but there are sufficient numbers of nonaggressive creatures living even today to suggest that co-operation was becoming the habit of evolving mammals before the primates developed. What, therefore, has happened? Man obviously is an aggressive animal. We have lost both the peacefulness and the inhibition against killing others of our own kind. Is there an explanation?

As Lorenz points out, aggressiveness can be taught. It is also intensified when it is exercised (and atrophies when it is not). When men began to settle in communities, they learned the irritations of being crowded. By then they had probably learned the use of weapons, originally for the purpose of killing game. And since they had already acquired at least a rudimentary speech, they could absorb from one another, and preach, animosity. With words, they could incite hatred against neighboring tribes. A leader, coveting power or property, could, with propaganda, instill in his subjects admiration for warlike attitudes.

Perhaps that is the way—culturally rather than genetically—that human aggressiveness arose. As for sadism, something no animal displays, it is my belief that the trait is psychotic.

Nothing could more effectively prolong man's fighting behavior than a belief that aggression is in our genes. An unwelcome cultural inheritance can be eradicated fairly quickly and easily, but the incentive to do it is lacking while people believe that aggression is innate and instinctive with us, as both Ardrey and Lorenz declare.

More than 100 years ago, the philosopher William Whewell wrote: "There is a mask of theory over the whole face of nature." Anyone writing about the wilderness has a great responsibility not to accept too readily a belief that the mask is nature's true face. In a chaotic and perfidious world, nature is all we have that is infallibly real.

If writers assert their own, unproven

It is an easy matter to foresee the trend of physically dramatic events during the next 21-year generation. We will go to the moon and start communicating with humans in other parts of the universe and open up entirely unexpected new realizations of the significance of man in the universe. We will probably learn that Darwin was wrong and that man came to earth from another planet and monkeys are hybrids degenerated by over-long inbreeding of isolated humans.
R. Buckminster Fuller,
"The Prospect for Humanity"

hypotheses as the truth, civilized people, so isolated from the wilderness that they cannot recognize a fallacy when they hear or see one, will be deprived of their one lifeline to what may be felt intuitively as sane and good. Then, even the intuition will be lost—what is there left for anybody but madness?

Photograph courtesy of United Press International.

I had decided in 1927 that there are two things you could do if you want to improve the total existence of man on earth. You could try to reform man himself or you could reform the environment, and the environment, if properly reformed, would allow man to really behave well.

I don't think I can improve on man. He's quite an extraordinary piece of design. He simply has been spoiled. He's not something you improve; you preserve the very high potential with which he is born. ... So I thought I could do best with the environment.

R. Buckminster Fuller

"The child is born perfect."

From the recording *R. Buckminster Fuller Thinks Aloud.*
Photograph courtesy of Emme Gilman, Larkspur, California.

"The more ingenious and determined the attempt to assign to life a purely rational value, the more cruelly and viciously will the irrational burst through to reestablish its own neglected values," writes Alan McGlashan in *The Savage and Beautiful Country*. Laurens van der Post, in reviewing McGlashan's book, points out that "the country of the title is not one of the rapidly diminishing lands in a fast-shrinking physical world. It is the great unknown in the swiftly expanding universe of the mind."

from THE SAVAGE
AND BEAUTIFUL COUNTRY

Alan McGlashan

The mind of a child is a mystery and a paradox. Outwardly all clarity and innocence—*O ces voix d'enfants!*—all ignorance and dependence, all rainbow tears and laughter; inwardly the rapt secret communion with realities of another order, with opposites and correspondences of which the golden key is lost to us, with the world of witch and dwarf and monster: the archetypal Fairy-Tale World. A child lives largely in the Unconscious, and is more than a little mad.

Here is one playing alone in a garden: listen to the earnest dialogue with imaginary beings, watch the bizarre gestures and queer grimaces. For less than this adults have been put quietly away. And yet it is a madness which wisdom envies, for to a child the world is meaningful, is urgently alive with meaning. And this in the last analysis is wisdom's goal. Having in childhood possessed it, and lost it again, there persists in the adult mind a forlorn sense of estrangement.

John Keats once said that the life of a man of any worth is a continual allegory. It is the corroding certainty of having lost the key to this translucent kind of living that eats the heart out on quiet summer evenings. In such an hour men and events seem contingent, pointless, formless; and Reason, that tireless choreographer of "the bloodless ballet of concepts," grows sick of its own success.

Three paths there are that lead out of this wilderness. One is a fatal path, with a fatal fascination. Through the iron gates of War man suddenly re-enters the fluid and phantasmagorial world of the child and the madman. With what helpless dread and what infinite weariness the rational part of the mind, critic of millennial sad experience, watches the old stock figures strut confidently onto the stage, as the curtain rises yet again on the deadly, dreary drama! With what enormous distaste it foresees the futile finale before the opening word is spoken. Even the protagonists' names are hardly altered—Khan, Caesar, Kaiser, Führer—

Permission to reprint from Alan McGlashan, *The Savage and Beautiful Country* granted by the author and by Chatto and Windus Ltd.

though the players' stature seems to shrink, the crown and robes to sit more grotesquely, with each preposterous re-enactment. Everything is stale, false, seen-before, senseless. Beauty vanishes, darkness falls from the air. One man finds the perfect phrase: "The lamps of Europe are going out," said Sir Edward Grey in 1914; "they will not be relit in our time." To the eyes of reason War is the total eclipse of meaning.

Exactly here lies the inevitable paradox. While reason cries out on the insanity of War, feverishly searching out its causes, shuffling and rearranging its determinants, the Unconscious sees only this: that War allows the reappearance on earth of certain meaningful figures. Like Walpurgis Night it is a privileged occasion, when the portals of the Unconscious swing wide. And what a nightmare throng streams up through those unguarded gates! Monstrous and unreal they are, yet charged with a terrible energy: Führers and Duces with the implacable faces of blood-loving Baal and child-devouring Moloch; women spies, the Lamias of the twilight hour, sliding like jeweled snakes through the ruined cities; Renegades, loaded with infamy and shame, whispering dark secrets to the enemy; and here and there, crawling up from remotest swamps of the archaic psyche, furtive bearers of unnameable evil, men who make bonfires of living bodies, women who make lampshades of human skin.

Jostling these grisly figures come the shining band of Saviors: hero generals haloed with golden legend; Unknown Warriors; triumphing martyrs; divinely compassioned Mother-figures like the Lady with the Lamp. The qualities of all things good and evil are fiercely intensified. Opposites collide to form new truths and new falsehoods. Faith blooms, born of despair; at Mons once, ten thousand hopeless eyes see Angels close above them. The whole world suddenly brims with clear and terrible meaning. Silenced and appalled, the conscious part of man looks on, while the Unconscious eagerly releases these tremendous avatars of good and evil, each one a secret but immortal aspect of the human psyche.

War is the punishment of man's disbelief in these forces within himself. It is the cruel reaffirmation of those powers which the ego can never command or subdue. And disastrous as the cost may be, something in the depths of man is mysteriously assuaged by this release of daemonic and destructive energies. There is a fierce satisfaction in living under the rule of the Early Gods. There is a dignity in facing powers beyond us, and indifferent to us. To be blind to this, to fail to grasp its difficult meaning, is to let slip the golden Ariadne's thread that may lead man at last out of the stinking labyrinth of War.

In *The Green Table*, that terrifying ballet of the 1930's the cause of War is shown to lie in the criminal futilities of power-politics. The intolerable blame is comfortingly projected on to wrangling statesmen. It may well be so. But causal chains belong to the conscious level, while War springs from the Unconscious, which is concerned not with causes but with meanings. And meaning, as Lao Tzu has said, is that which exists through itself: it is the Secret of the Golden Flower. War has causes—social, political, and economic—but it also has a meaning. To reach this meaning in time may be man's last and best hope. For in the moment it is reached, a question rises urgently in the heart: is there no other way to release these primordial powers, no other path to wholeness?

If indeed there were none, mankind could well yield to despair. But another does exist; a curious path, this one, that winds its secret way through very different regions, but leads there no less surely. Children, the pre-elected freemen of the world of the Unconscious, stray along this path—or perhaps are blown along it like brightly colored leaves. Swayed by intimations from an unknown source, the games and group-ings of children left entirely to themselves have an unmistakable air of ritual. They seem to be half remembering something, and their move-ments, made often with the tranced certainty of sleepwalkers, awaken memories that have slept for centuries in the adult human heart. . . .

And not children only: kings and queens, priests and mystics, the very wise and the very simple, have always intuitively sought and found this path that leads to the fourth-dimensional world of meaning. From Delphos to Westminster Abbey, from shrouded oracle to impeccably laundered Archbishop, from primitive fertility rite to the crowning of a young and radiant Queen, the magic of ritual binds and releases the soul of man and reveals to him the world of meaning that logic can never reach.

In their final significance the forms of ritual are far more than forms: they are the intricate beautiful patterns, the delicate temporal webs, in which man has striven to enmesh that which lies outside his space and time. And sometimes with their help (as also sometimes without it, a sheer, lovely irrelevance) a door suddenly opens, revealing for an instant the timeless world of primordial images in whose depths the meaning of life is contained. As in the monstrous instance of War, the forces of the Unconscious surge eagerly through the momentary opening, and something in the heart of man responds, as always, with the deep, indefinable sense of assuagement.

How subtle a thing is this feeling of assuagement! The thirst it allays, the terrible thirst to find a meaning in life, is one of which a man is at first only obscurely aware. He feels only a vague deepening sense of dis-comfort, of missed harmonies as faint as the wave-music in a small seashell—which Science reassures us is nothing but illusion. O keep still, keep still, and listen. Once the inner ear is attuned to this music, there is no other it will wish to hear; no other reality in the world of time and space that compares with this "illusion"—this sweet assuaging harmony —heard only on that Everest-peak of inner experience where the temporal touches, however briefly, the eternal. "Man has come into this world," said William Law, "on no other errand than to arise out of the vanity of time."

There is no alternative. The more ingenious and determined the attempt to assign to life a purely rational value, the more cruelly and viciously will the irrational burst through to re-establish its own neg-lected values; on the social level by War, on the individual level by neurotic conflict, on the intellectual by such epileptic reactions as the

Surrealists and the neo-abstractionists. Humility is the key. Man must return to his origins, personal and racial, and learn again the truths of the imagination. And in this task his strange instructors are the child, who has but half-entered the rational world of time and space, and the madman, who has half-escaped from it. For just these two are in some measure released from the remorseless pressure of daily events, the ceaseless impact of the external senses, which burdens the rest of mankind. They travel light, this curious pair, and go on far and solitary journeys, sometimes bringing back a gleaming branch from the Gold Forest through which they have wandered.

... [T]he fantasies of the child, the intuitions of the madman, are more than moonshine. Concealed within them are realities, though of a different order from those of which guns and computers are made.

It is no accident that John Custance, who has written a travel book of a new kind, has given it the curious title of *Wisdom, Madness, and Folly*. It records a grim, heroic journey of the spirit through the fear-haunted realm of lunacy; from which he is perhaps the first modern ever to return strengthened and enriched. Time and again on his wild Odyssey he comes to perilous regions where the madman and the child are the only companions that Wisdom has, or can have. For these three know, what we have fatally forgotten, that we carry within us that which must, at however tragic a cost, keep its contacts with the world of myth and fairy tale, the world beyond human space and time. beyond human cause and effect. It is man's chief aim. We have come into this world on no other errand.

There is a third path—unfashionable now, and unfrequented—along which dark elements of the soul, the monstrous apparitions and wild pageantry of the inner world, are allowed for a few dream-like days and nights to irrupt into conscious life. For that brief period law and order abdicate, and all the forces of the irrational make hasty holiday. In Catholic countries this strange interlude in men's lives has been christened Carnival, and its culminating day—*Mardi Gras*, "Fat Tuesday"—is a shrewdly permitted license to the faithful on the eve of Lenten austerities. But its origins are worldwide, and more ancient by many centuries than Christian belief.

Carnival is a phenomenon of cultured societies. Primitive man had no need of it, for the return of chaos loomed over him every hour of his life. But as soon as men began to create for themselves conditions of stability and some measure of the rule of reason, at once the necessity for a compensating period, however brief, of anarchy and license became manifest. In all ages and in all parts of the earth, from China to the Amazon—with the sole exception of the petrified, death-obsessed culture of Dynastic Egypt—the most intelligent societies have recognized this need and tried to canalize it, to contain it within the specified dates of their local calendar.

The history of Carnival is the history of the socially unacceptable impulses in human nature, and their insistent demand to be admitted into life....

... The claim of the irrational forces for recognition will recur—*must recur*. In the contemporary world there are already signs of this among the adolescents of many countries. Boys with feminine haircuts and gaudy clothes, girls as masculine and bizarre as they can make themselves, are appearing in the streets, the harbingers of masquerade. Their outbursts of violence—still vaguely connected with public holidays—against each other and against the community and the police are, of course, an ebullition of youthful high spirits; but not simply that. There is also present, for those who dare to look for it, an unmistakable flavor of the sinister. What these adolescents are rousing is the sleeping urge to anarchy that hides not only in their hearts, but in ours. And we must somehow make room for its reawakening demands. It is a task of enormous difficulty. To crush these anarchic impulses by superior power is to invite catastrophe. Yet to handle them indulgently and "understandingly" is to risk, as in the past, the release of vicious mass frenzies of a kind that is fortunately peculiar to the human animal.

We are compelled, nevertheless, to take the second of the two risks. For the truth is that these recurrent irruptions of unconscious imagery into everyday life express in their own fantastic terms a not unworthy aim: *to fling in the world's face the Dionysiac challenge*—life lived like a mountain torrent, sparkling and tumbling in the sunlight, carrying all before it, crowned with beauty in the instant of its own destruction. ... Over against it forever stands the Classic attitude, marmoreal, calm, clear thinking; verbalized once and for all in the sonorous syllables of St. Augustine—PAX, ORDO, LEX, SOCIETAS; the four great pillars of Apollonian life.

No one in his normal senses would wish for the total victory of either side. A world of Romantics would end in unendurable chaos, a world of pure Classics in a static perfection; and "perfection," as Kenneth Clarke has said, "closes the door." Both attitudes are valid and indeed complementary. What is deplorable is that each, in its brief moment of victory, can treat the other with such savagery and lack of comprehension.

Perhaps after all, Carnival, the answer given by so many earlier civilizations, is the best we can do. For all its look of lunacy and its inherent dangers, it is an answer that rises up from the deepest levels of the psyche. The giant phantoms of Carnival are direct, unmediated creations of the dreaming mind. Set free for a time they release and act out its negative, nonconforming aspect. Swaying monstrously past startled eyes, the figures of Carnival grant us a warning glimpse of the iconoclastic impulses of man's unconscious mind—as War reveals its homicidal madness, and Ritual hints at its fragile and inexpressible beauty.

For modern man there is a new and promising possibility: to go down boldly into the darkness of the underworld, and there to claim his bride, his shadow-self, his wholeness. For the truth is, full human consciousness has still to be won. It is waiting to be born from a marriage that has not yet taken place, that only *can* take place at the deepest level of the psyche —the marriage between thinking and feeling. In everyday life these two functions tend to be antagonistic except in certain moments of high crisis. And while this is so, human consciousness is a crippled thing.

Moreover, when operating in isolation each function is essentially destructive. The thermonuclear bomb is a typical end-product of the kind of thinking that is disconnected from feeling. But feeling is also a mode of consciousness. The kind of feeling that is disconnected from thinking has as its end-product—war. Autonomous thinking provides the cataclysmic weapon. Autonomous feeling provides the setting in which the weapon can be used. The appalling danger presented by the operations of these isolated functions can be countered at the individual level in one way only: by a fusion of these two modes of consciousness so perfect and indissoluble as to make it impossible for the human mind ever again to use them separately.

They should never be so used. For isolated thinking and isolated feeling are, in fact, classic forms of madness: they constitute the two dangerous, closed-in worlds of the schizophrenic and the manic-depressive. But to marry thinking to feeling is not merely to restore sanity to the operations of the human mind; it is also to open new and urgently needed dimensions in human consciousness.

Out of the royal union of thinking and feeling will be born the inner force that alone can pull man back to safety from the high and narrow window ledge on which he now stands, screaming silently.

the search for the self

If you tried to explain what it is like to be human, where would you place the heart of the experience? In our capacity to think? To feel? To create? In the union of thinking and feeling? In conscious awareness? In awareness of the unconscious? In objective rationality? In subjective irrationality? In independent self-sufficiency? In interdependent relationships with others? Take your pick; you can find writers who advance each of these notions, separately or in combination.

The novelist Ayn Rand sees true humanity in the creative functioning of the independent, reasoning mind. Unfortunately, few persons measure up to her standards of what it means to be human. Most of mankind, she contends, is comprised of two kinds of despicable half-men. These are the men of force and the men of feeling. They are united in mutual, manipulative dependence—a relationship profoundly destructive of human potentiality. She contrasts these with that rare, creative, reasoning person who is willing to stand alone in his affirmation of his own free self.

In condemning manipulative, dependent relationships and applauding the creative power of the man who is truly free, Rand is in accord with Erich Fromm, Eric Berne, Otto Rank, Abraham Maslow, and others concerned with the human potential. It is not uncommon in a democracy to denounce authoritarian relationships. Erich Fromm writes:

> The paralyzing effect of power does not rely only upon the fear it arouses, but equally on an implicit promise—the promise that those in possession of power can protect and take care of the "weak" who submit to it, that they can free man from the burden of uncertainty and of responsibility for himself by guaranteeing order and by assigning the individual a place in this order which makes him feel secure.
>
> Man's submission to this combination of threat and promise is his real "fall." By submitting to power = domination he loses *his* power = potency. He loses his power to make use of all those capacities which make him truly human; his reason ceases to operate; he may be intelligent, he may be capable of manipulating things and himself, but he accepts as truth that which those who have power over him call the truth. He loses his power of love, for his emotions are tied [in a symbiotic relationship] to those upon whom he depends. He loses his moral sense, for his inability to question and criticize those in power stultifies his moral judgment with regard to anybody and anything. . . . Indeed, freedom is the necessary condition of happiness as well as of virtue; freedom, not in the sense of the ability to make arbitrary choices and not freedom from necessity, but freedom to realize that which one potentially is, to fulfill the true nature of man according to the laws of his existence.

remember
Big Nurse
and Harding?

Otto Rank's definition of the creative artist, as described by Sidney Jourard in *Personal Adjustment*, reads in every detail like a description of the heroes of Rand's novels:

> Rank regarded the creative artist as a pinnacle of human growth. The artist was seen as one with courage to assert his difference from the mass of men and who dared to shape reality as he wished it to be, rather than passively "adjusting" to a fixed, frozen reality. Rank saw neurotics as persons with strong wills and strong creative urges but who lacked the final courage to impose their individual stamp on the world. Instead, they "shaped" their own personalities (as a sculptor shapes his clay) *in order to please others*. Healthy personality, for Rank, implied the courage to become a separate, distinct person, the courage to express one's difference from others, and the courage to be inventive and creative in various spheres of existence.

Unlike these writers, however, Ayn Rand emphasizes "I" almost to

Reprinted from Erich Fromm, *Man for Himself* (Greenwich, Conn.: Fawcett, 1965), pp. 247–248.
Reprinted with permission of The Macmillan Company from *Personal Adjustment* by Sidney M. Jourard. © by The Macmillan Company 1958.

the exclusion of "we." Her focus on the choice between dependence and independence excludes the range of rich relationships which can be called *interdependent*. In her insistence that men share only what stems from the reasoning mind, she misses much of what "we" can mean. In this respect she differs, too, from Ardrey and Mumford, who hold that in the "we" of civilization lies man's only possibility for survival.

While the free, rational, self-affirming man she portrays in her heroes is one we can all admire, as a human being he is incomplete; his only meaningful experience is that of his own uniqueness and of what stems from his reasoning mind. Ayn Rand neglects an entire dimension of experience—that of authentic, fulfilling, feeling-ful, growth-fostering, creative interaction based on shared needs, goods, and goals.

It is a technique of the fiction writer to deal in heroes and villains, good guys and bad guys. But in our search for the self, we are likely to find both hero and villain in each of us.

Novelists like Ayn Rand and Ken Kesey isolate certain qualities they wish to display, and assign them to one or another character. They—and we too, for that matter—would do well to remember that these "purified" types represent only a part of a real person. Indeed, as James Moffatt suggests in *Drama: What Is Happening*, all of the characters of a work are parts of the writer and represent the internalized "voices" of society—the aspects of human nature he himself experiences as real.

Let us look now at the views of some psychologists who believe that no man is fully creator or fully manipulator and who address the range of interactive capacities of human beings.

Eric Berne, author of *Games People Play* and *Transactional Analysis in Psychotherapy*, and Everett Shostrom, author of *Man, the Manipulator*, believe that, while manipulative relationships are common and in fact encouraged in our society, most people have the capacity to transcend them. Genuine, authentic interaction with others, they contend, is part of the process of self-actualization, of being a real self.

Berne believes that game-playing characterizes most interpersonal relationships. Each person carries within him a child, an adult, and a parent. Each of these aspects of a person engages in transactions with those of other persons. Out of these transactions grow our games. Some games are destructive, others are less so; all are basically dishonest. People derive considerable satisfaction from such vigorous games as "Kick Me," "Now I've Got You, You S.O.B.," "See What You Made Me Do," "Let's You and Him Fight," "Rapo," "Harried," "Let's Pull a Fast One on Joey." Games may be played in deadly seriousness; the grimmest of all is "War."

Berne describes 36 all-too-recognizable games. He believes, however, that what is important is not to avoid all game-playing, but to be aware that one is doing it and to be capable of more fulfilling relationships as well. The attainment of autonomy, or the freedom to be beyond games, is characterized by "the release or recovery of three capacities: awareness, spontaneity, and intimacy."

from GAMES PEOPLE PLAY

Eric Berne

Awareness. Awareness means the capacity to see a coffeepot and hear the birds sing in one's own way, and not the way one was taught. It may be assumed on good grounds that seeing and hearing have a different quality for infants than for grownups, and that they are more esthetic and less intellectual in the first years of life. A little boy sees and hears birds with delight. Then the "good father" comes along and feels he should "share" the experience and help his son "develop." He says: "That's a jay, and this is a sparrow." The moment the little boy is concerned with which is a jay and which is a sparrow, he can no longer see the birds or hear them sing. He has to see and hear them the way his father wants him to. Father has good reasons on his side, since few people can afford to go through life listening to the birds sing, and the sooner the little boy starts his "education" the better. Maybe he will be an ornithologist when he grows up. A few people, however, can still see and hear in the old way. But most of the members of the human race have lost the capacity to be painters, poets, or musicians, and are not left the option of seeing and hearing directly even if they can afford to; they must get it secondhand. The recovery of this ability is called here "awareness." . . .

Spontaneity. Spontaneity means option, the freedom to choose and express one's feelings from the assortment available (Parent feelings, Adult feelings, and Child feelings). It means liberation, liberation from the compulsion to play games and have only the feelings one was taught to have.

Intimacy. Intimacy means the spontaneous, game-free candidness of an aware person, the liberation of the eidetically perceptive, uncorrupted Child in all its naïveté living in the here and now.

Reprinted by permission of Grove Press, Inc. Copyright © 1964 by Eric Berne.

While Berne describes manipulative relationships in terms of maneuvers or games, Shostrom describes them in terms of life-styles, deeply established patterns of games. He isolates eight kinds of manipulator—Bully, Calculator, Dictator, Judge, Weakling, Clinging Vine, Nice Guy, and Protector—and shows how each can become an actualizor.

from MAN, THE MANIPULATOR

Everett L. Shostrom

A manipulator's style of life involves four fundamental characteristics: deception, unawareness, control, and cynicism. The actualizor's philosophy of life is marked by four opposing characteristics: honesty, awareness, freedom, and trust. (See Table 1.) The change from manipulation to actualization is in general on a continuum *from* deadness and deliberateness *to* aliveness and spontaneity.

TABLE 1

FUNDAMENTAL CHARACTERISTICS OF MANIPULATORS AND ACTUALIZORS CONTRASTED

Manipulators

1. Deception (Phoniness, Knavery). The manipulator uses tricks, techniques, and maneuvers. He puts on an act, plays roles to create an *impression*. His expressed feelings are deliberately chosen to fit the occasion.
2. Unawareness (Deadness, Boredom). The manipulator is unaware of the really important concerns of living. He has "Tunnel Vision." He sees only what he wishes to see and hears only what he wishes to hear.

3. Control (Closed, Deliberate). The manipulator plays life like a game of chess. He appears relaxed, yet is very controlled and controlling, concealing his motives from his "opponent."
4. Cynicism (Distrust). The manipulator is basically distrusting of himself and others. Down deep he doesn't trust human na-

Actualizors

1. Honesty (Transparency, Genuineness, Authenticity). The actualizor is able honestly to be his feelings, whatever they may be. He is characterized by candidness, *expression*, and genuinely being himself.
2. Awareness (Responsiveness, Aliveness, Interest). The actualizor fully looks and listens to himself and others. He is fully aware of nature, art, music, and the other real dimensions of living.
3. Freedom (Spontaneity, Openness). The actualizor is spontaneous. He has the freedom to be and express his potentials. He is master of his life, a subject and not a puppet or object.
4. Trust (Faith, Belief). The actualizor has a deep trust in himself and others to relate to and cope with life in the here and now.

ture. He sees relationships with
humans as having two alternatives:
to control or *be* controlled.

... We have suggested, for purposes of exposition, that man comes in two broad categories, the manipulator and the actualizor, and yet, as Tolstoy says, man has within himself the potential for every human quality. Each man is a manipulator, as we have seen, but he is also an actualizor. The important fact seems to be that he has a continuing choice—freedom to choose one or the other. By freedom we do not mean simply freedom *from* the control of others, but rather freedom *to actualize*. Freedom is the choice and responsibility taken for a style of expression we use. Erich Fromm believes that man "has the freedom to create, to construct, to wonder, to venture." He goes on to define freedom as the capacity to make a choice, to choose between alternatives. Only when we are aware of our manipulations are we free to experience them and to derive from them actualizing behavior. The actualizor is free to be master of his life; he is a subject and not a puppet or an object.

The actualizor is free in the sense that, while he may play the game of life, he is *aware* he is playing it. He plays it "tongue in cheek," Alan Watts says. He realizes that he manipulates sometimes and is manipulated at other times. *But he is aware of the manipulation.* He does not try to change the manipulator lest at that moment he becomes himself a manipulator. Taking the responsibility to change another is, you see, only to be manipulated by that person. One may *describe* him or *confront* him with his manipulation, but one need not take responsibility to change him. The actualizor recognizes that each person must ultimately take that responsibility for himself.

The actualizor is aware that life need not be a serious game at all, but rather is more akin to a dance. No one wins or loses in a dance; a dance is a process. The actualizor dances or skates between all his complimentary potentials. What is important is enjoying the *process* of living rather than achieving the *ends* of living. Since actualizing people appreciate the doing itself, for its own sake, they enjoy the process of getting someplace as much as the arriving. One psychologist believes it is possible for them to make an intrinsically enjoyable game or dance or play out of the most trivial and routine activity. The actualizor swings with life and does not take it with dead seriousness. The manipulator, on the other hand, sees life as a rat race and takes it so seriously he is frequently the candidate for a nervous breakdown.

other as brother

from INTERPERSONAL RELATIONSHIPS:
U.S.A. 2000

Carl R. Rogers

closeness and intimacy in the year 2000

For the first time in history man is not only taking his future seriously, but he also has adequate technology and power to shape and form that future. He is endeavoring to *choose* his future, rather than simply living out some inevitable trend. And we do not know what he will choose. So we do not know what man's relation to man will be in this country 32 years from now. But we can see certain possibilities. . . .

In our affluent society the individual's survival needs are satisfied. For the first time, he is freed to become aware of his isolation, aware of his alienation, aware of the fact that he is, during most of his life, a role interacting with other roles, a mask meeting other masks. And for the first time he is aware that this is not a *necessary* tragedy of life, that he does not have to live out his days in this fashion. So he is seeking, with great determination and inventiveness, ways of modifying this existential loneliness. The intensive group experience, perhaps the most significant social invention of this century, is an important one of these ways.

What will grow out of the current use of basic encounter groups, marathons, "labs," and the like? I have no idea what *forms* will proliferate out of these roots during the coming decades, but I believe men will discover new bases of intimacy which will be highly fulfilling. I believe there will

be possibilities for the *rapid* development of closeness between persons, a closeness which is not artificial but is real and deep and which will be well suited to our increasing mobility of living. Temporary relationships will be able to achieve the richness and meaning which heretofore have been associated only with lifelong attachments.

There will be more awareness of what is going on within the person, an openness to all of one's experience —the sensory input of sound and taste and hearing and sight and smell, the richness of kaleidoscopically changing ideas and concepts, the wealth of feelings—positive, negative, and ambivalent, intense and moderate—toward oneself and toward others.

There will be the development of a whole new style of communication in which the person can, in effect, say "I'm telling you the way it *is*, in me— my ideas, my desires, my feelings, my hopes, my angers, my fears, my despairs," and where the response will be equally open. We will be experimenting with ways in which a whole person can communicate himself to another whole person. We will discover that security resides not in hiding oneself, but in being more fully known, and consequently coming to know the other more fully. Aloneness will be something one chooses out of a desire for privacy, not an isolation into which one is forced.

This paper was part of a symposium sponsored by the Esalen Institute, San Francisco, entitled "USA 2000," on January 10, 1968. Reprinted by permission of the author.

In all of this I believe we will be experimenting with a new ideal of what man may become, a model very *sharply* different from the historical view of man as a creature playing various appropriate roles. We seem to be aiming for a new *reality* in relationships, a new openness in communication, a love for each other which grows not out of a romantic blindness, but out of the profound respect which is nearly always engendered by reality in relationships.

I recognize that many individuals in our culture are frightened in the depths of their being by this new picture of man—this flowing, changing, open, expressive, creative person. They may be able to stop the trend, or even to reverse it. It is conceivable that we will go in for the manufactured "image," as on TV, or may insist more strongly than ever that teachers are *teachers*, parents are *parents*, bosses are *manipulators*—that we may rigidify every role and stereotype in new and more armor-plated ways. We may insist with new force that the only significant aspect of man is his rational and intellectual being, and that nothing else matters. We may assert that he is a machine and no more. Yet I do not believe this will happen. The magnetism of the new man, toward which we are groping, is too great. Much of what I say in the remainder of this paper is based on the conviction that we are, for better or for worse, in labor pains and growth pains—turning toward this new view of man as becoming and being—a continuing, growing *process*.

man-woman relationships

What do the coming decades hold for us in the realm of intimacy between boy and girl, man and woman? Here, too, enormous forces are at work, and choices are being made which will not, I believe, be reversed by the year 2000.

In the first place the trend toward greater freedom in sexual relationships, in adolescents and adults, is likely to continue, whether this direction frightens us or not. Many elements have conspired together to bring about a change in such behavior, and the advent of "the Pill" is only one of these. It seems probable that sexual intimacy will be a part of "going steady" or of any continuing special interest in a member of the opposite sex. The attitude of prurience is fast dying out, and sexual activity is seen as a potentially joyful and enriching part of a relationship. The attitude of possessiveness—of owning another person—which historically has dominated sexual unions—is likely to be greatly diminished. It is certain that there will be enormous variations in the quality of these sexual relationships—from those where sex is a purely physical contact which has almost the same solitary quality as masturbation, to those in which the sexual aspect is an expression of an increasing sharing of feelings, of experiences, of interests, of each other.

By the year 2000 it will be quite feasible to insure that there will be no children in a union. By one of the several means currently under study, each individual will be assured of lasting infertility in early adolescence. It will take positive action, permissible only after a thoughtful decision, to re-establish fertility. This will reverse the present situation where only by positive action can one *prevent* conception. Also by that time computerized matching of prospective partners will be far more sophisticated than it is today and will be of great help to an individual in finding a congenial companion of the opposite sex.

Some of the temporary unions thus formed may be legalized as a type of marriage—with no permanent commitment, with no children (by mutual agreement), and—if the union breaks up—no legal accusations, no necessity for showing legal cause, and no alimony.

It is becoming increasingly clear that a man-woman relationship will have *permanence* only to the degree to which it satisfies the emotional, psychological, intellectual, and physical needs of the partners. This means that the *permanent* marriage of the future will be even better than marriage in the present, because the ideals and goals for that marriage will be of a higher order. The partners will be demanding more of the relationship than they do today.

If a couple feels deeply committed to each other, and mutually wish to remain together to raise a family, then this will be a new and more binding type of marriage. Each will accept the obligations involved in having and raising children. There may be a mutual agreement as to whether or not the marriage includes sexual faithfulness to one's mate. Perhaps by the year 2000 we will have reached the point where through education and social pressure, a couple will decide to have children only when they have shown evidence of a mature commitment to each other, of a sort which is likely to have permanence.

What I am describing is a whole continuum of man-woman relationships, from the most casual dating and casual sex relationship to a rich and fulfilling partnership in which communication is open and real, where each is concerned with promoting the personal growth of the partner, and where there is a long-range commitment to each other which will form a sound basis for having and rearing children in an environment of love. Some parts of this continuum will exist within a legal framework, some will not.

One may say, with a large measure of truth, that much of this continuum already exists. But an awareness of, and an open acceptance of this continuum by society will change its whole quality. Suppose it were openly accepted that some "marriages" are no more than ill-mated and transitory unions, and will be broken. If children are not permitted in such marriages, then one divorce in every two marriages (the current rate in California) is no longer seen as a tragedy. The dissolving of the union may be painful, but it is not a social catastrophe, and the experience may be a necessary step in the personal growth of the two individuals toward greater maturity.

Photograph courtesy of Oliver McMillan.

parents and children

What of the relationships between parents and their children? Here it is terribly difficult to foresee the future. If parents in general hold to the static views which have served reasonably well through the centuries of little change—"I know the values that are important in life," "I am wiser than my child in knowing the direction his life should take"—then the generation gap will grow so large that our culture will literally be split wide open. This may be the course of future events.

But there are straws in the wind which point in another way. Some parents wish to be *persons*—growing, changing persons—living in person-to-person relationships with the youngsters in their families. So we see the development of family encounter groups (still in their infancy) in which parents learn about themselves from their own and other's children, and children learn about themselves from their own and other's parents. Here the self-insights, the awareness of how one comes across to the other generation, bring changes in behavior, and new ways of relating, based on an open respect for oneself, out of which can grow a genuine respect for the other.

A new type of parent education is also developing, in which there is respect for the parent as a person with feelings and rights, as well as for the child and his feelings and rights. We find family groups where parent and child each *listen* to the other, where honest, open expression is also mutual. Parental authority and childhood submission give way before a realness which confronts realness. Such family relationships are not necessarily smooth, and the problems of process living are as perplexing as the problems brought on by static views—but there is communication and there is respect, and the generation gap becomes simply the communication gap which to some degree separates all individuals. . . .

learning in interpersonal relationships

What of education in the year 2000, especially as it involves interpersonal relationships?

It is possible that education will continue much as it is—concerned only with words, symbols, rational concepts, based on the authoritative role of the teacher, further dehumanized by teaching machines, computerized knowledge, and increased use of tests and examinations. This is possible, because educators are showing greater resistance to change than any other institutional group. Yet I regard it as unlikely, because a revolution in education is long overdue, and the unrest of students is only one sign of this. So I am going to speculate on some of the other possibilities.

It seems likely that schools will be greatly de-emphasized in favor of a much broader, thoughtfully devised *environment for learning*, where the experiences of the student will be challenging, rewarding, affirmative, and pleasurable.

The teacher or professor will have largely disappeared. His place will be taken by a facilitator of learning, chosen for his facilitative attitudes as much as for his knowledge. He will be skilled in stimulating individual and group initiative in learning, skilled in facilitating discussions-in-depth of the *meaning* to the student of what is being learned, skilled in fostering creativity, skilled in providing the resources for learning. Among these resources will be much in the way of programmed learning, to be used as the student finds these learnings appropriate; much in the way of audio-visual aids such as filmed lectures and demonstrations by experts in each field; much in the way of computerized knowledge on which the student can draw; but these "hardware" possibilities are not my main concern.

We will, I believe, see the facilitator focusing his major attention on the prime period for learning—from infancy to age six or eight. Among the most important learnings will be the personal and interpersonal. Every child will develop confidence in his own ability to learn, since he will be rewarded for learning at his own pace.

Each child will learn that he is a person of worth, because he has unique and worthwhile capacities. He will learn how to be himself in a group—to listen, but also to speak, to learn about himself, but also to confront and give feedback to others. He will learn to be an individual, not a faceless conformist. He will learn, through simulations and computerized games, to meet many of the life problems he will face. He will find it permissible to engage in fantasy and daydreams, to think creative thoughts, to capture these in words or paints or constructions. He will find that learning, even difficult learning, is fun, both as an individual activity and in cooperation with others. His discipline will be self-discipline.

His learning will not be confined to the ancient intellectual concepts and specializations. It will not be a *preparation* for living. It will be, in itself, an *experience* in living. Feelings of inadequacy, hatred, a desire for power, feelings of love and awe and respect, feelings of fear and dread, unhappiness with parents or with other children—all these will be an open part of his curriculum, as worthy of exploration as history or mathematics. In fact this openness to feelings will enable him to learn content material more readily. His will be an education in becoming a whole human being, and the learnings will involve him deeply, openly, exploringly, in an awareness of his relationships to himself, an awareness of his relationships to the world of others, as well as in an awareness of the world of abstract knowledge. . . .

persons in industry

In view of my past prejudices I find it somewhat difficult but necessary to say that of all of the institutions of present-day American life, industry is perhaps best prepared to meet the year 2000. I am not speaking of its technical ability. I am speaking of the vision it is acquiring in regard to the importance of persons, of interpersonal relationships, and of open communication. That vision is, to be sure, often unrealized, but it does exist. . . .

If I were to hazard a guess in regard to industry in the year 2000, it would be something different than the predictions about increasing technical skill, increasing automation, increasing management by computers, and the like. All of those predictions will doubtless come true, but the interpersonal aspect is less often discussed. I see many industries, by the year 2000, giving as much attention to the quality of interpersonal relationships, and the quality of communication, as they currently do to the technological aspects of their business. They will come to value persons as persons, recognizing that only out of the *communicated* knowledge of all members of the organization can innovation and progress come. They will pay more attention to breakdowns in personal communication than to breakdowns of the circuitry in their computers. They will be forced to recognize that only as they are promoting the growth and fulfillment of the individuals on the payroll will they be promoting the growth and development of the organization. . . .

Historically, much of man's life has revolved around his relationship to his God or gods, and his relationship to others who share his religious views. What will be the situation three decades from now?

It is definitely conceivable that out of a deep fear of the rapidly changing world he is creating, man may seek refuge in a sure dogma, a simplistic answer to life's complexities, a religion which will serve him as a security blanket. This seems unlikely, but I can imagine the circumstances under which it might occur.

The more likely possibility—or so it appears to me—is that by the year 2000 *institutionalized* religion, already on the wane as a significant factor in everyday life, will have faded to a point where it is only of slight importance in the community. Theology may still exist as a scholastic exercise, but in reality the God of authoritative answers will not only be dead but buried.

religion as interpersonal living

This does not mean at all that the concerns which have been the basis of religion will have vanished. The mysterious process of life, the mystery of the universe and how it came to be, the tragedy of man's alienation from himself and from others, the puzzle of the meaning of individual life—these mysteries will all be very much present. There may, indeed, be a *greater appreciation* of mystery as our knowledge increases (just as theoretical physicists now marvel at the true mystery of what they have discovered).

But religion, to the extent that the term is used, will consist of tentatively held hypotheses which are lived out and corrected in the interpersonal world. Groups, probably much smaller than present-day congregations, will wrestle with the ethical and moral and philosophical questions which are posed by the rapidly changing world. The individual will forge, with the support of the group, the stance he will take in the universe—a stance which he cannot regard as final, because more data will continually be coming in.

In the open questioning and honest struggle to face reality which exists in such a group, it is likely that a sense of true community will develop—a community based not on a common creed or an unchanging ritual, but on the personal ties of individuals who have become deeply related to one another as they attempt to comprehend, and to face as living men, the mysteries of existence. The religion of the future will be man's existential choice of his way of living in an unknown tomorrow —a choice made more bearable because formed in a community of individuals who are like-minded, but like-minded only in their searching.

In line with the thread which runs through all of my remarks, it may well be that out of these many searching groups there may emerge a more unitary view of man, a view which might bind us together. Man as a creature with ability to remember the past and foresee the future, a creature with the capacity for choosing among alternatives, a creature whose deepest urges are for harmonious and loving relationships with his fellows, a creature with the capacity to understand the reasons for his destructive behaviors, man as a person who has at least limited powers to form himself and to shape his future in the way he desires —this might be a crude sketch of the unifying view which could give us hope in a universe we cannot understand.

the self and the world

from THE BOOK:
ON THE TABOO AGAINST
KNOWING WHO YOU ARE

Alan W. Watts

This book explores an unrecognized but mighty taboo—our tacit conspiracy to ignore who, or what, we really are. Briefly, the thesis is that the prevalent sensation of oneself as a separate ego enclosed in a bag of skin is a hallucination which accords neither with Western science nor with the experimental philosophy-religions of the East—in particular the central and germinal Vedanta philosophy of Hinduism. This hallucination underlies the misuse of technology for the violent subjugation of man's natural environment and, consequently, its eventual destruction. . . .

It is said that humanity has evolved one-sidedly, growing in technical power without any comparable growth in moral integrity, or, as some would prefer to say, without comparable progress in education and rational thinking. Yet the problem is more basic. The root of the matter is the way in which we feel and conceive ourselves as human beings, our sensation of being alive, of individual existence and identity. We suffer from a hallucination, from a false and distorted sensation of our own existence as living organisms. Most of us have the sensation that "I myself" is a separate center of feeling and action, living inside and bounded by the physical body—a center which "confronts" an "external" world of people and things, making contact through the senses with a universe both alien and strange. Everyday figures of speech reflect this illusion. "I came into this World." "You must *face* reality." "The conquest of nature."

This feeling of being lonely and very temporary visitors in the universe is in flat contradiction to everything known about man (and all other living organisms) in the sciences. We do not "come into" this world; we come *out* of it, as leaves from a tree. As the ocean "waves," the universe "peoples." Every individual is an expression of the whole realm of nature, a unique action of the total universe. . . .

The hostile attitude of conquering nature ignores the basic interdependence of all things and events—that the world beyond the skin is actually an extension of our own bodies—and will end in destroying the very environment from which we emerge and upon which our whole life depends. . . .

. . . The sensation of "I" as a lonely and isolated center of being is so powerful and common-sensical, and so fundamental to our modes of speech and thought, to our laws and social institutions, that we cannot experience selfhood except as something superficial in the scheme of the universe. I seem to be a brief light that flashes but once in all the eons of time—a rare, complicated, and all-too-delicate organism on the fringe of biological evolution, where the wave of life bursts into individual, sparkling, and multicolored drops that gleam for a moment only to vanish forever. Under such conditioning it seems impossible and even absurd to realize that myself does not reside in the drop alone, but in the whole surge of energy which ranges from the galaxies to the nuclear fields in my body. At this level of existence "I" am immeasurably old; my forms are infinite and their comings and goings are simply the pulses or vibrations of a single and eternal flow of energy.

The difficulty in realizing this to be so is that conceptual thinking cannot grasp it. It is as if the eyes were trying to look at themselves directly, or as if one were trying to describe the color of a mirror in terms of colors reflected in the mirror. Just as sight is something more than all things seen, the foundation or "ground" of our existence and our awareness cannot be understood in terms of things that are known. We are forced, therefore, to speak of it through myth—that is, through special metaphors, analogies, and images which say what it is *like* as distinct from what it *is*. At one extreme of its meaning, "myth" is fable, falsehood, or superstition. But at another, "myth" is a useful and fruitful image by which we make sense of life in somewhat the same way that we can explain electrical forces by comparing them with the behavior of water or air. Yet "myth," in this second sense, is not to be taken literally, just as electricity is not to be confused with air or water. Thus in using myth one must take care not to confuse image with fact, which would be like climbing up the signpost instead of following the road.

Myth, then, is the form in which I try to answer when children ask me those fundamental metaphysical questions which come so readily to their minds: "Where did the world come from?" "Why did God make the world?" "Where was I before I was born?" "Where do people go when they die?" Again and again I have found that they seem to be satisfied with a simple and very ancient story, which goes something like this:

"There was never a time when the world began, because it goes round and round like a circle, and there is no place on a circle where it begins. Look at my watch, which tells the time; it goes round, and so the world repeats itself again and again. But just as the hour-hand of the watch goes up to twelve and down to six, so, too, there is day and night, waking and sleeping, living and dying, summer and winter. You can't have any one of these without the other, because you wouldn't be able to know what black is unless you had seen it side-by-side with white, or white unless side-by-side with black.

"In the same way, there are times when the world is, and times when it isn't, for if the world went on and on without rest for ever and ever, it would get horribly tired of itself. It comes and it goes. Now you see it; now you don't. So because it doesn't get tired of itself, it always comes back again after it disappears. It's like your breath: it goes in and out, in and out, and if you try to hold it in all the time you feel terrible. It's also like the game of hide-and-seek, because it's always fun to find new ways of hiding, and to seek for someone who doesn't always hide in the same place.

"God also likes to play hide-and-seek, but because there is nothing outside God, he has no one but himself to play with. But he gets over this difficulty by pretending that he is not himself. This is his way of hiding from himself. He pretends that he is you and I and all the people in the world, all the animals, all the plants, all the rocks, and all the stars. In this way he has strange and wonderful adventures, some of which are terrible and frightening. But these are just like bad dreams, for when he wakes up they will disappear.

"Now when God plays hide and pretends that he is you and I, he does it so well that it takes him a long time to remember where and how he hid himself. But that's the whole fun of it—just what he wanted to do. He doesn't want to find himself too quickly, for that would spoil the game. That is why it is so difficult for you and me to find out that we are God in disguise, pretending not to be himself. But when the game has gone on long enough, all of us will wake up, stop pretending, and remember that we are all one single Self—the God who is all that there is and who lives for ever and ever.

"Of course, you must remember that God isn't shaped like a person. People have skins and there is always something outside our skins. If there weren't, we wouldn't know the difference between what is inside and outside our bodies. But God has no skin and no shape because there isn't any outside to him. [With a sufficiently intelligent child, I illustrate this with a Mobius strip—a ring of paper tape twisted once in such a way that it has only one side and one edge.] The inside and the outside of God are the same. And though I have been talking about God as 'he' and not 'she', God isn't a man or a woman. I didn't say 'it' because we usually say 'it' for things that aren't alive.

"God is the Self of the world, but you can't see God for the same reason that, without a mirror, you can't see your own eyes, and you certainly can't bite your own teeth or look inside your head. Your self is that cleverly hidden because it is God hiding.

"You may ask why God sometimes hides in the form of horrible people, or pretends to be people who suffer great disease and pain. Remember, first, that he isn't really doing this to anyone but himself. Remember, too, that in almost all the stories you enjoy there have to be bad people as well as good people, for the thrill of the tale is to find out how the good people will get the better of the bad. It's the same as when we play cards. At the beginning of the game we shuffle them all into a mess, which is like the bad things in the world, but the point of the game is to put the mess into good order, and the one who does it best is the winner. Then we shuffle the cards once more and play again, and so it goes with the world."

"The Ultimate Ground of Being" is Paul Tillich's decontaminated term for "God" and would also do for "the Self of the world" as I put it in my story for children. But the secret which my story slips over to the child is that the Ultimate Ground of Being is *you*. Not, of course, the everyday you which the Ground is assuming, or "pretending" to be, but that inmost Self which escapes inspection because it's always the inspector. This, then, is the taboo of taboos: you're IT! . . .

Hitherto the poets and philosophers of science have used the vast expanse and duration of the universe as a pretext for reflections on the unimportance of man, forgetting that man with "that enchanted loom, the brain" is precisely what transforms this immense electrical pulsation into light and color, shape and sound, large and small, hard and heavy, long and short. In knowing the world we humanize it, and if, as we discover it, we are astonished at its dimensions and its complexity, we should be just as astonished that we have the brains to perceive it. . . .

The people we are tempted to call clods and boors are just those who seem to find nothing fascinating in being human; their humanity is incomplete, for it has never astonished them. . . .

How is it possible that a being with such sensitive jewels as the eyes, such enchanted musical instruments as the ears, and such a fabulous arabesque of nerves as the brain can experience itself as anything less than a god? And, when you consider that this incalculably subtle organism is inseparable from the still more marvelous patterns of its environment—from the minutest electrical designs to the whole company of the galaxies—how is it conceivable that this incarnation of all eternity can be bored with being?

developing a creed

From all that has been said about change and the need to remain adaptable, it is clear that a statement of belief and commitment must be *for now*. Perhaps it is possible to write a creed that will pass the test of time; but only time will tell.

So, try your hand at developing a statement which answers the question, "Who am I—now?"

To prepare yourself for this, look at the models on the following pages. If there are others that you know of and like, think about them too. Next consider again the questions on pp. 293-4. If you can answer them, fine; but do not be afraid to be tentative.

Then weave your reflections, whatever they may be, into a verbal tapestry, a statement of belief which you can date and sign.

HOW A MAN OF THAT AGE MIGHT DESCRIBE
HIS VIEW OF THE WORLD

I
THE AGE OF
PRIMITIVE
REALISM
*From ? B.C.
to 650 B.C.*

"We are two, the world and me. The world is just as I sense it (see it, touch it, taste it, smell it, hear it). The world is like me. In me there is a spirit; in the world as a whole, and in each part of the world that I deal with, there are spirits who rule. I have come to terms with these spirits. I do so by rituals, by magic. *The superior man is the magician or witch doctor who knows the spirits and how to*

Marginal material between quotation marks is from "Explorations in Awareness" by J. Samuel Bois. © 1957 by Harper & Row Publishers, Inc.
    The Dynamics of Change, Kaiser Aluminum & Chemical Corporation, copyright © 1967.

deal with them." (In many parts of the world today, in all cultures and societies, there are still people who believe that there are "spirits" whose help can be invoked, or whose wrath avoided, through incantation of magic words and the performance of rituals.)

"the world is what i feel it to be."

**II
THE AGE OF
REASON**
*From 650 B.C.
to 350 B.C.*

From Thales Through Aristotle. "We are now three: the world, I, facing the world, and I, observing myself looking at the world. To put order into the world, I classify things, qualities and actions in the world and in me. I take this classification into account when I want to guide my behavior. My ideal is to be as 'objective' as possible. My thinking must be orderly, as the world is orderly. My brain mirrors the world; to each thought corresponds a fact; to each word corresponds a thing, a person, an action or a quality. If my thinking goes from one thought to another according to logic, it directs me through the world from one fact to the next. *Within my brain there is a miniature of the universe.*" (Even after 2,000 years, there are still many people who think this way today. They are the 'practical' people; they accumulate 'facts' and pin labels on them, and base their conduct—and their appraisal of others—on 'facts' and labels.)

"the world is what i say it is."

**III
THE AGE OF
SCIENCE**
*From 1500 A.D.
to 1900 A.D.*

From Copernicus to Planck. "I do not confer with the spirits as did the primitive. Nor do I deceive myself as did the Metaphysician (II) who mistook his own voice for that of Nature. I ask Nature definite questions and Nature gives me clear-cut answers. I translate these answers into mathematical formulas that project my conclusions into the unknown, where I discover other facts that Nature has kept hidden since the beginning. *The superior man is the experimenter-mathematician, the man who expresses relations in formulas that reveal how the properties and the actions of men and things follow measurable sequences.*" (The man of affairs today; the one who runs business and industry, serves in high governmental posts; writes and edits our journals and newspapers, is the product of colleges and universities whose curriculum is largely based on the experimenter-mathematician concept; he speaks in charts and graphs and figures, and bases his conduct upon them and his appraisal of others on the extent that they do so.)

"the world is an immense machine and i can discover how it works."

**IV
THE AGE OF
RELATIVISM**
*From 1900 A.D.
through
1966 A.D.*

From Roentgen Through Russell. "I find that the further I ask questions, the less and less the world seems like a giant machine. I have trouble even asking the 'right' questions and the answers frequently baffle me. Even when I ask the 'right' questions and get the 'right' answers, I find that the answers are in terms of my frame of reference to the world I have *myself* created through centuries of observations. The structure of my world is built of *my own* postulates, which must be re-examined relentlessly. They appear to be relative to my own space-time relationship with the cosmos, and with every unique event that I single out for study. What the primitivists thought of as spirits in nature, and the philosophers considered the 'facts' of nature, and the rationalists considered the 'laws' of nature, I find now to be but gross irregularities in the world as I see it through my inadequate senses and instruments. The only 'laws of nature' I can discover are statistical averages that provide rough indications of probabilities."

"the world consists of probabilities that i create by my way of looking at them."

**V
THE AGE OF
UNITY**
*From 1966 A.D.
to ? A.D.*

From Peirce Through Einstein and Reiser to? "Having discovered that I cannot separate what I observe from my own act of observation, I begin to study my own way of observing. When I do this, I find that my observation does not consist solely of what goes on in my brain, but that my total organism, with all of its history, is also engaged.

"I discover that my most clever formulations take their origin and their significance from an immediacy of felt contact, of fusion and oneness with what is going on, beyond the dimensional limits of symbols, and without the distinction between the self and the non-self. Out of this knowledge comes an awareness of my inter-relatedness with everything, from blind cosmic energy to fellow human beings; the old, verbal distinctions between art and science and religion disappear—becoming an overall oneness of experience." (This concept, which after 2,000 years offers the promise that the powerful ethical systems of Christ, Buddha and Mohammed may fuse with the relativistic world of Einstein, the cyclic, recreative universe of Hoyle, the "participative iconology" of McLuhan and Ellul, is a still, small voice in our world of today. It can be heard in the enclaves of a handful of universities; in the words of a bearded poet somewhere east of mid-

"my world has a structure that no formulation can encompass; i conceive of the world as my own total experience with it, and i play with my own symbolic constructs in a spirit of easy detachment."

night; and in the voiceless contemplation of a Zen disciple beside the dripping water and stone pools somewhere west of a Shoji screen. But it *can* be heard.)

SELECTIVE SERVICE SYSTEM SPECIAL FORM FOR CONSCIENTIOUS OBJECTOR

Stephen Gordon

Question one—Do you believe in a Supreme Being?

Question two—Describe the nature of your belief which is the basis of your claim made in Series I above, and state whether or not your belief in a Supreme Being involves duties which to you are superior to those arising from any human relation.

MAN'S BASIC NATURE IS GOD. God is not only a universal object removed from this world, but He is everything that exists in this world. He is the living creatures, and also everything inanimate. Man, therefore, is a part of God, or in other words man and God are of the same substance. Life is a gift given to man by God. It is the only gift God gave to man. Consequently life is the basic right of man. All other ideals that man has come to call rights are conceived by man and developed by him. Therefore these rights are subordinate to the basic right to live.

Because of these convictions, I find it impossible to justify killing. First of all, killing another man is in essence killing God. Secondly, killing a man is destroying his basic freedom. Thus killing is the most grievous sin against God, and against man's own nature. In destroying another's basic right of life, one destroys one's own basic right to live.

I find it impossible to support any military organization whose actions result in the destruction of human lives. For this is to make oneself the equal of God, who alone has the right to give life and to take it away.

Reprinted from Stephen Gordon, "Creed" (Santa Barbara, Calif.: Unicorn Press) by permission of the publisher and the author.

from TIME'S FUTURE IN OUR TIME

John R. Seeley

If we had looked for that trace, that first, faint, foreshadowing, twenty years ago, of what the new society might be like, we should perhaps have looked toward San Francisco and Venice and North Beach—to "The Beatniks." There, then, visibly, audibly, sensibly, in joy and grief, ecstasy and agony, wail and laughter, mad motions and quiet contemplation, orgy and debate, what was to be was being sought and seized and shaped, with leadings and misleadings, tremolo and blatancy, false start and brave beginning. There, then, in the quiet womb of time, reposed and stirred that whose spiritual issue and descent today is what is being variously called The New Generation, The New Youth, The New Left, The Movement. . . .

What is it that I see in the range of the young, in what might best be loosely termed, "The Movement," that makes me suggest that the seed of the transition society is there highly visible and palpitating?—

Disavowing work as intrinsically and inherently valuable—and particularly the glorification of work to avoid coping with the problems of aggression . . .

The abandonment of overdrawn distinctions, particularly dualisms like good-evil, masculine-feminine, right-wrong, in favor of a sense of the spectrum of similarities that underlies experience . . .

Refusal to accept combative and competitive approaches in nearly all of their forms . . .

A foreswearing of the furious enjoyments of fanaticism; the food and fuel of most previous movements . . .

Withdrawal from the idolatry of self and those merely projected and extended selves—my family, my city, my class, or race or religion or nation—in favor of something more than tolerance . . .

A heightened appreciation for goods that are good only in the giving (such as folk song singing or the playing and reproducing of music) as against the standard goods that are mere counters in a game, based on heightened envy . . .

An enormously enhanced and increased valuation of love in all its extended and various manifestations, its range of aims and objects . . .

Discarding rules as the tools of principal reliance, preferring, instead, a unique and personal response to a situation that is viewed in its own uniqueness and novelty . . .

From "Time's Future in Our Time," a paper for the Minister's Conference on Recreation, Toronto, November 1966 by John R. Seeley of the Center for the Study of Democratic Institutions.

twenty

the taste of space,
the scent of time

The evolution of the entire universe—stars, elements, life, man—is a process of drawing something out of nothing, out of the utter void of non-being. The creative element in the mind of man—that latency which can conceive gods, carve statues, move the heart with the symbols of great poetry, or devise the formulas of modern physics— emerges in as mysterious a fashion as those elementary particles which leap into momentary existence in great cyclotrons, only to vanish again like infinitesimal ghosts. The reality we know in our limited lifetimes is dwarfed by the unseen potential of the abyss where science stops. In a similar way, the smaller universe of the individual human brain has its lonely cometary passages, or flares suddenly like a super nova, only to subside in death while the waves of energy it has released roll on through unnumbered generations.

Loren Eiseley,
"The Mind as Nature"

We form our impressions of human nature primarily from our own subjective experience of it. Yet we know that our experience is limited by what our five senses convey to our central nervous system, and controlled by the pattern of relationships built up over time of brain to mind to consciousness to awareness. There is more—perhaps infinitely more—to heaven and earth than is dreamt of in our philosophy.

In "Coping with Change" we explored ways in which early conditioning (imprinting), social fictions, and the "filter" system control our experience of ourselves and the world. We also examined some agents of change which can "shock" us into new ways of perceiving and conceiving. Let us look now at agents of change in a different way.

Let us imagine a huge kaleidoscope with an infinite number of different pieces of glass. If we think of what we experience as what we see when we look into it, then an agent of change is something that twists the kaleidoscope, bringing a different pattern into focus. Today we are discovering more and more ways to twist the kaleidoscope and thus expand our capacity for experience.

In a sense, human nature is what we experience it to be. Human nature, then, changes as our capacity for experience changes. For mankind generally, extensions of human experience supply new knowledge—and even alter what we mean by "knowledge." For each of us individually, they permit and in fact coerce us to experience differently.

Our sensations, perceptions, and conceptions are interrelated. A change in one is accompanied by changes in the other two. To see the complexity of human experience, it might be helpful to reshape our earlier definition of agents of change and distinguish four kinds.

An agent of change is:

Any piece of equipment which extends one or more of our senses, permitting us to experience something otherwise beyond our sensory range. Radar, microscopes, telescopes are examples. What others can you think of? What changes do they bring?

sen-sa-tion

sen-sa-tion (sen-sa'shen), n. [LL. sensatio < sensatus; see SENSATE], 1. the power or process of receiving conscious sense impressions through direct stimulation of the bodily organism or of the sense organs: as, hearing, seeing, touching, tasting, and smelling are sensations. 2. an immediate reaction to external stimulation of a sense organ; conscious feeling or sense impression: as, a sensation of cold. 3. a generalized feeling or reaction, often vague and without reference to immediate stimulus: as, a sensation of happiness. . . .

Anything which changes the filtering of sense data to the mind, permitting us to become aware or conscious of appearances otherwise ignored. Drugs are agents of this kind of change. What else?

From *Webster's New World Dictionary of the American Language*, College Edition. Copyright 1968 by The World Publishing Company, Cleveland, Ohio.

per-cep-tion

per-cep-tion (per-sep′shen), n. [< OFr. & L.; OFr. perception; L. perceptio < pp. of percipere; see perceive], 1. consciousness; awareness. 2. the awareness of objects or other data through the medium of the senses. 3. the process or faculty of perceiving. 4. the result of this; knowledge, etc. gained by perceiving. 5. insight or intuition, as of an abstract quality.

Anything which alters the action of our "censor," permitting us access to our own buried self. Encounter, shock, introspection are examples. What others can you think of?

con-cep-tion

con-cep-tion (kən-sep′shen), n. [ME. concepcioun; OFr. conception < L. conceptio, a comprehending, conception < conceptus; see conceive], 1. a conceiving or being conceived in the womb. 2. that which is so conceived; embryo; fetus; hence, 3. the beginning of some process, chain of events, etc. 4. the act, process, or power of conceiving mentally; formulation of ideas. 5. a mental impression or image; general notion; concept. 6. an original idea, design, plan, etc.—SYN. see idea.

Anything which reveals or creates new patterns, structures, relationships, permitting us to reorganize our perceptions into new meanings. Art is an instance. What are others?

With the rapid development of extensions of human experience, we must anticipate that change in subjective experience—and thus in the quality of human life—will be as great as change in the environment.

Among the changes we can anticipate are changes in the way we experience space and time, big and little, figure and ground, self and world. How are we to insure that these changes will create new meanings and a richer life, and not merely disintegrate old structures and leave us with chaos?

The key word here is *create*. Let us look first into the relationship between *creativity* and *chaos*. Then let us experiment.

twisting the kaleidoscope

The purpose of the set of materials following "The Creative Process" is to give you an opportunity to twist the kaleidoscope—to shake up your usual patterns of sensation, perception, and conception. Let your mind range freely, even erratically, among these stimuli. Explore your own capacity to create new realms of meaning.

the creative process

THE WORLD OF
$A^n + B^n \longleftrightarrow C$!

Not everyone likes formulas, having been scared to death by them during tender and impressionable years. Yet formulas are not only a shorthand way of expressing an enormous amount of human experience, but they can be fun, as well. They are like Tinker Toy sets; you can form all sorts of things out of them, providing you abide by the simple rules that certain things fit together only in a certain way.

When it comes to creativity, a formula that seems particularly pertinent is:

$$A + B \longleftrightarrow C$$

Here A and B represent two concepts established by the mind, which come together in some way to produce the new thing C. The arrow means "yields" or "produces." Thus when you put A and B together, you get something different—C. It is like biological creation, the offspring are something different than either parent.

The formula is not ours, but was created by John W. Haefele and described in his book *Creativity and In-*

novation, and we trust he doesn't mind our playing around with it; that's what formulas are for.

To begin with, we would put a little n just to the right and a little above A and B—like this: A^n and B^n. We say that n means any number of or condition of, the ingredients A or B. We do this to remind ourselves that both A and B can be very complex phenomena, and not necessarily just little, discrete things like a snail and a ball bearing (which might yield us a "snail-mobile"). The n is a shorthand way of saying, "all those things that make up A" and "all those things that make up B." When put together, they yield C, which is something quite different than either A or B.

For instance:

Let A be:
A^{n1}—A ball when rolling touches only a small part of its surface to the surface it rolls on.
A^{n2}—When a ball is enclosed in a socket, it can still roll but its movements can be controlled.

Kaiser Aluminum NEWS, © 1968.

Let B be:

B^{n1}—When a dry surface is exposed to a wet medium, it will pick up a thin layer of the wet medium.

B^{n2}—When a wet surface is pressed against a dry surface, a portion of the wet will transfer to the dry.

If we combine A^n with B^n we get something new—namely a ball-point pen—C. (We haven't the slightest idea if that's the way the ball-point pen was invented, but if it wasn't invented that way, it should have been.)

Now, two more changes in our formula. We would put an arrow at *both* ends of $\longleftrightarrow$ to indicate that the process is reversible and thus applies to discovery, too. Given C, we may be able to find that it is made up of A^n and B^n. (Given water, we might discover that it has two components, hydrogen and oxygen, as someone seems already to have done.)

Finally, we would add "!" to C, making it $C!$ This would indicate that it is an original (and often surprising) pattern.

After all this tinkering, we come up with $A^n + B^n \longleftrightarrow C!$—which may not be much of an improvement after all, but comes closer to what we are trying to say; namely, that the creative process appears to be a rather simple one. It seems to require only putting two or more systems in juxtaposition to yield an original combination or pattern.

If we can assume that $A^n + B^n \longleftrightarrow C!$ is at least one way of describing the creative act, can we figure out what particular steps an individual must take to make the formula work? We think it can be done. Let's assume that most, if not all, of the following steps are followed by each person who successfuly completes the creative act:

Desire. The person must for some reason *want* to create something original. It may be that he wants to solve a problem that bothers him. He may simply be curious about something he doesn't understand. He may want to express some personal experience (as in the arts). He may want to make more money through the introduction of a new invention, process or technique. Or it may simply be a response to a change in the environment. Whatever the reason, creativity starts with motivation. For some reason, many people simply are not motivated, and with them the process never gets started.

Preparation. As the first step toward satisfying the desire, both pertinent and seemingly impertinent information are gathered. This may be through research, experimentation or exposure to experience. It is here that the substance of A^n and B^n is determined. The process is analytical, and is a way of "making the strange familiar."

Manipulation. Now, with all this material before him—in his mind, on the workbench, or in piles of notes on slips of paper—the creative person begins to try to find some new pattern. He pokes at the material, shuffles it around, turns it upside down, looks at it sideways. He may seek metaphors, just as in literature poets seek them. ("She walks in beauty like the night.") Or, in invention, one may conceive that the flow of electricity outside a conductor is *like* the flow of water inside a pipe. The manipulative process is an attempt at synthesis, the putting together of hitherto unrelated concepts, and what it hopes to do is "to make the familiar strange."

Incubation. In most instances, the solution does not appear immediately. The problem is "dropped" and the person turns to some new problem. For reasons we do not fully understand, the unconscious mind keeps wrestling with the original problem. Here, the process of manipulation continues, possibly now considering other aspects of A^n and B^n that had not consciously been considered before. Anyway, something goes on, perhaps driven by the psychic tensions set up by the original desire and its unfulfillment.

Intimation. Suddenly, there may be a feeling that a solution is about to be found. It wells up into the conscious mind like the light before the dawn. There is a feeling of premonition.

Illumination. C! is suddenly revealed; there is a "flash," an "insight," a "sudden dawning." Sometimes the experience is described as "A-Ha!" or "Eureka!" Both are cries of joy, and seem to arise from the sudden release of strong psychic tensions. The experience appears to be closely related to the release of physiological tension in the sexual act, and sometimes has been described that way.

Verification. This is the process by which the new pattern C! is examined and valued. If mathematical, it is susceptible to proof; if a theory, it can be tested; if a work of art, it can be exhibited for social reaction or examined to see if it is (personally) satisfying to the artist; if an invention, it can be tried to see if it "works."

Not all these steps are necessarily the part of every creative act; certainly some creative acts appear to be purely fortuitous. Pure luck probably plays a greater part in discovery than in invention.

It should be emphasized that although the sequence can be plotted, the mechanism by which the sequence occurs is only partially understood. In order to come up with some acceptable mechanism, we have to invent entities we call the conscious, the preconscious (or sub-conscious) and the unconscious. These are signs we hang on the parts of the transactions that occur between an organism and its environment.

Let us consider that the organism —any organism—is constantly bombarded by stimuli of all sorts from its environment—electromagnetic waves, both visible and invisible, pour in from all sides; electronic vibrations are communicated from the ground through the soles of the feet, through the hand from the object it holds; the whole inner part of the organism is engaged in pulsating, highly complex electrochemical reactions. Everything is going on at once.

Survival, not to mention sanity, depends on the deliberate selection, out of the multitude of stimuli pouring in, of those which enable the organism to maintain its equilibrium. Certain sights, certain sounds, certain bodily sensations, will be selected from moment to moment; this is what we call consciousness. It is a ritualistic, rigidized, stereotyped set of responses, derived from previously successful confrontations of the organism with its environment.

Then, on the periphery of those deliberately selected stimuli, there is a dim awareness of other stimuli, not quite conscious—but preconscious. Here may be found what is barely seen at the edges of vision, what is hardly heard in the background, subtle changes in temperature; felt, but scarcely observed, changes in body chemistry. These are the "halo" effects; like the halo of a religious painting, they surround the head but are not quite a part of it.

Beyond the conscious and the preconscious, it is generally held that there is something called the unconscious. Here is the reservoir of life, and the wellspring of creativity. Into the unconscious, like snow sifting down on the ocean, go all the stimuli that pour in upon the organism. . . .

"Psychology has little to tell us of what is happening here," says Henry Eyring in *Scientific Creativity.* "In dreams and half-dreaming states the mind is filled with a throng of images and fantasies. The whole unconscious is presumably occupied with such, their source lying in memory and the experiences of the past, and perhaps also directly in the processes of life itself. Here, we should remember, is the place where matter, life and mind are most inextricably mixed. Here the natural tendencies and predilections of living stuff come to expression. . . . Here the organizing power of life fashions into orderly patterns the floating fantasies of the unconscious mind. Here, if anywhere, new patterns may be created."

Earlier we described consciousness as the interaction between stimuli and response. In a stable environment stimuli tend to be repetitive, and so do the responses. Satisfactory responses are repeated until they become as formalized as printed circuits. When stimuli change, or are experienced in a new way, then new responses have to be made, and this is the act of creativity.

Since human experiences are believed to be converted into wave pulses which can be translated into symbols, we can see that in the act of creativity we are dealing with forming and manipulating patterns of symbols.

This brings us to metaphor, which is a statement of a new relationship between what had previously been considered unrelated. The statement sets up psychic tensions because the established responses are not adequate to the new experience. The organism seeks to establish a new equilibrium that will accommodate the new transaction between itself and its environment. A new pattern of response results and the tension is relieved. . . .

By stating similarities between the dissimilar, or new systems of relationships among the hitherto unrelated, metaphor makes the familiar strange, an operation that lies at the heart of the creative act. Through metaphor our concept of the world changes: despite commonsense evidence to the contrary, the world becomes like a ball, and not flat; seemingly changeless species of animals and plants are seen to be but the most recent phase of a continually changing shape; the seemingly immutable laws of the physical universe are seen to be relative to the observer.

The interesting thing about metaphor is that it can be consciously directed. We can deliberately seek new relationships between seemingly unrelated phenomena and thus create new paths for interaction between ourselves and our environment. Thus,

creativity can be learned, and we can endlessly change ourselves and our world.

In addition to psychological theory, little by little we are beginning to discover the physiological basis of creativity. "Brain surgeons are now linking emotions with imagination," says Alex F. Osborn in *Applied Imagination.*

"Their knives are proving that every brain has a section that can create ideas. It is called the "silent area" since it controls no bodily movement, and has naught to do with what we see or hear or physically feel. Back of this area is a lump of tissue called the thalamus. In this lobe our basic emotions are centered. We have always known that ideas flow faster under emotional stress. Now we know that our emotional lobe is wired by nerves to the frontal area in such a way as to affect creative thinking.

Having determined the area (which ultimately, of course, extends to the whole system of the organism) it is interesting to conjecture about what goes on there. One such theory involves "clusters." An idea cluster may be defined as the group of words and ideas that are associated in one person's mind with a given word or sign.

Thus it might be suggested that in the act of preparation during the creative process, one is engaged in building clusters, and during the process of manipulation is trying to find new relationships between them; to construct metaphors, if you like. The wider and more varied the field of experience, the more there is in each cluster, and the more opportunities there are for original patterns to be produced.

It is quite possible that the external disorder that characterizes most creativity—the littered laboratory, the disorder of the inventor's workbench, the artist's studio—are all outward expressions of the inner chaos of the unconscious. The storm of stimuli from the disordered environment may often be an important part of the creative process.

Ben Shahn put it best, the cry of the creative person against the orderly and logical world of "reason," when, at the Aspen International Design Conference in 1966, he said, "Give me more chaos!"

CREATIVE PROBLEM-SOLVING

The best problem-solving comes from *diverse* groups—where many different backgrounds and viewpoints are represented. But how to release the potential of such a group?

1. Get someone to state the *problem as given*. Ask him questions. Get it as clear as you can. Make the strange familiar, until you are all clear on what the problem is.

2. At this point you have the *problem as understood*. This may be quite different from what you or the problem-stater thought it was at the beginning.

3. *Purge.* Now just throw out all the solutions you think of right away to the problem. Get rid of them. They are all the easy, obvious things that never work, that people say, "Yes, but ..." to. Purge yourselves of these ideas—otherwise they will get in your way.

4. *Make analogies.* Now your job is to "make the familiar strange." To do this, you have to let go of tightly-organized rational thinking. Instead, try analogies, things that "feel like" the problem. Suppose the problem is making an easy-open package:

Direct Analogy: It's like a clam shell, opening and shutting. If you heat the clam he opens.

Personal Analogy: I'm the clam. The heat is terrible. I push out the edges of my shell, but I'm afraid I'll die. If some cool water came now, I'd close up with relief.

Symbolic Analogy: It's like the missionary being boiled in the pot by the cannibals. He came to save them, but they had different objectives. Like, they were hungry.

Fantasy Analogy: I wish the damn package would open up just by saying some words: "Open, Sesame!" Or, "Open, poppy seeds!" You say what's in the package, and pow! It breaks open.

These guidelines were developed and adapted by M. B. Miles, Stanford Research Institute, from the ideas in W. J. J. Gordon, *Synectics: The Development of Creative Capacity* (New York: Harper & Row Publishers, 1961). Reprinted by permission of M. B. Miles.

Any or all of these kinds of analogies can be used. Some principles for making analogies: choose a realm (biological, mechanical, social, physical) that's *far* from the problem. *Example:* biological analogies are excellent for mechanical or social problems. Let go. Follow your impulses. Say what wells up in you, especially if it seems crazy or irrelevant. Speculate about the impossible. Say, "What if the law of gravity didn't apply?" Have fun. Build on others' analogies. Leave the original problem sitting there, and move as far out from it as you can. Farther. Play, joke, embroider on ideas.

5. *Flip the analogy back on the problem.* What is the essence of your analogy? How might it apply to the problem? Develop a viewpoint toward the problem, using the analogy:

Example: Maybe we could develop a package that would open by heat and stay open. You put it in the oven, first it opens, then it cooks.

Do *not* worry at this point about feasibility, whether others would think the idea crazy, whether it would run into administrative trouble, etc. Just ask: How might this analogy apply to this problem? Then start getting specific.

6. *Develop specific solutions* using the viewpoint:

Example: A metal package sealed with gelatin sides, which melt away and permit roasting of the product.

Stages 5 and 6 often have a strong feeling of delight, pleasure, joy to them. The solution "feels right," is elegant, "fits." It's like coming through to something beautiful which has a life of its own.

In both Stages 5 and 6, *experts* can be helpful to provide technical information. They can "reality-test," say what might work, explain principles, etc.

7. *Plan for development/implementation.* Decide on what needs to be done to make the solution workable. Where, how, will a trial model be set up, tried out, etc. Who will do it? Future users of the solution and experts needs to work along with the inventors. The test here is: will it work? And what kinds of resistance and support can we expect from others?

Example: It's necessary to find out whether a durable gelatin can be found that won't melt in sunlight, but will in an oven without sticking on. Also problems of the metal-to-gelatin bonding. And will the vice-president for marketing support or block the idea?

the "aha!" experience

What do you see?

from GESTALT THERAPY

Frederick Perls, Ralph F. Hefferline, and Paul Goodman

In this drawing the figure may be seen as a white chalice on a black ground; or, if the white area be taken as ground, then the figure becomes two heads in profile silhouette. One may, upon continued inspection of this ambiguous picture, become adept at shifting from one way of organizing it to the other, but one can never organize it both ways at once. Furthermore, please note that when a change in what is seen occurs, it is not a consequence of some modification in what is "objectively" given on the printed page—that was fixed once and for all when the book went to press—but is, rather, brought about by the activity of the seeing organism. Also, notice the three-dimensional quality of the two-dimensional picture. When one sees the white figure, the black ground is *behind* it. Likewise, a similar depth effect occurs when the two heads are seen as if outside a lighted window.

Figure 2 again presents an ambiguous picture, this time one in which there is more detail. In glancing at this, you will probably see at once a young woman in three-quarter view to the left. On the other hand, you may be that one person in about five who immediately sees an old

Reprinted from Frederick Perls, Ralph F. Hefferline, and Paul Goodman, *Gestalt Therapy* (New York: The Julian Press, Inc., Publishers, 1951), pp. 26–28, by permission of the publisher. A Delta Book.

hag facing to the left and forward. If you do not for a time spontaneously reorganize what you first saw—that is, destroy it as such and use its parts to make the new picture—there are ways in which we can assist you. . . .

First, though, there are several important points that we can make with the situation as it stands. Unless we had told you that there was a second picture, you certainly would not have suspected it or looked for one. You would have been quite satisfied with the correctness and adequacy of what you saw at first glance. What you now see, whichever picture it is, *is* correct. It solves for you, in terms of the way your seeing is at the moment organized, the question of "What is this a picture of?" In the context of our present discussion of figure and ground, you are probably willing to concede that we are not trying to dupe you and that the alternative organization, if it has not by this time been achieved by you, will as you now see the first one. In another context, you might regard someone who claims to see something that you do not as mistaken or "nuts," and pass on.

If you see a young woman where we say there is an old woman, you might, if a compliant type, decide to submit and say what we say. If we greatly outnumber you—if we, for instance, are "society" and you an "individual"—then, if you will yield and agree with us, we shall reward you by acknowledging that now you are behaving "normally." Please note, however, that in such case your acceptable behavior will have been imposed upon you and you will not be living it *on your own*. You will be in agreement with us only on a verbal basis, not on the basis of *seeing*, which is *nonverbal*.

This picture has been constructed so that various of its details have a dual function. The long promontory which is the old hag's nose is the whole cheek and jaw-line of the young woman. The hag's left eye is the young woman's left ear, her mouth the young woman's velvet neckband or choker, her right eye a bit of the young woman's nose, etc. If we could trace these for you it would be more helpful, but by now you probably have seen the second picture. It will have come suddenly, perhaps startling you into a little exclamation of surprise. This is what gestalt psychologists call the "aha!" experience. Their formal name for it is insight.

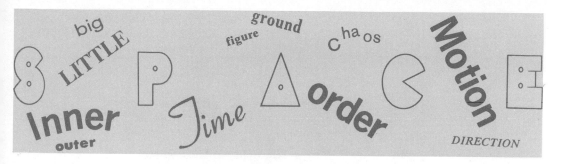

We all "know" that time is the fourth dimension. But do we experience it as the fourth dimension? Will we in the future? And a fifth?

If you took a trip around the entire rim of our galaxy, averaging 99 percent of the speed of light, you would return having aged 30 years while the earth would have aged 30,000. So take her along if you love her!

Can we experience permanence—or only change?

When you watch the sea, does its great age make a difference in your experience?

Is a paper flower a better metaphor than a plastic flower?

Time itself is a variable quantity; the rate at which it flows depends upon the speed of the observer.

Observed space is getting bigger—and smaller. Oddly, human beings remain in the middle. That is, the *macrocosm* we observe with our telescopes is as many times bigger than us as the *microcosm* we observe with our microscopes is smaller. With a sweep of the arm . . .

From PACE Magazine, Aug. 1969 (Compiled by Yvonne Mozee)

we can indicate where the macrocosm is. But where do we point to show the microcosm?

Is there anything in the universe, big or small, that is, even for an instant, *stationary?*

If there is, would we know about it?

Everything we experience moves through time, as do we. Can we even conceive of "something" which does not?

The sun is 4–5 billion years into its life span; it has 5–6 billion years to go.

There are no straight lines or right angles in nature. Why don't we wonder why?

Astronomers are discussing the possibility that one of the moons of Saturn may be artificially made, and that life on Jupiter may have evolved to fish.

Look closely at the picture on the cover. What do you see? As you look at it, think about big-little-space-time-inner-outer-order-chaos-motion-direction-figure-ground.

What are your sensations?

Then read the passages from *The Universe and Dr. Einstein* and look again at the picture.

In what ways have your perceptions of the picture changed?

In what ways have your *conceptions* about time-space, etc., changed?

from THE UNIVERSE
AND DR. EINSTEIN

Lincoln Barnett

the delicate
pressure of
starlight . . .

All the phenomena of nature, visible and invisible, within the atom and in outer space, indicate that the substance and energy of the universe are inexorably diffusing like vapor through the insatiable void. The sun is slowly but surely burning out, the stars are dying embers, and everywhere in the cosmos heat is turning to cold, matter is dissolving into radiation, and energy is being dissipated into empty space.

The universe is thus progressing toward an ultimate "heat-death," or as it is technically defined, a condition of "maximum entropy." When the universe reaches this state some billions of years from now all the processes of nature will cease. All space will be at the same temperature. No energy can be used because all of it will be uniformly distributed through the cosmos. There will be no light, no life, no warmth—nothing but perpetual and irrevocable stagnation. Time itself will come to an end. For entropy points the direction of time. Entropy is the measure of randomness. When all system and order in the universe have vanished, when randomness is at its maximum, and entropy cannot be increased, when there no longer is any sequence of cause and effect, in short when the universe has run down, there will be no direction to time—there will be no time. And there is no way of avoiding this destiny. For the fateful principle known as the Second Law of Thermodynamics, which stands today as the principal pillar of classical physics left intact by the march of science, proclaims that the fundamental processes of nature are irreversible. Nature moves just one way.

There are a few contemporary theorists, however, who propose that somehow, somewhere beyond man's meager ken the universe may be rebuilding itself. In the light of Einstein's principle of the equivalence of mass and energy, it is possible to imagine the diffused radiation in space congealing once more into particles of matter—protons, neutrons, and electrons—which may then combine to form larger units, which in turn may be collected by their own gravitational influence into diffuse nebulae, stars, and, ultimately, galactic systems. And thus the life cycle of the universe may be repeated for all eternity. Laboratory experiments have indeed demonstrated that photons of high-energy radiation, such as gamma rays, can, under certain conditions, interact with matter to produce pairs of electrons and positrons. Astronomers have also determined recently that atoms of the lighter elements, drifting in space—hydrogen, helium, oxygen, nitrogen, and carbon—may slowly coalesce into molecules and microscopic particles of dust and gas. And still more recently Dr. Fred L. Whipple of Harvard has described in his "Dust Cloud Hypothesis," published in 1948, how the rarefied cosmic dust that floats in interstellar space in quantities equal in mass to all the visible matter in the universe could in the course of a billion years condense and coagulate into stars. According to Whipple these tiny dust particles, barely one fifty-thousandth of an inch in diameter, are blown together by the delicate pressure of starlight, just as the fine-spun tail of a comet is deflected away from the sun by the impact of solar photons. As the particles cohere, an aggregate is formed, then a cloudlet, and then a cloud. When the cloud attains gigantic proportions (i.e., when its diameter exceeds six trillion miles), its mass and density will be sufficient to set a new sequence of physical processes into operation. Gravity will cause the cloud to contract, and its contraction will cause its internal pressure and temperature to rise. Eventually, in the last white-hot stages of its collapse, it will begin to radiate as a star. Theory shows that our solar system might have evolved, in special circumstances, from such a process —our sun being the star in question and the various planets small cold by-products condensed from subsidiary cloudlets spiraling within the main cloud.

Presupposing the possibility of such events as these, one might arrive ultimately at the concept of a self-perpetuating pulsating universe, renewing its cycles of formation and dissolution, light and darkness, order and disorder, heat and cold, expansion and contraction, through never-ending eons of time.

The cover picture and the picture introducing *Grokking the Problem* show how the extension of our senses through the inventions made possible by modern science can combine with the creativity of the artist to produce a new order of experience.

from MACRO COLOR 67

Manfred P. Kage

How did these pictures come into being? They are one of the latest expressions of pictorial art, called "polychromatic variations" based on the principles of crystal optics.

From Macro Color 67, a calendar of abstract color photography by Manfred P. Kage. The photograph on the cover and that on facing p. 2 are the result of this process.

The pictures ... are the result of an attempted synthesis between the scientist's physical and technological methods and the artist's creative intentions. It is a type of work which, in addition to extensive familiarity with chemical and physical phenomena, requires increased perceptive ability with regard to the transformation potential of crystallizing substances. This is necessary in order to control the process of crystallization with all its accidental appearances by means of a series of highly differentiated interventions in the normal sequence of the natural process.

The procedure is based on the crystallization processes of chemical substances, either from a smelting or from solutions with appropriate solvents added. In these circumstances, creative activity is not limited to the simple transportation and arrangement of matter, as in classical pictorial art (e.g., painting), but by influencing the physical conditions of crystallization during the process, it is possible, above all, to bring about a change "in the natural order of the *energetic* states of matter."

Thus, the anisotropic conditions of energy in crystallizing substances provide the latent source for unfolding their chromatic potential in the form of an *immaterial*, aerial image, made of nothing but light. For this chromatic potential to unfold, the conditions of energy in the crystallizing object have to be "translated" into shades of color, i.e., made visible, by means of a specially designed optical instrument called "polychromator" (developed by the author), in conjunction with polarized light. The mode of translation—while, of course, subject to the laws of optics —is variable and, hence, open to deliberate programming. Its control produces an infinite variety of hues of color, ranging from pure tones of gray through turbid shades of coloring all the way to maximum satiation of primary colors.

Whereas the classical scientist—minerologist or crystallographer—will use crystal pictures occurring in connection with his research only as evidence in the interpretation of measurement data, the author is primarily interested in the perception and creative control of the "crystalline landscape," figuratively speaking—or, in other words, in the aesthetic mastery of form and color.

A different synthesis of science, technology and art produced the picture introducing *Evolution or Revolution*. Here, a color-coded photograph, "Tongue of the Ocean", highlights depths on the Great Bahama Bank. Scientists at Philco-Ford isolated each tone from a photograph taken by Gemini 5 from an altitude of 140 miles. Projecting twelve tones one at a time, they assigned a color to each. Red shows depths to six feet; yellow, six to nine feet. Clouds appear in shades of purple, and great depths in white, because no color was given to darkest tones.

In each of the full-color pictures in the book, the impact is in the picture's ability to startle us into unaccustomed ways of seeing and thinking.

Look at each of these in turn.

What is it "saying"? That is, what do you see? And, what does it mean? *How* is it saying?

Each is based on some form of ambiguity. Which pictures are based on perceptual ambiguity? Which on conceptual ambiguity? Do you find that any of your visual perceptions or conceptions change, as you look at a picture and contemplate its meanings? What were they before, and what are they now?

How do you think each picture relates to the part of the book it introduces? That is, what is it saying in the context of the book?

---

the universe within

To reveal what we experience to be the relationship between *self* and *world* (not what we have been told it is, but what we *experience* it to be), we necessarily do so metaphorically, creatively, as artists. This is true because the revelation is a *construct*. No two persons have the same experience; therefore, each of us must make—create— his own construct.

> "In the act of creativity we are dealing with forming, and manipulating patterns of symbols."
> **(p. 340)**

Of course, since human beings have much in common, we may share a great deal. And the artist who speaks to us is the one whose experience we can enter into and make our own. To make it our own, we must be creative too. Our response to the work of art is to reform and manipulate the pattern of symbols through which the artist reveals to us his world of experience.

"Metaphor makes the familiar strange. . . . Through metaphor our concept of the world changes."
(p. 340)

What will the art of the future be like? At the dawn of the era of the airplane, Picasso painted as though from an aerial perspective, though he had never been in a plane. How would an artist give us an experience of space flight? Of curved space? Of genetic change? Of time travel? Of immortality? What would these experiences do to the universe within us?

We now expect the work of art to create a *situation* in which we create our own values, make our own connections, and shape our own forms, whereas traditionally the work of art . . . was valued precisely because of its capacity to do these things for us.

Louis Kampf,
On Modernism

Some metaphors to think about.
Ardrey's *Cain's children*
Watts' *Vedanta myth*
Kesey's *wolf and rabbit*

When we spoke of *experience* metaphorically as *what we see when we look into a huge kaleidoscope,* we did not say what the kaleidoscope "stands for." What is it, then? The kaleidoscope is neither *self* nor *world* but the interaction or continuum between them; it is *process.*

William Cozart, in his review of Louis Kampf's *On Modernism,* presents Mr. Kampf's views on change and creativity:

Our old epistemological assumptions that there is an empty space between ourselves and the external world, that there is some kind of objective reality "out there," must be discarded. Just as the work of art does not have a solid, impenetrable "frame" around it allowing us to view it with dispassionate detachment, so the world in which we live must be seen not as a configuration of objective substances but as an amorphous process of change challenging us to give it whatever order, value, and direction we choose to impose. The dizzying speculative freedom which this new situation engenders can, as Mr. Kampf sees it, "lead to intellectual despair . . . or it can lead to a desire for order at almost any cost . . . or it can renew our capacity to connect."

Here, then, are two final twists of the kaleidoscope:

I Think of Time . . .

Richie Havens

I think of time as it was then,
something to speak of in tangible
  terms,
when I am young,
    when I was young
    and knew not false within my
    egg,
    the things so well involved,
    that lurked just outside my
    frosted shell,
    a modern thing,
    already cracked,
    upon entering the
    decompression chamber.
    Which still to me through
    breath, yield daylight visions,
    in the most vivid detail now,
    silently.
    When I was young and thought
    not much of time
    for it evaded me in transparent
    dress
    barefooted, laughing and dancing
    through my youth
    disguised in the floral gaiety of
    reality unknown
    what I know now to be either the
    feelings of exhilarated vibrations
    (which is all we are at the point of
    complete freedom and
      awareness)
    or on another plateau,—
    the worlds of knowing or doing
    (which is parallel to the previous,
    to the same end).
When I was young
discovering and plucking from trees
the bitter and the sweet fruit
to place upon my tongue
the experience of both
to lend to self the highest shadow
illumined by the sun and the moon,

wind and rain, night and day,
to dwell beyond environment
  (physical
and mental) seeking all other's way,
individual under gods.
Having made ready the acceptance of
the immediate trail.
To add to love
the vastness of is,
the validity of was,
the solidity of now,
    forever.
When I was young
I spent my eyes
in noisy places, only seeing
and recording every vision
within the illusion
true and false it mattered not.
But that it was
that day to be
as I went on investigating
the in-between worlds.
When I was young
time seemed so vague
so transparent there,
as I sat spending my ears
in quiet places
time or rather its concept
was withering away
and I realized that all springtime has
  felt
ever
was winter's cold hand upon her back
and yet I knew, not a single tear
was shed for herself
but for April's sake.
I watched the wind becoming
  hypnotized
by nature's long misunderstood mind
and function
I saw it run off following a songless
  bird

From the album "Mixed Bag" by Ritchie Havens. Reprinted by permission of the author.

nowhere
time still withering away
all but springtime's fear
will perish hence.
When I was young
following my pre-adolescent true
  nature
through subway tunnels
involved rhythmically with the spaces
between the tracks
in all its ever clacking
glorious existence
and I thought "Oh hear the real
  heartbeat
of transportation"
while all the time, I knew
that it was only a physical artery
placed deep beneath the skin of
the earth
and although the heartbeat was its
  own,
it was only the sound I could relate
to my mother
and not the feeling
my adventures, predestined only
by the patronage of me to myself
ofttimes cast me upon worlds
of shattered dreams
glowing of broken joys
floating
and I realized it was only Times
  Square
or Grand Central Station, or home.
When I was young
and inner misty, lurking shadows
fell upon the light of day
when the steadiness of the sea
was fatal
I stretched myself on a long beach
under the greyest of skies
and the brightest horizons thinking,
days upon days I pondered,
my thoughts most inverted,
whispering underneath my mind's
  ears
"Oh the fate of mankind,
the most disastrous
of time and space,
the epitome of forever."
When in the brightest darkness,

below, above, about,
wherever we lie, and/or
stripped of moral behavior patterns
and cleansed of physical chains,
that bound our minds
to physical means, (Adam
a petty thing within us be).
    How I am young
    when I am the realization
    of the universe within
    a single thought,
    which traced an infinite
    string over the edge of
    individuality into the realm
    of heaven (realm of ideas)
    for the first time without
    fear of death,
    Adam's folly.
    Desecrating his temple (body)
    with age
    as if it were not a part
    of his soul, never aging.
    And worshipping it as if
    it were master
    and watching it all die in
    a silver eye, the steadiest
    sea, upon the wall,
    unnecessarily
How I am young,
when I realized
the universe within
the actuality of all
that is.
All that is yet beyond
me, save acceptance.
All that is without
me
and all that is within
me, where all is
and cannot help but
wonder
who tells you who you are?
    How I am young
    as I am the master
    of my ship, its rudder,
    its gale, its port from
    which it no longer needs
    to sail. Which is today, this
    very moment, now

Giacometti's Dog

Robert Wallace

LOPES in bronze:
  scruffy,
      thin. In

the Museum of Modern Art
  head
      down, neck long as sadness

lowering to hanging ears
  —he's eyeless—
      that hear

nothing, and the sausage
  muzzle
      that leads him as

surely as eyes:
  he might
      be

dead, dried webs or clots of flesh
  and fur
      on the thin, long bones—but

isn't obviously,
  is obviously
      traveling intent on his

own aim: legs
  lofting
      with a gayety the dead
          aren't known

for. Going
  onward in one place,
      he doesn't so much ignore

as not recognize
  the well-
      dressed Sunday hun-

dreds who passing, pausing make
  his bronze
    road

move. Why
  do they come to admire
    him?

They wouldn't care for real dogs
  less raggy
    than he

is? It's his tragic
  insouciance
    bugs them? or is

it that art can make us
  cherish
    anything—this command

of shaping and abutting space—
  that makes us love
    even mutts,

even the world, accept
  even
    the starry wheels by which
      we're hurled

toward death, having
  the rocks and
    wind for comrades?

It's not this starved hound,
  but Giacometti seeing
    him we see.

We'll stand in line all day
  to see one man
    love anything enough.

There lies before us, if we choose, continual progress in happiness, knowledge, and wisdom. Shall we, instead, choose death, because we cannot forget our quarrels? We appeal, as human beings to human beings. Remember your humanity, and forget the rest. If you can do so, the way lies open to a new Paradise; if you cannot, there lies before you the risk of universal death.

The Russell-Einstein Appeal

PART VII **inventing the future**

from HUMAN IMAGINATION
IN THE AGE OF SPACE

William R. Cozart

In a living room, frozen in an armchair, a young man sits speechless. He has just been asked a terrible question, a question all the more terrifying for its seeming simplicity: Out of all that life can offer, what do *you* want? A silence ensues that seems longer than the uncrossable spaces between galaxies; then, haltingly, he stammers out an answer:

> Something—I'm not sure. Yes—I think I want . . . to achieve something that only I could do. I want to fall in love with just one person. To know what it is to bless and be blessed. And to serve a great cause with devotion. I want to be *involved.*

The young man is Clive Harrington, the hero of a play which is being staged with increasing frequency on college campuses across this country. The play is *Five Finger Exercise* by Peter Shaffer. And the answer that Clive so painfully pieces together to this question of human desire is far more than a climactic moment in modern theatre. It is the kind of answer that every post-modern man must struggle to find to the anxious question of what he is going to do with his time and space in an ever-changing, expanding universe.

For this is the question that is posed to contemporary civilization: Out of all the possible futures toward which man can direct his continuing evolution, which one does he really *want*? The spectacular advances in basic science which have produced man's accelerating technology have given him almost unlimited power over his environment. What, then, is the kind of world that he really desires? Today almost any kind of future is technically within his reach. Knowing this, post-modern man feels that the greatest adventure into which he can channel his energy is the adventure of inventing the most imaginative and liberating future possible for human life on this planet. And, like Clive, man of the Space Age feels that all individual achievements, all deep relationships with those he loves, find their meaning and fulfillment within this overarching task. And in this task he wants to be *involved.*

Is it possible, beneath the myriad number of future-designing projects and programs that currently are underway, to isolate any *basic* dimensions of what it means to be involved in shaping the world of tomorrow? Perhaps there are at least three major concerns which suggest themselves —concerns which, one feels, continue to keep the Clive Harringtons of the world lying awake far into the night.

Reprinted from *motive*, March/April 1967, by permission.

First, to be involved would mean that one is engaged in *the recon-struction of our fundamental world-picture.* It is now an axiom of the social sciences that every man is fundamentally controlled by the pictures of the world which he carries in his head. His most basic image of an order, of an intelligible world, is the dominating factor in all his thinking, loving, hating, creating, destroying, rebuilding. For the past three hundred years, Western thought has been dominated by the world-picture of Newtonian physics: an image of a mindless and impersonal machine made up of particles exerting force upon other particles pushed along by unalterable causal laws. This world-image sees man as an alien intruder upon a vast, indifferent landscape—or, as E. A. Burtt was moved to describe him, "as a puny, irrelevant spectator lost in a vast mathematical system." Of course, this world-picture has been enormously successful in terms of the scientific discoveries and technological marvels it has produced. And, indeed, such a picture became accessible to man only at the price of removing from it everything that had to do with man as a conscious, perceiving and feeling self and of assuming that particles arranged in space alone constitute the "real world." But to conceive man as being *outside* the real world as an insignificant and irrelevant spectator had thunderous consequences in the subsequent history of thought. It gave rise to the modern philosophical conception of the universe as a senseless, absurd and irrational void encircling and isolating the es-tranged human self. As Albert Camus (whose thought is deeply colored by the Newtonian world-view) expressed it, "In a universe suddenly divested of illusions and lights, man feels an alien, a stranger." Home-less in a neutral landscape of particles and mechanical forces, man senses that the divorce between his life and that of the universe, between "the actor and his setting, is properly the feeling of absurdity."

Yet, in the last few decades, a remarkable change has taken place in this world-picture, beginning, perhaps, in an alteration of science's own vision of what it is doing. The ablest scientists now are realizing that Newton's world-image was, in fact, literally an *image* or "model"—a great canvas across which a hypothetical world was painted, a work as much of the imagination as of observation. The consensus now emerg-ing among scientists is that reality is not merely a datum, but a mental construction which man makes in dialogue with given discoveries in the various scientific disciplines. The image of the great machine and the alien human observer has thus come under direct attack by science itself. As Werner Heisenberg summarizes the change in attitude: "Science no longer is in the position of observer of nature, but rather recognizes itself as a part of the interplay between man and nature. . . . The mathe-matical formulae no longer portray nature, but rather our knowledge of nature."

Thus, man-made conceptions are now seen to be at the heart of science, and the progress of science now rests in the replacing of those concep-tions by other conceptions, which may enlarge or even contradict them. Herbert Dingle sees this process as unceasing: "We can no longer say, The World is like this or The World is like that. We can only say, our experience up to the present is best represented by a world of this char-acter; I do not know what model will represent the world of tomorrow, but I do know that it will coordinate a greater range of experience than that of today."

We are recognizing today, therefore, that the order of the universe is not just passively observed but is imposed, at least partially, by man's mind. And the great task awaiting us is to distinguish between all the different kinds of order that can be constructed out of the given materials of the scientific *and* humanistic disciplines. Science alone cannot accomplish this task. The old idea that only the truths of science are significant is rapidly disappearing. We see instead that there are many kinds of truth, each reached by many different methods. The constructs of science and the other constructs which men built out of their confrontation with reality are seen, in Paul Obler's phrase, as "complementary modes of engagement." Our *total* meaningful world-picture must be a structure in which the many different symbolic constructs of the sciences and humanities are held together in a new and reintegrated way. The structure of knowledge of tomorrow will at last fulfill the vision de Chardin held of a genuine cosmology, a "true physics" which would "one day achieve the inclusion of man in his wholeness in a coherent picture of the world."

our image of personal destiny

Then, secondly, to be involved in inventing the future would mean that one is engaged in *the reconstruction of our image of personal destiny*. As we have seen, Newtonian cosmology has severely damaged our conception of human destiny by divorcing the human actor from his setting, by pulling the earth—the arena of our decision-filled historical action—from beneath our feet and substituting in its place a vast, mathematical system. Now that very earth is being given back—no longer as an impersonal machine, but as a map which we are continually redrawing. And no longer are we divorced from the real world, but enmeshed in its very fabric and texture. Now we must, as Ortega y Gasset has suggested, "construct for ourselves—as the physicist constructs his 'models'—an imaginary life of the individual," a kind of graph of his "possible life." Everyone senses that his actual life is not synonymous with what his life could be. Yet, a "possible life" today cannot be constructed arbitrarily or abstractly; a model of destiny must be analogous to the model of the world in which it is enmeshed. For the microcosm of the human self can be grasped today, for the first time since the Renaissance, as a replica of the macrocosm, of the universe itself. Therefore the model of destiny must duplicate the great drama between life and energy, order and disorder which is fundamental in the constructs of physics, biology, astronomy, history, and literature.

It is in the field of physics that the cosmic conflict between order and disorder has been dramatized most clearly. "The laws of physics are the decrees of fate," Whitehead once observed; and no recognition scene in classical Greek tragedy could more forcefully demonstrate the fateful working of Necessity than can the "laws" of thermodynamics in the twentieth century. Lincoln Barnett's summary of thermodynamics' Second Law reads like the chilling denunciations of the old prophet Teiresias to a disbelieving Oedipus. (p. 347?.)

Though this process is irreversible, many scientists have felt—Norbert Wiener was one—that the phenomenon of life may be an exception to the Second Law of Thermodynamics. "While the universe as a whole . . . tends to run down," Wiener reasons, "there are local enclaves whose direction seems opposed to that of the universe at large and in which there is a limited and temporary tendency for organization to increase. Life finds its home in some of these enclaves." Is it just possible that life reverses the stream of disorder by its organizing systems of ever greater complexity in its immense journey of evolution? The anthropologist, Loren Eiseley, is persuaded that this is the case and fixes the image of this dramatic conflict thus: "The enormous mindlessness of space, a universe running toward a black nothingness of dispersed radiation. But within it a shadowy pulse that out of nothingness arranges itself into form and spaces the notes of a skylark's song."

Man, the most recent and most complex expression of that "shadowy pulse" is now conscious of directing his own evolution, of being the creator of his organic as well as of his spiritual destiny. It is his brain, the organ of imagination, and his nervous system that furnish him the power to impose his intentions upon the world and to contradict these random, disintegrating tendencies of nature and history. Human nervous systems, or so the field of cybernetics tells us, are goal-seeking, self-regulating mechanisms steering their way through an ocean of messages toward a dark, unknown shore whose horizon seems to take the shape of our dreams. The messages, the signals from our environment, are received in the brain, stored, recombined, and retrieved in the act of decision; then —in the form of intentions—they are imposed upon our environment. This "ability to make decisions," Wiener concludes, "can produce around us a local zone of organization in a world whose general tendency is to run down." Our image of human destiny, then, must be formulated in terms of what we intend to do to the world about us, in terms of the zones or orders—the structures of society—which we purpose to build for the future on our ever-shrinking earth.

our global human community   Finally, then, to be involved, it would seem that one must be engaged in *the re-construction of our global human community*. In the midst of the disorder that exists in our cities, in our structures of civil justice, in our system of international relations, we are summoned to join in the many revolutions of "rising expectations" which are literally re-designing the face of the entire world. Ours is not a time when one can afford to cling to private worlds of parochial loyalties. We are fast approaching a world-wide civilization, perhaps a single world-city, and it is imperative that we extend our loyalties—political, social, economic, cultural—to encompass the single globe of which we are citizens. . . .

Such gigantic tasks await the human imagination in this Age of Space. But in spite of the great discovery of the outrush of the galaxies and the pioneering work in space travel and communication, perhaps our age will best be remembered for its great breakthroughs in psychic or mental space—the breakthroughs achieved when human imagination is forced to envisage the theoretical, personal and communal spaces which man will inhabit. The fundamental job of the imagination, in Northrop Frye's phrase, is "to produce, out of the society we have to live in, a vision of the society we want to live in." Thus, the vast revolutions of our day, the enormous changes in our environment, may in the last analysis be leading us toward a new meeting with ourselves. Facing such a possibility, we can only accept the fate and the promise of this age of adventure, of this moment of human evolution when, as geneticist Theodosius Dobzhansky believes:

> Man and man alone knows that the world evolves and that he evolves with it. By changing what he knows about the world man changes the world he knows; and by changing the world in which he lives man changes himself.

BILL OF RIGHTS FOR 1984

Richard E. Farson

At the risk of sounding naïve, I am going to describe an optimistic view of our future. Unquestionably, it seems difficult at the moment to make hopeful predictions about life twenty years from now. Many present trends, if continued, seem to point to an Orwellian world, depersonalized and dehumanized by the technological Juggernaut. On a world-wide scale, we face the prospect of irreversible pollution and destruction of our natural environment; mass starvation in the southern hemisphere as the industrialized northern half grows richer; the possibility of nuclear catastrophe. The entire globe is in a tumult of violent conflict and upheaval as people everywhere demand a share in the benefits of technology. Even in America, the freest, richest nation in history, there are scenes reminiscent of the French Revolution in city after city as police and militia battle deeply angry citizens—not only the poor and segregated, but, on occasion, middle-class protesters as well. All this makes the pessi-

mists among us seem merely hardheaded, down-to-earth realists.

Nevertheless, I think there are grounds for optimism in the very phenomena that seem most disquieting —in the ghetto riots, the rebellion of youth, the "crisis in values" . . . for it looks as though we are entering upon an age of protest. And in the West, it seems to me, this protest reflects a radically new attitude toward life—a radically new view of man himself.

People are never satisfied. Once their needs are met at the survival level, they move on to needs of a higher order. They begin to need freedom, democracy, education. And while it is true that these needs are interrelated with the demands of technology in a positive feedback system, I think they are evidence, on a deeper level, of a revolutionary change in our feelings and beliefs about the purpose of life and about the human potential.

The infants of 1967 will be the high school graduates of 1984. And though

This paper is prepared from a presentation to the International Design Conference at Aspen, Colorado, June 26, 1966. An adaptation appeared in the January 1967 issue of *Glamour* under the title, "The World of 1984." Reprinted by permission of the author.

the world has changed enormously since the Second World War, I don't think we can smoothly extrapolate those changes to the world of 1984; about all we can be certain of is that life will be vastly different from life today. Every change follows more quickly on the heels of the previous change; if we plot the curve of innovation we can see that it rises more and more sharply and that the plateaus are fewer and fewer. In the past, however, man has always been able to make a change and coast awhile, rest on the new plateau, and catch his breath until what seemed alarmingly radical became acceptable and then traditional. In the future, *change will be a way of life*. It is hard to imagine what that will mean, but we can be sure of this: not only will life be very different, but concepts, values, patterns of living, the way people feel about themselves, will be quite different from anything we can easily imagine today. Human nature is *not* immutable, and a world in which change is a way of life will give rise to new human needs.

Marshall McLuhan has said that, "Technological changes recast the entire character of the individual and compel him to rediscover himself in depth instead of in detachment and objectivity." I agree that this is already taking place, and that the age of protest springs not only from man's attempt to rediscover himself, but from a radically new view of the human potential. And in the future, people will demand above all the right to fulfill their potentialities. This, not material possessions as such, will be seen as the means to the good life.

We have had a limited view of what people can do and be. We have assumed that only the sensitive and gifted few can create or appreciate beauty; that only the mystic is capable of transcendental experience; that only certain kinds of cognitive activity constitute "intelligence" which is possessed in high degree by only a few. I think man is beginning to take himself much more seriously. As we begin to be-lieve that we are all playing with a full deck, we will change the rules of the game. And as each of us comes to believe that he is *potent*, he will demand the right to develop and fulfill his potential. Simply by virtue of his humanness, he will demand the right to experiences that have in the past been considered luxuries to be enjoyed by the few. For the high school seniors of 1984, the good life will be focused on *experiencing their humanness*; their values, I think, will be experimental rather than utilitarian, and the purpose of life will not be to use themselves for ulterior goals, but to experience themselves, not to use others, but to experience others, not to use their environment, but to experience it in the fullness of its possibilities for richness and beauty. So I want to talk about the realistic, practical demands I think people will be making to help them attain this.

People will be demanding a new Bill of Rights—not a replacement of our constitutional Bill of Rights guaranteeing civil liberties, but a Bill of Rights guaranteeing *human* liberty. But since the satisfaction of one set of needs gives rise to a new set, my suggested Bills of Rights can only be an interim measure, based upon needs we can now foresee.

right to leisure

My first item in the new Bill of Rights is the Right to Leisure. That is a safe one to start with because we already have leisure. But by today's definition, leisure means time-off-from-work. I am talking about a society in which leisure will not mean time off, but the *right not to work* and still be considered a worthy human being. Work, today, means labor-for-pay. Many authorities believe that this kind of labor will be done by a relatively small percentage of the population, so that the chances for many of us to have jobs in the traditional sense—to "bring home the bacon"—will be limited. This poses a serious problem. How are we going to feel worthy, achieve self-esteem and the esteem of others, without feeling useful?

I think that in the world of post-technical man our whole idea of the usefulness of things and of people will be quite changed. For the past two hundred years or so, we have been thoroughly imbued with the notion that the way to achieve self-respect is to work hard, deny the present for the sake of the future, be of service to others. We require that objects and processes be useful, functional—"Does it *work?*" We even defend beauty, pleasure, leisure as being useful: "Good design is good economics." "Recreation and leisure enable people to work more productively." "Good interpersonal relations are important for smooth organizational functioning." Curiously, though, we don't ask "Does it work?" of the things that we value most. We never ask that of a sunset, of a symphony, of a love affair. We believe these experiences are in some way enriching, of value in and of themselves. It is my guess that we will ask this utilitarian question less and less often, for I think we are discarding the value system, derived from the Protestant ethic, in which work is an end in itself.

In the future we will see a fusion of work and play. Play will be our work, as it is for children. Work will be our play; we will demand the right to occupy ourselves with deeply fulfilling activities that we can cry about and laugh about and be engrossed in for many, many hours at a stretch; and so we will demand that our homes, buildings, and cities be designed not just for efficiency, but for leisure, for delight, for romance, for play.

right to beauty Second in my new Bill of Rights is the Right to Beauty. I think this, too, is a safe one to predict because people are already beginning to rebel against ugliness in their surroundings; they are proposing legislation to remove billboards, establish green belts, hide junkyards, renovate and beautify our cities. "Beauty," "culture," and "life" will not be compartmentalized as they are today. As human energy is replaced by cybernetic slaves, as

culture, leisure, work, and play are fused, people will increasingly turn to experiences that refresh the spirit and expand the senses. We are discovering that beauty is a human need; ugliness will be regarded, literally, as a crime against life.

right to health The next right will surely be the Right to Health. Logically, perhaps, that should come first, but though at present the idea that medical care should be guaranteed to all is controversial, in 1984 the right to health will surely seem as fundamental and as essential to society as the right to an education. We will redefine "health," however, to mean not merely the *absence* of illness, but the *opposite* of illness—a positive condition of well-being, with peak moments of vigor, strength, coordination, ease. I can't help wondering what methods, what experiences, what chemical agents will we use to bring about or enhance these peak moments and open the way to new realms of sensory experience?

The same will be true for mental health. We will no longer be talking about the mere absence of symptoms; we will talk about emotional *wellness*, a positive state of well-being in which our emotions are integrated with our behavior, giving us a feeling of potency, of euphoria. We will increasingly be concerned with the normal problems of normal people, the problems of everyday life—loneliness, superficiality, frustration, fear, guilt, anxiety, despair. And we will deal with these problems not only in clinics, but in the basic institutions of our society—in schools, churches, in homes, in industries, in the neighborhood. This job can't be left to psychologists. We will learn how to make use of the therapeutic resources that exist in all human beings. People are very good for each other. They can be enormously helpful if we arrange circumstances in which they can really reach each other. How are these circumstances to be designed? Perhaps intensive small-group experiences—"group therapy"—increasingly used today in all sorts of settings, will become as normal and everyday a form of human interaction as the cocktail party, the discussion group, or the social club.

right to intimacy

The fourth right is the Right to Intimacy. In this busy, urbanized, crowded society, our complicated relations with so many people seem inevitably to lead to appalling superficiality, and physical proximity has, paradoxically, brought emotional distance. Millions of Americans have never had, and never will have, in their entire lives one moment of intimacy with another human being, even with those who are closest to them—one moment in which they could be honestly, authentically, genuinely themselves. People need to get acquainted with their own feelings, and they need to be able to share those feelings. But in our society, we are actually embarrassed about intimacy; we have the notion that it should occur only in the privacy of the family circle; the trouble is that the shared-feeling of intimacy seldom takes place even there. I think that we will intentionally search for authentic, intimate relationships and, at the same time, be relatively satisfied with relationships that may be only fleeting or transient. For intimacy need not, as we seem to think, be the outgrowth of time. We need intimate relationships, whether of long or short duration, to remind us of our membership in the human race, to give us a sense of community, to help us be less afraid of one another, to permit us to laugh and cry with one another. We need new designs for living which will encourage unforced emotional intimacy. This will be one of the ways we will meet our need to experience ourselves and others more fully.

right to truth

Fifth on my tentative list is the Right to Truth. Some sociologists distinguish between two styles of behavior in relations, "presenting" and "sharing." You can "present" yourself to another person, try to insure that you make a favorable impression on him, or you can "share" yourself with him by letting him in on what it is like to be you at that particular moment. Almost all our relationships—at work, at school, at parties, even at home—are of the "presenting" kind. Sharing of oneself is much more common among the younger generation—which has been called the "Honest Generation." Teen-agers and college students seem much less likely to censor what they say; they seem to want more of the truth from themselves and from others, more honest relationships, and they reject what they call "adult hypocrisy."

When I think of how much we censor our thoughts before speaking, I am reminded of a little experiment which a friend of mine conducts. He asks the people he interviews to wear earphones that feed them "white noise"—something like radio static combined with the sound of a jet plane getting ready to take off. The noise is activated by the subject's voice, but he can't hear himself talking. In this situation, where the interviewer can both talk to the subject and hear what he says, but the subject can only hear the interviewer, some interesting phenomena turn up. One of them is that people lose some of their ability to control and censor their speech. For example, a man asked, "How do you and your wife get along?" might reply, "We get along just fine," and then add very quietly, "That's a lot of crap." When the taped recording is played back to him, he doesn't remember making the second statement.

Our demands for the right to truth are more and more evident, I think, as we move toward a more open society. We seem less willing to go along with the deceptions and secrets we have tolerated for so many years. We are demanding truth in product claims, in packaging, in advertising. As science and technology give us more and more control over heredity, and over the thoughts and behavior of others, we are becoming alarmed about wire-tapping, psychological testing, computerized dossiers, psychologically coerced confessions, and the like. I believe we must deal with our new power by reducing deception and secrecy. In the long run, for example, I doubt that people will permit information about themselves to be collected and stored in data banks or in thick personnel folders to which they have no access. Furthermore, I doubt that people will submit to psychological tests of any kind unless they are sure that such tests are designed to benefit them. People will resist giving personal information to anyone; they will refuse to subject themselves to unclear procedures as they become more aware of the controls that can be exercised over them. I believe there will soon be sweeping legislation that will radically change our practices of record-keeping, testing, experimentation, investigation, and communication **right to** —and I believe these changes will not **travel** be in the direction of Orwellian, cradle-to-the-grave surveillance, as some writers have suggested, but rather in the opposite direction. Moreover, as the communication network becomes larger and more finely meshed, it will be harder, not easier, to conceal or distort the "facts behind the news," and thus manipulate or control opinion.

right to Right number six on my tentative **study** list is the Right to Study. I was going to call this the Right to Education, but that's not what I'm talking about, for "education" is presently designed to prepare people to earn a living, enter a profession, serve the needs of technology and industry, and we have the right to that sort of education pinned down. I am talking about the right to life-long study and learning, to the enriching experience of *learning* as an end in itself. The quest for knowledge and understanding is uniquely human, but we often act as though people must be driven to it by competition for grades, by discipline or fear **right to** of failure, by all sorts of pressures. In **sexual** the future, learning will be an integral **fulfill-** part of creative living; we will be **ment** studying and learning throughout our lives because it is as enjoyable as becoming a good skier or improving one's backhand.

Leading educationists have broadened their concept of education so that they now talk about it in terms of experiences that develop the total person. So the concept of "learning" will be broadened to include the affective, emotional, interpersonal dimensions as well as the cognitive, intellectual aspects of development. We are beginning to realize that learning must encompass all these dimensions if people are to live fully human lives in a world of machines, to cope with unceasing change and enjoy it, to meet the human and social problems of such a world. So we will be educating for awareness, for honesty, intimacy, and interpersonal competence—and people will continue to develop these skills, too, throughout their lives.

The seventh right is the Right to Travel. Soon travel will be so inexpensive, so delightful, and so rapid, the exotic places of this world so accessible, that people will insist on the right to travel. I can foresee the possibility that union contracts written in the coming decades will demand as a fringe benefit the right to travel at company expense. An inevitable consequence of large-scale travel is that we shall develop a new kind of citizen, a citizen of the world. He will return from his travels changed in many ways. Take the Peace Corps volunteer for example. One of the major benefits of the Peace Corps is the new attitude it instills in its members, for quite apart from what they are able to contribute to the countries in which they work, it is clear that their experiences have tremendous impact on them. Probably the most important changes accomplished by the Peace Corps are within the volunteers themselves, and certainly they are returning to the United States as knowledgeable citizens of the world.

The eighth right is the Right to Sexual Fulfillment. We are still plagued by ignorance and guilt and fear, but I think and hope that we are the last generation to settle for so much less than full enjoyment of our sexuality. Sexual pleasure will be as legitimate as the pleasures of eating or drinking or listening to music, and we will be freed to derive erotic enjoyment from all sorts of experiences. We might as well face it, the sexual revolution is already well under way. We might as well relax and enjoy it, but I think it will bring about some unexpected changes, particularly in our ideas of sexual roles and role differentiation. When sex is no longer simply a means to an end—procreation, or economic security for women and ego-security for men—we will be able to deploy and enjoy the range of our sensory and emotional potential. For the generation that comes of age in 1984, sexual fulfillment and erotic experience will not only be a delightful and taken-for-granted aspect of life, as it has been in many cultures other than our own, but I think it will be more than that. We will explore the possibilities of sex to find new ways of experiencing our-selves, new ways of expanding our physical, mental, and emotional poten-tials, and new ways of relating to others.

right to peace   Ninth in my new Bill of Rights is the Right to Peace. Of the apocalyptic Four Horsemen, War has usurped the place of Pestilence and Famine as the most devastating threat to mankind. I think we can hope for international peace of a sort by 1984, in which the current unstable "balance of terror" has been replaced with a more stable form. But I am not envisioning a world of brotherly love and tranquility, either. In the age of protest, revolu-tionary ferment will probably increase in the underdeveloped half of the world. But already in the widespread support for the UN, in the increasing number of peace-oriented groups and peace demonstrations, in the use of nonviolent techniques to achieve civil rights legislation, in the "hippie" phe-nomena, people in the Western nations are voicing their demand for the right to peace. Our growing understanding of social processes is being applied to problems of international conflict, and all over the world behavioral scientists are studying and developing new non-violent techniques for conflict resolu-tion—devising, for example, research models of the world community by which the outcomes of various strat-egies can be tested in a simulated "world."

The great majority of mankind has always desired peace; today I think that fewer and fewer of us see violence as the only or ultimate solution to conflict. Indeed, we are rediscovering what children know: that in many situations we can achieve our "ends" by transforming them into "means." Negroes who want to desegregate a lunch counter do not picket—they simply sit down at the lunch counter; college students are showing that the way to achieve a relevant education is to create their own free universities.

right to be unique   Finally, I think we will demand the Right to be Unique, to be different, to be autonomous. Today the pressures toward conformity are enormous and they will become even greater as the inevitable consequence of living and working in groups. The War on Pov-erty has been called the war of the middle class against the lower class. If the middle class wins, a homoge-nized society will be the result—and I think we will be very sorry. For ex-ample, we look at Skid Row as the embodiment of failure and misery, but some sociologists who recently studied Skid Row society report that they really liked it. Apparently something *truly* exists in Skid Row culture that we *say* exists in middle class culture: people do care about one another on Skid Row; they go the distance with each other; they help each other; they truly regard themselves as their brothers' keepers. One sociologist said, "You know, if I didn't have a family I think I'd live there."

We will delight in diversity, we will value and accentuate variation. We will want to preserve the customs, prac-tices, ethnic differences among us; we will delight in whatever is idiosyn-cratic, unique, evidence of the strange and wonderful inventiveness of man as he invents himself. We will preserve these differences in depth, not just as traditional pageants that we revive once a year. As we redesign our cities, we will have to decide not only what to change, but what to preserve. I don't mean only historical landmarks, but other places—charming, quaint, romantic, sentimental, highly valued and highly functional places. What smelly delicatessens, what smoky taverns, what dim and dusty old-bookshops, what meeting places for old people do we want to keep?

But the right to be unique poses some fundamental questions today. How can we enable people who are trapped in ghettos to improve their lives and enjoy full citizenship and, at the same time, help them retain for the benefit of all of us the richness of their culture? It may be that celebrating these ethnic differences rather than pretending to ignore them will do more to achieve full citizenship, full humanity for all of us. Young Negroes are turning away from "white" values, discovering in the history of black Africa a source of pride and dignity; wearing their hair "natural," they are proclaiming their autonomy, and that to be different is *good*. They are demanding the right to full citizenship without being required to assimilate, and they are right, I think, for how can we realize the multiformity of the human potential if we set up boundaries for its expression?

It's not easy to talk about the human potential because there is probably no limit to it. The human potential is not only what it *is* at any given moment, but it is also determined by what we *believe* it is; what we think it is or want it to be has a lot to do with what we find it to be. We simply do not know much about the conditions that evoke high-order behavior. We do know that environment is an important determinant of human potential, that environment can expand or stultify cognitive functioning, sensory acuity, emotional response and awareness. And as a matter of fact, probably the best way to predict a person's behavior is to study the *situation*, not the person's life history. For example, people don't smoke in church.

It doesn't make any difference what their life histories are, nobody smokes in church.

As people demand the right to fulfill their potential, their rights to beauty, leisure, intimacy, honesty, autonomy, the environments and situations must be designed to meet these needs. But the most difficult, the most frustrating fact of life is this: the more progress we make, the more we must make. The more needs we satisfy, the more needs we develop. Improvements bring higher expectations and demands for more improvements. We have seen this in the civil rights movement. We keep thinking, "Okay. Now we've provided the Negroes with legislation for equal educational benefits, equal chance at the polls, equal job opportunities. That's been a difficult struggle for all of us. Why don't they appreciate these improvements, rest a minute, and let us catch our breath? Then we'll do something more. Can't we just coast for a little while first?" But of course we can't. On the contrary, as a result of our successes we must step up the pace even more. The closer people come to their goals, the more anxious and impatient they become, so the business of trying to make life better is endless and frustrating.

When people feel their potentialities are not being realized, they grumble or rebel. But these grumbles and rebellions are to be valued because they reflect high-order motivation—what Abraham Maslow calls "meta grumbles." Actually, of course, we would not hear such grumbles were it not for the fact that man's future and the quality of life are for the first time within our control. I think we can have the better life that humanity is demanding if we can understand that the real barrier to a better world is our own resistance to change. William Carlos Williams writes, "The mind is the cause of our distresses, but of it we can build anew. . . . A new world is only a new mind."

The most beautiful and most profound emotion we can experience is the sensation of the mystical. It is the sower of all true science. He to whom this emotion is a stranger, who can no longer wonder and stand rapt in awe, is as good as dead. To know that what is impenetrable to us really exists, manifesting itself as the highest wisdom and the most radiant beauty which our dull faculties can comprehend only in their most primitive forms—this knowledge, this feeling is at the center of true religiousness.

Albert Einstein,
quoted in *The Universe and Dr. Einstein*
by Lincoln Barnett.

when the walls began to fall . . . .

There is a little bit of science in painting and poetry. There is a great deal of art in economics, history, politics, and life. We are really artists, not scientists.

Robert Bickner,
"After the Future, What?"

Personally, I have a great faith in the resiliency and adaptability of man, and I tend to look to our tomorrows with a surge of excitement and hope. I feel that we're standing on the threshold of a liberating and exhilarating world in which the human tribe can become truly one family and man's consciousness can be freed from the shackles of mechanical culture and enabled to roam the cosmos. I have a deep and abiding belief in man's potential to grow and learn, to plumb the depths of his own being and to learn the secret songs that orchestrate the universe. We live in a transitional era of profound pain and tragic identity quest, but the agony of our age is the labor pain of rebirth.

I expect to see the coming decades transform the planet into an art form; the new man, linked in a cosmic harmony that transcends time and space, will sensuously caress and mold and pattern every facet of the terrestrial artifact as if it were a work of art, and man himself will become an organic art form. There is a long road ahead, and the stars are only way stations, but we have begun the journey. To be born in this age is a precious gift, and I regret the prospect of my own death only because I will leave so many pages of man's destiny—if you will excuse the Gutenbergian image—tantalizingly unread. But perhaps, as I've tried to demonstrate in my examination of the postliterate culture, the story begins only when the book closes.

Marshall McLuhan

from THE JOURNEY

Lillian Smith

A century from now, men may think it strange that we so long spoke of our times as the age of anxiety; that we let the greed of ordinary men and the power-lust of dictators and demagogues get out of bounds even for a brief span of years; for parallel with the anxiety and the terror and the inquisitors and exploiters and the awful poverty and ignorance there is another way of life building firmly, steadily, swiftly on scientific facts and technics and on men's newly discovered humility and dignity and on their concern for each other. . . .

I believe future generations will think of our times as the age of wholeness: when the walls began to fall; when the fragments began to be related to each other; when man learned finally to esteem tenderness and reason and awareness and the word which set him apart forever from other living creatures; when he learned to realize his brokenness and his great talent for creating ties that bind him together again; when he learned to accept his own childhood and in the acceptance to become capable of maturity; when he began to realize his infinite possibilities even as he sees more clearly his limitations; when he began to see that sameness and normality are not relevant to human beings but to machines and animals; when he learned never to let any power or dictator cut his ties to the great reservoir of knowledge and wisdom without which he would quickly lose his human status; when he learned to live a bit more comfortably with time and space; when he learned to accept his need of God and the law that he cannot use Him, to accept his need of his fellow men and the law that he cannot use them, either; when he learned that 'what is impenetrable to us really exists,' and always there will be need of the dream, the belief, the wonder, the faith.

To believe in something not yet proved and to underwrite it with our lives; it is the only way we can leave the future open. Man, surrounded by facts, permitting himself no surmise, no intuitive flash, no great hypothesis, no risk is in a locked cell. Ignorance cannot seal the mind and imagination more surely. To find the point where hypothesis and fact meet; the delicate equilibrium between dream and reality; the place where fantasy and earthy things are metamorphosed into a work of art; the hour when faith in the future becomes knowledge of the past; to lay down one's powers for others in need; to shake off the old ordeal and get ready for the new; to question, knowing that never can the full answer be found; to accept uncertainties quietly, even our incomplete knowledge of God: this is what man's journey is about, I think.

Reprinted from *The Journey* by Lillian Smith by permission of W. W. Norton & Company, Inc. Copyright 1954 by Lillian Smith.